Illiberal Politics in Southeast Europe

The world is increasingly becoming less democratic and this trend has not left Southeast Europe untouched. But instead of democratic breakdown what we are witnessing is a gradual decline and the rise of competitive authoritarian regimes.

This book aims to give a country-by-country overview of how illiberal politics has led to a decline in democracy and the re-emergence of autocratic governance in Southeast Europe, more specifically in the Western Balkans. It defines illiberal politics as the everyday practices through which ruling parties undermine democratic institutions in order to remain in power. Individual chapters examine recent political developments and identify practices of illiberal politics that target electoral institutions, rule of law, media freedom, judicial independence, and enable political patronage, while several thematic chapters comparatively explore cross-regional patterns.

This book addresses academics, policymakers, and practitioners with professional interest in Southeast Europe or democratic decline and is both timely and relevant as the European Union attempts to reengage with the countries of the Western Balkans.

The chapters in this book were originally published as a special issue of *Southeast European and Black Sea Studies*.

Damir Kapidžić is Associate Professor of Comparative Politics at the Faculty of Political Science, University of Sarajevo in Bosnia and Herzegovina. His research looks at ethnic conflict, political parties, power-sharing, and processes through which democratic or authoritarian politics are institutionalized.

Věra Stojarová works as Academic Researcher and Associate Professor at the Department of Political Science at the Faculty of Social Studies at Masaryk University in Brno, Czech Republic. She specializes in security and politics in the Western Balkans.

The Southeast Europe and Black Sea Series
Journal Editor: Ioannis Armakolas
Managing Editor: Julianne Funk

Today's crises in the eastern Mediterranean, the multivalent developments in Turkey, and European integration and democratisation challenges have focused scientific and political attention on Southeast Europe and the wider Black Sea area. The Southeast Europe and Black Sea Series publishes multidisciplinary original research about these current hotspots on the margins of Europe. The volumes include comparative and individual country analysis, as well as innovative research that develops deep and fruitful understanding of these regions. The series engages academic and original policy-oriented books with such themes as the politics of state-building and reform, foreign and security policy, socio-cultural phenomena and socio-economic dynamics, EU enlargement and neighbourhood policies. The series also publishes books that advance our understanding of recent history in this broad area – from Slovenia to Ukraine, south to Greece, Cyprus and Turkey, and east to the Caucasus – and its relevance for contemporary problems.

Most recent titles in the series include:

Jewish Life in Southeast Europe
Diverse Perspectives on the Holocaust and Beyond
Edited by Kateřina Králová, Marija Vulesica and Giorgos Antoniou

Islam, Populism and Regime Change in Turkey
Making and Re-making the AKP
Edited by M. Hakan Yavuz and Ahmet Erdi Öztürk

The National Politics of EU Enlargement in the Western Balkans
Edited by James Ker-Lindsay, Ioannis Armakolas, Rosa Balfour and Corina Stratulat

International-Led Statebuilding and Local Resistance
Hybrid Institutional Reforms in Post-Conflict Kosovo
Edited by Arolda Elbasani

Illiberal Politics in Southeast Europe
How Ruling Elites Undermine Democracy
Edited by Damir Kapidžić and Věra Stojarová

For more information about this series, please visit:
www.routledge.com/The-Southeast-Europe-and-Black-Sea-Series/book-series/SEBSS

Illiberal Politics in Southeast Europe

How Ruling Elites Undermine Democracy

Edited by
Damir Kapidžić and Věra Stojarová

LONDON AND NEW YORK

First published 2022
by Routledge
2 Park Square, Milton Park, Abingdon, Oxon OX14 4RN

and by Routledge
605 Third Avenue, New York, NY 10158

Routledge is an imprint of the Taylor & Francis Group, an informa business

Chapters 1–9, 11 and 12 © 2022 Taylor & Francis
Chapter 10 © 2019 Marko Kmezić. Originally published as Open Access.

With the exception of Chapter 10, no part of this book may be reprinted or reproduced or utilised in any form or by any electronic, mechanical, or other means, now known or hereafter invented, including photocopying and recording, or in any information storage or retrieval system, without permission in writing from the publishers. For details on the rights for Chapter 10, please see the chapter's Open Access footnote.

Trademark notice: Product or corporate names may be trademarks or registered trademarks, and are used only for identification and explanation without intent to infringe.

British Library Cataloguing in Publication Data
A catalogue record for this book is available from the British Library

ISBN: 978-1-032-07689-8 (hbk)
ISBN: 978-1-032-07691-1 (pbk)
ISBN: 978-1-003-20832-7 (ebk)

DOI: 10.4324/9781003208327

Typeset in Minion Pro
by Newgen Publishing UK

Publisher's Note
The publisher accepts responsibility for any inconsistencies that may have arisen during the conversion of this book from journal articles to book chapters, namely the inclusion of journal terminology.

Disclaimer
Every effort has been made to contact copyright holders for their permission to reprint material in this book. The publishers would be grateful to hear from any copyright holder who is not here acknowledged and will undertake to rectify any errors or omissions in future editions of this book.

Contents

	Citation Information	vii
	Notes on Contributors	ix
1	The rise of illiberal politics in Southeast Europe *Damir Kapidžić*	1
2	The political economy behind the gradual demise of democratic institutions in Serbia *Dušan Pavlović*	18
3	Institutional and symbolic aspects of illiberal politics: the case of North Macedonia (2006–2017) *Borjan Gjuzelov and Milka Ivanovska Hadjievska*	39
4	The elephant in the room: illiberal politics in Montenegro *Olivera Komar*	59
5	Subnational competitive authoritarianism and power-sharing in Bosnia and Herzegovina *Damir Kapidžić*	79
6	Soft competitive authoritarianism and negative stability in Kosovo: statebuilding from UNMIK to EULEX and beyond *Adem Beha and Arben Hajrullahu*	100
7	Influencing votes, winning elections: clientelist practices and private funding of electoral campaigns in Albania *Gentiana Kera and Armanda Hysa*	120
8	Structural weaknesses and the role of the dominant political party: democratic backsliding in Croatia since EU accession *Dario Čepo*	137
9	Media in the Western Balkans: who controls the past controls the future *Věra Stojarová*	156

10 Rule of law and democracy in the Western Balkans: addressing the gap between policies and practice 177
Marko Kmezić

11 Big dreams and small steps: comparative perspectives on the social movement struggle for democracy in Serbia and North Macedonia 193
Gazela Pudar Draško, Irena Fiket and Jelena Vasiljević

12 Moving towards EU membership and away from liberal democracy 214
Věra Stojarová

Index 230

Citation Information

The chapters in this book were originally published in *Southeast European and Black Sea Studies*, volume 20, issue 1 (2020). When citing this material, please use the original page numbering for each article, as follows:

Chapter 1
The rise of illiberal politics in Southeast Europe
Damir Kapidžić
Southeast European and Black Sea Studies, volume 20, issue 1 (2020), pp. 1–17

Chapter 2
The political economy behind the gradual demise of democratic institutions in Serbia
Dušan Pavlović
Southeast European and Black Sea Studies, volume 20, issue 1 (2020), pp. 19–39

Chapter 3
Institutional and symbolic aspects of illiberal politics: the case of North Macedonia (2006–2017)
Borjan Gjuzelov and Milka Ivanovska Hadjievska
Southeast European and Black Sea Studies, volume 20, issue 1 (2020), pp. 41–60

Chapter 4
The elephant in the room: illiberal politics in Montenegro
Olivera Komar
Southeast European and Black Sea Studies, volume 20, issue 1 (2020), pp. 61–80

Chapter 5
Subnational competitive authoritarianism and power-sharing in Bosnia and Herzegovina
Damir Kapidžić
Southeast European and Black Sea Studies, volume 20, issue 1 (2020), pp. 81–101

Chapter 6
Soft competitive authoritarianism and negative stability in Kosovo: statebuilding from UNMIK to EULEX and beyond
Adem Beha and Arben Hajrullahu
Southeast European and Black Sea Studies, volume 20, issue 1 (2020), pp. 103–122

Chapter 7

Influencing votes, winning elections: clientelist practices and private funding of electoral campaigns in Albania
Gentiana Kera and Armanda Hysa
Southeast European and Black Sea Studies, volume 20, issue 1 (2020), pp. 123–139

Chapter 8

Structural weaknesses and the role of the dominant political party: democratic backsliding in Croatia since EU accession
Dario Čepo
Southeast European and Black Sea Studies, volume 20, issue 1 (2020), pp. 141–159

Chapter 9

Media in the Western Balkans: who controls the past controls the future
Věra Stojarová
Southeast European and Black Sea Studies, volume 20, issue 1 (2020), pp. 161–181

Chapter 10

Rule of law and democracy in the Western Balkans: addressing the gap between policies and practice
Marko Kmezić
Southeast European and Black Sea Studies, volume 20, issue 1 (2020), pp. 183–198

Chapter 11

Big dreams and small steps: comparative perspectives on the social movement struggle for democracy in Serbia and North Macedonia
Gazela Pudar Draško, Irena Fiket and Jelena Vasiljević
Southeast European and Black Sea Studies, volume 20, issue 1 (2020), pp. 199–219

Chapter 12

Moving towards EU membership and away from liberal democracy
Věra Stojarová
Southeast European and Black Sea Studies, volume 20, issue 1 (2020), pp. 221–236

For any permission-related enquiries please visit:
www.tandfonline.com/page/help/permissions

Notes on Contributors

Adem Beha, Faculty of Philosophy, Department of Political Science, University of Pristina, Pristina, Kosovo.

Dario Čepo, Faculty of Law, University of Zagreb, Zagreb, Croatia.

Irena Fiket, Institute for Philosophy and Social Theory, University of Belgrade, Belgrade, Serbia.

Borjan Gjuzelov, School of Politics and International Relations, Queen Mary University of London, London, UK.

Arben Hajrullahu, Faculty of Philosophy, Department of Political Science, University of Pristina, Pristina, Kosovo.

Armanda Hysa, Institute for the Study of Crimes and Consequences of Communism, Tirana, Albania.

Milka Ivanovska Hadjievska, Department of Political Science, Lund University, Sweden.

Damir Kapidžić, Faculty of Political Science, University of Sarajevo, Sarajevo, Bosnia and Herzegovina.

Gentiana Kera, Faculty of History and Philology, University of Tirana, Tirana, Albania.

Marko Kmezić, Centre For Southeast European Studies, University of Graz, Graz, Austria.

Olivera Komar, Faculty of Political Science, University of Montenegro, Podgorica, Montenegro.

Dušan Pavlović, Faculty of Political Science, University of Belgrade, Belgrade, Serbia.

Gazela Pudar Draško, Institute for Philosophy and Social Theory, University of Belgrade, Belgrade, Serbia.

Věra Stojarová, Faculty of Social Studies, Department of Political Science, Masaryk University, Brno, Czech Republic.

Jelena Vasiljević, Institute for Philosophy and Social Theory, University of Belgrade, Belgrade, Serbia.

The rise of illiberal politics in Southeast Europe

Damir Kapidžić (iD)

ABSTRACT
Democracy is backsliding throughout Southeast Europe but there are no signs of full democratic breakdown. Instead, political parties and their leaders incrementally undermine challenges to governmental authority while keeping electoral contest largely intact. This article introduces a special issue that aims to examine and explain democratic decline by looking at the prevalence of illiberal politics across countries and issues. In order to overcome the limitations of fixed regime classification we adopt a procedural lens and look into governing practices that gradually tilt the electoral playing field. Utilizing the concept of Illiberal politics allows us to examine sets of policies enacted by political parties in government with the aim to remain in power indefinitely. By tracing democratic decline in Serbia, North Macedonia, Montenegro, Bosnia and Herzegovina, Kosovo, Albania, and Croatia we observe different patterns of weakness, but also common causes arising from weak institutions and inherited governance practices that preserve executive dominance, patronage, and informality.

1. Introduction

Has the third wave of democratization come to an end? This question is debated among scholars with no clear answer in sight. Diverging trends show continued, albeit weak, democratization but also erosion or collapse of democracy in different countries of the world. In the multiple instances of democratic backsliding, including some long-standing and consolidated democracies, authors notice an emerging global trend where some elements of democracy are kept intact while others have eroded (Bermeo 2016; Levitsky and Way 2015; Lührmann et al. 2018). The countries of Southeast Europe are no exception to these developments. It is possible to identify instances of incremental democratic backsliding in each throughout the past 10 years, although the speed of change and the final outcomes vary. This special issue aims to look at how the emerging democratic decline has and continues to play out in the countries politically labelled the 'Western Balkans'.[1] We utilize the procedural concept of illiberal politics that gives prominence to the role of political parties and their leaders. At the same time, it is our aim to include as many contributions of local academics coming from the region who live and work under conditions of deteriorating democracy and have strong personal investments in the countries they study.

In recent years, several authors have developed increasingly precise and empirically grounded classifications for regimes that are not fully democratic, but not authoritarian either (Merkel 2004; Schedler 2013; Levitsky and Way 2010). Still, there is no agreement on where to set the borderline between highly deficient democracies (democracies with adjectives) and authoritarian regimes that incorporate some elements of democracy (autocracies with adjectives). Classifying countries in this grey zone along a democracy–autocracy continuum, especially those with weak and unconsolidated governing institutions such as in Southeast Europe, is not straightforward. This is where it makes sense to initially focus on the aggregate of policies enacted by governing parties and rulers in order to map the direction of change taking place. By utilizing the concept of liberal politics, we aim to do just that. Illiberal politics are sets of policies that extend an electoral advantage for governing parties with the aim to remain in power indefinitely. This includes perpetuating advantageous socio-economic structures and governing practices, as well as specific and targeted restrictive actions against political opponents and independent institutions. By comparing the magnitude and intensity of illiberal politics we are able to draw conclusions on democratic and authoritarian trajectories of countries and the region as a whole.

Southeast Europe has seen its fair share of illiberal politics in recent years. Some of the most noticeable include the abuse of power with regard to elections, media, rule of law and public finances by the VMRO-DPMNE[2] in North Macedonia, the SNS[3] in Serbia, the SNSD[4] in Bosnia and Herzegovina, and the DPS[5] in Montenegro. Yet all countries have been affected by politicians willing to bend the rules of the game to create an advantage for themselves and their party. This trend is confirmed by several indices that measure the quality of democracy, including the Varieties of Democracy index (V-Dem) used in this article. While elections are currently not under threat, what comes before and after elections very much is. A level playing field can no longer be taken for granted.

The rationale behind this special issue is to address the perceived lack of academic literature on the topic and to look more specifically into the practices and structures behind non-democratic governance. While there have been several recent publications addressing democratic backsliding in Southeast Europe (Bieber 2018; Kmezić and Bieber 2017; Perry and Keil 2018; Bieber et al. 2018; Bieber 2020), they either do not specifically look into the role of governing political parties, or do not cover most countries and several crucial topics, such as media, rule of law, and social movements. With this special issue, we want to examine the prevalence of illiberal practices, explore similarities across countries, and examine whether they are grounded in structural weaknesses particular to the region. This will allow us to draw conclusions on consequences for party competition and democracy in countries that aspire to join the European Union. An additional aim is to unpack the concept of democratic backsliding and the related concept of autocratization by adopting a procedural lens and looking into practices that, while not undermining democracy on their own, incrementally add up to create regimes that can no longer be called democratic.

This special issue adds value to the recent renewal of both academic and policy interest for democracy in Southeast Europe. A first set of articles consists of individual country case studies covering Serbia, North Macedonia, Montenegro, Bosnia and Herzegovina (BiH), Kosovo, Albania, and Croatia. The authors highlight a common issue where governing parties readily use executive power to circumvent checks and balances for political and economic gain, while undermining institutions through reliance on informal politics. A second set of comparative articles examines the control of media, rule of law, and social movements, showcasing structural weaknesses while at the same time addressing the possibility to increase governmental transparency and accountability.

Our argument is that countries in Southeast Europe are not experiencing a sudden democratic reversal or breakdown of democracy. Rather, structural deficiencies centred around a strong executive, weak checks and balances and institutionalized informality are exploited by political parties to tilt the electoral playing field through the use of illiberal governing practices, while maintaining competitive elections. The following section gives a theoretical perspective on what makes these countries structurally similar and what constitutes illiberal politics. The subsequent section provides a comparative analysis of democracy in Southeast Europe using data from V-Dem. Finally, we give an overview of the contributions to this special issue.

2. Going, going, gone! Situating the concept of illiberal politics

Countries regularly experience slight shifts in levels of democracy, while sudden and noticeable regime change is rare. When small change is continuous and moves in a single direction, either towards democracy or authoritarianism, we can speak of incremental regime change. Most of academic literature is focused on the classification of regimes (Zakariah 1997; Merkel 2004; Levitsky and Way 2010; Schedler 2013). Yet it is equally important to look at the sum of processes affecting democratic institutions in order to understand incremental democratic decline. Almost all countries in Southeast Europe are in the midst of incrementally moving towards authoritarian rule.

This is well encompassed by what Bermeo calls democratic backsliding, especially in the form of gradual changes 'that are legitimated through the very institutions that democracy promoters have prioritized' but that do not lead to outright regime change (Bermeo 2016, 6). A conceptually broader but related term is autocratization that captures any deliberate change that move a regime away from a full democracy, including democratic backsliding, breakdown and authoritarian consolidation (Lührmann et al. 2018, 896). Such incremental changes largely target challenges to governmental authority, while keeping the electoral process intact. The term we use to describe the policies behind these changes is illiberal politics. By illiberal politics, we understand policies that are enacted (or proposed) by political parties in government with the aim to remain in power indefinitely while maintaining competitive elections. The resulting regimes maintain competitive multiparty elections but are neither democratic nor fully authoritarian. They have alternatively been described as 'illiberal democracy' (Zakariah 1997), 'defective democracy' (Merkel 2004), 'competitive authoritarianism' (Levistky and Way 2010), and 'electoral authoritarianism' (Schedler 2013).

Of the several attempts to classify regimes in the grey zone between democracy and authoritarianism, we will elaborate on the most relevant for regimes in Southeast Europe. All countries in this region can be described as hybrid regimes and Zakariah's illiberal democracy is applicable to most of them. These are regimes that, while democratically elected, ignore constitutional limits to their power and limit basic rights and freedoms of citizens (Zakariah 1997, 22). Yet, illiberal democracy is a vague concept as it groups countries with minor deficiencies together with those that display serious authoritarian traits. Levitsky and Way's competitive authoritarianism can be used to describe the regime in three countries, Serbia, Montenegro, and North Macedonia until 2017 (Bieber 2018), where competition is real but highly unfair. Regimes are competitive authoritarian when 'formal democratic institutions exist and are widely viewed as the primary means of gaining power [...] but they are not democratic because the playing field is heavily skewed in favour of incumbents' (Levitsky and Way 2010, 5). The authors specify empirical conditions for such a regime based on attributes of free elections, broad protection of civil liberties, and a reasonably level playing field.[6] The concept of competitive authoritarianism is currently the most suitable for classifying regimes in Southeast Europe as all regimes can be defined in relation to it. Other concepts, such as defective democracy (Merkel 2004) or electoral authoritarianism (Schedler 2013) have some value but are either imprecise or have limited applicability.

Classifications in the academic literature generally describe regime change once it has occurred, not the process of moving away from democracy. But using a single concept for the myriad of different ways that regimes (of Southeast Europe) move towards authoritarian rule does not allow us to understand this change in the absence of evident democratic breakdown. Therefore, more flexibility is needed to identify incremental erosion of democracy in regimes that are sliding towards competitive authoritarianism but are not 'gone' yet. This is exactly where illiberal politics is a useful tool for academic inquiry. By adopting a process-oriented approach that looks at governing practices of parties in power, illiberal politics can identify trends of incremental regime change that do not fully disregard democratic and liberal institutions and norms (to paraphrase, regimes that are 'going, going . . . '). Nevertheless, once a threshold is passed these regimes are considered 'gone' and can best be described as competitive authoritarian, or even as fully authoritarian. To put it in other words, while (competitive) authoritarianism is a strong symptom, illiberal politics are the disease that causes it, that can be identified, and ultimately addressed.

Illiberal politics play out in two broadly defined arenas, centred around the electoral component of democracy and the liberal component of democracy. What can be termed as constitutional liberalism is different from electoral democracy in a fundamental way, even though both are key components of a procedural understanding of democracy (Dahl 1989). While the electoral process serves to enable and concentrate political power, constitutional liberalism recognizes the need to restrict power through a protection of civil liberties and institutional checks and balances (Zakariah 1997, 22, 30). In this sense, the electoral lens has a positive, power-enabling view on democracy while the liberal lens has a negative power-restricting view on democracy. Both components are described in academic literature, both are empirically situated, and they can be challenged separately by actors with authoritarian agendas.

The electoral component of democracy can be subverted by manipulating free and fair elections as well as by creating an electoral playing field tilted in favour of incumbents. Illiberal politics erode the central electoral criteria of procedural democracy by limiting suffrage and the right to run for office, restricting freedom of expression, independent media and associational autonomy in the run-up to elections and in their aftermath (Dahl 1989). These measures target core elements of democracy and make rulers less accountable to citizens. Tilting the electoral playing field focuses on policies that limit the political opposition or that favour the ruling party in order to gain electoral advantage.

Also called strategic electoral manipulation (Bermeo 2016, 13) it occurs long before elections are held and is centred on access to resources, media, and the rule of law (Levitsky and Way 2010, 10). This can include monopolizing and abusing political and economic power and resources, the use of state resources and institutions for partisan purposes, restricting independent media or supporting media biased in favour of incumbents, a subverted legal process that targets opposition and favours the party in power, or a mix of the above.

Empirical examples of illiberal politics aimed at the electoral component of democracy that were identified in Southeast European countries include: legal or physical limitations enacted on parts of the population that restrict their right to vote or to run for office; changes to electoral rules so they favour incumbents; hampering of voter registration and tampering of electoral rolls; gerrymandering electoral districts; political party control of electoral commissions; intimidation and restriction of opposition parties and independent candidates, whether legally, financially or physically, and keeping them off the ballot; laws or regulations that penalize public government criticism or discussing certain topics; prohibitions or restrictions of public assembly and association and other limitations to the freedom of expression; policies and actions that target the editorial, financial, and personnel independence of media and journalists and that censor media or lead to self-censorship; the use of government funds for partisan purposes and campaigning; and budgetary allocation preferences that closely align with partisan aims and party structures.

The liberal component of democracy is undermined by a lack of horizontal accountability and in more extreme cases by a dominance of executive power unrestrained by checks and balances. What Bermeo terms executive aggrandizement 'occurs when elected executives weaken checks on executive power one by one.' They accomplish this through legal channels by gradually disassembling institutions that effectively might challenge them and by restraining opposition (Bermeo 2016, 10–11). Targets usually include institutional and/or professional autonomy of the legislature, judiciary, media, and independent agencies (for example anti-corruption agencies). Constitutionally guaranteed civil liberties are a key element in protecting individuals and groups from the tyranny of the majority. If such protections are removed, limited or restricted through illiberal politics, parties in government can target vulnerable groups, minorities, or issues such as gender equality and reproductive rights for political gain. Democracy is thus subverted into unchecked rule of the majority dominated by the discourse of the governing party.

There is certain overlap of policies between the electoral and liberal components of democracy. A non-extensive list of illiberal politics in Southeast Europe that target the liberal component of democracy includes: stronger and persistent executive control over the legislature, judiciary and independent institutions; actions that circumvent existing legislative and judicial procedures; appointment of loyal individuals as heads of independent agencies instead of merit-based appointments; a roll back of checks and balances; policies that weaken the rule of law; an increased reliance on informal and non-institutional executive decision-making; legal, financial or thematic restrictions enacted on civil society; intimidation and harassment of protesters by police and government officials; conscious indifference in upholding and protecting civil liberties equally for all citizens; public shaming of vulnerable groups, minorities and government critics as tainted and a threat to the nation; and the removal of constitutionally protected civil liberties and group rights.

Policies from both components can be used to reinforce the position of the governing party, to weaken accountability or to counteract opposition politics. While (mostly) borderline legal, illiberal politics tend to create governance structures and practices that tend to reproduce themselves over time and that exert influence both formally (through policies and institutions) and informally (through networks and perceptions). In order to enact and implement policies that stabilize a competitive authoritarian regime both strong parties and coercive state capacities need to be in place (Levitsky and Way 2010). When they are not, competitive authoritarianism is more easily challenged by opposition, such as in the case of North Macedonia. Due to historical institutional legacies, we understand that there are distinct features of politics in each country studied in this issue. Therefore, we do not propose a common codebook of illiberal policies that are widely applicable. The contributing authors are given the freedom to identify and describe illiberal politics in a given context.

In order to identify common trajectories among countries, it is necessary to explore theoretical explanations for illiberal politics that are rooted in structural conditions specific to Southeast Europe. Here we rely on historical institutionalist insights on post-communist power relations and informality. For this purpose, we need to understand the moment of regime change that occurred across most of the Southeast Europe in the early 1990s. As a critical juncture, a historical moment of unusually high contingency, regime change from communist rule proved crucial in directing subsequent outcomes (Dolenec 2013, 6). Instead of paving the way for democracy like in most countries of East Europe, the introduction of competitive elections in the early 1990s led to the establishment of competitive authoritarian regimes that exploited structural weaknesses, and governance practices left over from the period of state socialism. The newly elected 'democratic' parties set themselves as an impendent to the development of free and fair electoral competition. Violent conflict that engulfed many countries shortly thereafter solidified the competitive authoritarian regimes. Structural constraints arising out of the over-lapping political, social, and economic transitions (Offe 2003), as well as from transitions towards independence and from war to peace, made democratization all the more difficult and led to the entrenchment of newly elected elites.

To explain the governance practices that coalesced into competitive authoritarian rule Zakošek (1997) highlights the absence of the rule of law and identifies three processes of post-communist power mutation, which are further elaborated by Dolenec (2013). First is the concentration of power in the executive over parliamentary and judiciary branches of government, where the balance in division of power is subverted through legal means. Second, a conversion of political into economic power which helps create new economic elites out of political party affiliates and leads to the establishment of a clientelist relationship centred around the perpetuation of economic benefits. Finally, third, is a power dispersion from state administration and public institutions into a web of informal, party-controlled networks accompanied by a weakening of state capacity (Dolenec 2013, 20–24, 46–48, 55). The authoritarian parties that dominated regime change and politics in the 1990s used variations of these three processes to consolidate power and to remain in power.[7] The practices they adopted became a new norm for electoral contestation that inhibited future democratization. While regimes did become noticeably more democratic in the 2000's by adopting sets of liberal democratic policies, the engrained party practices of executive dominance, patronage and informality did not disappear. It is merely the tools, the illiberal politics used to achieve party aims, that have become more sophisticated, less repressive, and more informal (Vladisavljević and Krstić 2019). In this sense the 'democratic rupture' of the 2000s was real but at the same time shallow. The party leaders pushing illiberal politics today still rely on processes established decades ago as enduring obstacles to substantive democratization (Dolenec 2013).

Illiberal politics has produced an array of contemporary more or less misaligned 'frankenstates' in Southeast Europe (Krastev and Holmes 2018). These regimes combine elements of liberal democracy in a way that subverts its original meaning, leaving only empty shells of liberal democratic institutions as a façade to retain outside recognition. Beneath are established authoritarian practices of executive dominance, patronage, and informality that are used to enforce political stability. To sum up, the theoretical argument that this introductory article advances is that today's illiberal politics have their roots in the post-communist power mutation set up in the early 1990s and with strong links to socialist governance practices. Actions of parties in government that manipulate elections, tilt the electoral playing field, disassemble checks and balances, and restrict civil liberties arise out of inherited governance practices that preserve executive party dominance, maintain clientelist linkages between the party and economy, and instrumentalize weak state institutions through informality.

3. Tracking democratic backsliding in Southeast Europe

Comparative measurement of democracy is always an imperfect business as there are few objective criteria to compare levels of democracy among regimes. Some of the most widely used indices of democracy, such as the Freedom in the World Index, rely on expert surveys or expert-coding. The complexity of the concept of democracy and its multiple meanings guarantee that each measure is a reflection of the selected attributes, coding decisions of authors, rules of aggregation, and structural conditions the experts are familiar with (Munck 2009).[8] In this sense, democracy indices measure how well countries match scholarly and expert perceptions of a specific definition of democracy.

The V-Dem data we use in this article, more specifically the Liberal Democracy Index (LDI), are based on a definition of democracy well suited to measure democratic backsliding as defined earlier. The index adopts an empirical measure for a 'thin' definition of democracy 'which recognises that liberal-democratic systems are the sum of two core components, democracy and liberalism' rather than one that includes all desirable characteristics under a single definition (Mounk 2018, 99). This allows us to identify threats to independent institutions, the rule of law, and minority rights in countries that uphold competitive elections.

The V-Dem LDI is composed of two empirically distinct components that individually measure the electoral and liberal aspects of democracy. The Electoral Democracy Index (EDI) measures the elements of Robert Dahl's polyarchy definition as it conforms to electoral democracy where rulers are responsible to citizens (Lührmann et al. 2018, 1322). It is an essential component for any understanding of democracy and is based on indicators of free and fair electoral contest and a level playing field, both before and in between elections. The Liberal Component Index (LCI) supplements electoral democracy in a way that reflects the presence of executive constraints, rule of law, and civil liberties that protect individual and minority rights against abuse from the state and the elected majority (Coppedge et al. 2019). As each indicator is available for comparison before aggregation, the 'nuanced nature of the V-Dem data also makes it possible to discern unevenness across different traits of democracy, down to the level of specific indicators' (Lührmann et al. 2018, 1330). The index is based on expert surveys and on a mix of additive and multiplicative aggregation rules. All data below are from V-Dem Dataset version 9 (Coppedge et al. 2019), while figures and tables are calculated by the author.

The general trend for Southeast Europe, according to the LDI, shows stagnation at best and democratic regression at worst. The data cover the past 7 years, coinciding with the final year of the European debt crisis, just before Croatia joined the European Union, and the last year data is available for at the time of writing. There are significant differences between countries and components of the index. As demonstrated in Figure 1, the level of democracy in the region as a whole has not changed significantly. In fact, the countries ended up becoming more similar in 2018. Throughout the whole period levels of liberal democracy in Croatia are well above the regional average, largely due to high standards in the electoral process, but are in decline here as well. The onset of democratic backsliding did not occur simultaneously, and in some cases, it happened many years prior to the data presented here. For example, while decline in levels of liberal democracy in Croatia was preceded by a continuous rise until 2012, in North Macedonia they were already declining since 2004. During this period change has been most dramatic in Serbia, North Macedonia, and Croatia, while Montenegro, BiH, and Albania generally show a pattern of stagnation.

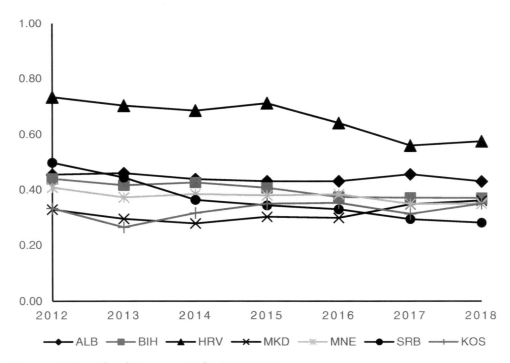

Figure 1. V-Dem Liberal Democracy Index 2012–2018.

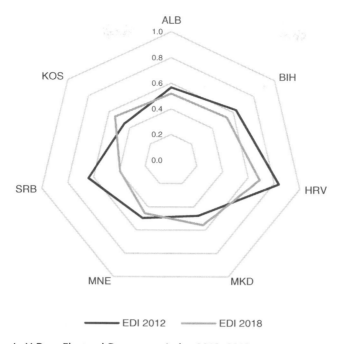

Figure 2. Change in V-Dem Electoral Democracy Index 2012–2018.

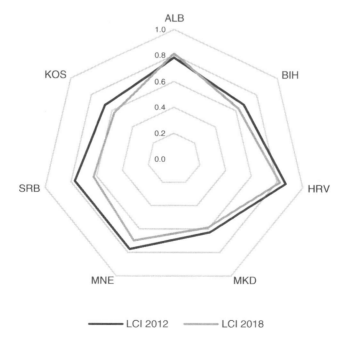

Figure 3. Change in V-Dem Liberal Component Index 2012–2018.

Disaggregating the LDI, it is possible to identify the challenges and weaknesses that each country faces. Also, change does not occur equally across both electoral and liberal components of democracy and not along the same components in all countries (Figure 2 and Figure 3). Looking at the change between 2012 and 2018 across the EDI and LCI indices confirms relative stagnation in Albania while showing that Croatia and BiH largely experienced decline in the electoral component of democracy. Montenegro and Kosovo show decline in the liberal component, along with an improvement on the EDI in the latter country. Serbia shows sharp decline along both components, while recent developments in North Macedonia boosted its EDI score above the 2012 levels, with the LCI still remaining low. The regional average indicates incremental decline in levels of both liberal and electoral democracy.

Observing the aggregate yearly change over a longer period of time (since the 2004 European Union expansion) shows us the amount and direction of change in each country during those 14 years. All countries have experienced a decline in levels of liberal democracy (LDI) or stagnation, while Kosovo's improvement is negligible. Decline is most pronounced in Serbia and North Macedonia, despite recent improvements in the latter (Table 1). Decline in the electoral component (EDI) is again noticeable in all cases except Albania and Kosovo, and most significant in Serbia, followed by BiH and Croatia. The liberal component (LCI) shows an improvement in Croatia and Albania, while decline is most pronounced in North Macedonia and Serbia. In other words, the level of democratic backsliding is largely due to deficiencies related to the electoral process in Serbia, Croatia, Montenegro, and BiH, and due to shortcomings of the liberal component in North Macedonia and Kosovo.

The intensity of change can be observed by aggregating the absolute values of yearly change for LDI (Table 1). We notice that Kosovo and Croatia have experienced significant change over the past 14 years, as well as North Macedonia and Serbia. These four regimes can be described as dynamic. Whereas Serbia largely experienced democratic decline, Croatia experienced both an increase and decline in levels of liberal democracy that largely evened out the final LDI score. On the other hand, BiH, Albania and Montenegro have seen very little change over the same period and can best be described as static regimes.

It is also possible to identify variables for each country that significantly contribute to democratic backsliding using the V-Dem data (Coppedge et al. 2019). For the three regimes identified as static, any backsliding happened largely due to issues related to tilting the playing field before elections and executive aggrandizement that ignores judicial and legislative competences. The dynamic group exhibits a much more diverse set of flaws. The main issue in Croatia is lacking freedom of expression, little media

Table 1. Aggregate change for LDI, EDI and LCI, 2004–2018.

Country	LDI	EDI	LCI	Absolute LDI
Albania	0.000	0.012	0.010	0.234
BiH	−0.102	−0.137	−0.044	0.190
Croatia	−0.043	−0.108	0.092	0.419
Kosovo	0.008	0.038	−0.021	0.432
Montenegro	−0.038	−0.051	−0.016	0.168
N. Macedonia	−0.139	−0.072	−0.186	0.359
Serbia	−0.254	−0.274	−0.154	0.302

independence, and media censorship. This is also the case in Serbia, along with tilting the playing field before elections and a lack of legislative constraints on the executive. Kosovo has a problem with judicial constraints on the executive, as well as civil liberties and equality before the law. Finally, North Macedonia has issues with all forms of executive constraints, deficient freedom of expression and media independence, as well as civil liberties.

The literature on democratic backsliding in Southeast Europe is very recent, although the trend became evident at least as far back as 2012. Countries where democratic decline has been ongoing for almost a decade are present in the literature as case studies. Yet, there have been few attempts to explore systemic issues that cross-cut individual cases or the important role of political parties in shaping this change.

Dolenec (2013) authored one of the first works that looks at how authoritarian practices persist in the region. While not specifically examining democratic backsliding, her book addresses both systemic explanations and the role of political parties and leaders, with most of the empirical analysis limited to Croatia and Serbia. A policy study by the Balkans in Europe Policy Advisory Group (edited by Kmezić and Bieber 2017) was an early foray into exploring the crisis of democracy in Southeast Europe through the lens of local adaptation to external (European Union) policy, resulting in what the authors term 'stabilitocracies'. Under a stabilitocracy regime actions that may be considered repressive are legitimized domestically with reference to European standards and through piecemeal adoption of European Union policy guidelines. The personal legitimation of national leaders with authoritarian traits is also important and occurs through multilateral summits and supportive statements from European leaders. Survey-based research with a focus on youth in Southeast Europe has found that support for leaders with an authoritarian style of governance, unchecked by legislative and judicial institutions and unquestioned by media, is significant and with marginal differences between countries (see Turčilo et al. 2019). This corresponds to the processes of post-communist power mutation that emphasize the political, economic and personalized power of strong leaders. Even though these young peoples had no experience of communist authoritarian rule, their perceptions of a leader's qualities are shaped by the institutional legacy and practices inherited from and embedded during early post-communist democratization.

In his forthcoming book, Bieber (2020) expands on an earlier article (Bieber 2018) and examines the return of competitive authoritarianism by looking at internal and external driving factors and restrictions. He notices a different type of non-democratic rule than in the 1990s, one that pays more attention to maintaining a semblance of competitive elections while exploiting an institutional weakness to undermine civil liberties and tilt the electoral playing field. A special issue of Southeastern Europe (edited by Perry and Keil 2018) explores the emergence of various forms of state capture by predatory elites. Their aim, according to the authors, is not to explicitly undermine democracy, but to capture weak state institutions in order perpetuate clientelist forms of economic power. In the end, these regimes end up weakening democracy in their path. Bochsler and Juon (Forthcoming) look at the systemic effect of populist governments on the quality of democracy in the region and find a consistent negative effect on the quality of competition, while effects on the quality of democracy are context dependent. Finally, a volume edited by Bieber et al. (2018) tackles issues of democratic backsliding by examining the role of political elites through a large number of case studies from Eastern Europe but does not cover more recent events in North Macedonia, Serbia or BiH.

The region of Southeast Europe is clearly regressing in quality of democracy, with exceptions in few countries and segments. Albania, in particular, presents a case where it is necessary to look deeper into governance and electoral practices and trace whether democratization has been able to make a break with the past. The reasons for the recent regression in Croatia warrant further attention, as does Kosovo's failure to make a significant move towards democracy. The change of government in North Macedonia has created possibilities for a new push to further democratize and it is pertinent to follow those developments and learn from the past. Recent civic protests in Serbia and BiH could have potential to halt democratic breakdown and induce change if they are able to mobilize a broad, national following. But all progress is tentative and uncertain as the region has for several decades remained volatile and stuck between a historical legacy of authoritarian rule and a democratic future that has not materialized.

4. Contributions to the special issue

This special issue aims to examine democratic backsliding by looking at the prevalence of illiberal politics across countries and issues. The case studies of Serbia, North Macedonia, Montenegro, BiH, Kosovo, Albania, and Croatia all roughly follow a common structure. These articles give a brief description of the country context, including the party system and contentious political issues. The main section of each focuses on governance practices or enabling factors of democratic decline. The authors identify proposed or enacted policies by governing parties that are aimed at perpetuating their rule. This includes policies targeting the electoral and liberal components of democracy and their four dimensions: explicit electoral manipulation, tilting the electoral playing field, removing checks and balances on the executive, and restricting civil liberties. As specific illiberal policies are context dependent and differ between countries, the authors of the case studies are left to decide which ones to prioritize. Finally, the case study articles address possible causes for the rise in illiberal politics. The authors explore whether these can be linked to structural factors embedded in a historical understanding of institutions, or to actors' motivations driven by opportunity, threat perceptions or identity-related narratives.

The first article by Dušan Pavlović examines the gradual demise of democratic institutions in Serbia. He argues that since coming to power in 2012, the SNS has undermined almost all elements of democracy, including free and fair elections and independent media, and has extensively misused public resources. Especially the latter is important as the party improved an existing system of extractive institutional design. The system rewards privileged access to public resources in exchange for electoral support, thus creating and reinforcing an uneven electoral playing field. The sum of illiberal policies has propelled the regime in Serbia back into the competitive authoritarianism of the 1990s.

Borjan Gjuzelov and Milka Ivanovska Hadjievska examine the case of North Macedonia by looking at the institutional and symbolic aspects of illiberal politics during the 11-year rule of VMRO-DPMNE. The institutional aspect examines party abuse of electoral processes, media reporting, access to rule of law, and distribution of public resources with the aim to create an uneven electoral playing field. The symbolic aspect looks into the intertwined Macedonian nationalism and 'antiquization' policies of VMRO-DPMNE that sought to legitimize illiberal politics and discredit opposition through a focus on identity politics. As a prime example of competitive authoritarianism in Southeast Europe, North Macedonia is also the only country that, at least seemingly, has been able to break the trend of democratic backsliding.

The case study of Montenegro, written by Olivera Komar, examines a country that is touted as the front-runner of European integration but where critical voices have been systematically weakened. She focuses on three illustrative examples of illiberal politics that have been successful at keeping the DPS party (and its party leader) continuously in government for almost three decades. Through cases of party control over public broadcasting, use of public resources to secure votes, and curtailing the independence of academic institutions, Komar examines illiberal policies enacted by DPS that have incrementally positioned Montenegro as a competitive authoritarian regime.

Damir Kapidžić looks at illiberal politics at the subnational level in order to explain the absence of democratic breakdown in BiH. He finds that autocratization is contained within subnational arenas by dominant parties representing a single ethnic group and constrained by multi-level and cross-ethnic checks and balances. While consociational power-sharing enables subnational leaders to establish competitive authoritarian regimes, it limits the spread and ramifications of illiberal politics to higher levels of government. Kapidžić analyses three cases of illiberal politics dealing with restrictions to the freedom of assembly, weakening independent media, and patronage in elections. He identifies deliberate attempts by ruling parties, especially the SNSD, to create and maintain an uneven electoral playing field. The result is differentiated democratic backsliding where parts of the country are significantly more authoritarian than others.

Writing on Kosovo, Adem Beha and Arben Hajrullahu trace how policies aimed at democratization and Europeanization have been misused by political elites to remain in power and to capture public resources. Policy priorities for Kosovo were largely defined by international actors and focused on keeping the country stable rather than on democratization and sustainable development. However, policy development and implementation relied on Kosovar political parties that use weak state institutions to subvert policymaking into a struggle for power and resources, while masking the effort as democratization and Europeanization. The weak economy, incomplete international recognition and divided society all contribute to the primacy of strong party-based clientelist networks.

The case study of Albania by Gentiana Kera and Armanda Hysa examines clientelist practices and private funding of election campaigns. Backed up by interview data, they adopt an ethnographic lens in order to identify donors, recipients and the impact of informal clientelism. Their research uncovers a widespread practice where, in order to gain an electoral advantage, parties engage in informal contracts with private donors, thus side-lining official regulations on party financing. Undeclared private money or services during election campaigns are found to increase the risk of future political favours for involved actors. The repercussion is a general dissatisfaction with the electoral process, especially in regard to influence of money on politics, and a perception of implicit reliance on clientelism for employment, education and services even beyond electoral contest.

The article on democratic decline in Croatia, written by Dario Čepo, focuses on the period after the country's accession to the European Union. The author finds that during this time the ruling HDZ[9] was able to maintain an electoral advantage by relying on structural weaknesses of the political system it had shaped during the transition in the 1990s. Through illiberal politics the party systematically weakened autonomous institutions, preserved influence over the judiciary, and subverted independent media. While the extent of all these practices is still limited, their impact adds up to consistent but incremental democratic backsliding that is still ongoing.

The comparative articles focus on specific issues across several (but not necessarily all) Southeast European countries. Their aim is to gain a broader understanding of the relevance of individual aspects of democracy in Southeast Europe. As these issues have central importance in defining liberal democracy, any deficiencies and restrictions can significantly reduce democratic quality. At the same time, they are most often the target of government policies and practices that we have identified as illiberal politics.

Věra Stojarová's comparative article looks at control of media and constraints on media independence in Southeast Europe. She argues that illiberal politics target all aspects of the profession not with the explicit aim to eliminate independent media or silence dissent, but to overpower it with pro-government reporting. Her article examines the legislative framework and the role of regulatory bodies, issues of defamation and media ownership, economic pressure and censorship, as well as physical and verbal intimidation of journalists. Throughout the region the role of independent media is found to be weak and compromised. Instead of being a watchdog, the most influential and relevant media outlets engage in favourable reporting of executive leaders while critical voices are side-lined.

The second comparative article focuses on the nexus between rule of law and democracy. Marko Kmezić argues that the absence of a democratic rule of law is purposefully exploited by ruling elites in order to misuse fragile institutions to their advantage. He demonstrates this through a comparative analysis of elements related to electoral processes (exploitation of public resources, media dominance, electoral registers and voter fraud) and media freedom (historical legacies, weak regulation, informal pressure and government influence). In this sense, he argues that due to deficiencies in rule of law, the countries of the region lack the substance not just of liberal but also of formal democracy.

Gazela Pudar Draško, Irena Fiket and Jelena Vasiljević examine the role of social movements and their potential to generate democratic change in authoritarian societies. Based on an ethnographic approach and in-depth interviews the authors compare social movements in Serbia and North Macedonia and assess their capacity to act as a corrective when other institutions are subverted, when trust in official public institutions is critically low and when competitive electoral contest is no longer certain. They conclude that while there are several similarities across the two cases, the Macedonian movements displayed greater capacity to cooperate with each other, as well as with other social players, in comparison to emerging social movements in Serbia, to greater effect.

In the concluding article to this special issue, Věra Stojarová focuses on the central themes which link all articles: undermining free and fair elections, weakening independent media, limiting the role of judiciary, gaining privileged access to public resources, and independent institutions and executive oversight. She examines the prevalence of illiberal politics and similarities among Southeast European countries across these themes. In searching for causes of democratic decline she explores the impact of structural deficiencies, unrestrained executives, and institutionalized informality.

Tracing the recent rise of illiberal politics in Southeast Europe is not straightforward. So far there has not been an abrupt democratic breakdown or descent into authoritarianism in any country of the region. Instead what we notice are incremental changes, executed by governing parties through illiberal policies, that target a broad range of issues and actors with the aim to reduce governmental accountability and electoral competitiveness. The contributions to this special issue aim to shed light on a region-wide political process and to examine the causes of democratic decline in each country individually and comparatively. By examining structural deficiencies that were institutionalized during the post-communist transition period the authors highlight country-specific enabling factors that allow political parties and their leaders to subvert democracy to their own gain. The topic of this special issue is both timely and relevant as the countries of the Western Balkans redefine their relationship towards the European Union or adopt to shifting internal policies of the European Union, in the case of Croatia.

In a region where democracy has not been fully consolidated it is not prudent to advance an agenda of political stability at the expense of liberty. With the European Union accession process at a standstill and third actors exerting increasing influence, it becomes necessary to assess threats to democratic institutions in Southeast Europe arising from illiberal politics of their elected leaders.

Notes

1. The countries we examine are: Albania, Bosnia and Herzegovina, Croatia, Kosovo, Montenegro, North Macedonia, and Serbia. We include Croatia because it shares very many traits with other countries, even though it is no longer officially part of the Western Balkans after joining the European Union in 2013. While we acknowledge the difference between the terms 'Western Balkans' and 'Southeast Europe', individual articles in this special issue use the terms interchangeably.
2. Internal Macedonian Revolutionary Organization – Democratic Party for Macedonian National Unity.
3. Serbian Progressive Party.
4. Alliance of Independent Social Democrats.
5. Democratic Party of Socialists.
6. To calculate their measures for classification, the authors exclusively rely on multiplicative aggregation of variables which leads to an exaggeration of single structural flaws in the classification (Levitsky and Way 2010, 365–371).
7. Vladisavljević (2008) argues that these trends have roots even further back in the past, in the radical decentralization of political and economic power in Yugoslavia in the 1970s and 1980s, and were propagated by centrifugal nationalist mobilization in the early 1990s.
8. The Democracy Barometer attempts to provide an alternative solution by relying on objective and comparable data instead of expert assessments but is (still) limited in scope and therefore comparability (Merkel et al. 2018).
9. Croatian Democratic Union.

Acknowledgments

The author is grateful to Nebojša Vladisavljević, Daniel Bochsler, and Věra Stojarová for their insightful comments on earlier drafts of this article.

Disclosure statement

No potential conflict of interest was reported by the author.

ORCID

Damir Kapidžić http://orcid.org/0000-0002-8619-3530

References

Bermeo, N. 2016. On democratic backsliding. *Journal of Democracy* 27, no. 1: 5–19. doi:10.1353/jod.2016.0012

Bieber, F. 2018. Patterns of competitive authoritarianism in the Western Balkans. *East European Politics* 34, no. 3: 337–54. doi:10.1080/21599165.2018.1490272

Bieber, F. 2020. *The rise of authoritarianism in the Western Balkans*. Cham: Palgrave Macmillan.

Bieber, F., M. Solska, and D. Taleski, eds. 2018. *Illiberal and authoritarian tendencies in Central, Southeastern and Eastern Europe*. Bern: Peter Lang.

Bochsler, D., and A. Juon. forthcoming. Authoritarian footprints in Central and Eastern Europe. *East European Politics*.

Coppedge, M., J. Gerring, C.H. Knutsen, S.I. Lindberg, J. Teorell, D. Altman, M. Bernhard, et al. 2019. *V-Dem [Country-Year/Country-Date] dataset v9*. Varieties of Democracy (V-Dem) Project. doi:10.23696/vdemcy19.

Dahl, R. 1989. *Democracy and its critics*. New Haven: Yale University Press.

Dolenec, D. 2013. *Democratic institutions and authoritarian rule in Southeast Europe*. Colchester, UK: ECPR Press.

Kmezić, M., and F. Bieber, eds. 2017. *The crisis of democracy in the Western Balkans. An anatomy of stabilitocracy and the limits of EU democracy promotion*. Balkans in Europe Policy Advisory Group. https://biepag.eu/wp-content/uploads/2017/05/final.pdf.

Krastev, I., and S. Holmes. 2018. Imitation and its discontents. *Journal of Democracy* 29, no. 3: 117–28. doi:10.1353/jod.2018.0049

Levitsky, S., and L.A. Way. 2010. *Competitive authoritarianism: hybrid regimes after the cold war*. Cambridge: Cambridge University Press.

Levitsky, S., and L.A. Way. 2015. The myth of democratic recession. *Journal of Democracy* 26, no. 1: 45–58. doi:10.1353/jod.2015.0007

Lührmann, A., V. Mechkova, S. Dahlum, L. Maxwell, M. Olin, C. Sanhueza Petrarca, R. Sigman, M.C. Wilson, and S.I. Lindberg. 2018. State of the world 2017: Autocratization and exclusion? *Democratization* 25, no. 8: 1321–40. doi:10.1080/13510347.2018.1479693

Merkel, W. 2004. Embedded and defective democracies. *Democratization* 11, no. 5: 33–58. doi:10.1080/13510340412331304598

Merkel, W., D. Bochsler, K. Bousbah, M. Bühlmann, H. Giebler, M. Hänni, L. Heyne, et al. 2018. *Democracy barometer. Methodology. Version 6*. Aarau: Zentrum für Demokratie.

Mounk, Y. 2018. The undemocratic dilemma. *Journal of Democracy* 29, no. 2: 98–112. doi:10.1353/jod.2018.0030

Munck, G. 2009. *Measuring democracy*. Baltimore: Johns Hopkins University Press.

Offe, C. 2003. *Herausforderungen der Demokratie: Zur Integrations- und Leistungsfähigkeit politischer Institutionen*. Frankfurt: Campus Verlag.

Perry, V., and S. Keil. 2018. The business of state capture in the Western Balkans. An introduction. *Southeastern Europe* 42, no. 1: 1–14. doi:10.1163/18763332-04201001

Schedler, A. 2013. *The politics of uncertainty. Sustaining and subverting electoral authoritarianism*. Oxford: Oxford University Press.

Turčilo, L., A. Osmić, D. Kapidžić, S. Šadić, J. Žiga, and A. Dudić. 2019. *Youth study 2018. Bosnia and Herzegovina*. Sarajevo: Friedrich Ebert Stiftung.

Vladisavljević, N. 2008. *Serbia's antibureaucratic revolution: Miloševic, the fall of communism and nationalist mobilization*. Basingstoke: Palgrave Macmillan.

Vladisavljević, N., and A. Krstić. 2019. Competitive authoritarianism and populism in Serbia under Vučić in political cartoons. Unpublished manuscript.

Zakariah, F. 1997. The rise of illiberal democracy. *Foreign Affairs* 76, no. 6: 22–43. doi:10.2307/20048274

Zakošek, N. 1997. Pravna država i demokracija u postsocijalizmu. *Politička misao* 34, no. 4: 78–85.

The political economy behind the gradual demise of democratic institutions in Serbia

Dušan Pavlović (iD)

ABSTRACT
This paper aims to accomplish two goals. First, to present recent empirical evidence supporting the claim that Serbia is on the path towards embracing a more radical version of electoral authoritarianism. This is accomplished by examining most recent illiberal politics aimed at controlling electoral processes and the media sphere, and extracting public funds for partisan purposes. I claim that the incomplete design of democratic institutions in Serbia set up between 2001 and 2012 is primarily responsible for the democratic decline. The second goal is more general and aims to emphasize the importance of extracting public funds for hybrid regimes. Extractive institutions matter because they directly impact other critical segments of electoral authoritarianism (notably, elections and media freedom), but also because they explain the type of leadership they promote in politics. If public resources remain without proper institutional oversight and are simply 'up for grabs,' this will attract leaders more willing to dismantle democratic institutions and violate democratic procedures. Serbia serves as a good and current example of this linkage.

1. Introduction

There is a widespread academic consensus that Serbia under Milošević (1990–2000) represents a kind of hybrid regime (Pavlović and Antonić 2007; Stojiljković 2012; Dolenec 2013; Donno 2013; Spoerri 2014). Such regimes are sometimes referred to as examples of electoral authoritarianism (Schedler 2006, 2009; Levitsky and Way 2010) and are based on the illusion of democracy (Puddington 2017). From the outside, they look democratic, but when one digs deeper, it is a travesty of democracy. Elections are rigged, the most influential media are censored (or they self-censor), judges and prosecutors are blackmailed and are at risk of losing their jobs if they apply the law impartially and investigate politically sensitive cases, and corruption runs rampant.

A number of studies published recently put forward the claim that Serbia (and several other countries in the Western Balkan region) is experiencing a democratic rollback accompanied by the rise of authoritarian practices (Günay and Džihić 2016; Bieber 2018a; Bieber 2018b; Kmezić and Bieber 2017; BIEPAG 2017; Keil 2018; Krastev and Holmes 2018; Kapidžić, 2020). This is an interesting development because Serbia appeared to have improved its democratic record after Slobodan Milošević was forced to step down in October 2000 (Bunce and Sharon 2011; Bieber 2011; Spoerri 2014). After 12 years of sluggish democratic consolidation from 2001–2012 (Stojiljković 2012), in 2013 Serbia started again to move towards becoming a competitive authoritarian regime, which accelerated following the 2014 parliamentary elections when the incumbent cabinet led by Aleksandar Vučić launched institutional reversal, gradually stripping nascent democratic institutions of their democratic substance. Why did this happen?

I offer an institutional explanation. As a start, I adopt Bieber's thesis that the democratic decline in Serbia is a consequence of 'the failure of reformist governments during the early 2000s to decisively break with authoritarian practices and establish independent and democratic institutions, thus facilitating the return of competitive authoritarian regimes' (Bieber 2018b, 339). Rather than building strong democratic institutions that would prevent electoral manipulation, media control, public office abuse, and various sorts of extraction, the post-Milošević political elite did a poor job, thus leaving democratic institutional design unfinished. When the younger generation of the Milošević-era politicians returned to office in 2012, they found weak institutions and unrestrained access to public funds and rents. They used this opportunity to abuse public funds for their private gain, but to be able to do this they had to block access to the opposition (former incumbents) and prevent their return to office. Put another way, the recent rise of electoral authoritarianism in Serbia is a consequence of the preference towards creating a hyper-incumbency[1] to be able to continue with extraction.

My second goal is to argue that extraction[2] matters more than is usually recognized in the research on hybrid regimes. An analysis of access to public funds and rents is essential for both electoral competition and media access in electoral authoritarianism. For one thing, the incumbent does not only use public funds for private gain, but also to skew the previously-level playing field. We, therefore, cannot fully understand how incumbents win elections if we do not understand what kind of advantage the unrestrained access to public funds provides. Secondly, the institutions that enable the plundering of asset and the extraction of public funds draw a specific type of person into politics, thereby producing a specific type of leadership. If extractive institutions are strong and public resources are unprotected, they will attract political agents who are prone to violating and abolishing democratic procedures to be able to pursue public resource extraction. Such dynamics, in my view, lie at the heart of the most recent democratic rollback in Serbia.

This article is divided into two parts. Part I (sections 3–4) describes the emergence of the Serbian multiparty system after 1990 and the failed attempt to consolidate democracy from 2001–2012. Part II (sections 5–7) is focused on the institutions of the hybrid regime: elections, the media, and the extraction of public funds. Section 8 discusses these findings.

2. Theoretical concepts

As previously mentioned, during the 1990s Serbia was a hybrid regime, otherwise known as competitive (electoral) authoritarianism. After Slobodan Milošević stepped down in October 2000, some research classified the country as democracy (Schedler 2009), some said that it can arguably be classified as democracy (Roberts 2018), some claimed that it has embarked upon its path of democratization (Levitsky and Way 2010), or that 'the early 2000s marked the highpoint of the democratic transformation' (Bieber 2018b). The first statement was probably too soon. Granted, Serbia's democracy score according to many international rankings after 2000 improved significantly. However, after the collapse of communism in 1990, Serbia has never attained the level of a consolidated democracy.

Indeed, international ranking houses were united in claiming that Serbia was not a democracy after 2000. From 2000–2012, Serbia was classified as a semi-consolidated democracy under the Freedom House's project Nations in Transit, partly free under the Freedom in the World project, a flawed democracy under the EIU's democracy index, and defective democracy or democracy in consolidation by the Bertelsmann transformation index. All these ranking houses (except one) demoted Serbia's democratic rating after 2012. The Serbian democratic path from 1990–2019 suggests a non-linear, or zigzagged pattern (Bieber 2018b; Vladisavljević 2019).

Although Serbia has never been a consolidated democracy, there was an apparent attempt by the four post-Milošević cabinets to build new democratic institutions from 2000–2012. In that period, a whole array of new institutions emerged that did not exist prior to Milošević's downfall (see section 3 for the list). However, despite some tangible success in departing from Milošević' version of electoral authoritarianism after 2000, the post-Milošević political and economic elite failed to strengthen these institutions to safeguard future democratic development. Under some interpretations, Serbia and the whole region (not only the Western Balkans but the whole of Central and Eastern Europe; see Kapidžić, 2020) never reached the level of real democracy, so that the usage of the term 'democratic backsliding' is rather misleading because one cannot slide from something that did not exist (Cianetti et al. 2018). The region's post-communist governments established 'relatively stable forms of bad governance that serve to block the path to fuller democracy and, in some cases, might open opportunities for democratic deterioration' (*Ibid.* p. 246). We can only talk about the degree as to how far one government goes towards fuller autocracy or moves away from it.

This sits comfortably with the central category of this volume, namely – illiberal politics, under which there is a thin line between weak democracy and electoral authoritarianism. 'While (competitive) authoritarianism is a strong symptom, illiberal politics are the disease that causes it, that can be identified, and ultimately addressed' (Kapidžić, 2020). It is also in agreement with the thesis under which the post-Milošević elite failed to adopt a strategy of self-restraint, thus failing to design strong institutions that would limit the abuse of office. When Boris Tadić lost the presidency and the post-Milošević political parties were out of office in 2012, the political agents from the Milošević era who returned to office started an institutional reversal – their aim was to go back to the 1990s, towards a more radical version of electoral authoritarianism. A number of academic research papers that recognized this return to a more radical hybrid regime type significantly increased over the past few years (Günay and Džihić 2016; Bieber 2018a, 2018b; Keil 2018; Vladisavljević 2019; Pavlović 2019; Stojanović and Bértoa 2019). Even the European Parliament's research division recognized the risk of Serbia reverting to a more autocratic form of government (Russel 2019).

Before I explain what happened, let me briefly invoke some critical elements of electoral authoritarianism that are relevant for further discussion. Electoral authoritarianism (EA) is a relatively new concept in comparative political science. It signifies a regime type in which electoral manipulation runs so high that it cannot qualify as a democratic regime (Schedler 2009). Yet, such a regime has a rather developed institutional design that looks like a democracy. The design is a mere façade but with a strategic purpose. It serves the incumbents to mask attempts to hinder or block democratic competition that would enable meaningful political change, but may also be a consequence of 'international pressure and domestic legitimacy' (Miller 2017).

EA regimes are different from autocracies or dictatorships. Some examples of such non-democratic countries, such as Saudi Arabia, China, or Eritrea, do not organize elections, while some other, like Laos and Swaziland, do organize them but with only one, or no party (Gandhi and Lust-Okar 2009; Levitsky and Way 2010). Like in a democracy, in EA elections are fiercely contested,[3] but in contrast to a true democracy, elections are heavily rigged. The incumbent does not only manipulate the election results but also controls a whole array of institutions which are supposed to vouch for a free and fair electoral process. The incumbents in such regimes are known for the alteration of electoral lists, gerrymandering, the intimidation of voters, harassment of the opposition, media and campaign funding control, but also outright fraud that involves falsifying the ballot counts (Schedler 2002, 2006, 2009; Levitsky and Way 2010). To give one of the most recent examples, the Turkish incumbent who disliked the outcome of the 2019 Istanbul mayoral election (won by the opposition contender) simply ordered that voting be re-run.

Since the electoral process is heavily manipulated and rigged, the opposition has an extremely hard time winning elections. But since elections in EA are competitive and do contain a degree of uncertainty (Schedler 2009, 2015), it is not entirely impossible that the opposition removes the authoritarian incumbent from office, especially when it is united and receive international support to accomplish this goal (Donno 2013). The protest and the removal often take place by way of mass street demonstrations in response to electoral theft (Vladisavljević 2014, 2016). The clashes between the incumbent and the opposition may not always be about a mere cabinet change. When the clash is a so-called nested game (Tsebelis 1990), the outcome is a more thorough regime change (Levitsky and Way 2010).

As stated, I discuss the extraction aspect in EA in some more detail because I believe it is somewhat under-theorized in this type of literature. For example Schedler's *Electoral Authoritarianism. The Dynamics of Unfree Competition* (2006) largely focuses on elections. The same goes for Levitsky and Way's seminal *Competitive Authoritarianism* (2010). A substantial number of articles about the general character of EA, or on the most recent trends in such regimes are also focused on elections and media (Schedler 2002; Levitsky and Way 2002; Ottaway 2003; Howard and Roessler 2006; Lust-Okar 2006; Gandhi and Lust 2009; Donno 2013; Miller 2017), or some other practical issues (Rodriguez 2018). This is expected given the fact that electoral victory provides a major source of legitimacy for the incumbent and can explain a large part of regime change dynamics. Yet, to fully grasp the functioning of such regimes, it is critical to explain how electoral dynamics are influenced by extractive institutions and what the political agents are fighting for.

Extraction matters for at least two reasons. First, extractive institutions directly affect electoral and media dynamics. Political agents that can freely extract public funds from state and municipal budgets enjoy a massive advantage over the opposition which does not. The incumbent is not only able to financially support their electoral campaign but also to support the media that are close to them, financially starving media outlets that pledge no political affiliation. Sections 4–5 provide some details and recent practice about how unequal public funds access adversely impacts electoral politics and media freedoms.

The second aspect of extraction is even more important because in Serbia it relates to the institutional reform that was carried out from 2001–2012. This reform did not go deep enough in building protection from the abuse of power and the prevention of democratic decline after 2012. More precisely, the institutional design built from 2001–2012 did not provide for the proper oversight of public resources, leaving them unprotected and attractive to the type of leadership already mentioned. Non-transparent budget spending, unregulated privatization procedures, and the absence of accountability of public officials for mismanaging public funds attracts into politics a specific kind of people who are unprepared to accept the outcome of democratic procedures and are more prone to violate democratic rules in order to defend their exclusive privileges, stemming from the incumbent position they occupy. This is what happened in Serbia after 2012. When the younger echelon of the Milošević elite returned to office in 2012, it just continued in a gradual way from where Milošević left off in October 2000. Section 7 describes some such mechanisms, emphasizing that some of them were in place before Vučić became President.

3. The consolidation of democracy in Serbia after 2000

Serbia under Milošević (1990–2000) was a hybrid regime built during the years of war in former Yugoslavia. Despite this hybrid regime, the opposition parties reorganized and united into an 18-member coalition called the Democratic Opposition of Serbia (DOS), which ousted Milošević and the SPS in October 2000. With Milošević gone, the DOS coalition launched economic and institutional reforms with the aim to transform the institutions of the hybrid regime of the 1990s.

The DOS coalition fell apart by mid-2001, but the parties that were part of it remained in the next four post-Milošević cabinets (2001–2012), thus carrying on with reforms of the political, economic, and judicial institutions. Parliamentary, presidential, and local elections were free and fair with no major procedural objections coming from participants, internal or international observer (OSCE 2007; 2008; 2012), although there were a lot of rooms to improve on electoral procedures (Jovanović 2008, 138). Some media reports revealed serious objections to ownership of the media (Anti-Corruption Council 2011), but the media system was fairly open – all political agents could appear on all TV channels, radio programmes and in print media, including the public broadcaster, which at the time organized almost daily televised debates between incumbent and opposition representatives. In general, the media in 2000–2012 reflected a much more balanced coverage of political conflicts (Vladisavljević 2019). A special institution called the Republic Broadcast Agency, and then renamed as the Regulatory Authority for Electronic Media (REM), was the first regulatory agency established in 2003 with the aim of overseeing media content and media ownership. It was supposed to act as a politically-independent institution that would insure a fair balance of media representation for all parliamentary agents. Although the REM has never, even before 2012, performed its role in its entirety, media freedom was significantly stronger compared to developments since 2012.[4]

REM was not the only institution in this new institutional design. Several other institutions that make up the fourth branch of government (Schedler 1999) and that are critical for overseeing and controlling the executive branch of the government but did not exist in Milošević's Serbia, were established from 2001–2012. These are the Prosecution for Organized Crime (2003), the Commissioner for Information of Public Importance and

Personal Data Protection (2004), the State Audit Institution (2005), Human Rights Protector (2007), the Anti-Corruption Agency (2009) etc. The new institutional design that emerged underneath the rubble of the Milošević era was no accident. The DOS leaders were truly more democratic and less prone to abusing public office. The crucial confirmation of this statement comes from the fact that they were prepared to compete for office under free and fair institutions. The two DOS leaders who occupied important political posts surrendered them to their successors without attempting to rig elections in order to stay on. Vojislav Koštunica, the Serbian Premier from 2004–2008, left office in 2008 after unsuccessful 2.5 month-negotiations to put together a third cabinet. Boris Tadić, Serbian President from 2004–2012, did the same after he lost presidential elections to Tomislav Nikolić of the Serbian Progressive Party (SNS) in May 2012.

4. Free and fair elections

As mentioned, the democratic rollback in Serbia started in 2013. Figure 1 displays the democratic score, an average taken from seven democratic areas according to Freedom House's *Nations in Transit* study.[5] We can observe two things. Firstly, Serbia's democracy score deteriorated from 2014 to 2018. (According to the methodology, a higher score is worse, lower is better. When a country reaches the score of 4, it is classified as a hybrid regime). Secondly, we can observe that the average score for the four central categories for electoral authoritarianism – elections, independent media, judicial independence, and corruption – ranks above the average.[6] The average score for Serbia in 2018 is 3.96, meaning it is only 0.04 points away from being classified as a hybrid regime under the FH classificatory standards. The average for the four categories is 4.25, which is well into the

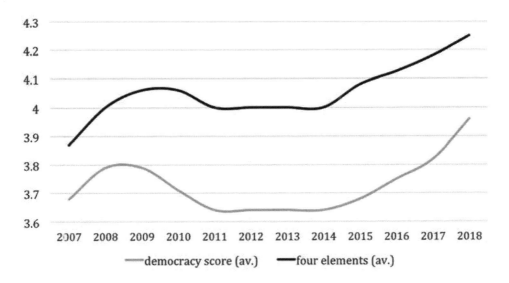

Figure 1. Serbia. Democracy score and the averages for electoral process, media, judiciary and corruption 2007–2018.
Source: Freedom House, Nations in Transit. https://freedomhouse.org/report-types/nations-transit

hybrid regime domain. (Figure 2 displays separate rankings for each of these dimensions for the same period.)

Serbian elections became increasingly illiberal in 2014. As in many modern non-democratic regimes, they do not serve to select the best leaders but rather to validate autocracy through the ballot, albeit under fraudulent conditions (Puddington 2017). The central institution in Serbia intended to vouch for free and fair elections is the Republic Electoral Commission (REC). It is given a large prerogative to be involved in the electoral process, including a right to act as a quasi-judicial institution when solving electoral issues. If necessary, it can order a recount, or even cancel the elections. In practice, the REC appears to do the opposite: it either does not get involved when it should, or it takes political sides by allowing collusion among its members. Both things have a detrimental effect on free and fair electoral competition.

The behaviour of the REC is only one item in the menu of manipulation that an incumbent (sometimes in alliance with opposition parties) can use to skew the electoral playing field in order to get the preferred electoral outcome. There are more. Electoral roll has become all the messier since 1990. The roll does not get updated when a voter dies, so often dead people are kept on the list long after they have passed away and even receive a formal letter, inviting them to vote. The list is full of people who do not exist with fake addresses. The electoral roll is supposed to be taken care of by the Ministry of Local Administration, but the Ministry fails to keep the roll up to date (Branković and Cvejin 2018). A corrupt practice called Bulgarian train, where voters are forced or blackmailed to use previously prepared ballots, has been on the rise after 2012, notably on the 2016 parliamentary, and the 2018 Belgrade and Lučani local elections (Dragojlo 2016; Russel 2019).

The SNS field activists become increasingly aggressive on the election day. Since 2014, they started organizing a 'get out and vote' campaign that involves intimidation and job

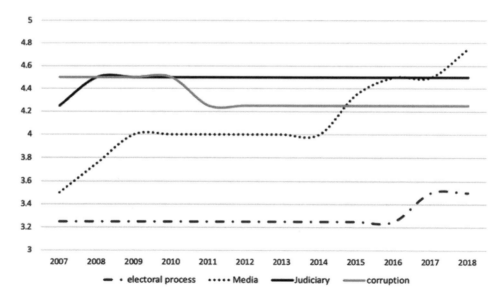

Figure 2. Serbia. Separate ranking for electoral process, media, judiciary and corruption in 2007–2018.
Source: Freedom House, Nations in Transit. https://freedomhouse.org/report-types/nations-transit

loss threats on the potential electorate. (Lots of people in Serbia are employed in the public sector, so the threat of losing the job is real). Very often in smaller settlements and villages, citizens would report skin-head thugs driving around town in black jeeps and SUVs with no licence plates visiting every house, knocking on everyone's doors and getting people out to vote. SNS activists are seen standing by polling stations and the electoral booths with a paper list, taking down the names of the people who voted (CRTA 2018; Branković and Cvejin 2018; Damnjanović 2018).

According to the CRTA, an independent NGO that monitors elections in Serbia, the level of fraudulent electoral behaviour is on the rise. In the last local elections that took place on 16 December 2018 in the municipality of Lučani, the SNS won 66 per cent of the votes. CRTA reports blatant violations of electoral procedure in 12 out of 43 polling stations: people voted without IDs, the secrecy of voting was violated, voters' fingers were not marked (to avoid multiple voting), a UV lamp was not used (to identify if the voter had already voted), the SNS activists stood by pooling stations, keeping parallel voting lists and taking down who showed up to vote etc. (CRTA 2018; CESID 2018; Branković and Cvejin 2018). The organization of such people requires money. Most of them are the public sector's employees who participate in such activities under the threat of losing their jobs.

5. Media freedom

Compared to the other critical areas of electoral authoritarianism, media freedoms saw the most rapid decline after Vučić came to power (Figure 2).

Since Freedom House monitors media indicators in the post-communist countries, only in one year did Serbia have a worse score for media freedom than in 2018. This was in 1999 (score 5.75), when Aleksandar Vučić was the Minister of Information in the cabinet of Mirko Marjanović. Vučić's main responsibility was to control the media. In October 1998, Vučić proposed the Information Act, which enabled magistrates to issue draconian fines for media that violated the act within 24 hours. The peculiarity of this act was that it did not involve the presumption of innocence, so the media had to prove to the court that they were not guilty rather than the other way around. Between October 1998 and February 2001, the act was applied 67 times and the total amount of fines was €1.25 million (Stevanović 2018).

During the 1999 NATO bombing, Vučić rounded up the editors of the largest print media and instructed them what to print on a daily basis. They would come to his offices with a copy of the next day's front page and followed his instructions as to how to amend it (Andrejić 2017). Since media freedom is anyhow limited during wartime, one could say that the situation in 1999 was an outlier, which makes 2018 (i. e. 2017) the worst year for independent media in Serbia ever.

Several surveys that were carried in Serbia over the past few years show a rather dominant presence of Aleksandar Vučić in the major national broadcasters as well as in the print outlets with the highest circulations, both of which are controlled by the executive (BIRODI 2016; 2017; Jaraković 2019). Only during the 2017 presidential campaign, Vučić received ten times more airtime than all other candidates combined (Maksić and Gruska 2017). A study that looked into the media content after 2000 found that political conflicts in 2010 (while the DOS political elite was still in office) were portrayed as pluralistic, thus reflecting greater media freedom. In contrast, in 2015 political conflicts were portrayed as rather monolithic, thus reflecting stronger political influence of the incumbent (Vladisavljević 2019).

The pressure on public media appears in direct and indirect way. Direct control is exerted on the public broadcasters' management and editorial content, while indirect control is exerted through finances. Two publicly-owned stations, Televizija Srbije (RTS) and Radio Televizija Vojvodine (RTV), are the examples of both. They reach over 90 per cent of Serbian households. As state-sponsored broadcasters (RTS employs over 3,000 people and RTV over 1,000), these are under the direct political control of the incumbent. The Serbian Assembly appoints the members of the RTS Supervisory Board.[7] It is the RTS Supervisory Board that later appoints the RTS general manager who is then obliged to follow the political line set by the majority in the Assembly and the executive. Besides, every year when it adopts the state budget, the Serbian Assembly sets the total share of the budget for RTS and RTV (Jaraković 2019). This is a significant amount of money (€26.2 million for 2019), without which these two public broadcasters would not be able to survive. This serves as an annual reminder to every RTS and RTV employee that there will be no salaries if they do not follow the incumbent party line. This is a gross violation of democratic principles in public institutions because both RTS and RTV are financed from the state budget, meaning they are financed by all citizens. Yet the opposition leaders, who represent a significant chunk of the population, are rarely seen on these two stations' programmes.

RTS and RTV are public broadcasters owned by the state, so some degree of political influence is probably unavoidable. There is, however, a number of private broadcasters that are even more politically biased. TV PINK, O2, Happy, and TV Prva openly prioritize news in favour of Aleksandar Vučić, the SNS and its coalition partners (BIRODI 2016; 2017). The only national TV broadcaster that has a more balanced approach, but leans towards the opposition, is TVN1, which was established in the region in October 2014, but as it is only available on cable, it has a reach of no more than 10 per cent of households.

The institutional agent that is most responsible for such a biased media is the Regulatory Body for Electronic Media (REM) which is, under the 2014 Electronic Media Law, tasked with ensuring the diversity of media services as well as the protection of freedom of opinion in a democratic society. This task is well-defined, but if the REM fails to act on it, there is no sanction for its members (Jaraković 2019).

The REM is a regulatory institution that takes the main decisions about who may enter the Serbian media market. It does that by way of issuing broadcasting licences. Only broadcasters which are granted a national licence can broadcast programmes across the whole territory of Serbia. Licences are issued by the REM Council whose members are, just like in the case of the RTS Supervisory Board, appointed by the Serbian Assembly.[8] They have to follow the political line set by the incumbent. Consequently, the REM will issue a licence, but only if the owner of the private broadcasters who apply for it informally declare upfront that they will favour the incumbent. Should the private owner later defect (by not privileging the incumbent), the REM can withdraw the licence. According to Nenad Cekić, the first REM head (2006–2008), the REM has manipulated the process of issuing the licences since 2008. Although the law explicitly forbade that one owner can have more than one broadcasting licences, the REM allowed Antena Group to buy a licence for two broadcasters, the then TV Fox Serbia (later renamed into TV Prva) and the then TV B92 (later renamed into O2). In 2014, the law was changed, so it explicitly allowed that one owner can buy more than one broadcasting licences (Cekić 2018).

ILLIBERAL POLITICS IN SOUTHEAST EUROPE

Apart from TVN1, there are several print media outlets that are rather critical about Aleksandar Vučić and his government. However, the print circulation of these is rather small and, compared to other print outlets, insignificant. The print circulation of the most popular weeklies *NIN* and *Vreme* do not exceed 10,000, while the daily *Danas* does not run over 20,000 copies. In contrast, the total combined daily circulation of *Blic, Informer, Kurir, Srpski telegraf, Alo* can reach 333,000 a day in 2016.[9]

Perhaps most telling is the fact that since the 2012 parliamentary electoral campaign, televised debates between the incumbent and the opposition have been dying down and at some point were totally taken off the air (except on TVN1). Even the parliamentary sessions, which are mandated by law to be broadcast live on RTS2 (a publicly-owned broadcaster), are often interrupted by commercials and live sport event coverage. Aleksandar Vučić himself has literally not met with any opposition leader for a televised debate since 2012. Even during the 2017 presidential campaign, he refused to have one with any of the contenders. Since 2014, the journalists from the electronic media which is not controlled by the government have to struggle with Vučić's PR team in press conferences to ask him even a simple question. Rather than getting a straightforward answer, they would receive a salvo of offence and accusations. The last interview Vučić gave for a media outlet which is critical of him was on 14 April 2016. Since 2013, he appears regularly on TV RTS, TV Pink, Happy TV, O2, and TV Prva – all of which almost weekly rearrange their programming to make room for the 1–2 hour long interviews he gives sitting alone in the studio.

The situation is even worse with the local media. Since 2011, the Serbian Government, encouraged by the EU within the context of the enlargement process (Chapter 23), adopted the policy of getting the Government out of media ownership (Poznatov and Vukojičić-Obradović 2012). The strategy implied that local administrations must sell all publicly-owned media – TV and radio stations – by mid-2015. This policy measure appeared to have dealt a deadly blow to the independence of local media but also have led to the deterioration of the media content's quality. Instead of getting a preferred outcome under which the market would allocate resources so as to enhance media freedom in the Serbian municipalities, local TV and radio stations were sold off to tycoons affiliated with the SNS, with rigged sales administrated by the Privatization Agency, which itself was a corrupt institution, 'infected' by massive party patronage. Local tycoons connected to the SNS bought several dozen local TV stations and transformed them into a SNS propaganda service (Gotev and Poznatov 2016).

Although the media were privatized, the local administrations continued to finance them from their local budgets (Jaraković 2019). For example, TV Novi Pazar was sold to a consortium linked to Rasim Ljajić, Minister of Trade in the Vučić cabinet, for €89,500. The same year the city council of Novi Pazar gave €4.2 million to this TV station as a kind of subsidy for the next three years (TCD 2016). In 2019, only the city of Niš gave away €655,000 to local media. Fourth fifth of this sum went to the people connected directly to the SNS. Some of these media are owned by the sons of the top-ranked SNS members (Miladinović 2019). Apart from this free direct financial support, flagship broadcasters (such as TV Pink) receive indirect financial support, such as tax debt write-offs (CINS 2018).

State financing of private media led to poorer quality of the outlets. Most media that receive financial support promote fake news, hate speech and violate the journalist code adopted in 2006 jointly by the two Serbian national journal associations. According to a research made by KRIK, an NGO for criminal and corruption research, the newspapers that print most false news are the newspapers that receive most money from the budget. Newspapers *Informer, Srpski telegraf,* or *Alo* printed altogether 730 false front page news in 2018. Most of these news were about 'upcoming wars' and some other country's 'imminent attack on Serbia' as well as about smearing the oppositional leaders. Nonetheless, these newspapers received over €50,000 each from municipal budgets for various media projects in 2018 (Radojević 2018).

Violence against journalists is also on the rise. A report titled 'Freedom of expression and media freedom in Serbia in the EU integration process' produced by Civic Initiatives, an NGO, reported that 57 journalists were attacked in the first eight months of 2018 (Teofilović et al. 2018). Reporters without borders ranked Serbia 76 (out of 180) in 2018, which equated to a drop of 10 positions compared to 2017.

6. Extractive institutional design

Aleksandar Vučić and the SNS won the 2012 parliamentary elections by promising to stamp out corruption and to launch an investigation into the 24 rotten privatizations of socially-owned enterprises from 2001 to 2012. They also promised to shut down or reform hundreds of state agencies and introduce corporate governance principles into public enterprises. (Agencies and public enterprises have been widely seen as channels for party patronage and the illicit extraction of public funds for maintaining the political party machinery.) This never happened. Instead, under the Vučić government, the extractive institutions of contracts with confidentiality clauses, non-transparent budgets, large economic subsidies without proper oversight, and party patronage in the public sector did not only continue but were upgraded with the aim to enable even more substantial extraction. In sections 4 and 5, I gave some examples of how privileged access to public resources can skew an otherwise level playing field in electoral politics and the media sphere. Here I list some of the most frequent extractive institutional mechanisms which were upgraded after 2014 and identify what kind of leadership such institutions create. It is critical to emphasize that most of these extractive mechanisms emerged well before 2012 and that the Vučić government served mostly to simply 'improve' the manners of extraction.

6.1. Contracts with a confidentiality clause

Even before the return of Vučić, the Serbian Government was known for signing public economic investments contracts containing a confidentiality clause, which is against the Serbian constitution (art. 51). The contracts that were signed between the public Serbian Government and FIAT (2008), NIS (2008), Air Serbia (2013), Smederevo steel factory (2014), the Belgrade Waterfront[10] (2015), Belgrade Airport (2018) etc. were either blacked out or completely hidden from the public eye, in spite of the facts that they involved public investment and subsidies. The electorate never learned if these contracts are harmful to the Serbian budget.

Such contracts by definition ought to be public and cannot contain a confidentiality clause. Yet, not only did they contain one, but it is also not possible to establish individual accountability of the public officials who signed them. The example of the Smederevo steel factory is indicative of this. In 2014, the Serbian Government hired a team of 12 professional managers for the state-owned Smederevo steel factory at the cost of €300,000 a month. The contract between the Ministry of Economy and the management contained a confidentiality clause. After two years, the management made a loss totalling €144 million. When Rodoljub Šabić, the then Commissioner for Information of Public Importance, officially requested the details of the contract from Željko Sertić, the then Minister of Economy, the Minister refused to disclose them. The Commissioner fined the Minister twice, albeit only symbolically. The fines, however, were paid not from the Minister's pocket, but rather from the Ministry's budget. This is nothing more than moving money from one pocket to another. There was no personal responsibility, which sent signals to other public officials that the rejection of information disclosure pays off. This not only encouraged officials to carry on with such practices, but also kept attracting people to politics who are prone to violating legal and democratic procedures that would prevent extraction.

6.2. Budgetary non-transparency

Most budgetary items are still expressed in the budget law as a lump sum whose detailed composition cannot be analysed. The most critical items in each ministry, office, or agency are under budgetary economic classification 242, 422, 423, 424, 454, which involve subsidies, travel costs, contractual services etc., which are expressed as a lump sum in every budget, and can sometimes total up to several billion dinars (1 billion dinars = €8.4 million) per budget item. Most shady public spending is carried out under these classifications, which explains why the government does not submit a report on how budget revenues are spent. (It has done this only twice – in 2002 and in 2014, but the latter was never adopted.)

Some spending details cannot be accessed even after the information has been requested via the Commissioner for Public Information. The only accessible information is sometimes provided by another institution that belongs to the fourth branch of government. A report produced by the State Audit Institution (SAI) found out that 18% of the 2017 Serbian budget was misspent (State Audit Institution 2018). The SAI can press criminal charges against public officials for such abuse, but the law permits the officials to settle with the public prosecutor by paying a fine. Again, most such settlements result in public officials paying their fine out of the budget of the institutions in which they are employed, thus failing to establish any individual responsibility for misspending.

6.3. Public procurement

A practice that is most closely related to budget non-transparency is that of rigged public procurement procedures. It is usually done via corrupt commissions which are instructed to select a private firm that is close to the incumbent, or whose requirements are designed so that only a specific applicant can win.

One of the most recent examples was revealed by an NGO, the Whistle, in December 2017. It revealed that the Belgrade City Secretariat for Defence paid €83,000 for a ceremonial 18-metre high artificial Christmas tree that was supposed to beautify the centre of Belgrade for New Year's Eve. A similar tree could be found at the Rockefeller Plaza in New York which cost 'only' €25,000, or by the Emirates Palace, which cost

€10,000. This kind of extraction of public funds was only accidentally discovered because the Whistle somehow got access to the contract where it could see the excessive 'price' of €83,000 (Đurić and Živančević 2017).

The supplier of the Christmas tree is the private company *Keep Light* that 'won' several more handsome deals from the Belgrade city administration. Since 2014 when the SNS won the Belgrade elections, this firm kept winning public tenders for New Year's decorative illuminations in Belgrade, despite the fact that it increased its price 100 times in five years (Figure 3). Nobody really understands what the public justification for such an increase is except for the fact that, as the years pass by, the lights are put up and switched on earlier and earlier (in September and October, respectively) and switched off later and later (in the early spring).

The Belgrade Waterfront is another kind of extractive project that involves the construction of a large living and office space in central Belgrade that would physically stand out against the rest of the downtown area. This is reflective of a more general trend in non-democracies according to which incumbents incline to engage in physically impressive, but socially wasteful projects (Gjerløw and Knutsen 2019). The explanation of such megalomaniac trends is that such projects enable more effective extraction, maintain a link with the incumbent's clientele (in this case, the private firms which are selected to build the Belgrade Waterfront apartments, office spaces and shopping malls), and impress voters. These projects are more easily done in non-democracies precisely because media do not inform the electorate about the real costs or the level of corruption.

6.4. State agencies and other bodies

Almost every ministry in the Serbian Government has under its authority several state agencies and committees that distribute public money for public purposes. Most of these state agencies' operations are non-transparent. An analysis of the Ministry of Economy

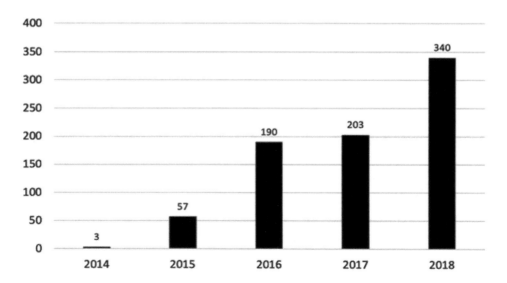

Figure 3. Belgrade New Year's city illumination costs 2014–2018. (In million dinars).
Source: Belgrade city's budgets.

showed that several state agencies – notably the Development Fund and the Agency for Export Promotion – recorded a massive loss by misallocating public funds into the pockets of tycoons and party members of the incumbent coalition (Anticorruption Council 2014; Pavlović 2016a; Pavlović 2016b).

6.5. Party patronage in public companies and local administration

Public companies have remained a hotbed of corruption and one of the most lucrative resources that distorts the playing field for political agents (Transparency Serbia 2017). Unreformed public enterprises' top positions generate corruptive behaviour, which is why the people in them are frequently a legitimate target of the Prosecutor for Organized Crime. For example, the general manager of Resavica, a state company for coal exploitation, was arrested in 2015 for graft and was sentenced to four years in prison. Already in April 2017, the next manager of the same company was charged with graft and sentenced to 2.5 years in prison. Both managers were appointed by the cabinet of Aleksandar Vučić, who regularly repeats that he 'would not tolerate the irresponsible behaviour of public companies' general managers,' albeit keeps avoiding the provisions of the Public Company Law provisions, under which public companies' general managers are not permitted to be party activists and must be qualified for the job.

The abuse of public companies and the public administration with the aim of maintaining party machinery goes to the heart of the problem of how democratic performance backslides and why electoral authoritarianism (re)emerges under weak or incomplete democratic institutions. The openness of institutions for party patronage and extraction attracts specific types of people. These are the people with low educational credentials, those who are prone to aggressive and violent behaviour, and the people who outright lie. The prevalence of such people in politics adversely affects the democratic process.

One of the most famous examples of the first kind is Milorad Grčić, first appointed as the general manager of the public company Kolubara in 2012, and then to the position of general manager of Elektroprivreda Srbije, the largest public company in Serbia, in 2015. He ran a barbecue shop before 2012. The former Minister of Defence had to step down in early 2016 for making a sexually offensive comment to a female journalist in front of the cameras, only to reappear one year later as a director of the state security agency whose annual budget exceeds the annual budget of several ministries. Before he entered politics and joined the SNS in 2008, he was a tile setter.

Another sort of people is those with a criminal record. A number of local administration presidents and mayors are SNS members who previously spent time in prison, or had been under police investigation for criminal offences including but not limited to violence, theft, drug possession, abuse of public office, sexual harassment, etc. After they joined the SNS and occupied top administrative positions, the charges were either dropped or shelved (Stamenković 2019). Several top executive officials – the Minister of Finance, Minister of Interior, Governor of the National Bank, and the former President of Serbia – have been under suspicion for several years of plagiarizing their doctoral dissertations, or paying for an MA diploma.

Arguably, such people are critical for these positions on account of their unconditional loyalty and preparedness to tolerate the extraction of public companies' and public offices' resources for political purposes which frequently take on the form of party patronage, a resource of utmost importance when it comes to maintaining this kind of regime. The SNS has a large team of nearly 3,500 people whose only task is to leave comments on Twitter, Facebook, and media portals. Most of them receive training and modest financial compensation, but their main motivation is to get a job in the public sector if they perform well (Bukumirović 2014; Mališić 2016). Party patronage is then implemented by either a top public company manager or a municipal mayor. Blagoje Spaskovski, the general manager of the public company RTB Bor since 2000, who was known for changing party membership as soon as there is a change in government, became 'famous' for employing 500 people at RTB Bor in only one day in 2014. Milutin Jeličić Jutka, former president of the Brus municipality, admitted that he found jobs for his whole family in the Brus municipal administration, because 'the whole Brus is his family' (Blagović 2019). These examples are not accidents. They happen every day, only are much smaller in scale, because of which they frequently go under the radar.

By installing such people at top of the executive, public companies, and in administrative posts, the incumbent mobilizes an army of people who more easily accept and participate in the incumbent's preference to create and maintain a non-democratic order. This acceptance will not arise merely out of obligation. Such people will support it willingly because most of them, when they get to these positions, realize that extraction is the only way by which they can prosper in life. Their preference to keep these posts by blocking the opposition from accessing them arises as a natural consequence of this.

7. Discussion and conclusions

In this paper I argued two things. The first has to do with the most recent democratic reversal towards a more authoritarian regime under the government of Aleksandar Vučić, who returned to office in 2012. I gave a number of empirical examples of electoral violations, the control of the media, and the abuse of public funds that increased in both number and scope after 2012, thus moving Serbia back to a form of EA that existed under Milošević from 1990–2000. I agree with the claim defended by a number of authors that under strict definitions, Serbia never really left electoral authoritarianism behind, although the post-Milošević elite from 2001–2012 did accomplish a significant institutional distinction in order to move away from Milošević, and closer to democracy.

My second goal is to discuss the role of extractive institutions and how they matter for the (re)emergence and strengthening of hybrid regimes. The extractive aspect of such regimes is analytically salient for two reasons. First, extractive institutional design can directly impact the two other critical areas of competitive authoritarianism – namely, elections and the media. This aspect is, in my mind, under-theorized in research on EA. The extraction of funds from state and municipal budgets, contracts with a confidentiality clause, party patronage, or shady land concession deals enable the incumbent to buy votes by way of maintaining clientelist networks and bribing members of the electorate who make less than the minimum wage or who live under the poverty line. Party patronage (also financed from the budget) is critical to keep the incumbent party going when it has to do its 'get out and vote' campaigns (section 4). Opposition parties do not have this kind of privilege and are therefore handicapped in the electoral process.

A similar kind of practice can be observed in the media sphere. A significant number of private media outlets under the control of SNS-affiliated owners receive subsidies from municipal budgets which they then use to propagate the incumbent's public policy and demonize the opposition. The extractive mechanisms discussed in section 5 have a direct impact on the electoral process and media freedom, thus creating an unfair political arena whilst undermining democratic institutions. All this helps the incumbent to use informal mechanisms to maintain their power advantage.

Extractive institutions are at the very heart of the most recent authoritarian strengthening in Serbia under Vučić. As I mentioned at the outset, I accept the claim that the causes for the re-emergence of competitive authoritarianism in Serbia should be sought in the previous incumbent's failure to consolidate democracy (Bieber 2018a). The post-Milošević elites set up a system of political institutions which belong to the so-called fourth branch of government with the task of protecting human rights and boosting future democratic processes. They, however, failed to solve the principal-agent problem, thus allowing the continued extraction of public resources and abuse of office (Pavlović 2016a). The phenomenon was known from the early 1990s and is linked to the post-collapse phenomenon in most post-communist countries. The collapse of communism in 1989 opened up an opportunity for the incumbent to plunder the state. Public resources and assets were unprotected, which encouraged massive asset-grabbing, notably in the former Soviet Union and Yugoslav countries (Roland 2002). Roughly speaking, the outcome of transition depended on what kind of political and economic elite a society happened to have at the moment of the breakdown of socialism, and if this elite 'developed the capacity to decide on rules that are meant to be self-binding, and to comply with these rules, once adopted, *as if* they had been enforced and imposed by some hierarchically superior actors' (Elster et al. 1998, 30).

The removal of Milošević was supposed to solve this problem in Serbia. The new political elite promised to establish the fourth branch of government – a system of checks, balances and oversight that would subject the executive and administrative powers to the threat of sanctions (Schedler 1999) – with the aim to halt plundering and asset-grabbing and to provide procedures ensuring the peaceful turnover of government. But with few exceptions the new institutions have proven toothless – they have been unable to fight rotten privatizations and have allowed contracts with a confidentiality clause, massive party patronage as well as budgetary non-transparency that resulted in huge wasteful spending and illegitimate economic redistribution. Public officials could still abuse public office and for the most part get away with it. When the DOS elite was out of office, public resources were still up for grabs and the fourth branch of government was too weak to protect them. This opportunity – to continue with the institutional extraction that began under Milošević – gave the Milošević elite an incentive to return to a more radical version of a hybrid regime. The authoritarian path under Vučić since 2012 has been a product of these dynamics.

This is an important conclusion because it offers an alternative to a number of competing explanations, according to which democratic rollback in the Western Balkans is a result of ethnic divisions, historic hatred, the EU's inability to sanction wayward member- and candidate-states, the 2008 financial crisis, the 2009 Eurozone crisis, the rise of populist parties in Hungary and Poland, or the geopolitical impact of Russian interest in the Western Balkans. Of course, all these trends have contributed to the most recent rise of autocratic trends in the Western Balkans and Serbia, but institutional extraction and its enduring attractivity for political agents remains the primary cause.

Notes

1. This term is borrowed from Greene (2007). Some level of incumbency advantage is inevitable even in democratic systems. Hyper-incumbency goes beyond this, indicating a massive abuse of public posts and resources in favour of the incumbent.
2. I borrow the concept of extractive institutions from Acemoglu and Robinson (2012). Extractive institutions hamper economic growth and lead to stagnation and poverty. Such institutional design allows one group of people privileged access to the nation's public and private resources.
3. This is why some authors call such regimes competitive authoritarianism (Levitsky and Way 2010). Electoral authoritarianism is a term proposed by Andreas Schedler (2006). I take these two concepts – electoral and competitive authoritarianism – to be cognates.
4. See Section 6 in this article for details.
5. Nations in Transit's score for one year always reflect the previous years' events. Therefore, a gradual decline that can be observed in the year 2014 actually took place in 2013. Freedom House's methodology for constructing the score can be accessed here: https://freedomhouse. org/report/nations-transit-methodology .
6. I selected these four categories because they reflect the major areas of manipulations in EAs, thus constituting the essence of illiberal politics (see Kapidžić, 2020).
7. Identical pattern applies to the Vojvodina Assembly which appoints the RTV supervisory board.
8. The incumbents deliberately keep the REM Council incomplete, and appoint people who had poor, or no experience in broadcasting and sometimes media in general. At the end of 2018, the Serbian Assembly, with no official explanation, still failed to elect the three missing members of the REM Council, including the head of the Council. Out of six members, two previously had no professional journalistic or media experience (one previously worked in an association for the deaf, and the other as a clinical psychologist). Although this is a regulatory body that should not reveal its political preferences, one of the members is constantly quarrelling with several opposition leaders.
9. http://uns.org.rs/sr/desk/UNS-news/42197/vucicevic-septembarski-tiraz-informera-106-603-lista-danas-3-966.html.
10. The Belgrade Waterfront contract itself was made public in 2015, but the details contained by the Belgrade Waterfront Investment Plan are still a secret. This Plan contains the detailed cost structure.

Disclosure statement

No potential conflict of interest was reported by the author.

Funding

This work was supported by the Ministry of Education and Science, Republic of Serbia [179076].

ORCID

Dušan Pavlović http://orcid.org/0000-0003-3941-1539

References

Acemoglu, D., and J. Robinson. 2012. *Why nations fail. The origins of power, prosperity, and poverty.* New York: Crown Business.

Andrejić, B. 2017. Kod Vučića na cenzuri [At Vučić's, for Cenzorship]. *Danas*, January 9. https://www.danas.rs/dijalog/kod-vucica-na-cenzuri/.

Bieber, F. 2011. Popular mobilization in the 1990s: Nationalism, democracy and the slow decline of the Milošević regime. In *New perspectives on Yugoslavia: Key issues and controversies*, ed. D. Đokić and J. Ker-Lindsay, 161–75. London: Routledge.

Bieber, F. 2018a. Patterns of competitive authoritarianism in the Western Balkans. *East European Politics* 34, no. 3: 337–54. doi:10.1080/21599165.2018.1490272.

Bieber, F. 2018b. Belated transitions in South Eastern Europe. In *The routledge handbook of East European politics*, ed. A. Fagan and P. Kopecky, 27–38. Abingdon, Oxon: Routledge.

Blagović, K. 2019. Tačno je. Celu familiju sam zaposlio [It's true. I found jobs for whole my family]. *Kurir*, May 14. no. 1889: 4–5. https://bit.ly/2w0OBX0.

Branković, T., and Ž. Cvejin. 2018. *Izbori u Srbiji - demokratija zamagljena kampanjom* [Elections in Serbia – Democracy tarnished by the campaign]. Belgrade: CRTA.

Bukumirović, D. 2014. On je prošao obuku, sad može da bude stranački bot [He has been trained. Now he can be a party bot]. *VICE*, December 29. https://www.vice.com/rs/article/qk8755/provela-sam-nekoliko-dana-sa-botovima-i-saznala-da-ne-rade-za-sendvice.

Bunce, V., and W. Sharon. 2011. *Defeating Authoritarian Leaders in Postcommunist Countries.* Cambridge: Cambridge University Press.

Cekić, N. 2018. Ovo je trgovina uticajem, a ne kapitalom [This is influence peddling, not a capital exchange]. *Nedeljnik*, no. 362: 12–13.

CESID. 2013. *Belgrade local elections report.* CESID: Belgrade. http://www.cesid.rs/wp-content/uploads/2018/04/Belgrade-Local-Election-2018_Report-by-CeSID.pdf.

Cianetti, L., J. Dawson, and S. Hanley. 2018. Rethinking "democratic backsliding" in Central and Eastern Europe – Looking beyond Hungary and Poland. *East European Politics* 34, no. 3: 243–56. doi:10.1080/21599165.2018.1491401.

Damnjanović, M. 2018. Serbia 2018. In *Nations in transit 2018*. New York: Freedom House. https://freedomhouse.org/report/nations-transit/2018/serbia.

Dolenec, D. 2013. *Democratic institutions and authoritarian rule in Southeast Europe.* Colchester: ECPR Press.

Donno, D. 2013. Elections and democratization in authoritarian regimes. *American Journal of Political Science* 57, no. 3: 703–16. doi:10.1111/ajps.2013.57.issue-3.

Dragojlo, S. 2016. Serbian elections deemed fair despite irregularities. *Balkan Insight*, April 25. https://bit.ly/30nJi1U.

Đurić, S., and B. Živančević. 2017. Jelka u centru Beograda za 83,000 evra postavljena pre kraja tendera [A Christmas Tree for €83,000 installed before the public call was over]. *pištaljka.rs*, December 21. https://pistaljka.rs/home/read/687.

Elster, J., C. Offe, and U.K. Preuss. 1998. *Institutional design in post-communist democracies. Rebuilding the ship at the sea.* Cambridge: Cambridge University Press.

Gandhi, J., and E. Lust-Okar. 2009. Elections under authoritarianism. *Annual Review of Political Science* 12: 403–22. doi:10.1146/annurev.polisci.11.060106.095434.

Gjerløw, H., and C.H. Knutsen. 2019. Leaders, private interests, and socially wasteful projects: Skyscrapers in democracies and autocracies. *Political Research Quarterly* 72: 504–20. doi:10.1177/1065912919840710.

Gotev, G., and M. Poznatov. 2016. Serbia's media privatisation leaves bitter aftertaste. *Euractiv.rs*, September 19. https://bit.ly/30xf7pe.

Günay, C., and V. Džihić. 2016. Decoding the authoritarian code: Exercising 'legitimate' power politics through the ruling parties in Turkey, Macedonia and Serbia. *Southeast European and Black Sea Studies* 16, no. 4: 529–49. doi:10.1080/14683857.2016.1242872.

Howard, M.M., and P.G. Roessler. 2006. Liberalizing electoral outcomes in competitive authoritarian regimes. *American Journal of Political Science* 50, no. 2: 365–81. doi:10.1111/ajps.2006.50.issue-2.

Jaraković, V. 2019. *Četvrti deo: Mediji u Srbiji – U slobodnom padu* [Part 4: The freefall of the Serbian media]. Belgrade: CRTA.

Jovanović, M. 2008. Predsednički izbori u Srbiji od 1990. do 2008. godine [Presidential elections in Serbia from 1990 to 2008]. In *Oko izbora 16* [The electoral watch 16], ed. S. Mihailović, 73–139. Belgrade: CESID.

Kapidžić, D. 2020. The rise of illiberal politics in southeast Europe. *Southeast European and Black Sea Studies* (introductory article of this special issue).

Keil, S. 2018. The business of state capture and the rise of authoritarianism in Kosovo, Macedonia, Montenegro and Serbia. *Southeastern Europe* 42, no. 1: 59–82. doi:10.1163/18763332-04201004.

Kmezić, M., and F. Bieber. 2017. *The crisis of democracy in the Western Balkans. An anatomy of stabilitocracy and the limits of EU democracy promotion.* Graz: BIEPAG.

Krastev, I., and S. Holmes. 2018. Imitation and its discontents. *Journal of Democracy* 29, no. 3: 117–28. doi:10.1353/jod.2018.0049.

Levitsky, S., and L.A. Way. 2002. The rise of competitive authoritarianism. *Journal of Democracy* 13, no. 2: 51–65. doi:10.1353/jod.2002.0026.

Levitsky, S., and L.A. Way. 2010. *Competitive authoritarianism. Hybrid regimes after the cold war.* Cambridge: Cambridge University Press.

Lust-Okar, E. 2006. Elections under authoritarianism: Preliminary lessons from Jordan. *Democratization* 13, no. 3: 456–71. doi:10.1080/13510340600579359.

Maksić, T., and U. Gruska. 2017. Who owns the media in Serbia? *Reporters Without Borders Report*, June 21. https://bit.ly/2sPZo67.

Mališić, A. 2016. Provela sam nekoliko dana sa botovima i saznala da ne rade za sendviče [I spent several days with bots and found out they don't work for sandwiches]. *VICE*, February 26. https://www.vice.com/rs/article/qk8755/provela-sam-nekoliko-dana-sa-botovima-i-saznala-da -ne-rade-za-sendvice.

Miladinović, Z. 2019. Za propagandu vlasti bliskim familijama skoro ceo budžet [The whole budget to the families close to the government]. *Danas*, May 24. no. 7907: 6.

Miller, M. 2017. The strategic origins of electoral authoritarianism. *British Journal of Political Science*: 1–28. doi:10.1017/S0007123417000394.

Ottaway, M. 2003. *Democracy challenged: The rise of semi-authoritarianism.* Washington, DC: Carnegie Endowment for International Peace.

Pavlović, D. 2016a. *Mašina za rasipanje para. Pet meseci u ministarstvu privrede* [Money-wasting machine. Five months inside the ministry of economy]. Belgrade: Dan Graf.

Pavlović, D. 2016b. Extractive Institutions in the Westen Balkans. In *Decline or eclipse of democracy in Europe's new democracies*, ed.. I. Vujačić and B. Vranić, 127–40. Belgrade: Fakultet političkih nauka and Udruženja za političke nauke Srbije.

Pavlović, D. 2019. When do neoliberal economic reforms cause democratic decline? Evidence from the post-communist Southeast Europe. *Post-Communist Economies* 31, no. 1: 671–97. doi:10.1080/14631377.2019.1607436.

Pavlović, D., and S. Antonić. 2007. *Konsolidacija demokratskih ustanova u Srbiji posle 2000* [The consolidation of democratic institutions in Serbia after 2000]. Belgrade: Službeni glasnik.

Poznatov, M., and S. Vukojičić-Obradović. 2012. Strategijom do boljih medija u Srbiji [Toward better media in Serbia by way of strategy]. *Euroactiv*, September 4. http://www.euractiv.rs/ mediji/4638-strategijom-do-boljih-medija-u-srbiji.

Puddington, A. 2017. *Breaking down democracy: Goals, strategies, and methods of modern authoritarians.* New York: Freedom House.

Radojević, V. 2018. Najmanje 60 miliona dinara za naprednjačke medije [At least 60 million dinars for progressivist media]. *Raskrikavanje*, November 20. https://www.raskrikavanje.rs/page.php?id=313.

Roberts, A. 2018. Democracy and democratisation in post-communist Europe. In *The routledge handbook of East European politics*, ed. A. Fagan and P. Kopecký, 9–26. London: Routledge.

Rodriguez, G.S. 2018. *Implications of ideology in the endurance of competitive authoritarian regimes - Case studies of Venezuela under Hugo Chavez and Peru under Fujimori, left versus right, Bolivarianismo and Chavismo.* Washington DC: Progressive Management Publication.

Roland, G. 2002. The political economy of transition. *The Journal of Economic Perspectives* 16, no. 1: 29–50. doi:10.1257/0895330027102.

Russel, M. 2019. Serbia at risk of authoritarianism? Briefing for European Parliament. Brussels. https://bit.ly/2JthSm7

Schedler, A. 1999. Conceptualizing accountability. In *The self restraining state: Power and accountability in new democracies*, ed.. A. Schedler, 13–28. Boulder CO: Lynne Rienner.

Schedler, A. 2002. The menu of manipulation. *Journal of Democracy* 13, no. 2: 36–50. doi:10.1353/jod.2002.0031.

Schedler, A. 2006. *Electoral authoritarianism: The dynamics of unfree competition.* Boulder: Lynne Rienner.

Schedler, A. 2009. Electoral authoritarianism. In *The SAGE handbook of comparative politics*, ed. T. Landman and N. Robinson, 381–94. London: SAGE.

Schedler, A. 2015. *The politics of uncertainty: Sustaining and subverting electoral authoritarianism.* Oxford: Oxford University Press.

Spoerri, M. 2014. *Engineering revolution: The paradox of democracy promotion in Serbia.* Philadelphia: University of Pennsylvania Press.

Stamenković, I. 2019. Lokalni šerifi odranije poznati policiji [Local thugs previously known to the police]. *NIN*, no. 3554: 10–13. Belgrade: Ringier, Axel Springer.

Stojanović, B., and F.C. Bértoa, 2019. Orbanization of Serbia: Vucic's path towards competitive authoritarianism. *The Global Post*, April 29. https://theglobepost.com/2019/04/29/serbia-vucic-orbanization/.

Stojiljković, Z. 2012. Serbia between electoral authoritarianism and consolidated democracy. *Serbian Political Thought* 5, no. 4: 5–21. doi:10.22182/spt.622012.1.

Tsebelis, G. 1990. *Nested games: Rational choice in comparative politics.* Oakland: University of California Press.

Vladisavljević, N. 2014. Popular protest in authoritarian regimes: Evidence from communist and post-communist states. *Southeast European and Black Sea Studies* 14, no. 2: 139–57. doi:10.1080/14683857.2014.901725.

Vladisavljević, N. 2016. Competitive authoritarianism and popular protest: Evidence from Serbia under Milošević. *International Political Science Review* 37, no. 1: 36–50. doi:10.1177/0192512114535450.

Vladisavljević, N. 2019. Media discourse and the quality of democracy in Serbia after Milošević. (Paper accepted for publication in *Europe-Asia Studies).*

Documents and Reports

Anticorruption Council. 2014. Analiza političkog uticaja na poslovanje Fonda za razvoj Republike Srbije [The analysis of political influence on the development fund's operations]. 72, no. 023-00-7791/2014. Released on 15 July 2014. Belgrade: The Anticorruption Council. Accessed May 3, 2019. http://www.antikorupcija-savet.gov.rs/izvestaji/cid1028-2585/izvestaj-analiza-politickog-uticaja-na-poslovanje-fonda-za-razvoj-republike-srbije.

Anti-Corruption Council. 2011. *Izveštaj o pritiscima i kontroli medija u Srbiji* [A report on the pressures and control of media in Serbia]. (No: 07-00-6614/2011-01). Belgrade: Savet za borbu protiv korupcije.

Balkans in Europe Policy Advisory Group (BIEPAG). 2017. *The crisis of democracy in the Western Balkans. Authoritarianism and EU stabilitocracy.* Graz and Belgrade: European Fund for the Balkans and Centre for Southeast European Studies.

BIRODI. 2016. *Media and elections.* Belgrade: The Bureau for Social Research. http://www.birodi.rs/wp-content/uploads/2016/07/Mediji_i_izbor_2016_ENG.pdf.

BIRODI. 2017. *Mediji, javnost i izbori* [Media, public and elections]. Belgrade: The Bureau for Social Research. http://www.birodi.rs/wp-content/uploads/2018/02/BIRODI_IZBORI_2017_DIGITAL.pdf.

CINS. 2018. Podaci o poreskim dugovanjima moraju da budu javni [The information on tax debts has to be public]. https://www.cins.rs/srpski/news/article/podaci-o-poreskim-dugovanjima-moraju-da-budu-javni.

CRTA. 2018. *Lokalni izbori 2018. Izveštaj dugoročnih posmatrača* [The 2018 local elections. Long-term reporters' report]. Belgrade: CRTA.

OSCE. 2007. Republic of Serbia early parliamentary elections, 21 January, OSCE/ODIHR limited election observation mission final report. Warsaw: OSCE. https://www.osce.org/odihr/elections/serbia/24806?download=true.

OSCE. 2008. Republic of Serbia early parliamentary elections, 11 May, OSCE/ODIHR limited election observation mission final report. Warsaw: OSCE. https://www.osce.org/odihr/elections/serbia/33212?download=true.

OSCE. 2012. Republic of Serbia parliamentary and early presidential elections. 6 and 20 May, OSCE/ODIHR limited election observation mission final report. Warsaw: OSCE. https://www.osce.org/odihr/elections/92509?download=true.

State Audit Institution. 2018. *Izveštaj o reviziji završnog računa Republike Srbije za 2017. godinu* [A report on auditing of the 2017 final statement of Republic of Serbia]. No. 400-575/2018-03/36. Belgrade. https://www.dri.rs/php/document/download/1518/1.

Transparency Serbia. 2017. *Politički uticaj na javna preduzeća i medije* [Political influence on public enterprises and media]. Belgrade.

Toplički centar za demokratiju i ljudska prava (TCD). 2016. *Civic Oversight of the Media Privatisation in Serbia*. Prokuplje.

Teofilović, I., T. Zahirović, M. Stojanović, and D. Popović. 2018. *Sloboda izražavanja i medijske slobode u Srbiji u procesu EU integracija* [Freedom of Expression and of the Media in Serbia in the EU Integration Process]. Belgrade: Građanske inicijative. https://www.gradjanske.org/wp-content/uploads/2018/12/Sloboda-izražavanja-i-medijske-slobode-u-Srbiji-u-procesu-EU-integracija.pdf.

Films (documentaries)

Stevanović, V. 2018. *Dvadeset godina posle Zakona o informisanju* [20 years after the information Act]. Belgrade: TVN1 Production. http://rs.n1info.com/Vesti/a429899/Susa-i-Skrozza-o-Zakonu-o-informisanju-1998.html.

Institutional and symbolic aspects of illiberal politics: the case of North Macedonia (2006–2017)

Borjan Gjuzelov and Milka Ivanovska Hadjievska

ABSTRACT
The paper discusses the underlying characteristics of Macedonian illiberal politics during the 11-year rule of the centre-right party VMRO-DPMNE (2006–2017) focusing on two aspects: institutional and symbolic. We argue that the unfair political competition was enabled by the weakness of pre-existing institutions and the population's clientelist preferences, which were systematically exploited and expanded by VMRO-DPMNE. We also argue that the multi-ethnic character of the country, the disputed Macedonian national identity and the lack of viable international prospects allowed VMRO-DPMNE to construct a strong nationalist narrative that appealed to voters and further isolated the opposition.

Introduction

In the period between 2006–2017, North Macedonia, ruled by a coalition government led by the Internal Macedonian Revolutionary Organization – Democratic Party for Macedonian National Unity (VMRO-DPMNE) became an illustrative example of how illiberal politics are made. During this period, the country diverged from its democratization trajectory due to incumbents' active monopolization of power and abuse of state institutions and resources (Bieber 2018; Crowther 2017). In addition, this undemocratic turn was characterized by strong populist and ethno-nationalist narratives which 'purposefully deepened divisions in the society' (Crowther 2017, 752; Petkovski and Nikolovski 2018) and promoted 'an atmosphere of uncertainty' (Günay and Dzihic 2016, 537).

North Macedonia is not an isolated example of such developments. In recent years the scholarly attention on hybrid regimes in post-communist countries of both Central East Europe and the South East Europe has significantly gained traction (see Bieber et al. 2018; Greskovits 2015). In the first group of countries, the debate is focused on the growing tendencies of democratic deconsolidation, de-democratization, backsliding, and regression (Bogaards 2018; Cianetti et al. 2018; Bustikova and Guasti 2017) presuming that these countries, as EU member states have already reached some satisfying democratic benchmarks. Regarding the second group of countries, the literature is still dealing with the stalled and constrained democratic consolidation (Bieber and Ristić 2012), weak states (Bieber 2011; Kostovicova and Bojicić-Dželilović 2006) and inability to secure functioning rule of law (Dolenec 2013). Despite these differences, countries in both groups face similar 'authoritarian tendencies' that endanger constitutional division of power, political competition and some fundamental civil liberties (Bieber et al. 2018). One of the underlying characteristics of most of these hybrid regimes which exist between the poles of democracy and authoritarianism is the actions by governing elites used for monopolization of power beyond constitutional limits.

Illiberal politics is understood in this issue as a specific set of policies and actions undertaken by governing parties with the aim of creating an uneven playing field to be able to remain in power indefinitely. Whilst the focus on the sum of illiberal policies and actions avoids the complicated task of classifying regime types on the democracy-authoritarianism continuum, it provides a good analytical tool for capturing directions of change – away or towards authoritarianism (Kapidžić, forthcoming). Similar approach has been used in the volume by Bieber et al. (2018, 16) focusing on 'authoritarian tendencies' as a political development and not an outright shift towards full authoritarianism. Building on this theoretical foundation, we further distinguish between institutional and symbolic elements of illiberal politics.

Under *institutional aspects* of illiberal politics, we understand policies and actions by governing parties involving political abuse of state institutions and resources that generate unfair political competition. This is similar to what Levitsky and Way (2010) define as competitive authoritarianism. They underline the importance of an even playing field for fair contest between political parties as a democratic precondition and consider it skewed when: (1) there is abuse of state institutions for partisan ends; (2) ruling parties are systematically favoured, and (3) the opposition's ability to successfully compete in elections is notably limited. As a consequence, they conceptualize uneven playing field as an outcome of the incumbent's privileged, *uneven access to resources, media and law* (Levitsky and Way 2010, 10). Taking a process-oriented approach, the institutional illiberal politics of the governing elites that we focus on encompass those policies which aim to increase the privileged access to resources, media and law with the aim of creating an uneven playing field.[1]

By *symbolic aspects* of illiberal politics, we understand the policies and actions geared towards the monopolization of public discourse with ethno-nationalist, anti-communist or otherwise divisive discourse in order to legitimize incumbents and discredit political opponents (Bieber and Solska 2018; for similar emphasis on the elite's ability to frame the political debate see Schatz 2009). The distinction between institutional and symbolic elements of illiberal politics is important for two reasons: firstly, the two sets of mechanisms for maintaining power – institutional and symbolic – are related to different enabling circumstances; and secondly, institutional capture and symbolic politics in a given context skew the level playing field in a different way, hence the distinction helps in providing a richer empirical account on the intensity and the interrelatedness of these elements in a given context.

In this paper, we argue that the rule of VMRO-DPMNE and their ethnic Albanian coalition partner, the Democratic Union for Integration (DUI) between 2008 and 2017, especially in the second half of this period, is a typical case of illiberal politics (see Petkovski and Nikolovski 2018; Ramet 2017). In accordance with our conceptual distinction, we aim to describe the underlying characteristics of the rule of the VMRO-

DPMNE-led coalition by focusing on both *institutional and symbolic* elements and their interrelatedness. Whilst our account is agency-centred and focuses on the set of policies that VMRO-DPMNE actively implemented to skew the level playing field and maintain loyal support base, we recognize the different circumstances which enabled the rise of illiberal politics in the Macedonian context. In line with Dolenec (2013), the institutional mechanisms of illiberal politics we focus on in N. Macedonia were enabled by post-communist power mutations manifested through a strong executive, weak institutional check and balances, and clientelist political parties (see also Kapidžić, forthcoming). The symbolic illiberal politics has been enabled by the multi-ethnic character of the country (power sharing arrangements) and disputed national identity that culminated with the halt to EU and NATO integration.

To illustrate the usefulness of the conceptual distinction and our main argument we have conducted a case study analysis on illiberal politics in N. Macedonia in the period 2006–2017. The case study is based on media articles, monitoring reports from civil society and international actors and secondary sources (e.g., academic articles including N. Macedonia as a case).[2] The data from different sources was triangulated and information for which we had at least two independent sources were included in the case study narrative (Hammersley 2008; Yin 2018).

The structure of the paper is as follows: the paper starts with a brief overview of N. Macedonia's general political context and the party-political scene developed since independence. Then the main institutional and symbolic aspects of Macedonian illiberal politics during the rule of VMRO-DPMNE are presented. Finally, in the discussion and conclusion section, we discuss the interrelatedness of institutional and symbolic aspects of illiberal politics and the distinct enabling circumstances behind these tendencies.

Background: the post-communist transition during the 1990s

Macedonian independence in 1991 triggered a 'triple transition' (Offe 2004) towards the establishment of new independent state institutions, multi-party democracy and market economy. During the first decade of independence, N. Macedonia faced multiple challenges: a national identity strongly contested by neighbouring Bulgaria and Greece; tensions related to the multi-ethnic composition of the country, with a sizable Albanian minority constituting one quarter of the population (Daskalovski 2004; Crowther 2017, 744); as well as very low levels of economic development and living standards due to the disintegration of the Yugoslav market, regional wars, and the Greek economic embargo in the first half of the 1990s (Boduszyński 2010). In the second half of the 1990s economic development was further constrained by UN sanctions on Yugoslavia and the Kosovo refugee crisis (Boduszyński 2010). These challenges continued to shape the transitional trajectory of N. Macedonia during the 2000s and represent crucial contextual anchors for understanding the failure to consolidate its democracy post-independence, and, specifically, the democratic reversal during VMRO-DPMNE's rule discussed in this paper.

According to Dolenec (2013, 48), in post-communist countries dominated by authoritarian parties and undergoing regime change, undemocratic practices from state socialism were not only perpetuated but also expanded with new forms of power abuse. The political parties that defined the new institutional rules during regime change, and led the redistribution and privatization of publicly owned capital, abused this opportunity for amassment of wealth and power (Dolenec 2013, 4). This was the case in N. Macedonia, where the process of democratization during the 1990s was marked by 'strong hold on power of the successor party to the local League of Communists', the Social Democratic Union of Macedonia (SDSM) (Bieber and Ristić 2012, 381). The SDSM government during the 1990s exercised control over the media and 'ruled in a competitive authoritarian manner' (Levitsky and Way 2010, 125).

The development of the party system in Macedonia in the first half of the 1990s thus happened in the context of very low levels of economic viability and high unemployment (Boduszyński 2010) exacerbated by the process of privatization of public companies implemented in 1995/1996 (Casal Bértoa and Taleski 2016). The privatization processes benefited managers of public companies who had close ties with the ruling party SDSM and who were later seen as the private sponsors of the party (Casal Bértoa and Taleski 2016, 551). These tendencies continued in the later stages of privatization during the first government of VMRO-DPMNE (1998–2002), when businessmen and individuals close to them also benefited from it. This is in line with Boduszyński's (2010, 144) observation that the political parties were the 'main site of corruption (...) and used quasi privatization to enrich their members'.

Similar to other Western Balkan countries, parties' mobilization capacity and their membership was and still is largely determined by their clientelist potential to redistribute public goods and serve as important informality brokers that provide their supporters with employment opportunities and privileged access to public services and resources (Bieber and Ristić 2012; Günay and Dzihic 2016; Bliznakovski et al. 2017). In this context, it is not surprising that the estimated percentage of citizens who are political party members in N. Macedonia is 13%, which is slightly higher than the estimated Western Balkan average of 10% (Bliznakovski et al. 2017) and the Eastern European average of 3% (van Biezen et al. 2011). Consequently, once they get in power, political parties tend to address population's clientelist 'shared expectations', and thus start to abuse public institutions and resources for party gains (Bliznakovski et al. 2017). As a result, incumbent parties capture state institutions through the 'employment of party members in the civil service' and in this way overpower the institutions that are supposed to constrain their behaviour (Bieber and Ristić 2012, 354).

In addition to the dominance of the 'authoritarian party' during regime change, the newly formed state faced challenges to its statehood (Dolenec 2013; Daskalovski 2004). During the first decade of independence, even though interethnic relations posed a 'security concern' (Casal Bértoa and Taleski 2016, 548), Albanian grievances were largely unaddressed (see Daskalovski 2004; Crowther 2017, 745) and an inter-ethnic conflict escalated in 2001 when ethnic Albanian paramilitary groups (National Liberation Army) clashed with the Macedonian army and police. The conflict ended with the signing of the Ohrid Framework Agreement (OFA) under the brokerage of the EU and NATO, which promised an acceleration of the Euro-Atlantic integration of the country (Ilievski 2007; Ilievski and Taleski 2009). The OFA entailed constitutional amendments and the adoption of a consociational model of democracy, characterized by qualified majority procedures in the parliament, decentralization, equitable representation in the public administration and extended rights for the use of minority languages (Aleksovska 2015, 55; Crowther 2017).

In the years after the inter-ethnic conflict, the relations between ethnic Macedonian and Albanian communities remained fragile and were characterized by limited social interaction due to the linguistic barriers and geographical separation (Crowther 2017, 746). The party competition mirrors the 'parallel societies' division, and even before the 2001 conflict, governments were formed by the two most successful parties in each ethnic block.[3] The Macedonian party system is mainly structured around VMRO-DPMNE on the ideological right, and SDSM on the left, and Albanian parties DUI[4] and DPA[5] competing for the votes of ethnic Albanians (Casal Bértoa and Taleski 2016; Crowther 2017). Such ethnicizing of party politics has been identified as a further obstacle to democratic consolidation (Dolenec 2013).

In addition, since independence, Macedonian national identity and language were challenged by neighbouring countries, which incited an atmosphere of external threat to sovereignty. Bulgaria, although it recognized the independence of the country, contested the existence of Macedonian ethnic identity and language, considering the Macedonian language to be a dialect of Bulgarian (Ilievski and Taleski 2009; Crowther 2017). Moreover, the name dispute became a serious obstacle for the integration of N. Macedonia in the EU and NATO (Vangeli 2011). Specifically, in 2008 Greece vetoed N. Macedonia's application to join NATO, whilst in 2009 Greece blocked the start of accession negotiation processes for EU membership. The prospects for joining the EU were further hindered by Bulgaria, which in 2012 supported Greece in delaying the accession negotiations (Ilievski and Taleski 2009; Crowther 2017). Due to the blockade, the EU's leverage to support the democratic consolidation of the country was seriously restrained (Ilievski and Taleski 2009).

Electoral politics during VMRO-DPMNE's rule, 2006-2017

Throughout the period 2006–2017, VMRO-DPMNE enjoyed a continuous electoral legitimization that helped them expand their political power at all levels and branches of government. After 2008, criticism by both international and domestic actors of abuse of state institutions and resources for party ends was increasing, as well as of their populist and nationalist rhetoric which had polarized society and endangered fragile inter-ethnic relations (Dolenec 2013, 91). However, during their 11-year rule, VMRO-DPMNE has been constantly re-legitimized via nine subsequent electoral wins between 2006 and 2017 in parliamentary, presidential and local elections. Throughout this period, they organized early elections before the end of each of their four-year terms[6]: four of their parliamentary election victories were victories on early elections. Early elections were justified as necessary due to political disputes with the opposition SDSM or with their coalition partner, DUI, as a pragmatic move to regain new legitimacy and take full advantage of their high political rating. With this practice, they kept their electorate continuously mobilized and maximized their political support. Moreover, as the opposition was disorganized and financially weaker than the incumbent coalition, such frequent election cycles have additionally increased the gap between the ruling and opposition parties.

Between 2006 and 2017, although elections were generally considered well administered, numerous deficiencies were noted, ranging from insufficient separation between state and party structures (particularly in 2011, 2013, 2014) to intimidation of voters and biased and pro-governmental media reporting (see Table 1 for an overview of general conclusions by OSCE/ODIHR Election Observation Mission).

Table 1. General conclusions of OSCE/ODIHR election observation mission reports.

Parliamentary elections 2006	'[E]elections largely met OSCE commitments for democratic elections, instances of violence and intimidation during the first half of the campaign, and a number of cases of serious irregularities on election day, cast a shadow over an otherwise generally well-administered election held in a competitive environment.' (OSCE/ODIHR 2006, 1)
Early Parliamentary elections 2008	'In most of the country the elections were procedurally well administered. However, expectations of progress were not realized because of a failure by some election stakeholders and relevant authorities to prevent violent acts in predominantly ethnic Albanian areas, including limited and selective enforcement of laws.' (OSCE/ODIHR 2008, 1)
Presidential and Municipal elections 2009	'[E]lections were administered in a professional and transparent manner. Some problems were evident, such as allegations of **intimidation of voters in the pre-election periods**.' (OSCE/ODIHR 2009, 1)
Early Parliamentary elections 2011	[E]lections were competitive, transparent, and well-administered throughout the country, although certain aspects require attention. These include measures to ensure an **adequate separation of state and party structures**, a thorough voter list audit, and clarification of certain provisions in the Electoral Code. (OSCE/ODIHR 2011, 1)
Local elections 2013	'[E]lections were efficiently administered and highly competitive. However, partisan media coverage and a **blurring of state and party activities did not provide a level playing field** for candidates to contest the elections. (OSCE/ODIHR 2013, 1)
Presidential and early parliamentary elections 2014	'[E]lections were efficiently administered, including on election day. Candidates were able to campaign without obstruction and freedoms of assembly and association were respected. However, the elements of the campaign indicated an **inadequate separation between party and state activities (…) Allegations of voter intimidation persisted throughout the campaign …**' (OSCE/ODIHR 2014, 1)
Early Parliamentary elections 2016	'The parties were generally able to campaign freely, and fundamental freedoms of association, assembly and expression were respected. (…) Allegations of **voter intimidation, coercion, pressure on civil servants, vote-buying, and the misuse of administrative resources** persisted through the campaign. (…) Such actions raised concerns about voters' ability to cast their vote free of fear of retribution …' (OSCE/ODIHR 2016, 1)

This constant electoral legitimization generated a vicious cycle of uneven political competition: on one hand, with continuous and convincing electoral wins the incumbents have expanded their informal power to control and misuse state institutions and resources, while on the other, their control and misuse of state institutions and resources have increased the unfair political competition which helped them continue winning elections. Thus, they became a model example of competitive authoritarianism using a wide variety of practices ranging from misuse of public resources for party gains and abuse of key state institutions such as the Ministry of Interior, the intelligence services and judiciary (Priebe 2015, 2017). As the lines between the three constitutionally divided branches of power were blurred, the executive, directly controlled and micromanaged by top VMRO-DPMNE officials, had excessive control over the parliamentary and judicial branch. This further weakened the already underdeveloped institutional checks and balances system that was overridden anyway by a parallel, informal hierarchy determined and controlled by the party in power.

Simultaneously, the opposition parties, which were successively on the losing side, struggled to convince voters with their political programme and had to use extra-institutional measures such as parliamentary boycotts and civic protests in order to regain political leverage and try to level the political field. As will be elaborated further in the chapter, opposition parties struggled to have their voice heard in the media, nor did they have any real opportunity to institutionally influence or constrain the policies of the incumbent coalition. A good illustration is an incident in 2012, when the SDSM's MPs were physically expelled from the plenary session of the Parliament by security while they were filibustering the procedure for enactment of new annual budget that they characterized as profligate and excessive (Casule 2012). Due to the lack of political dialogue, the opposition boycotted the parliament during periods of 2011, 2013 and 2014 (Marusic 2011, 2013, 2014), whilst mass civic protests were organized in 2015 and 2016 (Marusic 2016a). Civic protests were organized since 2009 by independent civil society actors and citizens not allied with the opposition parties (see Petkovski and Nikolovski 2018, 212–214), and they rose in scale in the last years of their rule (2015–2017).

In 2015 a wiretapping scandal revealed by the opposition hit the incumbent coalition. The scandal revealed mass abuse of the state intelligence apparatus (Marusic 2016b; Ramet 2017) and numerous corruption cases which were not properly investigated by the existing anti-corruption institutions (Priebe 2015; Keil 2018). As a consequence, in the summer of 2015, two internationally brokered agreements, the 'Przino Agreements'[7] were signed by the main incumbent and opposition parties. The agreements envisaged a number of provisions to address the problem of the uneven playing field for fair political competition through the formation of a pre-election interim government and the establishment of a Special Public Prosecutor's Office to investigate the allegations for mass abuses of public office and resources.

In 2017, after the early parliamentary elections in December 2016, in which VMRO-DPMNE won most number of parliamentary seats (51) but failed to form a post-election coalition with DUI to secure a parliamentary majority of 61 MPs, they started to obstruct the work of the Parliament and did not allow for a peaceful transition of power (Popovikj 2017). The obstructions culminated with organized violent riots in the Macedonian Parliament in April 2017, after the new parliamentary majority appointed a new President of the Parliament. This event showed the destructive consequences of VMRO-DPMNE's mass abuse of state institutions which on one hand enabled and, to a certain extent, supported the riots, and on the other hand the outcomes of their nationalist rhetoric which had mobilized supporters to engage in such violence. The crisis ended with a power transition and the establishment of a new government formed by SDSM and DUI in May 2017, a month after the aforementioned violence in the Parliament.

Institutional aspects of Macedonian illiberal politics

In the following pages, we will describe the crucial institutional policies and actions by which VMRO-DPMNE increased privileged access to state *resources, media and law* – and skewed the even playing field in their favour.

Uneven access to resources

Access to resources is uneven when ruling parties abuse their position and authority to take advantage of resources that are in serious disparity with the ones of the opposition. That might include partisan use of state resources, abuse of the state machinery (state buildings, vehicles, communication infrastructure) and public employees for campaign purposes as well as monopolized access to private sector finance (Levitsky and Way 2010, 10). In

N. Macedonia the uneven access to resources was most evident in the differences in political party financing and campaign expenditures. During electoral campaigns VMRO-DPMNE reported considerably higher incomes and expenditures in comparison with the major party in opposition, the SDSM. For instance, in the 2013 local elections, OSCE/ODIHR's report noted that they spent five times more than the second closest competitor. Besides these high inter-party discrepancies, there were notable differences between VMRO-DPMNE's reported incomes and expenditures, as they were reporting higher expenditures than their reported incomes (State Electoral Commission 2014, 2016).

The released wiretapped conversations in 2015 indicated that VMRO-DPMNE's top party officials, led by the prime minister Nikola Gruevski, were directly involved in abuse of public institutions and resources. For illustration, in one wiretapped phone conversation, the former Minister of Interior Gordana Jankulovska describes how the premises of her ministry were used for party campaign purposes and how there was an entire party call-centre within the ministry (Jordanovska 2015a). In another conversation, she explains that the police would obstruct the rally of the opposition by diverting the busses with opposition supporters to undergo a technical check. In other conversations, she and the Minister of Transport and Communications describe how they organized for ethnic Macedonians from Albania to get Macedonian citizenship and identity cards with Skopje addresses in order to vote for VMRO-DPMNE in the local 2013 elections (Jordanovska 2015a).

Clientelist employments and other benefits were used to mobilize political support. Top VMRO-DPMNE officials micromanaged their clientelist networks in order to maximize the benefits for their party (Petkovski and Nikolovski 2018). There are numerous wiretaps that confirmed the previous allegations that public sector employments had been largely controlled by the ruling party's bodies and officials. They organized and centralized the system of non-merit-based, party employments, making detailed lists of loyal party members that should be employed or promoted (Jordanovska 2015b). Party clients had to demonstrate not only their political loyalty, but to provide lists of 10 to 30 other voters who would certainly vote for the party. Besides this, clients were not only asked to be active during election campaign, but also to be involved in other initiatives of the party, including political rallies and 'spontaneous' protests and counter protests (Nikolovski 2013). Their presence was secured by the party's local branches which were responsible for mobilization through direct communication with the people and registering the attendance at party events of each and every party member on their lists (Blazevska 2018).

Moreover, election years were characterized by increased numbers of public sector employments (Cvetkovska 2013) and agricultural subsidies (Jankovska 2015), while there are examples in which even private companies mobilized their employees to vote for the incumbent political party (Delevska 2018). A good illustration is that although public sector employments were legally prohibited during election campaigns in order to prevent clientelist employments, during the local elections in 2013 there were numerous job advertisements for short-term employment in various public sector institutions (local self-government, education, health, etc.). Despite criticisms from experts who claimed that this was contrary to the law and would be used for clientelist electoral mobilization, the government officials and the State Commission for Prevention of Corruption (SCPC) considered these employments as legal and in accordance with the needs of the respective institutions (Cvetkovska 2013).

Uneven access to media

Another aspect of VMRO-DPMNE's competitive authoritarian regime was uneven access to both state-owned and private media. During their rule, media freedom deteriorated, with the majority of media outlets being favourable towards the government and hostile towards the opposition (Freedom House 2017; Spasovska and Rusi 2015). While the state-owned radio and television traditionally supported incumbent political parties, most of the private media outlets were tied to political and business interests that influenced their editorial policies. According to a comparative media freedom ranking issued by Reporters Without Borders, in the last 10 years' Macedonian media freedom decreased 80 places, from 36th place in 2007 (out of 169 ranked countries) to 118th place in 2016. Problems with media freedom were noted in European Commission (EC) and US Department of State's reports. EC reports constantly raised concerns over 'government control over media' and 'scarcity of independent reporting and lack of accurate and objective information being made available through mainstream media to the public and a lack of informed public debate' (EC 2014, 2). Similarly, the US State Department reports (2013, 10) noted that '[t]he mainstream media rarely published views opposing the government' while only a limited number of media were independent and offered a variety of views.

Media loyalty was incentivized through well organized media-political clientelism (Micevski and Trpevska 2015) conducted primarily via extensive state-financed advertising and concentration of media ownership by several businessmen close to the government (Apostolov et al. 2015). The government was the top advertiser on private national TV stations, spending large amounts on buying loyalty and favourable treatment (Apostolov et al. 2015). According to the former president of the Association of Journalists of Macedonia Naser Selmani, annually the government was spending an equivalent of the annual budget of the Ministry of Defence (20 million euros) on advertising and media: 'These advertisements have nothing to do with the public interest of the citizens, these funds are used for buying and corrupting the media in order not to criticise governmental policies' (Dimovski 2014).

Furthermore, some of the most influential TVs and newspapers were already owned, or taken over, by businessmen close to the government. Such was the case with TV Sitel and TV Kanal 5 which were owned by junior coalition partners of VMRO-DPMNE, who won seats in the parliament mainly due to their media ownership which had guaranteed favourable news reporting. In addition, three of the most influential daily newspapers, Dnevnik, Vest and Utrinski, were taken over by an oligarch close to VMRO-DPMNE. These and other media outlets which were taken over experienced rapid change in their editorial policies, destroying their earlier professional standards and becoming biased and unprofessional (Dimovski 2014).

Finally, journalists were faced with numerous defamation cases issued by high-ranking ruling politicians which put them under additional pressure, as the rulings in these cases were usually in the politicians' favour (Risteska 2015). For instance, Jadranka Kostova, editor of the critical weekly magazine Focus was ordered to pay 15.000 euros in fines to VMRO-DPMNE's former Minister of Foreign Affairs Antonio Milososki, while the Journalists' Association in 2012 estimated that there were more than 300 lawsuits against journalist in the Macedonian courts, mostly brought by ruling politicians and connected businessmen (Marusic 2012a). As a consequence, journalists were under continuous pressure to report in a biased, pro-governmental manner and self-censor their work in order to keep their jobs (Apostolov et al. 2015; Dimovski 2014).

One of the biggest blows for Macedonian media freedom was the closure of N. Macedonia's first private, and most influential television station, A1 TV, in 2011. While characterized as 'the best and the worst of Macedonian media industry' (Ordanovski et al. 2012, 98 in Spasovska and Rusi 2015), A1 TV had had a significant impact on the development of media pluralism and professional journalism. The television station was closed as an act of retaliation against its owner Velija Ramkovski who was initially close to Gruevski and VMRO-DPMNE but later, via A1 TV, had become a vocal critic of the government (Dimovski 2010; Ramet 2017). Ramkovski and number of his employees were charged and later sentenced for money laundering, tax evasion and criminal association (Spasovska and Rusi 2015).

Uneven access to law

Uneven access to law is conducted through structured abuse of power and control of legal institutions (judiciaries, electoral commissions and other supposedly independent arbiters) that instead of working independently to protect the legal and constitutional order, work under influence and in favour of the incumbents. This affects political competition because unlike the opposition, incumbents enjoy privileged treatment and impunity that enables them to avoid or violate certain democratic and legal procedures without sanctions (Levitsky and Way 2010). This was the case in N. Macedonia, as the work of the judiciary and other oversight and law enforcement institutions was under strong political pressure that led to double standards favouring ruling party officials and disfavouring their political enemies. These problems were noted in a number of domestic and foreign assessment documents where these issues were identified as key reasons for the country's backsliding in the process of EU accession and the spread of grand corruption and state capture (US Department of State 2011, 2012, 2013, 2014; EC 2015, 2016).

Political interference in the Macedonian judiciary became systemic during VMRO-DPMNE rule. It was mainly executed through control over the mechanisms for appointment, evaluation, promotion, discipline, and dismissal of judges, as these mechanisms were abused to reward the obedient cadres and punish those who did not conform with politically determined informal influence (Priebe 2015, 2017). Informal influence has been exercised primarily via the members of the Judicial Council, a body responsible for appointment, promotion and dismissal of judges. As can be heard in the wiretapped conversations, the decision-making of the Judicial Council was directly coordinated between the highest party officials (Petkovski and Nikolovski 2018). Furthermore, there were abuses regarding the dismissal procedures, which were later characterized as unlawful by the European Court of Human Rights (ECHR).[8] Political influence was also exercised through presidents of some of the key courts in the country. In 2017 the Ministry of Justice identified numerous irregularities related to abuse of the electronic system randomly assigning judges to cases (ACCMIS) in order to ensure that certain sensitive cases were allocated to specific judges (Akademik 2017). In 2015, when the Special Public Prosecutor started prosecuting high-level officials from VMRO-DPMNE, the political loyalty of some court presidents became evident as they were abusing their formal competences by frequently reallocating judges to different court departments. These reallocations were made to assign loyal judges to sensitive judicial cases in which top VMRO-DPMNE officials were trialled (Dimovski 2017).

The control of the judiciary and law enforcement institutions was used to silence and discipline political opponents and public critics. Such was the arrest and conviction of the opposition politician Ljube Boskovski who left VMRO-DPMNE to form his own party United for Macedonia, becoming a very vocal critique of Gruevski. He was arrested one day after the parliamentary elections in 2011 in a staged case on grounds of illegal election campaign financing. His arrest was filmed and the video was later broadcasted on YouTube and on the website of the Ministry of Interior. His case was noted by the US State Department as a case of political imprisonment (US Department of State 2011). Later he was sentenced on five years and was released in 2016 (MKD.mk 2016). Similar targeted cases include those against the investigative journalist Tomislav Kezharovki (US Department of State 2013; Spasovska and Rusi 2015), against the president of the council of the opposition-led Skopje-Centar municipality Miroslav Shipovic (US Department of State 2013) and against the physician Dejan Stavric who lead the doctors' union strike against the Ministry of Health (US Department of State 2011).

Besides the political interference on the judiciary, the party had an extensive influence on other independent bodies such as the State Commission for Prevention of Corruption (SCPC). The commission was composed of seven members appointed by and loyal to the stable parliamentary majority of VMRO-DPMNE and DUI. While corruption was repetitively labelled as prevalent and serious problem, through the years there were cumulatively fewer cases processed and almost no actions against any incumbent political officials (Petkovski and Nikolovski 2018, 217). The European Commission has continuously criticized SCPC as passive, ineffective and prone to political influence (EC 2013, 2014, 2015, 2016). However, despite its passive role in chasing high-level government officials, during the 2013 elections, the SCPC issued a public announcement about irregularity of the asset declaration of the opposition candidate for Mayor of the municipality of the Centre, Andrej Zernovski. The timing of this action of SCPC, which was used to discredit the opposition candidate, coincided with the peak of the electoral contest in this key Skopje municipality and raised further questions about its impartiality (EC 2013). VMRO-DPMNE's control over the SCPC was also visible when, in 2015, one a member was appointed who had previously been a donor to the party. One year later he became president of the Commission (Jovanovska 2017).

In summary, policies and actions that increased VMRO-DPMNE's privileged access to state resources, media space and law, over time created an uneven playing field where parties in the opposition and critical voices were marginalized. This enabled continuous electoral success and broad legitimization of VMRO-DPMNE. In the next section, we offer an overview of symbolic aspects of their illiberal politics which help us make better sense of the discursive mechanisms through which VMRO mobilized their support base among citizens.

Symbolic aspects of Macedonian illiberal politics

In addition to the institutional capture discussed above, VMRO-DPMNE's continued electoral success can be best understood in reference to their coordinated attempts to monopolize public discourse and mobilize support through ethno-nationalist narrative. The symbolic aspects of their illiberal politics include the process of antiquization, anti-communist, anti-minority, conservative narratives, and concerted discrediting and smear campaigns against political opponents and civil society. Particularly after the Greek blocking of N. Macedonia's accession at the NATO summit in Bucharest in 2008, ethno-nationalist discourse has been reinforced as a main strategy for political mobilization and one of the main factors of the party's subsequent electoral success even in the light of failed economic promises and international stalemate (Andreassen 2011). Besides, VMRO-DPMNE under Gruevski also reinforced the widespread perception among impoverished citizens that SDSM's party cadres have largely benefited from the 'unlawful privatization' during the 1990s (Petkovski and Nikolovski 2018), at the same time managing to distance itself from the old VMRO-DPMNE's elites who themselves participated in the late stages of the privatization. These policies and practices were a complementary strategy for skewing the level playing field through delegitimization of political opponents and critics and directing the attention away from the glaring abuse of resources and law.

As part of its nationalist agenda, VMRO-DPMNE launched a set of 'identitarian policies based on the assumption that there is a direct link between today's ethnic Macedonians and Ancient Macedonians', popularly referred to as the process of 'anti-quization' (Vangeli 2011, 13). This initially encompassed the renaming of the airport in Skopje as 'Alexander the Great', the Skopje stadium as 'National Arena Philip II', and the renaming of the main highway as 'Alexander of Macedonia'. The reconstruction of Skopje's city centre under the project 'Skopje 2014' aimed at glorifying the ancient history of Macedonians and served as a central symbol of the national renewal (Vangeli 2011; Keil 2018). As part of the project, dozens of monuments of historical figures were constructed and installed, among which the centre-stage is occupied by a massive statue of Alexander the Great. Several public buildings in neo-classical and baroque style were also built which, according to the architects, were aimed at obscuring the 'modernist constructions of the socialist period and the Ottoman-era architecture that indexes the city's Muslim heritage' (Graan 2013, 161). The reconstruction of national identity, while reinforcing ethnic divisions within the country, has also intensified the backlash from neighbouring Greece (Crowther 2017). Gruevski used this as an opportunity to con-solidate his and VMRO-DPMNE's role as the ultimate guardians of the Macedonian identity from both external and internal threats (Günay and Dzihic 2016).

The government of Nikola Gruevski has launched a parallel yet complementary discourse of anti-communism. According to Spaskovska (2014) '[...] the socialist legacy has been progressively erased from the public space and existing historical narratives forged around the common anti-fascist struggle been played down and redefined [...]'. In this context, a controversial Lustration Law was implemented which also encompassed the period of socialism up until 2006, the year when Gruevski's VMRO-DPMNE came to power. The Amended Law on Determining the Additional Condition for Performing Public Service (2011) extended its remit to apply to 'priests, journalists, NGO activists, lawyers and scientists', requiring them, in 2011–2012, to submit statements on their collaboration with secret services (Orlović 2013, 73). Though the Constitutional Court had, in a past ruling concerning the previous law on lustration, stated that such law can only apply for the period until 1991, the new law created by VMRO-DPMNE ignored this rule (Marusic 2012b).

The work of the Commission for the Verification of Facts [known as the Lustration Commission] was heavily criticized on the basis of alleged abuse of the law for discrediting and attacking political opponents and prominent civil society activists (Bohnet and Bojadzieva 2011). For example, the head of the Open Society Foundation in Macedonia and university professor Vladimir Milčin was publicly proclaimed as a collaborator with the communist security services on the basis of scarce evidence (Orlović 2013). Milčin, a vocal critic of Gruevski's policies, accused the head of the Lustration Commission of withholding documents that prove his innocence. He claimed that 'The goal of this lustration is not to settle the injustices of the past, but to tarnish people's reputation' (Marusic 2012b). The processes of lustration portrayed VMRO-DPMNE's political opponents as 'communist collaborators' harmful to the Macedonian interest.

The VMRO-led coalition through its extensive influence in the media led smear campaigns against civil society organizations, depicting them as being close to SDSM and serving the interests of foreign powers (Crowther 2017, 752; Keil 2018). Furthermore, the governing coalition enabled the 'proliferation of discriminatory discourses' against sexual minorities (Miškovska Kajevska 2018), reflecting the underlying conservative-religious consensus of VMRO-DPMNE and DUI (Spaskovska 2014). NGOs collaborating or being funded by the Open Society Foundation in Macedonia were under attack by media close to the government. For example, during civic protests against the building of a church on Skopje's main square, the earliest protests against VMRO-DPMNE's plan for the reconstruction of the city centre, media close to the government repeatedly tried to discredit the protest by pointing out the presence of members of the opposition party and employees of the Open Society Foundation (Nikolovski 2013, 23). Both the opposition party SDSM and the Open Society Foundation were associated with 'evil, conspiracy and treason' in the media (Nikolovski 2013, 24). This has been complemented by a wide-spread talk of 'de-Sorosization' of civil society and the emergence of patriotic NGOs and citizen initiatives for the protection of the name, tradition and identity of N. Macedonia (Jordanovska 2017; Petkovski and Nikolovski 2018). Many of the protests against the government's policies were faced with 'counter protests' organized by VMRO-DPMNE supporters. Citizens who opposed the government's policies were discouraged from joining public protests out of fear of being labelled as 'traitors' or 'Sorosoids'. Hence, SDSM had troubles mobilizing an effective opposition not only because of their limited institutional leverage but also because they were constructed as a symbol of all things-harmful for Macedonian national interests.

In summary, VMRO-DPMNE dominantly framed the public debate to mobilize and maintain its support base among ethnic Macedonians. By doing so, they met the demands for ethno-nationalist, conservative and anti-communist discourse among the population. The successful monopolization of the public debate was made possible not only due to the privileged access to resources and media as discussed before but also the existence of loyal support base who believed and reproduced VMRO's narratives (see Schatz 2009).

Discussion and conclusion

The paper focused on the institutional and symbolic aspects of the illiberal rule of the VMRO-DPMNE-led coalition and described the core characteristics of Macedonian illiberal politics in the period 2006–2017. The examples of abuse of political power presented demonstrate how the coalition led by VMRO-DPMNE, and their leader Nikola Gruevski, gained privileged access to resources, media and law that helped them to continuously win elections and legitimacy. While the creation of an 'uneven playing field' through the abuse of state institutions and resources is a necessary factor accounting for their high political support and continuous electoral victories, we showed that symbolic illiberal policies also significantly contributed to VMRO-DPMNE's attainment and maintenance of power.

We identify different enabling circumstances of institutional and symbolic aspects of the illiberal politics in N. Macedonia described above. In line with Dolenec (2013) we argue that the institutional capture during VMRO-DPMNE is rooted in the post-communist power mutations enabled by SDSM during the regime change, which created a dominant executive, weak institutional checks and balances and advanced clientelist practices. The low economic development and living standard during the transition period acted as an enabling factor for clientelist politics. Subsequent parties in power 'perpetuated state capture and continued to subvert the rule of law' (Dolenec 2013, 48). In addition, one of the key enabling factors of illiberal tendencies in N. Macedonia is the implementation gap between rules in the books (formal laws) and how they are implemented in practice (informal practices). For instance, although N. Macedonia's legal framework aims in theory at ensuring equal opportunities, impartiality and meritocracy, there is plenty of evidence that Macedonian society, similar to the rest of the Western Balkan region, largely operates in practice on the basis of nepotism, clientelism and corruption (Dehnert 2010; Bliznakovski et al. 2017; Gordy et al. 2019). Questions of democratic accountability and fighting clientelism and corruption are constantly pushed into the background due to the 'ethnification of politics' (Dolenec 2013, 89). In these conditions of weak institutions, clientelism and the threat of multi-ethnic conflict, VMRO-DPMNE and DUI abused their formal authority and informally controlled state institutions and resources to maintain and maximize their political power. International actors such as EU and the US, due to the halted NATO and EU integration process, were unable to constraint such developments (see Ilievski and Taleski 2009).

The symbolic illiberal politics of VMRO-DPMNE in the context of N. Macedonia emerged in relation to the entrenched feeling of threatened statehood and national identity by neighbouring Greece and Bulgaria and the internal multi-ethnic tensions underpinning the power-sharing arrangements. VMRO-DPMNE, as a right-wing nationalist party continuously maintained ethno-national questions on the domestic agenda. The failure to join NATO and start EU accession negotiations as a result of the escalating name dispute with Greece hindered opportunities for economic development and increased the feeling of threatened statehood. These processes created the sentiment among ethnic Macedonians that their position has been threatened and their rights have been diminished. Hence, VMRO-DPMNE's symbolic policies for national reinvigoration resonated well with ethnic Macedonians and were perceived as 'taking back control' over the state. In addition, the traumatic memory of SDSM-dominated post-communist transition period and its resulting economic uncertainty for the citizens who lost their jobs and economic standard helped VMRO-DPMNE to legitimize their 'reform agenda' and discredit the opposition SDSM.

The interplay between institutional and symbolic aspects of illiberal politics is particularly important. These two aspects can exist separately and independently from each other, as well as co-exist together and reinforce each other. Namely, abuse of state resources to skew the even playing field does not necessarily imply involvement in discursive, symbolic elements of illiberal politics as described above. Also, monopolization of historical and societal narratives to maximize political power can be performed without drastic interference in the work of state institutions or abuse of state resources. The presented N. Macedonian case, however, shows the use of combination of strategies by governing elites to maximize institutional and symbolic (discursive) capture. For example, policies for privileged access to media supported the establishment of a dominant ethno-nationalist and conservative frames of Macedonian identity. Also, the smear campaigns against government critics and the control of the public debate directed public attention away from the abuse of state resources. The institutional and symbolic aspects of illiberal politics reinforced each other resulting in a strong push towards authoritarianism.

The conceptualization of institutional and symbolic aspects of illiberal politics as two distinct but interconnected categories is important beyond the present case of N. Macedonia, because it can be used to compare and examine not only the emergence of illiberal and authoritarian tendencies but also the maintenance of hybrid regimes in other cases of analysis. For instance, some regimes may be characterized only with institutional or symbolic aspects of illiberal politics and therefore be more or less susceptible to democratic backsliding. Whilst we find some overlapping enabling factors of institutional and symbolic politics in the case of N. Macedonia, it would be valuable to further examine under which conditions elites decide to use both strategies as opposed to one.

Furthermore, this framework can be used to compare illiberal tendencies within a single country across different periods of time. For instance, N. Macedonia's new government that came into power in 2017, based on the new coalition between SDSM and DUI, have dramatically changed the course of the previous VMRO-DPMNE and DUI coalition, primarily in regard to the symbolic elements of illiberal politics. Instead of taking advantage of the Greek vetoes and the name dispute, they reached a historic agreement with Greece and opened the doors for Macedonian integration into NATO and the EU under the new name of the Republic of North Macedonia. They have also improved bilateral relations with Bulgaria and relaxed the interethnic tensions between Macedonians and Albanians. These actions have significantly transformed N. Macedonia's broader political context and restrained the major factors which enabled symbolic illiberal politics to thrive during VMRO-DPMNE's rule. In addition, there have been some improvements in the institutional aspects of governance: the previous governmental pressure on media has been relaxed, whilst state institutions have not (yet) been instrumentalized to generate unfair political competition. However, in the time of writing of this article, in spring 2019, the new political establishment has already started showing the first signs of some of the institutional aspects of illiberal politics elaborated above, primarily in regards to nepotism and clientelism, while there are still cases of non-universal and selective application of the law when interests of the incumbent parties or their officials are in question. Consequently, we expect institutional illiberal politics to continue to obstruct Macedonian democracy in the years to come.

Notes

1. With the help of institutional illiberal politics, we capture the process of creating privileged access over time. Only when the governing elites are successful in achieving such outcome, we can qualify the political regime as competitive authoritarian.

2. Both authors are native Macedonian speakers and in the past have worked in civil society organizations in N. Macedonia. This gives us the advantage to access documents, local media sources and civil society reports in the original language. To counterbalance potential biases, we rely on peer-reviewed international academic sources which analyse various aspects of Macedonian democratization.
3. The only exception to this practice occurred in 2006 when VMRO-DPMNE formed a coalition with the second-highest ranked Albanian party in terms of vote-share Democratic Party of Albanians (DPA). However, this changed following the 2008 snap elections when the 'unlikely' VMRO-DPMNE – DUI coalition was formed which lasted until 2016.
4. DUI was formed in 2002, emerging from former members of the National Liberation Army.
5. During the early 1990s the major party representing ethnic Albanians was the Party for Democratic Prosperity (PDP), and later the Democratic Party of Albanians (DPA) (Crowther 2017, 746).
6. This was the case with the early elections in 2008, in 2011 and 2014, while the early elections in 2016 were organized as part of an internationally mediated Przino agreements (elaborated further in the paper).
7. As the agreement negotiations were held in the residence of the EU ambassador of North Macedonia in the Skopje suburb Przino, these agreements became known as the Przino agreements.
8. Mitrinovski v. The Former Yugoslav Republic of Macedonia: ECHR 30 April 2015.

Disclosure statement

No potential conflict of interest was reported by the authors.

References

Akademik. 2017. Констатирани бројни неправилности во АКМИС-системот. *Akademik*, December 7. https://www.akademik.mk/konstatirani-brojni-nepravilnosti-vo-akmis-sistemot/.

Aleksovska, M. 2015. Trust in changing institutions: The Ohrid framework agreement and institutional trust in Macedonia. *East European Quarterly* 43, no. 1: 55–84.

Andreassen, M.D. 2011. 'If you don't Vote VMRO you're not Macedonian' A study of Macedonian identity and national discourse in Skopje. MA thesis, University of Bergen.

Apostolov, V., T. Chausidis, D. Georgievski, and S. Argirova. 2015. СТУДИЈА НА СЛУЧАЈ Медиуми, газди, новинари и работнички права. SSNM. http://www.merc.org.mk/Files/Write/Documents/01245/mk/Analiza_SSNM.pdf.

Bieber, F. 2011. Building impossible states? State-building strategies and EU membership in the Western Balkans. *Europe-Asia Studies* 63, no. 10: 1783–802. doi: 10.1080/09668136.2011.618679.

Bieber, F., and M. Solska. 2018. Introduction. In *Illiberal and authoritarian tendencies in Central, Southeastern and Eastern Europe*, ed. F. Bieber, M. Solska, and D. Taleski, 11–20. Bern: Peter Lang CH.

Bieber, F. 2018. Patterns of competitive authoritarianism in the Western Balkans. *East European Politics* 34, no. 3: 337–54. doi: 10.1080/21599165.2018.1490272.

Bieber, F., and I. Ristić. 2012. Constrained democracy: The consolidation of democracy in Yugoslav successor states. *Southeastern Europe* 36, no. 3: 373–97. doi: 10.1163/18763332-03603005.

Bieber, F., M. Solska, and D. Taleski. 2018. *Illiberal and authoritarian tendencies in Central, Southeastern and Eastern Europe*. Bern: Peter Lang CH.

Blazevska, K. 2018. 27 Април – Ден на срам, крв и неподелени сендвичи. *Prizma Birn*, April 26. https://prizma.mk/27-april-den-na-sram-krv-i-nepodeleni-sendvichi/.

Bliznakovski, J., B. Gjuzelov, and M. Popovikj. 2017. *The Informal Life of Political Parties in the Western Balkan Societies*. Institute for Democracy 'Societas Civilis'Skopje (IDSCS). http://formal-informal.eu/files/news/2017/Deliverables%20and%20Milestones%202017/IDSCS-Informal%20Life%20of%20Political%20Parties-Report-27092017.pdf.

Boduszyński, M.P., 2010. *Regime change in the Yugoslav successor states, divergent paths towards a New Europe*. Baltimore: The Johns Hopkins University Press.

Bogaards, M. 2018. De-democratization in hungary: Diffusely defective democracy. *Democratization* 25, no. 8: 1481–99. doi: 10.1080/13510347.2018.1485015.

Bohnet, H., and D. Bojadzieva. 2011. Coming to terms with the past in the Balkans the lustration process in Macedonia. *KAS International Reports*. https://www.kas.de/c/document_library/get_file?uuid=13c23ea7-0fa8-41f0-de9c-6fc558dc3ba3&groupId=252038.

Bustikova, L., and P. Guasti. 2017. The illiberal turn or swerve in Central Europe? *Politics and Governance* 5, no. 4: 166. doi: 10.17645/pag.v5i4.1156.

Casal Bértoa, F., and D. Taleski. 2016. Regulating party politics in the Western Balkans: The legal sources of party system development in Macedonia. *Democratization* 23, no. 3: 545–67. doi: 10.1080/13510347.2014.987664.

Casule, K. 2012. Macedonia opposition ejected from parliament in row. *Reuters*, December 24. https://www.reuters.com/article/us-macedonia-protest/macedonia-opposition-ejected-from-parliament-in-row-idUSBRE8BN0EX20121224.

Cianetti, L., J. Dawson, and S. Hanley. 2018. Rethinking 'Democratic Backsliding' in Central and Eastern Europe – Looking beyond Hungary and Poland. *East European Politics* 34, no. 3: 243–56. doi: 10.1080/21599165.2018.1491401.

Crowther, W. 2017. Ethnic condominium and illiberalism in Macedonia. *East European Politics and Societies: and Cultures* 31, no. 4: 739–61. doi: 10.1177/0888325417716515.

Cvetkovska, S. 2013. Анализа: Не запираат огласите за вработувања среде кампања. *Nova TV*, March 30. https://novatv.mk/analizane-zapiraat-oglasite-za-vrabotuvanja-srede-kampanja/.

Daskalovski, Z. 2004. Democratic consolidation and the 'Stateness' problem: The case of Macedonia. *Global Review of Ethnopolitics* 3, no. 2: 52–66. doi: 10.1080/14718800408405165.

Dehnert, S. 2010. *Elections and conflict in Macedonia country analysis*. Friedrich-Ebert Stiftung. https://library.fes.de/pdf-files/iez/07523-b.pdf.

Delevska, S.K. 2018. Не вртете вие, вртат моиве од ОРКА - Му вика Орце Камчев на Јанакоевски во бомбите за изборите 2013. *SDK.MK*, October 30. https://sdk.mk/index.php/makedonija/ne-vrtete-vie-vrtat-moive-od-orka-mu-vika-ortse-kamchev-na-janakieski-vo-bombite-za-izborite-2013/.

Dimovski, S. 2010. Velija Ramkovski - Shady Tycoon or Media Hero? *Balkaninsight*, December 2. http://www.balkaninsight.com/en/article/velija-ramkovski-shady-tycoon-or-media-hero.

Dimovski, S. 2014. Медиумските донации за политичките партии и сопственичката структура потенцијален извор на корупција во македонските медиуми. http://mediapedia.tamijov.webfactional.com/media/dokumenti/Korupcija-mediumi-final.pdf.

Dimovski, S. 2017. Скопска единица расчисти со побунениците против Панчевски, ги прати во прекршоци. Сведок, February 21. http://www.svedok.org.mk/mk/record.php?id=718.

Dolenec, D. 2013. *Democratic institutions and authoritarian rule in Southeast Europe.* Colchester: European Consortium for Political Research.

European Commission. 2013. *The former Yugoslav Republic of Macedonia 2013 Progress Report.* https://ec.europa.eu/neighbourhood-enlargement/sites/near/files/pdf/key_documents/2013/package/mk_rapport_2013.pdf.

European Commission. 2014. *The former Yugoslav Republic of Macedonia 2014 Progress Report.* https://ec.europa.eu/neighbourhood-enlargement/sites/near/files/pdf/key_documents/2014/20141008-the-former-yugoslav-republic-of-macedonia-progress-report_en.pdf.

European Commission. 2015. *The former Yugoslav Republic of Macedonia 2015 Progress Report.* https://ec.europa.eu/neighbourhood-enlargement/sites/near/files/pdf/key_documents/2015/20151110_report_the_former_yugoslav_republic_of_macedonia.pdf.

European Commission. 2016. *The former Yugoslav Republic of Macedonia 2016 Report.* https://ec.europa.eu/neighbourhood-enlargement/sites/near/files/pdf/key_documents/2016/20161109_report_the_former_yugoslav_republic_of_macedonia.pdf.

Freedom House. 2017. *Freedom in The World 2017 Macedonia Profile.* https://freedomhouse.org/report/freedom-world/2017/macedonia.

Gordy, E., P. Cveticanin, and A. Ledeneva, eds, 2019. *The gap between rules and practices: Informality in South-East Europe.* London: UCL Press, FRINGE Series.

Graan, A. 2013. Counterfeiting the nation? Skopje 2014 and the politics of nation branding in Macedonia. *Cultural Anthropology* 28, no. 1: 161–79. doi: 10.1111/j.1548-1360.2012.01179.x.

Greskovits, B. 2015. The hollowing and backsliding of democracy in East Central Europe. *Global Policy* 6: 28–37. doi: 10.1111/1758-5899.12225.

Günay, C., and V. Dzihic. 2016. Decoding the authoritarian code: Exercising 'Legitimate' power politics through the ruling parties in Turkey, Macedonia and Serbia. *Southeast European and Black Sea Studies* 16, no. 4: 529–49. doi: 10.1080/14683857.2016.1242872.

Hammersley, M. 2008. *Questioning qualitative research: Critical essays.* London: Sage

Ilievski, Z. 2007. *Ethnic Mobilization of Macedonia.* Eurac Research. http://www.eurac.edu/en/research/autonomies/minrig/Documents/Mirico/Macedonia%20Report.pdf.

Ilievski, Z., and D. Taleski. 2009. Was the EU's role in conflict management in Macedonia a success? *Ethnopolitics* 8, no. 3–4: 355–67. doi: 10.1080/17449050903086955.

Jankovska, S., 2015. Субвенции во земјоделството – Реална помош или промашена политика? *Prizma Birn,* June 15. https://prizma.mk/subventsii-vo-zemjodelstvoto-realna-pomosh-ili-promashena-politika/.

Jordanovska, M. 2015a. Седмата бомба на СДСМ ги откри изборните манипулации. *Prizma Birn,* March 6. https://prizma.mk/sedmata-bomba-na-sdsm-gi-otkri-izbornite-manipulatsii/.

Jordanovska, M. 2015b. Партиска агенција за вработување. *Prizma Birn,* April 14. https://prizma.mk/partiska-agentsija-za-vrabotuvane/.

Jordanovska, M. 2017. Се множат патриотските невладини организации. *Prizma Birn,* March 21. https://prizma.mk/se-mnozhat-patriotskite-nevladini-organizatsii/.

Jovanovska, M. 2017. Игор Тантуровски реизбран за претседател на Антикорупциска Комисија. *Nova TV,* April 13. https://novatv.mk/igor-tanturovski-reizbran-za-pretsedatel-na-antikoruptsiska-komisija/.

Kapidžić, D. Forthcoming. The rise of illiberal politics in Southeast Europe. *Southeast European and Black Sea Studies.*

Keil, S. 2018. The business of state capture and the rise of authoritarianism in Kosovo, Macedonia, Montenegro and Serbia. *Southeastern Europe* 42: 59–82. doi:10.1163/18763332-04201004.

Kostovicova, D., and V. Bojicić-Dželilović. 2006. Europeanizing the Balkans: Rethinking the post-communist and post-conflict transition. *Ethnopolitics* 5, no. 3: 223–41. doi: 10.1080/17449050600911091.

Levitsky, S., and L.A. Way. 2010. *Competitive authoritarianism: Hybrid regimes after the cold war.* New York: Cambridge University Press.

Marusic, S.J. 2011. Macedonian opposition say boycott goes on. *Balkaninsight,* February 10. http://www.balkaninsight.com/en/article/macedonian-opposition-continues-boycott.

Marusic, S.J. 2012a. Macedonian journalists cry foul over libel reform. *Balkaninsight*, June 15. https://balkaninsight.com/2012/06/15/macedonian-journalists-cry-foul-over-libel-reform/.

Marusic, S.J. 2012b. Macedonian NGO chief to sue lustration body. *Balkan Transitional Justice*, August 13. https://balkaninsight.com/2012/08/13/macedonian-ngo-chief-to-sue-lustration-body/.

Marusic, S.J. 2013. Last-ditch efforts made to solve Macedonia crisis. *Balkaninsight*, February 28. http://www.balkaninsight.com/en/article/last-ditch-efforts-to-solve-macedonian-crisis.

Marusic, S.J. 2014. Macedonia opposition toughens line on poll fraud. *Balkaninsight*, May 2. http://www.balkaninsight.com/en/article/opposition-cements-defiance-against-electoral-fraud.

Marusic, S.J. 2016a. Thirteenth night of protests ends in Macedonia. *Balkaninsight*, April 26. http://www.balkaninsight.com/en/article/thirteenth-night-of-protests-ends-in-macedonia-04-26-2016.

Marusic, S.J. 2016b. Macedonia's SJO says secret police ran illegal wiretapping. *Balkaninsight*, November 18. http://www.balkaninsight.com/en/article/macedonia-s-sjo-says-secret-police-ran-illegal-wiretapping-11-18-2016#sthash.IIVT8JS9.dpuf.

Micevski, I., and S. Trpevska. 2015. What the Macedonian phone-tapping scandal tells us about clientelism in the media. *International Journal of Digital Television* 6, no. 3: 319–26. doi: 10.1386/jdtv.6.3.319_1.

Miškovska Kajevska, A. 2018. A foe of democracy, gender and sexual equality in Macedonia: The worrisome role of the party VMRO-DPMNE. *Politics And Governance* 6, no. 3: 55. doi: 10.17645/pag.v6i3.1415.

MKD.mk. 2016. Љубе Бошкоски пуштен од затвор, 2016. *MKD.mk*, June 3. https://www.mkd.mk/makedonija/politika/ljube-boshkoski-pushten-od-zatvor.

Nikolovski, D. 2013. *Traitors hirelings and sandwich-protesters: Civil activism in Macedonian public discourse*. Skopje: Foundation Open Society – Macedonia. http://eurothink.mk/gridfs/data/id/5820fe8efffc7468d62a9bc7.

Offe, C. 2004. Capitalism by democratic design?: Democratic theory facing the triple transition in East Central Europe. *Social Research: An International Quarterly* 71, no. 3: 501–28.

Ordanovski, S., G. Ismail, D. Stankovski, and G. Ajdini. 2012. Заробена демократија: развојот на сопственичката структура на медиумите во република македонија. Skopje: Transparency Macedonia.

Orlović, S. 2013. *Transitional Justice in Post-Yugoslav Countries: Report For 2010-2011*. Belgrade: Humanitarian Law Center. http://recom.link/wp-content/uploads/2014/12/Transitional-Justice-in-Post-Yugoslav-countries-2010-2011.pdf.

OSCE/ODIHR. 2006. *The Former Yugoslav Republic of Macedonia Parliamentary Elections OSCE/ODIHR Election Observation Mission Final Report*. Warsaw: Office for Democratic Institutions and Human Rights. https://www.osce.org/odihr/elections/fyrom/20630?download=true.

OSCE/ODIHR. 2008. *The Former Yugoslav Republic of Macedonia Early Parliamentary Elections OSCE/ODIHR Election Observation Mission Final Report*. Warsaw. https://www.osce.org/odihr/elections/fyrom/33152?download=true.

OSCE/ODIHR. 2009. *The Former Yugoslav Republic of Macedonia Presidential and Municipal Elections OSCE/ODIHR Election Observation Mission Final Report*. Warsaw. https://www.osce.org/odihr/elections/fyrom/37851?download=true.

OSCE/ODIHR. 2011. *The Former Yugoslav Republic of Macedonia Early Parliamentary Elections 5 June 2011 OSCE/ODIHR Election Observation Mission Final Report*. Warsaw. https://www.osce.org/odihr/elections/FYROM/83666?download=true.

OSCE/ODIHR. 2013. *The Former Yugoslav Republic of Macedonia Municipal Elections 24 March And 7 April 2013 OSCE/ODIHR Election Observation Mission Final Report*. Warsaw. https://www.osce.org/odihr/elections/103411?download=true.

OSCE/ODIHR. 2014. *The Former Yugoslav Republic of Macedonia Presidential and Early Parliamentary Elections 13 And 27 April 2014 OSCE/ODIHR Election Observation Mission Final Report*. Warsaw. https://www.osce.org/odihr/elections/fyrom/121306?download=true.

OSCE/ODIHR. 2016. *The Former Yugoslav Republic of Macedonia Early Parliamentary Elections 11 December 2016 OSCE/ODIHR Election Observation Mission Final Report*. Warsaw. https://www.osce.org/odihr/elections/fyrom/302136?download=true.

Petkovski, L., and D. Nikolovski. 2018. Macedonia: Illiberal democracy or outright authoritarianism?. In *Illiberal and authoritarian tendencies in Central, Southeastern and Eastern Europe*, ed. F. Bieber, M. Solska, and D. Taleski, 205–224. Bern: Peter Lang CH.

Popovikj, M. 2017. Violence in the Macedonian parliament: What happened and how should the EU Respond? Blog. *LSE EUROPP – European Politics and Policy*, April 28. http://blogs.lse.ac.uk/europpblog/2017/04/28/violence-macedonian-parliament-what-happened-eu-response/.

Priebe, R. 2015. *The former Yugoslav Republic of Macedonia: Recommendations of the Senior Experts' Group on Systemic Rule of Law Issues Relating to the Communications Interception Revealed in Spring 2015*. Brussels. https://ec.europa.eu/neighbourhood-enlargement/sites/near/files/news_corner/news/news-files/20150619_recommendations_of_the_senior_experts_group.pdf.

Priebe, R. 2017. *The former Yugoslav Republic of Macedonia: Assessment and Recommendations of The Senior Experts' Group on Systemic Rule of Law Issues 2017*. European Commission. https://ec.europa.eu/neighbourhood-enlargement/sites/near/files/2017.09.14_seg_report_on_systemic_rol_issues_for_publication.pdf.

Ramet, S.P. 2017. Macedonia's Post-Yugoslav reality: Corruption, wiretapping, and stolen elections. In *Building democracy in the Yugoslav successor states: Accomplishments, setbacks, and challenges since 1990*, ed. S.P. Ramet, C.M. Hassenstab, and O. Listhaug, 287–320. Cambridge: Cambridge University Press.

Risteska, M. 2015. *Nations in Transit 2015 Macedonia*. Freedom House. https://freedomhouse.org/sites/default/files/NIT_2015_Macedonia.pdf.

Schatz, E. 2009. The soft authoritarian tool kit: Agenda-setting power in Kazakhstan and Kyrgyzstan. *Comparative Politics* 41, no. 2: 203–22. doi: 10.5129/001041509x12911362972034.

Spaskovska, L., 2014. From feudal socialism to feudal democracy - The trials and tribulations of the former Yugoslav Republic of Macedonia. Blog. *Opendemocracy*. https://www.opendemocracy.net/can-europe-make-it/ljubica-spaskovska/from-feudal-socialism-to-feudal-democracy-trials-and-tribulati.

Spasovska, K., and I. Rusi. 2015. From 'Chaos' To 'Order': The transition of the media in Macedonia from 1989 to 2014. *Southeastern Europe* 39, no. 1: 35–61. doi:10.1163/18763332-03901003.

State Electoral Commission. 2014. http://old.sec.mk/arhiva-rezultati/izbori-2014/predvremeni-parlam-2014/322-fin-izv-pretvremeni.

State Electoral Commission. 2016. http://www.sec.mk/predvremeni-izbori-za-pratenici-2016/.

US Department of State. 2011. *Country Reports on Human Rights Practices for 2011 Macedonia*. Bureau of Democracy, Human Rights and Labor. https://www.state.gov/documents/organization/186589.pdf.

US Department of State. 2012. *Country Reports on Human Rights Practices for 2012 Macedonia*. Bureau of Democracy, Human Rights and Labor. https://www.state.gov/documents/organization/204523.pdf.

US Department of State. 2013. *Country Reports on Human Rights Practices for 2013 Macedonia*. Bureau of Democracy, Human Rights and Labor. https://www.state.gov/documents/organization/220516.pdf.

US Department of State. 2014. *Country Reports on Human Rights Practices for 2014 Macedonia*. Bureau of Democracy, Human Rights and Labor. https://www.state.gov/documents/organization/236762.pdf.

van Biezen, I., P. Mair, and T. Poguntke. 2011. Going, Going, … Gone? The decline of party membership in contemporary Europe. *European Journal of Political Research* 51, no. 1: 24–56. doi: 10.1111/j.1475-6765.2011.01995.x.

Vangeli, A. 2011. Nation-building ancient Macedonian style: The origins and the effects of the so-called antiquization in Macedonia. *Nationalities Papers* 39, no. 1: 13–32. doi: 10.1080/00905992.2010.532775.

Yin, R. K., 2018. Case study research and applications. *Design and Methods*. Los Angeles.

The elephant in the room: illiberal politics in Montenegro

Olivera Komar

ABSTRACT
Montenegro is at the same time considered both a success story as the leader of European integration in South-Eastern Europe and a country with severe democratic deficiencies. This paper builds upon the theory of democratic backsliding and uses theory-building process tracing to detect and analyse systematic patterns in the illiberal policies that the governing party uses to maintain its position in power. The three typical cases examined here reveal that assuring external control and maintaining the pretence of legality seem to be important elements of illiberal policies and that independent institutions and European standards are often used to assert and maintain control.

Introduction

Recent Montenegrin history can be narrated in two quite distinct manners. One version would cite those EU officials or EU country representatives that describe this country as 'a leader in the integration process'[1] in the region, emphasizing the ongoing reforms concerning the rule of law and good governance. With 32 opened negotiating chapters[2] (out of which three provisionally closed) and without serious border disputes, Montenegro looks 'good' in comparison to the rest of its neighbourhood. Furthermore, the fact that the country managed to join NATO in spite of significant opposition from within represents a success story from the perspective of the Western international community.

Another narrative is also possible. The mere fact that the government at the national level has never been changed might not be sufficient proof of something not being entirely right, but it could be a fair indication. The fact that the government in question is dominantly constituted by a party that is a direct successor of the League of Communists in Montenegro adds to this 'suspicion.' When we consider the history of patrimonial power with some elements of national accommodative communism (Kitschelt et al. 1999), the lack of alternation in power (Magaloni 2006), and social dependence on state resources, the Montenegrin success story starts to look somewhat different.

Dolenec (2013) summarizes the literature on the development of political party competition in post-communist countries, outlining the following four preconditions: 'the exit of the Communist party from power at the first multiparty election, the existence of a strong enough democratic opposition to take its place, the prompt reform of the former Communist party into a modern Social Democratic party after losing office, and the subsequent regular alternation of political parties in power' (Dolenec 2013, 45). None of these conditions have been fulfilled in the Montenegrin case, so we might argue that proper or fair party competition has never fully developed. Additionally, if there was never a change in terms of the party controlling the public resources, we might expect that governmental control and oversight might not be at its most efficient. Both the international and the academic community (in addition to the media and opposition parties) have already noticed and described the consequences of such a prolonged position of power and privileged access to public resources in the Montenegrin case (Džankić 2013; Vuković 2013; Jenne and Bieber 2014; Komar and Živković 2016; Džankić 2018).

Montenegro is not an exception, however. There is already a body of scholarship that has identified reversing trends in democracies, especially new ones, towards authoritarian practices. While 'democratic backsliding' is not, it seems, solely confined to the Balkan region (Zakaria 1997; Levitsky and Way 2010; Öktem and Akkoyunlu 2016; Günay and Dzihic 2016; Bermeo 2016; Bieber et al. 2018), various authors have noticed several regional specificities, including the strategic use of ideology, external legitimacy, the creation and management of crises, re-establishing a loyal media and state capture (Bieber 2018b, 341). Dolenec adds 'the predatory conception of public office' to this list as a metaphor based on the example of a mayor from Serbia, who literarily emptied the offices he used to occupy 'taking the desk and chars; de-instaling the air-conditioning system and even removing electrical sockets from the walls' (Dolenec 2013, 4). Speaking of the reasons why democracy in the region has not reached levels 'comparable to those in Central Eastern Europe,' Dolenec points to socioeconomic parameters and regime legacies, the conditions of statehood, political party dynamics and EU democratization pressure (Dolenec 2013, 3). Additionally, as the main causes, Bieber identifies institutional weakness and authoritarian political actors that 'utilize these weaknesses to attain and retain power' (Bieber 2018b, 338). Bermeo describes this strengthening and concentration of power in the executive office as 'executive aggrandizement.' She notices that it is often accomplished through legal means and majority control in the decision-making bodies (Bermeo 2016, 12). We can also find evidence of deficiencies in both the electoral and liberal component of democracy in the region. The electoral component is disrupted through different mechanisms that directly or indirectly tilt the electoral playing field in favour of the incumbents (Levitsky and Way 2010; Bermeo 2016), while the liberal element is subverted by the dominance of executive power (Bermeo 2016) and the restriction of civil rights and freedoms.

This paper will not focus on the origins of one party's invincibility in Montenegro, since a lot has been written about the topic already. Rather, it will build upon the above-summarized literature on democratic backsliding and focus on one of the main mechanisms that have enabled such longevity in power – *illiberal policies*. Here, we mean policies that are proposed or enacted by political parties in government that create an uneven playing field, helping them to remain in power indefinitely. These policies include long term actions such as perpetuating illiberal socio-economic structures and governing practices, but also specific and targeted illiberal actions against political opponents and key institutions to reduce accountability (Kapidžić 2020). They involve the stretching or bending of the rules by the parties in government in order to create an advantage for themselves. The most prominent cases of such practices, besides the DPS in Montenegro, could include the rule of VMRO-DPMNE in Macedonia or the SNS in Serbia.

The goal of the paper is to look closely at specific examples of illiberal policies enacted by the ruling elites in Montenegro, so as to outline their common characteristics. Since illiberal politics are on the rise not only in the region but worldwide, understanding the mechanisms within them can help in building a general theory. We will use *theory-building process tracing* (Beach and Brun 2019) to examine specific cases of illiberal policies, identify commonalities and build a theoretical explanation of how they function.

Identifying all the individual incidents of illiberal policies in one country would be an impossible task. Therefore, our case selection strategy was to take three typical and highly visible incidences to unfold their elements. Bearing in mind that our goal is to examine empirical examples of illiberal policies, identify commonalities and necessary elements and build a theoretical explanation of how these policies work, the way forward is thus to select cases according to the most typical criterion (Gerring 2007, 91). We stared from one case, identified the main elements and then use a sort of 'snowballing' to test the outlined mechanism by adding more examples. Each case has been unfolded into a series of consecutive 'snapshots' which were then analysed. Through the 'snapshop' we understand a cohesive series of events and strategic actions concerning a specific issue or a policy that enable us to infer a systematic pattern and therefore unpack the causal mechanism underneath the particular illiberal policy in question.

For our analysis, we generally use primary sources – documents and records. However, those are further supported by secondary sources including interviews and media sources.

The paper is structured in the following way: in the next section, we will provide some information about the political system in the country. The overview will be minimalistic and focus on relevant points to provide references for understanding the empirical examples that follow. The main section will analyse three examples of illiberal politics in Montenegro. We will start from the case of the attempt to seize control over the National Broadcasting Service (NBS) as an example of monopolizing public resources and therefore limiting freedom of expression. After the key elements of the illiberal policy are identified, two more cases are used to see if these elements can also be found there and therefore substantiate the theory. The first is an example of tilting the electoral playing field in favour of the incumbents – the case of planning how to buy votes, and the second an example of taking political control over an independent institution – the case of exerting control over the State University. The final section discusses the identified elements and the implications of the evidence found for further theory building.

The context: the political system and democratic consolidation in Montenegro

Montenegro renewed its independence in 2006, thus becoming one of the last Yugoslav republics and territories to do so. Even though the country became independent only then, its administrative apparatus started to become self-sufficient after 1997, when an internal conflict split the predominant ruling party in two. Since the group that gave up its loyalty to the Serbian leadership prevailed after the first truly uncertain democratic elections[3], the slow but steady disintegration of the union with Serbia was initiated. This process was finally completed by the independence referendum in May 2006. After the referendum, the Constitution, stating that Montenegro is a parliamentary democracy with proportional representation, was adopted, thus formally completing the Montenegrin transition to independence.

Even though we might think that the consolidation of democracy should have been completed soon after the statehood issue was peacefully resolved, this might not be the case. Depending on the definition and the criteria of democratic consolidation, Montenegro could still be a pending case. In particular, one of the most important features of democratic consolidation – the peaceful replacement of the main party in government – has not yet happened. The Montenegrin party system could therefore be best described using Sartori's classification (Sartori 2005) as a *predominant party system*. The ruling Democratic Party of Socialists (DPS) is, in fact, the direct successor of the League of Communists of Montenegro. After winning the first regional elections under its old name in 1990, the party introduced a strategy of pragmatic reform (Bazoki and Ishiyama 2002, 6) which meant distancing itself from Communist ideology and reinventing itself as a party of technocrats and pragmatists that has continued to rule uninterruptedly at the national level ever since. Thus, democratization started from *patrimonial communism*, a type of system that emerged from pre-communist low bureaucratic institutionalization and the concentration of power in the hands of an individual leader or a small group with some elements of national accommodative communism, such as relying on cooptation to ensure compliance (Kitschelt et al. 1999). This system has continued without regime change towards the further personalization of politics.

The predominant party system in the Montenegrin case means that one party has controlled the national government without interruption since the 1990s. However, this does not mean that it rules alone. The Montenegrin system of proportional representation stimulates coalition governments. Recent history indicates the existence of 'preferred' coalition partners. In particular, the fact that ethnic minority parties and groups played an important role in obtaining Montenegrin independence in 2006 ensured their 'privileged' positions in the years to come. As a consequence, the DPS continues to invest in this relationship and often ignores the minimal coalition principle when forming the government, which representatives of all the major ethnic groups are usually invited to join (Bosniaks, Muslims, Albanians, and Croats). This, in turn, additionally antagonizes the opposition, constituted of parties that favoured the union with Serbia, who perceive this cooperation as a betrayal of Orthodox interests in the region.

The main cleavage remains the statehood issue, now 'disguised' in other visible manifestations, such as ethnic division (Montenegrins and ethnic minorities on the one hand vs. Serbs on the other) or the pro and anti-NATO blocks. The 'prostatehood' part of the cleavage is dominated by the DPS, the predominant party that presents itself as the main defender of Montenegrin statehood and identity and an ally of the EU and the West in general. Its average support is around 40%, which means that they sometimes need a partner to form a government. The necessary partner, besides minority parties, are usually small 'satellite' parties with just enough votes to achieve representation (according to the minimum vote requirement), such as the Social Democrats (SD) or the Liberal Party (LP). The usual members of the ruling coalition are the minority parties such as the Bosniak party (BS), the Croatian Civic Initiative (HGI) or the Democratic Union of Albanians (DUA). They have privileged access to representation, since the Montenegrin Election Law mandates a lower vote threshold for political parties representing ethnic minorities.

The other side of the cleavage is dominated by the Democratic Front, a rather radical, pro-East and anti-NATO group whose main constituents are New Serbian Democracy (NOVA) and the Movement for Change (PZP). There are other more explicit pro-Serbian and conservative parties in this block, but their strength individually usually means they fail to receive any seats in parliament.

The third group of parties is sometimes called the 'civic opposition.' Those are often new parties or parties emerging from either of the sides of the cleavage, who try to bridge the gap by proclaiming themselves 'neutral.' Neutrality in this sense means wanting to overcome the statehood and identity debate and engage in economics-based politics. There has been number of such parties since the independence referendum. Examples include the Movement for Changes (PZP) before they joined the Democratic Front, the Democrats (Demokrate), DEMOS, the Social Democratic Party (SDP), United Reform Action (URA) and at one brief point in time the Social People's Party (SNP). Most of the parties that start to gain significance in this 'neutral' terrain get pushed by the joint action of actors from both sides of the cleavage (Kapidžić and Komar 2019). The reason why the middle position is so important is the fact that without a strong party in that position, one that can attract both Montenegrin and Serbian votes, the DPS is mathematically irreplaceable (for the full overview of the main features of the party system, please refer to the table 1).

This system without alternations at the national level suffers from all the typical problems of predominant party systems, including an oversized public sector and dependence on public financing, state clientelism, corruption and nepotism, the lack of a meritocracy and low levels of bureaucratization.

However, due to external pressure and the 'carrot' offered in the form of independence and European integration, the trend at least seemed positive. Writing about democracy in transition, Levitsky and Way said that 'Such characterizations imply that these cases are moving in a democratic direction' (Levitski and Way 2002). In the Montenegrin case, the trend was positive, at least up to a point. Once independence was achieved and the political actors understood that the European integration process was not in fact directly contingent on the quality of the reforms they proposed, the tide started to shift. The Freedom of the World[4] report (see figure 1) captures the shift towards a more negative evaluation in terms of freedom and the political dimension since 2016[5]. This finding is supported by the V-Dem data[6], which has already been presented in the introductory article, which indicates stagnation with a prolonged decline after 2015.

The other way to describe the system is to use the Montenegrin National Election Study MNES, 2016[7]. According to this study, only 43.6% of Montenegrins believe that the results of the 2016 Parliamentary elections represent the reality, while only 21.6% believe that votes are 'always' and 15% that they are 'sometimes' counted correctly. On the other hand, 75.2% of respondents believe to a certain degree that voters are paid to vote in a specific way, and 71.6% believe that they are blackmailed into doing so. Finally, 13.3% admit that they have personally been offered money in exchange for their vote.

Using all this data, we can see that the functioning of democracy in the country is stagnating with a slow negative trend.

Table 1. Main features of political parties in Montenegro.

Party	Approximate strength[a]	Main trademark	True appeal	Position towards EU	Position towards NATO	Main problem
DPS	41.5%	'Statehood' defender party	Clientelism	No alternative	In favour	Negative selection, Internal clashes; Corruption scandals
BS	3.2%	Minority representation	Clientelism Ethnic politics	No alternative	In favour	DPS shadow party
SD	4%	DPS partner	Clientelism	No alternative	In favour	Dependence on DPS
Demokrate	20.7%	New and young	Ambivalence towards identity politics	In favour	Ambivalent	No clear position on identity politics
SDP	3.5%	'Statehood' defender party	Clearer statehood option	No alternative	No alternative	Lost access to privileges
SNP	6.8%	Conservative	Serbian moderate	Yes, 'but'	No	Ageing constituency
URA	2.8%	Reforms	Anti-DPS pro-independence option	No alternative	No alternative	Party infrastructure
DEMOS	2.6%	Reforms	Leader	Yes, 'but'	Ambivalence leaning towards against	Pro-Serbian voters and members
DF	10.1%	Anti-Đukanović	Anti-statehood, Pro-East Pro-Serbian	Ambivalent	Strongly against	Not coalition material

[a] According to the Centre for Democracy and Human Rights CEDEM's political public opinion survey conducted in December 2018, https://www.cedem.me/programi/istrazivanja/politicko-javno-mnjenje/send/29-politicko-javno-mnjenje/1917-politicko-javno-mnjenje-decembar-2018, accessed on 20 December 2018.

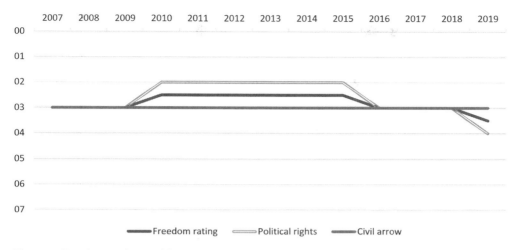

Figure 1. Freedom in the World report, Montenegro, 2007–2019.

Contentious political issues and illiberal politics

At least two conditions must be met for political elites to engage in illiberal political activity successfully: they must offer a believable justification that enough people accept and believe and there must be a reasonable belief that the activity will not be punished. In terms of the first condition, the usual justifications such as fighting crime, corruption or corrupt elites do not work in the case of Montenegro, since the ruling party has been in power for over a quarter of the century. Furthermore, ideological pragmatism and a number of EU-integration inspired laws remove social conservativism as an option. Migrants are also not a problem, yet. Finally, openly taking the pro-Western side by joining NATO in the context of a strong national division regarding the issue and the significant presence of Russian interests in the region additionally limits the options.

In such conditions, the logical choice seems to be the defence of Montenegrin statehood against external territorial appetites, primarily that of Serbia, as well as internal 'subversive' actors. The premise that Montenegrin statehood could be challenged often seems very plausible, bearing in mind the activities of part of the pro-Eastern opposition with regards to Serbian interests in Montenegro, as well as the enduring duality of Montenegrin identity (Džankić 2013). The argument could be articulated in the following way: *The DPS is the only political actor big enough to stand against anti-Montenegrin forces, whether from within or from the outside. It might be true that it misuses public resources and engages in clientelism and patronage, but the alternative is unacceptable, since it jeopardizes Montenegrin sovereignty.* Voters are continuously instructed and reminded to look 'at the broader picture'; that is, to consider the protection of Montenegrin identity and statehood and forgive certain 'petty' side-effects. Moreover, illiberal policies and practices are not recognized or admitted to as such. Quite on the contrary, most of the time, they are justified by the mere formal legality of the undertaken actions (Levitsky and Way 2010). The *rule of law* is understood in terms of *rechtsstaat* – if an action is compliant with the letter of the law, it needs no further justification. As will be seen from the examples in the following sections, when you have a sufficient majority, anything can be voted out. In this way, the ruling majority has evolved and adjusted itself to the requirements of the *forthcoming era* by using new, often very complicated and not quite 'fitting' European legislation to justify their actions. That, in turn, fulfils the second condition – if an action is not illegal, the actor cannot be punished. The system in place to monitor, adjudicate, punish, or remove is therefore subverted by illiberal politics and actions.

Here, we will analyse the successful attempt to regain control over the National Broadcast Company, to unfold the sequence of events and construct the pattern. We will look into specific events as individual 'snapshots' in the succession of developments that brought us the outcome in the case. Apart from being a very well-known and highly visible case, it is important because a free media can be considered to be one of the pillars of modern democracy. After establishing what we believe could be a systemic pattern of events, we will test the model on two more cases. The first will be the case of using public resources in order to tilt the electoral playing field in favour of the incumbents. Misusing public resources in order to gain an unfair electoral advantage has been one of the main problems of Montenegrin democracy given the almost three decades long incumbency of one party, and as such this element is often criticized by both civil society and international organizations.[8] The second will be the case of the successful attempt to gain full governmental control over an independent institution – the University of Montenegro. The existance of independent institutions, especially those that are supposed to harbour free thought and critical opinion is supposed to be one of the prerequisits of a functioning democracy.

Case 1: monopolizing public resources and limiting freedom of expression

There is only one public national broadcast company in Montenegro – Radio-Television Montenegro – RTCG. According to recent publicly available polls from 2018[9], it is one of the most trusted TV stations with full national geographical coverage in the state (22.5% of respondents share this opinion). Its main competitor is a private and openly anti-government TV station – *Vijesti*, whose news programme is usually the most-watched one. The rest of the broadcasting scene is mainly focused on entertainment but is nevertheless divided, with *Prva TV, Nova M* and *Pink M* on the side of the government and *A1*, at least until quite recently, against it. Additionally, a large share of the viewership watches TV stations from the wider region, predominantly from Serbia, via cable.

In 2002, RTCG was transformed from 'state television' into an entity that is often referred to as the *public broadcast service*. The idea of this concept was that since the national budget predominantly funds it, it should, therefore, be in the service of the citizens of Montenegro and the public in general and not specifically of the state, as was the case before.

For a considerable time, RTCG was perceived as a ruling party media outlet. Its reporting regularly reflected the position and interests of the DPS to different degrees. Numerous reports have shown, both quantitatively and qualitatively, that the selection of the news reported by RTCG, the tone and direction of the reporting, and the selection of guests significantly benefits the ruling party (Kerševan Smokvina et al. 2017).

Formally, since 2002, this influence was heavily asserted on RTCG through its two central managing bodies – the Executive Director and the RTCG Council. The RTCG

Council is especially important since it elects the Executive Director and is, in fact, the sole body that RTCG is responsible to. The members of the RTCG Council are appointed by the National Parliament and come from academia and civil society, including NGOs working in the field of culture, human rights or the media, trade unions and the Chamber of Commerce.

Snapshot 1, The Trigger – Loss of Control: Until 2016, the RTCG Council structure reflected the will of the parliamentary majority and directly or indirectly supported and promoted the interests of the DPS and its coalition partners. The channel (especially in its information and news output) supported the ruling coalitions' version of events and was under significant political influence[10] which was asserted through the Council. However, the political context briefly changed in 2016. Due to the break-up of a coalition formed by the DPS and the SDP, at the time the usual coalition partner, the ruling party lost its majority in the parliament and was forced to offer the opposition certain concessions. As a result, a new minority 'provisional government,' including ministers from the DPS and the traditional opposition was formed. In this way, a part of the opposition gained temporary influence over a number of political spheres. As might have been expected, one of the priorities for the opposition was the National Broadcasting Service – RTCG. The new RTCG Council members elected during this provisional time came, for the first time, from outside the zone of influence of the DPS. Indeed, the Council of Europe's Analysis of the Media Sector stated that RTCG was in fact for the first time 'controlled by the traditional opposition' (Kerševan Smokvina et al. 2017, 46).

Consequently, the reporting changed. According to the opposition – it became more open, inclusive, and objective. According to ruling party representatives 'even though it was considered independent, it was in fact oppositional' (interview with a DPS MP, to draft the report, Kerševan Smokvina et al. 2017, 46). Dissatisfaction with the way RTCG operated grew among the DPS leadership and culminated during the election campaign in October 2016, just as the 'provisional' government completed its mandate.

Snapshot 2 – Regaining Control by Building a Majority: After the elections, which resulted in a new DPS-controlled government, the Administrative Board of the Parliament, which consisted of a majority of DPS members, initiated the procedure to dismiss the RTCG Council members that were perceived to be 'independent', due to alleged conflicts of interest. At the Administrative Board's request, the Agency for the Prevention of Corruption (ASK) reviewed the cases of three RTCG Council members and found them all to be in a conflict of interest. Based on ASK's decision, the Administrative Board of the Parliament dismissed the three RTCG Council members, therefore tipping the scale of influence within this body in favour of the DPS once again.

Snapshot 3 – Assuring External Legitimacy: The Agency for the Prevention of Corruption is an independent body in charge of deciding whether the law on the conflict of interests has been violated. It was meant to be an independent body whose management is elected by the Parliament. The Director of the ASK is elected by the ASK Council whose members are elected by the National Parliament, based on a recommendation made by the Parliamentary Board for Anticorruption. The mechanism of the election of the ASK Council is meant to ensure its complete independence from the government and was such promoted as such by international organizations based on 'best comparative practice.' However, in a situation when the ruling party has strong control over the Parliament, the result is that DPS has seven out of 11 members of the Parliamentary

Figure 2. Elements of an illiberal policy in Montenegro.

Board for Anticorruption. This transforms a supposed mechanism of independence into an extremely -strong mechanism of control.

Snapshot 4 – Restoring Control: Whether the dismissed members of the RTCG Council were in fact in a conflict of interest was, to say the least, a legally controversial question. Probably the most questionable finding was in the case of a movie director by profession who was found to be in breach of the law on the conflict of interests because he directed a movie for a private company. ASK found that by making the movie, he could have come into a conflict of interests should this movie ever been submitted to the RTCG Council to decide whether it should be broadcasted on this television channel[11]. As a result, he was dismissed because of a hypothetical conflict which had never in fact happened. Needless to say, the movie in question was never submitted to the RTCG Council to be considered for broadcasting on national television.

Snapshot 5 – Democratic Epilogue: Later on, the Administrative Court ruled in favour of the movie director and annulled the decision of the ASK, but that has not so far changed the outcome. Court decisions have not produced any real change or instigated responsibility by the authorities. In a renewed procedure, the ASK reached the same decision[12], and the movie director was dismissed from the RTCG Council. The two other cases were less clear cut, but might also be seen as questionable decisions. The IREX Media Sustainability Report qualified the situation in the following manner: 'In the past year, the national public broadcaster Radio and Television of Montenegro (RTCG) was under immense political pressure' (IREX 2017, iii). The 2018 European Commission Progress Report comments on the decisions in a similar manner: 'Moreover, recent opinions issued by the Agency, including those concerning members of the Governing Council of the public broadcaster RTCG and the Council of the Agency for Electronic Media, have shown significant weaknesses in the application of the law, the establishment of the facts and proper reasoning. This opened a debate over the need to shield the Agency from undue external pressure' (European Commission 2018, 19). In the subsequent text it is also noted: 'Initial positive developments on RTCG's editorial independence and professionalism were challenged by instances of undue political interference and political pressure on its Council. Several members of the RTCG Council were dismissed and replaced by the Parliament in late 2017 and early 2018. In its new composition, the RTCG Council voted out its Chair, replacing him with one of the newly appointed members' (European Commission 2018).

Identified elements of illiberal politics

By identifying key 'snapshots' in this case (see figure 2), we could have posited a consequential chain of events that represent the 'skeleton' of an illiberal policy in

Montenegro. In this case, the trigger for illiberal political behaviour was a crisis in terms of the sudden loss of control over a provisionally independent institution – the National Broadcast Company. The loss of control was caused by the concessions the government had to make to the opposition to stay in power until elections could be held. However, after the elections were held and power was restored, the system was used to regain control over the RTCG. To do that several 'allegedly' independent institutions were used to vote out opposition figures in a series of legally questionable decision. This case shows how independent agencies, such as the ASK, created in fact for the protection of the rule of law, can be used to externally aid the selective and questionable enactment of legislation to gain political control. Ironically, the anti-corruption legislation was one of the emphases of the ongoing reforms within the European integration process. As a consequence, one could even argue that the field is overregulated, and that this meant the legal norms were skilfully misused in this case.

We can now use this 'pattern' to try to identify the same elements in other cases. In this paper, we will examine two more cases to do so.

Case 2: tilting the electoral playing field in favour of the incumbent

Snapshot 1 – The Trigger – Opportunity: Bearing in mind their privileged position and access to public resources, the DPS has often been accused of misusing them for their own political gain. The value of uninterrupted access to public resources becomes clear, bearing in mind the latest projections that almost one-third of all legally employed people in the country work in public administration[13]. In addition to the approximately 188,000 employed people in Montenegro, according to the National Statistical Office in 2016, a further 43.951 people were receiving some sort of welfare assistance which makes them directly dependent on the state. The fact that Montenegro has a total of 620,029 inhabitants according to the latest Census (2011) gives perspective to these figures. Džankić even goes so far as to label the level of the misuse of public resources in Montenegro as state capture (Džankić 2018). The recordings examined in this case illustrate how the DPS elites use their privileged access to create an uneven electoral playing field. However, the scandal also shows the weakness of the institutions that can be used to prevent such actions.

However, evidence has not always been easy to find. Most accusations have ended up being 'hear-say' and have never caught the attention of the official institutions. There have been some exceptions, though. One of them was infamous 'Audio recording scandal' that happened in February 2013. In this case, a recording from the official meeting of the Main DPS Council was leaked to the general public by an opposition party, which somehow managed to obtain it.

Snapshot 2 – Building a Majority by Buying Votes: During the session that was recorded, members of the DPS Council openly discuss how to use public resources, including IPA funded projects, to assure electoral victory. They talk about the strategy behind it, the specific mechanisms that could be used and report to their colleagues about activities that have already been implemented. For example, the director of the National Employment Agency, at the time, could be heard saying: *'One employed person means four votes. If we can manage to employ our man, we have taken one vote from them (the opposition) and increased the count for us (DPS). There is also the part regarding the family. 'Let's help this man get a job and as an effect we will gain four votes for the DPS'[14].* The same speaker goes on to explain in detail how publicly funded projects that create employment (even temporarily) can be used to employ 'our people'[15]. 'Through these projects, we will mainly employ DPS members,' he emphasized, therefore admitting that the projects and funds are used to incentivize people selectively and by doing that securing or buying votes.

Other Board members share similar plans and stories during the meeting[16]. The DPS Council members continue discussing how to use state projects, and public jobs and institutions, to gain votes. Furthermore, the recording gives a very rare insight into how party brokers use *hope* and *fear* to manipulate people into voting for the DPS, even without providing specific benefits.

Snapshot 3 – Assuring External Legitimacy: The first institutional reaction was the creation of a Parliamentary Committee of Inquiry into the alleged misuse of public resources for party gain. However, the committee concluded its work with a technical report which had no political consequences. The legal path was similarly limited. The general state prosecutor concluded that the recordings were not admissible evidence in the court and that they, in fact, did not contain evidence of a criminal act[17].

Snapshot 4 – Securing Control: Even though the leaked recording provoked a major public scandal facilitated by the anti-government media, there were no serious consequences. The party seemed to continue to use public resources to secure votes. Even though the prevalence of clientelist behaviour in Montenegro of different kinds is hard to estimate, there have been some attempts. For example, one of the recent studies using a *list experiment* estimates vote-buying during the 2016 local elections in Montenegro to be 24%, which is quite high (Batrićević and Komar 2018).

Snapshot 5 – Democratic Epilogue: There were some follow up judicial proceedings. The investigation that was initiated resulted in a few arrests of low-level brokers and had no significant political or legal consequences for the patrons.

Regardless of the legal value of the recording, the example also shows the passivity of the prosecution system and the judiciary, which should have been more decisive in obtaining actionable evidence and following up the story. The fact that it did not touch the main brokers (as it usually fails to) sent a clear signal to party operatives that regardless of what they do, they can count on the authorities to turn the blind eye, as long as they are not caught completely red-handed and as long as they are operating in the service of the ruling party's cause.

Case 3: political control over independent institutions

Finally, we will use the dismissal of the Rector of the State University by the government as an example of imposing political control over an independent institution. The value of the example is also in the fact that it illustrates a situation in which the ruling party seemed not to be unanimous in its view.

The University of Montenegro has never been especially political. Being rather new for a State University (founded in 1974) it rarely took any part in political events (Baća 2017, 1131). According to Baća 'Montenegrin students have been sporadically involved in collective actions' and even then the actions 'did not occur "organically" within autonomous student spaces' (Baća 2017, 1129). Moreover, for most of the post-communist period, it seemed as if there were some sort of 'gentlemen's agreement' between the University and the government. On the one hand, the University was rather passive concerning any social or political topic and, unlike its peers across the region, 'harmless' in terms of political mobilization or critique. In return, it was left alone, and individual professors were, at least most of the time, free to express their political views without consequence for their academic career. The authors writing about students' movements in ex-Yugoslavia rarely or never mention the social or political activism of students in Montenegro (Baćević 2015; Fichter 2016). The 'agreement' generally worked until the student protests of 2011 – 'the first highly visible mass student rally in the country's post-Yugoslav history' (Baća 2017, 3). The protests failed due to a disagreement within the student leadership as to whether they should maintain their 'apolitical' nature and limit themselves to mere 'expression of discontent over studying conditions' or should they join or even lead a broader coalition with civil society and labour unions for the purposes of initiating more 'radical sociopolitical change' (Baća 2017, 3). However, the protests had consequences – one of them being the increased interest among political elites in asserting more efficient control over the University as a potential 'troublemaker'. The changes coincided with the split of the ruling coalition between the DPS and its long-term partner the Social Democratic Party in the national government. In particular, the University was believed to be within the SDP's zone of influence since most of the Rectors and members of the University level administration were formally or informally affiliated with the SDP.

A number of actions that enabled subtle but firm control over the University followed. The officially given reason was centralization and the introduction of fiscal and quality controls. In reality, the University Governing Board, which used to be an irrelevant administrative body, strengthened its position and increased its power in relation to academic institutions such as the Faculty Boards or the University Senate. In addition, the Rector elected in 2014 was understood to be a controversial and politically motivated choice, someone who was perceived to be affiliated to the DPS and that was supposed to tighten control over the institution. The first few years of new Rector's mandate went as expected, involving extensive 'cleaning up.' The University was strongly centralized, those who were disobedient or not loyal enough as deans were dismissed, and various systems of control were put in place.

Snapshot 1 – The Trigger Crises: Rather unexpectedly, in 2017 a disagreement between the University administration headed by the Rector and the government of Montenegro emerged regarding the programme for the vocational training of nurses that was organized in Berane, a city in the north of the country. During reaccreditation, the University administration decided to move the programme to the capital, Podgorica, to reduce costs and increase the quality of the programme. The decision was passed by the relevant bodies, including the Council of the Medical Faculty, the University Senate, and the University Governing Board. Reaccreditation was officially approved. However, just before the relocation was to take place, the local community from Berane expressed their discontent, and this benign issue took on a strong political dimension. The relocation of the school seemed contrary to the government's efforts to 'revive' the north of the country, something that was especially sensitive given the forthcoming local election in Berane, which was at that time an opposition-governed municipality. A very noisy conflict between the University administration lead by Rector who was perceived as 'belonging' to the DPS and the DPS led government started. Many analysts saw this disagreement, which became very public, as a sign of conflict within the DPS between factional supporters of the current and the former prime minister, respectively.

The conflict quickly escalated with both sides refusing to back down – the University insisted that the school should move to Podgorica, citing university autonomy in deciding how to organize its programmes. On the other hand, the government and the Ministry of Education refused to allow the enrolment of students onto the programme in Podgorica, invoking the fact that the University is state-owned and should, therefore, follow state interests.

An unprecedented media campaign began. Both sides were very vocal and direct in expressing their opinion. It was the first time since 1996 that the Montenegrin public had witnessed such a public clash between what was perceived to be two factions of the DPS.

Snapshot 2 – Building a Majority: During this period, all the relevant University bodies voted in favour of the school transferring to Podgorica, including the University Governing Board. The Government of Montenegro had five representatives on the board, but most of them had an academic background and therefore sided with the University. Displeased, the government decided to change its representatives on the University Governing Board. Furthermore, during the summer recess, the student representatives on this Board changed their position and sided with the government. In the third vote about the same issue, the University Governing Board finally voted to support the position of the government. The programme for the vocational training of nurses would stay in Berane.

Snapshot 3 – Restoring Control: After winning the battle, the government representatives on the University Governing Board initiated the procedure to dismiss the Rector. According to the University Statute (Article 55), it is a two-step process, since the Rector cannot be dismissed without both the University Governing Board and the Senate voting for it. However, an exception is made if the Senate does not meet to discuss the proposal 'within a reasonable time;' in such circumstances, the University Governing Board can make the decision alone. There is no specification in the University Statute as to how many days are considered 'a reasonable time,' but the general idea of this provision was to prevent the Rector from blocking his/her replacement by not calling for a Senate session at all.

The Rector called for the Senate to meet on October 2nd. However, fewer than half of the Senators attended, so the Senate failed to reach a quorum. The Rector then called for another session to be held on October 6th (four days later). However, the University Governing Board decided that this was not 'a reasonable time', and certainly not soon enough. The decision was taken, solely citing the rule which states that the Board can do so if the Rector does not call for a new Senate session within 'a reasonable time.' As might be expected, the Rector was dismissed.

Snapshot 4 – Assuring External Legitimacy: In this case, the role of assuring external legitimacy came in an unexpected form. To be specific, even though the nongovernmental organizations and media tend to be very vocal about irregularities they notice in the work of the public University, in this case, at the time the reaction was pretty mild. The organizations that usually demand quick and determined action by the authorities commented on the event as something that the former rector 'deserved', citing her past actions 'which came back like a boomerang to her', therefore legitimizing it[18]. The dismissal was therefore signed off as a political conflict within the DPS, and the usually critical and oppositional public kept silent.

Snapshot 5 – Democratic Epilogue: Later, the dismissed Rector appealed to the courts, which reached the decision that the University Governing Board was not able to dismiss the Rector without the opinion of the Senate and that the proposed four days between the two sessions was not, in fact, an unreasonable delay that would justify the application of the Article 55. However, in the meantime, a new Rector had already been elected, so the court decision had no particular consequences, apart from perhaps offering moral satisfaction to the dismissed Rector. Most interestingly, the court refused to reinstate the dismissed Rector, since her mandate 'was limited' and 'since another person was already elected to that position.' The illegality of the decision regarding the Rector's dismissal was only viewed as grounds for compensation and damages in civil proceedings.

There are several lessons from this example, but the most important would be the lack of understanding of the concept of an autonomous and independent institution. As long as an institution does not operate in conflict with the general direction of party interests, it can 'practice' its autonomy. However, as soon as this perception changes, all the legal and factual options are invoked to bring it under control

The example also shows that the ruling party must not be viewed simply as a monolith and that there is a vivid, ongoing power struggle within it. Furthermore, it shows that it does not always have clear, single policy regarding issues and that even people close or connected to the DPS can themselves become 'victims' of illiberal actions. It also shows how usual watchdog subjects such are civil society and media can be used as tools in illiberal policies.

Discussion: the elements of illiberal policies in Montenegro

Here we would like to synthesize what we have learned from the three cases examined above.

First of all, the trigger for employing illiberal politics can be either crises or an opportunity. In the case of RTCG and the University, the trigger was the loss of control while in the case of the local elections, the trigger was the opportunity to use ongoing state and international projects to solicit votes. Nevertheless, **votes are the ultimate goal**. All these examples share the fact that the activity aimed to gain control and create a political advantage with the ultimate purpose of collecting votes and staying in power. In the case of RTCG, this advantage is the least direct – through controlling and influencing one of the most-watched television channels, thereby intending to influence the setting of the public agenda and the quantity and quality of the information that is being provided to the public. In the other two cases, obtaining votes either through providing or promising employment or as a part of the local election strategy, was more direct.

Secondly, the **outlook of legality** is essential. In each case, a creative but persistent effort was made to dress up illiberal actions in a legal form. The University Governing Board had to vote three times on the same issue before it passed the 'preferred' decision. In between, the votes, specific Board Members were changed, and student representatives influenced until a majority was in favour of the desirable outcome. The procedure for dismissing the RTCG Council Members was perhaps flawed in substance, but not in procedure. In the case of the 'Audio recording scandal,' the recording is, in fact, technically not admissible evidence in court. This fact does not, however, prevent the prosecution office from initiating their investigation of the matter and looking for other evidence. There is always a 'but' of a more substantive nature, where the institutions in question should have been more active, or should have followed up, or should have understood both the spirit and the purpose of the law. But strictly legally speaking, the procedures were at a minimum ambiguous and could be, and indeed were, defended in legal terms.

Third, **independent institutions and European standards are often 'used' to assert authority**. This means that, ironically, sophisticated legislation and European 'standards' are used as a shield to cover, or even a mechanism to implement, illiberal actions. For example, one of the main mechanisms to replace and control University bodies were the student representatives, which was one of the changes that were introduced as a 'European' standard. Thus, according to this 'progressive' practice, each decision-making body should include in its formation student representative, who must make up at least 25% of the total number of members of any given body; this is officially speaking, to ensure that their voice is heard, and their interests are protected. In reality, students' votes have proved to be the most easily influenced and manipulated and have often been used as a decisive vote to punish the 'disloyal' State University administration.

Moreover, one of the most profound reforms pushed by the European Commission in the process of integration was anti-corruption legislation. The Agency for the Prevention of Corruption, under pressure from the EU, has become a massive but weak administrative body with a huge level of responsibility but no real power. The fact that it is the Parliament which ultimately controls this organization is a fine democratic standard that appears to safeguard its institutional independence. However, if the majority party in the Parliament never changes, it becomes an alibi for controversial actions. Consequently, it is often misused (as in the example above) to assert control.

Conclusion

In this paper, we have used specific cases to detect and describe 'systematic patterns' (Beach and Brun 2013, 11) and therefore analyse the mechanisms and characteristics of illiberal policies and actions in Montenegro. First, we provided a very brief overview of the Montenegrin political system with a focus on those features relevant to understanding the specific cases that would follow. Then we used theory-building process tracing to analyse one typical case of illiberal politics and, by doing so, identify the sequence of events: trigger – building a majority – external legitimation – restoring/establishing control – democratic epilogue. Finally, we applied the identified pattern to two more cases, identifying the key elements of illiberal policies.

The first case was an example of monopolizing public resources and limiting freedom of expression through an attempt to seize control over the National Broadcasting Service. This example shows how formally independent agencies created and shaped by EU influence, such as the Agency for the Prevention of Corruption, can be used to perform the selective and questionable implementation of legislation to gain political control over public media. The second is an example of using public resources to tilt the electoral playing field in favour of the incumbents. It provides a rare insight into how party brokers use public goods, resources, and institutions to purchase votes. The last example shows a lack of understanding of the concept of an autonomous and independent institution. As long as University policies did not conflict with the general direction of party policies and did not jeopardize party interests, their autonomy remained intact. When that changed, mechanisms were employed to place that autonomy under State control. This happened even though the person that managed the institution was a member of the same party.

Even though Montenegro might seem too specific a case, bearing in mind the three decades of the governing party's invincibility, it is a useful extreme case that can depict the consequences of a dysfunctional system of checks and balances. The longevity of the party in power and the lack of true competitiveness helps us understand how 'newborn' institutions, which lack bottom-up legitimacy, can be substantively eroded without losing their appearance. In this case, the formal structures of democracy are kept intact. At the same time, substantial elements are, when necessary, eroded by practicing formal legalism. This pretence of legality seems to be necessary for 'stabilitocracy' (Kmezić and Bieber 2017), as a means of maintaining its external legitimacy.

We have argued that Montenegro is not experiencing some sort of a sudden democratic reversal. As the data shows and examples support, the democratic development in the country went through a formal and institutional transformation, moved towards substantial stagnation, and has returned to the old way of doing things in the new settings. It is a case in which the democratic institutions never really took off. Their introduction into the system was largely stimulated from the outside through 'carrot and stick' policies that the international community, and especially the European Union, played a significant role in creating.

In the case of Montenegro, we can see that the political elites in power have managed to adapt to the new rules of the game, while at the same time maintaining both control and rather unrestricted influence. The fact that the outer appearance of legality is deeply cherished shows clearly how countries with weak and fragile institutions, which are reformed primarily by external pressure, keep depending on the external view for their legitimacy.

In the case of Montenegro, the preconditions for such a situation are of a structural nature. The political landscape, including its deep ethnic cleavage and unchecked access to public resources, enables the predominant party to skilfully combine identity and clientelist politics and consequently remain in power. Thus, contentious political issues do not cause illiberal politics. Instead, they enable it. The structural deficiencies, such are personalized politics, an overly strong executive branch, as well as a lack of accountability and control are the very tools used by the governing party to adjust the system to their own needs.

Notes

1. http://ba.n1info.com/a256730/English/NEWS/Montenegro-is-making-headway-in-EU-integration-process.html, or https://azconsulting.me/montenegro-leader-eu-integration-process/ or https://www.cdm.me/english/montenegro-albania-leaders-european-integrations-says-mogherini/.
2. This information is correct as of 9 May 2019.
3. After 1997, the Agreement on the Minimum Principles for the Establishment of a Democratic Infrastructure in Montenegro (Sporazum o minimumu principa za razvoj demokratske infrastrukture u Crnoj Gori) was signed by all party leaders with the goal of ensuring free and fair elections.
4. https://freedomhouse.org/report/freedom-world/2019/montenegro, accessed 30 July 2019 .

5. The 2019 Freedom in the World states: 'In the Balkans, President Aleksandar Vučić of Serbia and President Milo Đukanović of Montenegro continued to consolidate state power around themselves and their cliques, subverting basic standards of good governance and exceeding their assigned constitutional roles.'
6. https://www.v-dem.net/en/.
7. Montenegrin National Election Study MNES 2016, www.mnes.defacto.me.
8. For example, see the European Commission's Report on Montenegro 2019.
9. http://www.rtcg.me/vijesti/drustvo/225510/gradjani-uocavaju-promjene-na-bolje.html .
10. For example, the Montenegro 2016 EU Progress Report criticizes the lack of editorial independence of the public broadcaster: 'The editorial independence of RTCG needs to be made a priority, since a well-functioning and truly independent public service broadcaster represents a key aspect of media pluralism. It is essential for RTCG to secure both editorial and financial independence from political influence and to ensure that all management changes are in line with the law.' https://ec.europa.eu/neighbourhood-enlargement/sites/near/files/pdf/key_documents/2016/20161109_report_montenegro.pdf.
11. Decision on the Nikola Vukčević case, the Agency for the Prevention of Corruption, 10 October 2017.
12. Decision on the Nikola Vukčević case, the Agency for the Prevention of Corruption, 26 January 2018.
13. According to the Ministry of Public Administration, there were 51,480 people employed in the public sector at the national and local level at the end of 2017.
14. *Content of the leaked conversation, reported by Radio Free Europe*: *https://www.slobodnaevropa.org/a/crna-gora-zoran-jelic-snimak-dri/28355897.html.*
15. *Content of the leaked conversation, reported by Kodex.me*: *https://kodex.me/clanak/10413/dps-zaposljavao-kako-bi-dobio-izbore.*
16. *Content of the leaked conversation, reported by Radio Free Europe:https://www.slobodnaevropa.org/a/transkripti-otkrili-dps-zaposljavao-kako-bi-dobio-izbore/24903362.html.*
17. The decision was reported in the media: http://www.rtcg.me/vijesti/drustvo/27691/tuzilastvo-odbacilo-prijave-za-aferu-snimak.html.
18. The full statement of the Director of the Centre for Civic Education to TV Vijesti can be seen at: https://www.youtube.com/watch?v=daJTBV7fXIU&feature=youtu.be.

Disclosure statement

No potential conflict of interest was reported by the author.

ORCID

Olivera Komar http://orcid.org/0000-0001-5723-1780

References

Baća, B. 2017. The student's two bodies: Civic engagement and political becoming of the post-socialist space. *Antipode* 49, no. 5: 1125–44. doi:10.1111/anti.12338.

Baćević, J. 2015. "They had sex, drugs, and rock 'n' roll; we'll have mini jobs and debts to pay": Transition, social change, and student movements in the post-Yugoslav region. In *Welcome to the Desert of Post-Socialism: Radical Politics After Yugoslavia*, edited by H. Srećko and I. Štiks, 223–242. London: Verso.

Batrićević, N. and O. Komar. 2018. An expensive loyalty: The role of ethnicity in vote buying. In *Working paper presented at the conference: Relational Studies on Global Conflicts*. Belgrade: Institut društvenih nauka.

Bazoki, A., and J. Ishiyama. 2002. *The communist successor parties of central and Eastern Europe*. New York: M.E. Sharpe.

Beach, D., and R. P. Brun. 2019. Process-Tracing Methods. Ann Arbor: University of Michigan Press.

Bermeo, N. 2016. On democratic backsliding. *Journal of Democracy* 27, no. 1: 5–19. doi:10.1353/jod.2016.0012.

Bieber, F. 2018a. Ethnopopulism and the global dynamics of nationalist mobilization. *Ethnopolitics* 17, no. 5: 558–62. doi:10.1080/17449057.2018.1532637.

Bieber, F. 2018b. Patterns of competitive authoritarianism in the Western Balkans. *East European Politics* 34, no. 3: 337–54. doi:10.1080/21599165.2018.1490272.

Bieber, F., M. Solska, and D. Taleski. 2018. *Illiberal and authoritarian tendencies in central Southeastern and Eastern Europe*. Oxford: Peter Lang.

Dolenec, D. 2013. *Democratic institutions and authoritarian rule in southeast Europe*. Colchester: ECPR Press.

Džankić, J. 2013. Cutting the mist of the black mountain: Cleavages in Montenegro's divide over statehood and identity. *Nationalities Papers: The Journal of Nationalism and Ethnicity* 41, no. 3: 412–30. doi:10.1080/00905992.2012.743514.

Džankić, J. 2018. Capturing contested states: Structural mechanisms of power reproduction in Bosnia and Herzegovina, Macedonia and Montenegro. *Southeastern Europe* 42, no. 1: 83–106. doi:10.1163/18763332-04201005.

European Commission. 2018. *Montenegro 2018 report: Accompanying the document communication from the Commission to the European parliament, the council, the European economic and social committee and the committee of the regions 2018 communication on EU enlargement policy*. Strasbourg: European Commission.

Fichter, M. 2016. Yugoslav protest: student rebellion in belgrade, zagreb, and sarajevo in 1968. *Slavic Review* 75: 99–121. doi:10.5612/slavicreview.75.1.99

Gerring, J. 2007. *Case study research: Principles and practices*. Cambridge: Cambridge University Press.

Günay, C., and V. Dzihic. 2016. Decoding the authoritarian code: Exercising 'legitimate' power politics through the ruling parties in turkey, macedonia and serbia. *Southeast European and Black Sea Studies* 16, no. 4: 529–549. doi:10.1080/14683857.2016.1242872

IREX. 2017. *Media sustainability index 2017: Montenegro*. https://www.irex.org/sites/default/files/pdf/media-sustainability-index-europe-eurasia-2017-montenegro.pdf

Jenne, E.K., and F. Bieber. 2014. Situational nationalism: Nation-building in the Balkans, subversive institutions and the Montenegrin paradox. *Ethnopolitics* 13, no. 5: 431–60. doi:10.1080/17449057.2014.912447.

Kapidžić, D. 2020. The rise of illiberal politics in Southeast Europe. *Southeast European and Black Sea Studies* 20, no. 1. pp crossreference. doi:10.1080/14683857.2020.1700880.

Kapidžić, D., and O. Komar. 2019. Segmented volatility in ethnically divided societies. In *Working paper presented at IPSA Diversity and Democratic Governance conference*. Sarajevo.

Krševan Smokvina, T., J.-F. Furnémont, M. Janssen, D. Mijatović, J. Surčulija Milojević, and S. Trpevska. 2017. *Analiza medijskog sektora u Crnoj Gori sa preporukama za usklađivanje sa standardima Savjeta Evrope i Evropske unije*. Podgorica: Council of Europe.

Kitschelt, H., Z. Mansfeldova, R. Markowski, and G. Toka. 1999. *Post-communist party systems.* Cambridge: Cambridge University Press.

Kmezić, M., and F. Bieber. 2017. *The crises of democracy in the Western Balkans. An anatomy of stabilitocracy and the limits of EU democracy promotion.* Graz: Balkans in Europe Policy Advisory Group.

Komar, O., and S. Živković. 2016. Montenegro: A democracy without alternations. *East European Politics and Societies* 30, no. 4: 785–804. doi:10.1177/0888325416652229.

Levitski, S., and L.A. Way. 2002. The rise of competitive authoritarianism. *The Journal of Democracy* 13, no. 2: 51–65. doi:10.1353/jod.2002.0026.

Levitsky, S., and L.A. Way. 2010. *Competitive authoritarianism: Hybrid regimes after the cold war.* Cambridge: Cambridge University Press.

Magaloni, B. 2006. *Voting for autocracy.* New York: Cambridge University Press.

Sartori, G. 2005. *Parties and party systems: A framework for analysis.* Colchester: ECPR press.

Vuković, I. 2013. Political dynamics of the post-communist Montenegro: One party show. *Democratization* 22, no. 1: 73–91. doi:10.1080/13510347.2013.814642.

Zakaria, F. 1997. The rise of illiberal democracy. *Foreign Affairs* 76: 22. doi:10.2307/20048274.

Öktem, K., and K. Akkoyunlu. 2016. Exit from democracy: Illiberal governance in Turkey and beyond. *Southeast European and Black Sea Studies* 16, no. 4: 469–480. doi:10.1080/14683857.2016.1253231

Subnational competitive authoritarianism and power-sharing in Bosnia and Herzegovina

Damir Kapidžić

ABSTRACT

Incremental democratic decline is evident in Bosnia and Herzegovina (BiH), but measures of democracy conceal an uneven subnational distribution of autocratization. So far there has been limited research on the drivers and constraints to subnational autocratization. This paper aims to contribute to the literature on power-sharing by exploring instances of illiberal politics enacted by parties in government at the subnational level in BiH. Evidence is gathered through semi-structured interviews and analysis of three specific cases of illiberal politics. We find that the political contest in BiH is purposefully contained within ethnic and subnational boundaries and constrained through several layers of institutionalized multilevel and ethnic checks and balances. The main drivers of subnational autocratization are opportunities that arise from the institutional framework established during early democratization and postwar structures that blend executive dominance with economic power and informal party networks, and occasionally from an individual actor's perceptions of threat. Democratization in BiH will need to address subnational politics and deep-rooted power structures if it is to be successful.

1. Introduction

Bosnia and Herzegovina (BiH) is commonly understood as one country consisting of two entities (essentially federal units), three constituent peoples (the main ethnic groups), and 14 semi-independent governments that retain some level of exclusive policymaking. It has one of the most complex political systems that exist. Different constellations of political parties govern at multiple levels, often using them as a power base to exert influence on and establish linkages with government levels above and below. While turnovers in government do happen, it is largely the same political parties that win elections. By creating an uneven playing field at the subnational level parties are able to remain in power while professing to uphold the democratic virtue of free and fair elections. In December 2018 the government of Republika Srpska (RS), a subnational unit of BiH run by the Alliance of Independent Social Democrats (SNSD), restricted freedom of assembly by cracking down on protesters demanding justice and accountability of police and banning any further gatherings. The media, under tight political control, half-heartedly reported on the events and those that did so objectively where labelled as traitors to the Serb people. All this occurred during a heated election campaign where the ruling SNSD managed to secure re-election, in part due to the control and use of public resources for patronage. Even though the elections were considered largely free and fair, it is safe to say that RS is a subnational competitive authoritarian regime. At the same time checks and balances between levels of governance, and parties representing different ethnic groups, temper authoritarian challenges at the national level. The essence of illiberal politics in BiH is multi-layered and complex as the political system of the country itself.

There is a rich literature on the political system of BiH (Chandler 2000; Bose 2002; Bieber 2006; Keil 2016). Set up as a postwar consociational democracy, the country enshrines principles of power-sharing among political parties representing the main ethnic groups in a way that emphasizes accountability towards one's own group rather than to citizens of the country as a whole. The political system closely mirrors an ideal consociation where grand coalitions, group veto, proportional representation and segmental autonomy are explicitly institutionalized (Lijphart 1999). Elections are held regularly and are mostly free and fair (OSCE 2019). Electoral contest is fought between parties representing the same ethnic group and cross-ethnic voting is almost non-existent. The party system of BiH closely reflects the ethnic structure of the country and subnational units of governance. Measuring democracy at the national level can, therefore, be misleading as both the electoral contest and the tools to affect it are largely present at the level of the two subnational entities, RS and the Federation of Bosnia and Herzegovina (FBiH).

This paper has the aim to study instances of illiberal politics at subnational levels of government and their effect on democracy at the national level. Under illiberal politics, we understand 'policies enacted (or proposed) by governing parties that create an uneven playing field with the aim to remain in power indefinitely' (Kapidžić 2020). The concept is useful in cases where we can witness an evident decrease in quality of democracy, but not extensive enough to warrant classification as competitive authoritarian (Levitsky and Way 2010). It also functions as an operationalization of democratic backsliding (Bermeo 2016) and a qualitative alternative to measures of autocratization (Lührmann and Lindberg 2019).[1] The case of BiH further gives an opportunity to address a gap in the literature on power-sharing and explore the impact of segmental autonomy, in the form of territorial ethnic self-governance, and ethnic party systems on democratization.

In this sense, the core purpose of the paper is theory building as a way to overcome limitations in the study of autocratization arising from the subnational arena in multi-level, multiethnic states. Through the case study of BiH the paper analyses the prevalence and distribution of illiberal politics. It explores the main drivers and inhibiting factors of (subnational) illiberal politics and whether these are structural in nature (institutional framework) or driven by an agent's perception of opportunity and threat (motivational framework)? To answer these questions, the paper relies on evidence gathered through 19 interviews with journalists, members of civil society, academics and political party members, in addition to 182 media reports, as well as surveys and research reports.

We find that structural issues arising from a combination of post-communist power distribution and postwar consociational democracy can explain most illiberal politics with the exception of challenges to ethnic legitimacy from in-group protests. Illiberal politics are deliberately contained within ethnic party systems and levels of government dominated by parties representing a single ethnic group. Where power-sharing in government is required illiberal politics are constrained by multilevel and cross-ethnic checks and balances. This leads to differentiated autocratization under asymmetric federalism in BiH where the predominantly Serb RS has become a competitive authoritarian regime while the joint Bosniak and Croat FBiH is still an electoral democracy.

The following section of the paper introduces the case study of BiH and gives a theoretical overview on illiberal politics and subnational autocratization. The third section introduces BiH's main ethnic parties. The fourth, fifth, and sixth sections explore three specific cases of illiberal politics and the drivers behind each of them: restrictions to the freedom of assembly in RS in wake of the *Justice for David* protests, political control of media, and the prevalence of patronage in elections tied to ruling parties. The final section concludes and explores both constraining and encouraging structural factors that make BiH a case of asymmetric subnational competitive authoritarianism within a weak national democracy.

2. Subnational autocratization in BiH's power-sharing democracy

The current political system of BiH was established through the Dayton Peace Agreement in 1995 following the dissolution of Yugoslavia and the Bosnian War. Designed to create a framework for postwar democracy to develop institutionalized power-sharing between the three main ethnic groups that fought against each other, Bosniaks, Croats, and Serbs. Each group is represented by several political parties and the country functions as a consociational democracy (Bose 2002). Elections are held regularly and there is turnover in government but with serious deficiencies in, among other, civic rights and rule of law. This includes illiberal elements in the country's constitution that bar citizens not belonging to the three titular ethnic groups and those not residing in 'their entity' from running for certain offices.[2] While reform of the political system is necessary and recognized by all domestic (and international) actors, the delicate postwar consociational power balance makes any attempt fraught with difficulty (Perry 2015, 34–35). Due to all this, it is not possible to speak of a liberal or consolidated democracy in BiH.

Nevertheless, the already low level of democracy in BiH is further declining, or is stagnant at best, according to several indices. Political leaders in power, such as Milorad Dodik from the SNSD, but also Dragan Čović from the Croatian Democratic Union BiH (HDZ BiH) and Bakir Izetbegović from the Party of Democratic Action (SDA), are more than willing to undermine democracy and subvert media and independent institutions in exchange for political gain. This trend is part of a broader, empirically verifiable and ongoing phenomenon of democratic backsliding in Southeast Europe that is selective as it affects some but not all segments of democracy (Bieber 2018; Solska et al. 2018). The Freedom House Index (FH) indicates a stagnation and slight decline of democracy in BiH while the downward trend is more evident in the Bertelsmann Transformation Index (BTI) and the Varieties of Democracy 'Liberal Democracy Index' (V-Dem). Even though they operate with different baselines, almost all indices display an identical trend of incremental decline over the past decade (Figure 1). The V-Dem index specifically highlights problems of media (self)censorship and harassment of journalists, civil society repression, autonomy of opposition parties, electoral irregularities and vote buying, noncompliance with judiciary and judicial constraints on the executive, and lack of effective legislative oversight (Coppedge et al. 2019). This indicates a selective dismantlement of

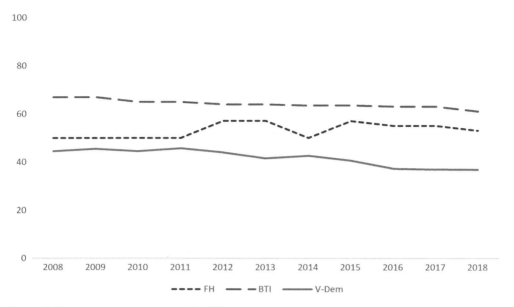

Figure 1. Democracy measurements for BiH.
Sources: Freedom in the World (2018); Bertelsmann Transformation Index (2018); Coppedge et al. (2019).

democratic institutions, especially executive constraints and independent checks and balances on executive power. However, in the BiH national context, this does not equate to the unrestrained rule of a single party and a descent into competitive authoritarianism.

To understand the stability of incremental democratic decline in BiH, it is necessary to look at structural factors and the institutionalization of consociational democracy in the country (see also Merdzanovic 2018). In this paper, we argue that ethnic power-sharing provides opportunities for subnational autocratization. Simultaneously, it curtails authoritarian leaders through checks and balances that arise out of multilevel and inter-ethnic competition, where they exist, by containing and constraining illiberal politics. The existing literature on power-sharing largely focuses on the role of segmental autonomy in managing ethnic conflict and neglects any functional role in facilitating democracy or autocratization (Horowitz 1985; Lijphart 1999; McCulloch and McGarry 2017). In the literature on BiH, autonomy and decentralization are generally seen political tools for ethnic conflict management rather than for development and democratization (Bojičić-Dželilović 2013). This creates a gap in our understanding of how relevant segmental autonomy is in creating opportunities for subnational authoritarian politics to develop, and of national-level power sharing in restricting such developments. The theory-building aspect of this paper aims to contribute to a better understanding of subnational authoritarian rule under power-sharing and the role of multilevel and inter-group checks and balances.

There is limited but recent literature on illiberal and authoritarian practices at the subnational level (Behrend and Whitehead 2016a; Behrend and Whitehead 2016b; Gibson 2012, 2005). These contributions build on what Guillermo O'Donnell described as 'brown areas' (O'Donnell 1993) and identify cases of either subnational authoritarianism or a broader category of subnational illiberal structures and practices. The authors show that large discrepancies in the quality of democratic governance exist and can persist at the subnational level. Gibson, who pioneered this research, introduces the concept of 'boundary control' as a measure by subnational authoritarian governments to isolate themselves from the influence of the national government (Gibson 2012, 24–25). The result is contained, localized illiberal politics that do not get attention from beyond the subnational unit. The observed cases in the literature are mostly large federations, such as the United States, Argentina, India, Russia or Mexico, where national governments have considerable power. Empirically this literature neglects cases with power-sharing between subnational units and weak central governance, such as BiH, where the national government cannot act as a check and balance to subnational autocratization (nor can it rely on a unifying national identity in doing so). An additional aspect of theory building in this paper aims to expand our understanding of subnational authoritarianism to consociational power-sharing settings, and countries with weak central but robust regional government.

In the literature, BiH is inversely defined as a confederation (Kasapović 2005; Bose 2002) or a highly decentralized state but is most accurately classified as a form of multinational federalism (Keil 2016) or an asymmetric ethnic federation with a weak central authority (Bieber 2006). It is divided into two subnational entities, the Serb dominated RS and the Croat and Bosniak FBiH where Bosniaks are a majority, and an independent unit, the District Brčko. FBiH is further divided into 10 cantons, local self-governance units with a high level of independence, while RS has a centralized government. There are only a limited number of exclusive or shared competences at the national level while most power resides with the entities (Marković 2012). FBiH and RS retain the major share of competences and resources and have their own constitutions, presidents, parliaments, governments and prime ministers. They grant citizenship and are primarily responsible for enforcing laws as the national level does not have the ability to do so (Foreign Policy Initiative BH 2008). The entities are the main level at which nationally collected financial resources are distributed and regulate the largest portion of civil and political rights. They are directly represented in national-level institutions and essentially have veto rights over all national policy. The cantons, which are specific to FBiH, retain their own police forces and are responsible for select policy areas. They do not have fiscal independence or direct influence on national-level governance, but strongly influence policymaking in FBiH. The division of competences among levels of governance in BiH is not clearly defined, resulting in a combination of dual and coordinative federalism. This introduces checks and balances between governments at different levels, especially when led by different parties.

Electoral competition in BiH is shaped by declared and perceived ethnicity of candidates, political parties and voters. It takes place within ethnically defined segments of the population. In the largely homogenous units of RS and the FBiH cantons it is also ethnoterritorial (Hulsey and Stjepanović 2017, 48). Political parties explicitly or implicitly position themselves towards ethnic identity, creating three ethnically bound party subsystems with a high degree of independence, and one not so well-defined multiethnic or nonethnic party subsystem. Previous research found very little competition for voters between these three or four distinct party subsystems (Kapidžić 2017; Hulsey 2015). Each party subsystem usually has one party that dominates electoral competition and represents a titular ethnic group. Within the Bosniak party subsystem, this is the SDA, within the Serb subsystem it is currently the SNSD, and within the Croat subsystem, it is the HDZ BiH. These three parties are not each other's main electoral competitors, rather their main oppositions are parties of their own ethnic group. It is possible to identify three distinct electoral playing fields corresponding to the three main ethnic party subsystems with different degrees of openness and impartial competition.[3] At the same time, all parties in BiH engage in interactions with each other, but do not seek cross-ethnic votes. The segmentation of the BiH party system serves as a further check and balance against the dominance of a single party at the national level, while allowing for subnational dominance.

The actions of the dominant ethnic parties and their leaders that constitute illiberal politics follow a political opportunity structure defined as 'the features of regimes and institutions that facilitate or inhibit a political actor's collective action' (Tilly and Tarrow 2007, 49), where opportunities and threats to remaining in power are assessed against institutional constraints. Further, we distinguish between illiberal politics that are centred around the electoral component of democracy and those that target the liberal component of democracy, where recent democratic backsliding selectively weakens restraints on executive rule, while keeping electoral provisions largely intact (Dahl 1989; Bermeo 2016).

A relevant question is whether illiberal politics arise from a structural framework centred around institutional opportunities or from an agent's framework centred around individual motivations. The institutional and regime features that facilitate illiberal politics are best described through the notion of 'post-communist power mutation' that includes a concentration of power in the executive, a conversion of political into economic power and a dispersion of power from state administration and public institutions into a web of informal, party-controlled networks (Zakošek 1997; Dolenec 2013, 20–24). This power mutation created an opportunity structure and governance practices that persist from early democratization of the 1990s to the postwar consociational democracy and until today. On the other hand, a motivational agent's framework can best be described by individual perceptions of existential threat arising from challenges to legitimacy within the same ethnic group. We argue that most illiberal politics in BiH can be explained by a structural framework that is defined at the subnational and ethnic party system level. Examples of illiberal politics as a motivational reaction to perceived intra-ethnic threats are recent, especially in RS where citizen's protests against a politicized police and judicial system loyal to the ruling party have gained momentum.

This paper argues that autocratization in BiH is incremental not because of strong institutions or active citizens' movements, but because political contest is purposefully *contained* within ethnic and territorial boundaries and *constrained* through several layers of institutionalized multilevel and ethnic checks and balances. We argue that illiberal politics can largely be explained by opportunities arising from the *institutional structural framework* based on three types of post-communist power mutation (concentration, conversion and dispersion) and postwar consociationalism, and only in isolated cases by an *individual actor's perceptions of threat*. While we recognize the relevance of external legitimization of semi-authoritarian leaders linked to the provision of internal stability (Kmezić and Bieber 2017), we disregarded it here in order to focus on domestic factors of autocratization at the subnational level.

Evidence was collected using methodological triangulation through interviews, media reports, research reports, and surveys. The three case studies were selected based on their prominence in media reports over the past 2 years, as well as their relevance to key aspects of democracy. Semi-structured interviews were conducted between February and April 2019 with a follow-up in June 2019, in person or via phone, with 19 individuals (four journalists, six civil society representatives, six academics, three members of political parties) from Banja Luka (eight), Mostar (two) and Sarajevo (nine). Interviewees were selected based on media reports, personal contacts and/or snowball sampling. Due to the sensitive topic and safety/privacy concerns, full anonymity was offered to all interviewees. 182 media articles were identified and collected from the websites of Al Jazeera Balkans, Buka magazin, Dnevni avaz, Klix, Nezavisne novine, Radio Slobodna Evropa and Radio televizija Republike Srpske in June 2019,[4] while utilized research reports and surveys are referenced.

3. Illiberal politics and ethnic party dominance

The three dominant BiH political parties, SNSD, SDA and HDZ, and their leaders Dodik, Izetbegović and Čović, respectively, are in a privileged position with access to power and resources to enact policies that can result in an uneven electoral playing field within their corresponding ethnic party subsystem. Each aims to reinforce their position as the primary representative of their own ethnic group within BiH's consociational democracy. Dodik and his SNSD have been in power in RS since 2006 and for most of this time at the national level as well. He has served as prime minister and president of RS and is now the Serb member of the BiH national presidency. Throughout his tenure, he has greatly increased political control of media in RS and stacked independent institutions with loyal supporters. By selectively distributing public funding, favouring business allies and controlling large state-owned enterprises (SOEs) he has 'managed to create a political machine that relies on patronage politics.'[5] More recently the SNSD has become active in restricting civil liberties as they perceive an increase of challenges to their rule. The regime in RS under Dodik can now best be described as subnational competitive authoritarianism (Bieber 2018).

Among Croat parties the HDZ BiH and its leader Čović are unrivalled, having won the majority of Croat votes in every election. In FBiH cantons where Croats are a majority the party has been in government since independence. Throughout this time HDZ BiH has established deep patronage networks, linking SOEs with party structures and remnants of the defunct wartime entity Herzeg-Bosnia (Bojičić-Dželilović 2006). These 'party affiliated SOEs employ a significant share of the local Croat population and in return create loyal voters'.[6] Illiberal politics among Bosniak parties are slightly more refined as intra-ethnic competition is more developed. The SDA, headed by Izetbegović, has always 'relied on a close-knit network of family and party officials to distribute public resources' in order to maximize electoral gain.[7] This includes managing SOEs and running public procurement procedures with patronage in mind. Likeminded civil society organizations with close ties to SDA leadership are supported through public funding only to 'serve as a pretence of broad grassroots support',[8] while light-handed control of media is used to temper criticism.

Through effective capture of public administration, all three parties are able to control economic resources and redistribute them to loyal supporters (Günay and Džihić 2016; Džankić 2018; Blagovcanin and Divjak 2015). Thereby each party primarily operates within their own ethno-territorial and party subsystem and does not interfere in other groups' interests. The following three sections will each focus on a set of illiberal politics surrounding a particular case or policy. The first will examine restrictions to freedom of assembly in wake of the Justice for David protests in RS. The second will look at the weakening of independent media in RS and FBiH, and control of the public broadcaster

Radio Television of Republika Srpska (RTRS). The final section will examine the influence of patronage in electoral contest and the role of SOEs as electoral prizes.

4. Restricting freedom of assembly: the justice for david protests

In late March 2018, the body of 21-year-old David Dragičević was found on the banks of the Vrbas River in Banja Luka after he went missing 6 days earlier. By the end of that month, the police investigation concluded that the death was accidental and that he drowned after tumbling into a swollen creek. The official report made an inept attempt to criminalize the young man. David's family did not accept the report and insisted that he had suffered a violent death that was covered up by RS police structures under control of the ruling SNSD party. Starting on March 26th a group called *Justice for David*,[9] led by the boy's father, gathered in the main Banja Luka square to demand a full investigation into David's death. The daily protests grew quickly in size and numbered over 10,000 participants by mid-April.

> The protests started out of a sense of frustration. Frustration with the police and justice systems, frustration with the ruling party elite. People feel like living in a state where some are more equal than others. It was a cause that a lot of people could relate to. That is why the movement was able to grow so big, so fast.[10]

Consistent public pressure and scrutiny revealed a botched police investigation with mishandled evidence, false claims and bullyish rhetoric of officials against the family of the deceased. This prompted the National Assembly of RS to form a Board of Inquiry to look into the matter. Their report concluded that David could have been murdered which was swiftly rejected by the ruling majority on the grounds of it being a politicized decision. Instead, the SNSD leadership insisted on an investigation by the prosecutor's office. At the same time, across the country in Sarajevo, another group was protesting for similar reasons: the unresolved death of the young Dženan Memić. Attempts to join the two causes and capture broader support that crossed ethnic and entity lines emerged. The young men's families held joint protests and exchanged support, and media coverage followed, painting a broader picture of unaccountable BiH institutions as a national policy issue. While both groups continued to portray themselves as ethnic patriots rather than civic ones, the joint cause of justice for David and Dženan was creating unwanted attention for the RS government.

The protests continued throughout the summer and into the national and RS election campaigns of October 2018. During this time several opposition figures expressed support for the movement but were not able to assume any leading role. The act of occupying the main Banja Luka square became a ritual, with the sculpture of a raised fist serving both as a shrine of mourning and a sign of solidarity and defiance. This attracted repeated of attention of local and international media (Zdeb 2019). The protests acted as a medium to voice anger at public institutions and the perceived lack of accountability, mostly at the entity level. The anger was directed at the police and judiciary for their direct involvement in the Dragicević case, but also at the ruling class in general and especially the SNSD. 'Bit by bit the protests became a symbol of a popular challenge to SNSD rule and to the power structures the party had put in place. They were not nationalist or anti-nationalist, definitely not against RS, but against the political elite and their economic partners in crime.'[11]

The October elections passed and SNSD emerged victorious within the BiH Serb party subsystem. Yet the protests did not stop, on one occasion bringing together 40,000 people in the streets of Banja Luka. After a new SNSD government in RS was formed in mid-December, official pressure on the protests increased with a set of illiberal policies aimed at restricting freedom of assembly. Top ranking SNSD politicians discredited the protesters as foreign agents through public broadcasts and blamed Western countries for meddling in internal affairs and plotting to abolish RS, a tactic previously used to discredit NGOs and independent journalists.

The showdown with the RS government and police forces came on December 25th when police officers in riot gear launched a violent crackdown on protesters. They arrested 18 of the group's leaders including Davor Dragičević, the father of David, and two oppositions MPs on charges of threat to public safety. The central square in Banja Luka was cleared and the makeshift shrine removed. The following day police released everyone but banned any further gathering. Foreshadowing what was to come, Dodik declared that 'the street will not model political decisions in RS' (Reuters 2018). Government-controlled media framed the protesters as violent individuals and citizens were advised to stay away. At the same time, a prosecutorial investigation into Davor Dragicević and other protest leaders was started. The final protest, held on December 30th, descended into violence as police and protesters clashed. In the following days, criminal charges were pressed against the movement's leaders while public intimidation continued. Davor Dragičević went into hiding and later fled the country. By separating the protest leaders, prosecuting them individually, and using force to disperse crowds gathered to support them, the RS police and government were able to repress the Justice for David movement. 'All is well as long as the problems remain in your house, or should I say entity. When your dirty laundry becomes an issue for neighbours to see you can get into trouble.'[12]

> It was easier for the ruling SNSD to stomp out a protest movement than to change their way of doing politics and increase transparency and accountability. But the citizens proved that they see through this charade, they are not afraid anymore. Once they have attention from outside BiH they will speak up.[13]

The following analysis does not focus on the unresolved death of David Dragičević or the subsequent investigation, but rather on illiberal politics enacted by the SNSD controlled government in light of prolonged civic protests and public criticism. Three phases of interaction between the government and protesters can be identified: 1) from the first protests in March 2018 until the October elections that year, 2) from the elections until the formation of a new RS government under SNSD in mid-December, and 3) following the establishment of the new government until the writing of this paper in June 2019.

The reaction of the SNSD government of RS towards the Justice for David movement does not follow an institutional opportunity framework. Rather, it can be seen as a reaction to a perceived existential threat. Both the timing and scope of illiberal politics show a gradual escalation in government and police actions in light of the perceived threat (Touquet 2012). In the initial phase, illiberal politics were limited and mostly consisted of spreading misinformation on the aim of the protests in order to discourage their spread to other cities in RS. The large turnout at the protests quickly made Dodik and other SNSD leaders aware that the movement could potentially ruin their chances at re-election. The movement's leaders and governing official also cooperated to inadvertently frame the protest as a singular and family-centred cause for justice, each out of their own interests. This diverted attention away from underlying socio-economic issues and did not let opposition parties co-opt the movement as a broader political platform.[14] In the lead-up to the elections, there was no room for sudden or forceful government action.

The second phase, following SNSD's electoral victory, was characterized by quiet tactical manoeuvring and preparation. During this time, outside attention had begun to shift away from BiH. As the protests did not subside but served as a cause to bring together weakened Serb opposition parties, the existential threat resurfaced.[15] Illiberal politics enacted during the third phase were swift and forceful, starting as soon as the new SNSD government assumed power. These included brief detention of the movement's leaders, especially the father of David, as well as opposition politicians who supported the protests; using violent police tactics to disperse protesters; 'cleansing' the protest site of any symbols and messages of support; denying protest permits to any gathering linked to the movement or its leaders; intimidating or prosecuting individual protest leaders through various means, such as judicial processes, media disinformation, administrative scrutiny, withholding employment, and denying public services.[16] The sum of these illiberal politics, while conducted behind the veil of legality and administrative procedures, amount to unmistakable restrictions in freedom of assembly and freedom of speech. This way the SNSD was able to remove a perceived threat to its continued rule originating from the Justice for David movement. The use of illiberal politics was reactionary and constitutes an agent's framework centred around individual motivations and perceptions of threat.

A strategy of containing protests within RS was pursued both by the SNSD and other national parties, relying on institutional opportunities. Containment is best illustrated through ethnic party spheres of influence in BiH power-sharing. As the predominant party among Serb voters, SNSD is in the position to shape political discourse within its party subsystem by interpreting ethnonational interests. By initially engaging in dialogue with the movement's leaders, and by framing it as a local issue, SNSD was able to limit the spread of protests and the emergence of an inter-ethnic and national call for justice, such as a joint Justice for David and Dženan movement, which the party would find more difficult to influence or obstruct. Political parties in FBiH, especially the SDA and HDZ BiH, complacently supported such action as not to 'import' unrest from RS. Therefore, the core of the movement remained subnational. This strategy was used with previous protests as well, such as the 2014 plenums where the issue was contained within FBiH (Gilbert and Mujanović 2015; Mujanović 2017).

At the same time, there was no effort to constrain SNSD in their use of illiberal politics from the national level as the RS government acted within its institutional competences. External actors, who still exert influence on BiH politics, only expressed declarative concern. Afterwards, the European Union (EU) launched an initiative to monitor and evaluate the rule of law system in BiH, with a focus on accountability and independence of judiciary (EU Delegation to BiH 2019).

To sum up the events, the RS government and Ministry of Interior banned citizens from holding peaceful protests, and public gatherings in Banja Luka were dispersed by force, open intimidation, judicial means, and through an artificially constructed atmosphere of fear. The illiberal politics by the SNSD were purposeful and actor-motivated in their aim to thwart a perceived threat to their continued rule. This was achieved through institutional opportunities to contain the protests within RS and from becoming a more

ILLIBERAL POLITICS IN SOUTHEAST EUROPE

prominent national issue, as well as through a lack of constrains which limited possibility for outside influence.

5. Weakening independent media and political control of RTRS

> Sometimes I am afraid to do my job, or at least to do it professionally and consciously. Journalists are not protected in BiH and when you report against politicians and their associates who have real power or are rich enough to buy it you feel vulnerable. And it is even worse for my colleagues in RS. I believe that many of them choose to be friendly with the regime not because they support it, but rather as a survival tactic.[17]

Media is supposed to give us a clear, unbiased view on politics and enable citizens to act as a check against those in power (Levitksy and Way 2010). Especially public media are envisaged as a non-partisan source of information that aims to promote public interests. In BiH, there are many media outlets but only few with significant impact, among which are the public broadcasters. The public broadcast system is as fragmented as the political system with three main outlets, the state-wide Radio and Television of Bosnia and Herzegovina (BHRT), the Radio-Television of the Federation of Bosnia and Herzegovina (FTV) in FBiH and the RTRS in RS. Each operates independently of each other, although they are supposed to function as one public corporation. Most citizens (66%) still get their daily political news from television, among which FTV and RTRS are the most viewed and trusted sources (Center for Insights in Survey Research 2018). They are also the most widely available, which gives them a lot of political leverage. It is no wonder that control of their broadcast agendas is high up on the priority lists of governing parties.

Control of public broadcasters is achieved through appointing politically loyal governing boards. They are, in turn, responsible for appointing directors, program committees, steering broadcast agendas, and approving budgets. The governing boards are appointed by the respective parliaments: the RS National Assembly for RTRS, the Parliament of FBiH for FTV, and the national Parliamentary Assembly of BiH for BHRT. By looking into the boards' compositions, we can notice that political control of the governing boards is, however, not equal. The BHRT governing board is largely professional and represents multiple interests. FTV has had no governing board at all for several years as ruling parties in FBiH could not agree on its composition. Differences between the SDA and HDZ BiH regarding programming language, editorial appointments, and broadcast agenda created a situation where a lack of political control is preferable to becoming a partner with minority influence. This has allowed FTV to maintain a level of professionalism and independence. In both cases, inter-ethnic consensus is required, and we can witness strategies of constraining potential misuse of public broadcasting.

RTRS has a governing board mostly composed of SNSD supporters and, consequently, a loyal director and supportive program committee. The current RTRS director, Draško Milinović, was previously head of office for the President of RS and Dodik's public relation officer. Opposition parties in RS have no influence on RTRS or ways to ensure its neutrality. This has real consequences for framing of political and contentious issues. In 2018 the BiH Communications Regulatory Agency, the national broadcast media oversight body, fined RTRS for 'continuous and biased promotion of the interests of the ruling party, favouring of individuals or entities in a positive context, with a constantly present critical tone towards the opposition parties' within its political news program (Communications Regulatory Agency 2018). The fine did not lead to a change of the broadcast agenda. 'The political program of RTRS only superficially attempts to be neutral. There may be a negative comment Dodik once a month. But there is almost no positive news on civil society and the opposition is just ignored.'[18]

> It is not sensible to be a real journalists and work at RTRS. From the director to the technician, everyone under control of the party can tell you how to report on issues. Those who value their professional dignity choose to leave, while others keep quiet and put their own economic benefit ahead of public interest or embrace the SNSD brainwash.[19]

It is possible to characterize RTRS a public propaganda tool of the SNSD, a regime-friendly outlet that can be used to influence public debate in ways favourable to Dodik, the party, and their allies. Exerting control over RTRS is an example of illiberal politics that has clear consequences on electoral competition and skews the playing field in SNSD's favour. The institutional framework defined by weak media regulation, insecure financing and a dominant executive has created conditions where parties in government are able to subvert independent and public broadcast media for partisan aim. By doing so with RTRS, the SNSD encountered almost no constraints as the company is institutionally contained in RS and largely Serb-controlled. In FBiH and at the national-level significant inter-ethnic constraints have managed to preserve some independence of public broadcast.

Parties in government also use other avenues to weaken independent and media through illiberal politics. These are mostly employed against commercial media that are not under the direct control of the government. Some illiberal politics are directed at outlets, such as a police raid of the popular news portal Klix in 2014, requested and carried out by RS police in cooperation with their colleagues in FBiH, after the portal uncovered a scandal implicating the SNSD in buying off MPs. Others are personal, such as Dodik's repeated hostility towards female journalists, the expulsion of an opposition-affiliated journalist from an SNSD press conference, accusations of treason to RS against investigative journalists, and threats and physical violence against journalists that are only half-heartedly condemned or prosecuted (Turčilo and Buljubašić 2017).

Various illiberal politics directed at media owners aim to create economic incentives or, alternatively, pressure to conform to more benign reporting. Although verifiable data on economic pressure is lacking, it is safe to say that public companies and SOEs offer significant support to regime-friendly media through lucrative advertising (Turčilo and Buljubašić 2017, 36–43; Cvjetićanin et al. 2019, 83). Regarding ownership, it is possible to identify strong links between media owners and political leaders, both personal and through political parties. For example, Fahrudin Radončić, the leader of a centric Bosniak party, is also the de-facto owner of the largest daily newspaper Dnevni avaz.

As a last resort, political party leaders increasingly make use of defamation lawsuits against journalists or their outlets in an attempt to censor and discredit their work (Sorguc and Rovcanin 2019). 'Defamation lawsuits are a highly effective tool as they portray the journalist in a negative light and consume their time and effort to deal with the charges instead of reporting. The outcome of the lawsuit is ultimately not important, but rather the Kafkaesque process itself.'[20]

Individually or combined, these illiberal politics lead to widespread self-censorship of media and individual journalists. The result is a weakening of media independence, poorer government oversight, and less professionalism. As with the control of public broadcasting, illiberal politics are enabled through an institutional framework and an ethnically segmented media sphere that creates opportunities for executive party dominance. The SNSD and Dodik have managed to largely subvert independent commercial media in RS, but the SDA and HDZ BiH have also used their fair share of illiberal politics to shape media coverage within their respective media spheres in FBiH. Even smaller regional parties use these tactics towards local-level media. Containment of illiberal politics to ethnic media spheres is evident in BiH making all dominant ethnic parties culpable. Constraints to executive actions are non-institutionalized, weak and lack enforcement mechanisms, mostly coming from professional associations and international observers.

Finally, governing parties resort to purposefully disseminating disinformation. This more recent phenomenon is increasingly present in the online media sphere. It is most evident in RS among media connected to the online presence of RTRS. Writing about online disinformation in BiH Cvjetićanin et al. find that 'public media are the largest individual sources of disinformation' where RTRS and the Serb news agency Srna 'stand out as single most prolific sources' forming a disinformation network with numerous media outlets in BiH and Serbia (2019, 7–8). The targets of negative disinformation campaigns are Bosniak parties and their leaders, the Serb opposition, Justice for David and other civic organizations, while disinformation portrays Dodik, the SNSD and members of the RS government, but also the HDZ BiH in a positive light. Another important disinformation source, the Dnevni avaz, aims to positively portray Radončić to Bosniak readers but is not part of a broader disinformation network (Cvjetićanin et al. 2019, 41–43, 60). The spread of disinformation is, again, conditioned on institutionally presented opportunities and lacking regulations, as well as ethnopolitical containment and very weak constraints.

It is currently not possible to speak of an independent and professional media sphere in BiH. Media is certainly not a mechanism to ensure control and accountability of ruling parties. Rather, it is increasingly dependent and disciplined by those in power. Nowhere is this more evident than in RS where Dodik and the SNSD are able to control public and private media through illiberal politics by taking advantage of structural circumstances and a weak regulatory framework. Their actions are self-contained within subnational boundaries an ethnic media sphere where multilevel and interethnic constraints are limited. Political parties in FBiH and the national level were not able to establish far-reaching media control. Constraints between national, entity and canton levels of government, as well as between ethnic party interests, limited their scope of action.

6. Patronage in elections: SOEs as electoral prizes

The electoral process in BiH is fraught with issues and segmented along ethnic lines, but elections are considered 'genuinely competitive' and largely transparent as most irregularities do not happen on election day (OSCE 2019). Political parties and BiH institutions make an effort to portray electoral contest as free and fair in order to emphasize the legitimacy they gain from electoral victory.[21] What happens before and after elections is much more problematic and ultimately undermines the democratic process by creating an uneven playing field. It is not possible to look into all problems of BiH elections such as a deficient legal framework, outdated voter registries, biased media coverage or manipulations in the composition of polling station commissions. Instead, we will focus on misuse of public resources for clientelism, more specifically patronage, through informality and illiberal politics of ruling parties. We understand clientelism as a non-programmatic distribution of material benefits combined with the conditionality of political support. Patronage is a form of clientelism 'used to refer to intra-party flow of benefits' (Stokes et al. 2013, 13–14). It is also described as relational clientelism that builds on long-term relationships and more permanent benefits, in contrast to electoral clientelism as an ad-hoc transaction focused on election day, such as vote buying (Gans-Morse et al. 2014). The most prominent feature of patronage is the use of public resources to reward individuals and strengthen party structures, such as employment or donations to party related causes.

Data from expert and population surveys illustrate the scope of the issue. According to the Electoral Integrity Project, elections in BiH suffer substantially from misuse of state resources for campaigning, influence of money on electoral outcomes, and non-transparent financial accounts of parties and candidates (Norris and Grömping 2019). Data from the INFORM project look in detail at informal mechanisms and clientelism in Southeast Europe and BiH, finding an exceptionally high dependence in regard to elections (Gordy and Efendić 2019). More specifically, 15.4% of respondents report to have been offered money in exchange for their vote during the 2014 general elections as a form of electoral clientelism. Also, 9.6% of respondents have turned to a party official for help which increases their likelihood to participate in a relational clientelist transaction seven-fold. This 'suggests that clientelist linkages are forged continuously, not only just before or after elections' (Popovikj et al. 2019, 106, 111). Our interviews confirm these findings.

> It is common knowledge that if you want a job in city or canton administration you need to talk to the right party officials. Openings are earmarked by political parties, one for HDZ [BiH] one for SDA, and they informally select the applicant who is most loyal or can deliver best. You need to have a *štela* to get a job there.[22]

Even with 14 distinct governments, the number of jobs in administration in BiH is limited. This is where control of employment opportunities and resources of SOEs becomes important. With numerous patronage opportunities, SOEs present an even greater electoral prize than ministerial positions. 'Access to sought-after jobs at SOEs is a principal means of political and ethnically based patronage' where political parties run the companies for their own purpose (McGill 2019). A recent IMF report on SOEs mapped out the staggering size of the sector. 'Roughly 80 thousand workers are employed in 550 SOEs across all sectors of the economy (about 11% of total employment)' most of them in the 20 largest, entity-owned SOEs (Parodi and Cegar 2019, 6). These include the FBiH and RS electricity companies, coal mines in FBiH, the RS forestry company, the BH Telecom company, and the FBiH and RS railways. A majority of SOEs are in a bad financial shape due to persistent mismanagement and an oversized workforce with large accumulated losses. At the same time, they maintain average salaries at 40% higher than in private firms.[23]

Employment opportunities and resources of SOEs are tightly controlled by political parties who appoint their governing boards.[24] As one interviewee stated 'the word state owned enterprise is actually a misnomer. We can talk about Serb, Bosniak or Croat SOEs but never of BiH SOEs. There is no state control there, just that of [ethnic] peoples.'[25] Just like with public broadcasting, the boards make all key decisions and the principal requirement to become a board member is party loyalty. These boards informally forward company information to the party leaderships while concealing full reports from oversight bodies and opposition parties in parliament (Centar za istraživačko novinarstvo 2018). SOEs are treated as electoral prizes that can be used to fulfil a party's electoral promises, such as employment, at the expense of public interest. Ethnic party control of SOEs is the main form of patronage in BiH. 'We pretty much know which SOEs [in FBiH] belong to the Croats and which belong to us [Bosniaks]. Those in RS are of course controlled by Serbs so we have no say. And of course, it is important to have people the party trusts in leading positions [at SOEs].'[26]

> There has not been a single BiH party that has not descended into clientelism. And the longer they are in government [at entity level] the more control they have. I can safely claim that BH Telecom [the largest telecom operator] is an SDA business affiliate. They use it as their intra-party employment bureau. The HDZ [BiH] has its own SOEs in Herzegovina, such as Aluminij [an aluminium smelter]. The opposition can offer nothing except electoral promises while SDA and HDZ [BiH] have means to deliver on theirs.[27]

Relational clientelism in the form of patronage based on control of SOEs is a major driver of electoral outcomes in BiH. It is also one of the most difficult to research thoroughly because it often entails illegal activities. Most patronage is concentrated at the level of the entities, and further shaped by ethnicity where parties that dominate each ethnic party subsystem control 'their' public companies. The institutional framework defined by post-communist power mutation is instrumental to executive exploitation of SOEs for electoral gain. Concentration of power enables unregulated executive control of public assets and leads to a conversion of political into economic power which is then reinforced by preferential dispersion into informal party networks. Ethnic parties, predominantly the SDA, SNSD and HDZ BiH, seek containment of SOE control within ethnic party systems and subnational levels of government as a form of ethnic oligopoly. They actively limit the market expansion of most SOEs into each other's territories, even where this makes economic sense, in order to keep jobs concentrated and appease core ethnic voters. Due to weak regulations and oversight, as well as limited market competitiveness in BiH, there are few constraints to exploitation of public companies. By using illiberal politics and informality as a mechanism to control SOEs, dominant ethnic parties are able to connect voting preferences to economic benefits. The result is a large number of ethnically defined political machines with stable voting patterns where opposition parties are at a significant disadvantage.

7. Conclusion

BiH is a unique political system where, in the aftermath of the Bosnian War, governance was divided between national and several subnational levels with a significant role for both ethnic parties and internationally intervention. Each level has distinct responsibilities, but many are shared. Competing interests of ethnic groups and colliding lines of authority ultimately merge to undermine accountability. This paper aimed to analyse cases of illiberal politics at subnational levels of government and their effect on democracy in BiH. We argue that subnational autocratization is possible due to opportunities arising from the institutional framework. At the same time, it is contained by asymmetric subnational governance and a segmented party system, as well as constrained by the checks and balances that arise out of multilevel and inter-ethnic competition. Incremental autocratization at the national level, or rather the lack of strong trends observed through several indices that measure the quality of democracy, can be explained by the structural constraints of BiH's consociational democracy.

By looking at three specific cases of illiberal politics at the subnational level, the paper aimed to identify drivers of autocratization and actions of governing parties aimed at remaining in power. First, restrictions to freedom of assembly in RS in wake of the Justice for David protests present the most forceful example of illiberal politics. The SNSD government under Dodik used a combination of intimidation, violence and judicial means to suppress the protests. The driver was the party's perception of existential threat arising from dissent within its own Serb ethnic group. By containing the issue within RS, the party was able to limit external constraints to its actions. Second, illiberal politics are heavily employed by governing parties to weaken and control media by taking advantage of structural circumstances and a weak regulatory framework. The SNSD was able to gain control of public broadcasting in RS as it contained the issue at subnational level, while SDA and HDZ BiH constrained each other's attempts to subvert public broadcasting in FBiH. Third, BiH political parties use illiberal politics to gain control of state resources, most notable SOEs, with the aim to create long-lasting forms of relational patronage that can be used in electoral contest on an uneven playing field. Thereby they rely on an institutional framework defined by executive dominance, a combination of political and economic power, and informality through party networks. All the while, illiberal politics and borderline lawlessness are masked behind a veil of legality as maintaining an appearance of rule of law is necessary for the legitimacy of parties and their leaders.

The paper finds widespread use of illiberal politics that add up to significantly impact the liberal component of BiH's democracy. The electoral component of democracy is largely left intact as most effects on electoral competition are indirect. We find substantial subnational variations between RS and FBiH where the former can be described as a competitive authoritarian regime and the latter as an electoral democracy.[28] The main drivers are found to be of institutional nature and can be traced back to democratic transition and subsequent wartime ethnic polarization in the 1990s. Back then several unfavourable aspects of communist governance transferred to the new newly established proto-democratic regime in the absence of effective rule of law (Zakošek 1997), and further consolidated into ethnic rule during the war. Additionally, threat to regime survival is a potent driver for illiberal politics that may become more important if protests in BiH continue. We also find that segmental autonomy in BiH's consociational democracy has the potential to contain illiberal politics at the subnational level. Such containment can be purposeful in order to avoid national and international scrutiny, a strategy pursued by all three ethnic elites. Where consociational democracy introduced checks and balances between levels of government or ethnic groups, strategies of constrainment are used to prevent illiberal politics being used to achieve ethnic dominance.

The theory-building aim of this paper was to contribute to a better understanding of subnational authoritarian rule under conditions of power-sharing and weak national government. In this sense, we can make several conclusions. First, where strong subnational governments are not inhibited by national government or other constraints at the subnational level, contained autocratization is possible and effective. Second, where subnational government is fragmented or inhibited by institutionalized constraints, autocratization is unlikely or partial. Third, under conditions of power-sharing subnational competitive authoritarianism is unlikely to spill over to the national level as this might break containment and endanger the subnational regime. Fourth, democratization of power-sharing regimes is not possible without fully addressing subnational governance practices. The relevance of this paper for the power-sharing literature is in highlighting the important role of autocratic subnational politics in cases where segmental autonomy and ethnic veto rights are institutionalized. In such cases, consociational democracy is found to inhibit autocratization where power-sharing requirements are high, and to promote autocratization where ethnic self-governance is far-reaching. As an effect, this makes democratization more complex and multi-layered.

Illiberal politics are likely to continue in BiH, especially at the subnational level. The three dominant parties have established mechanisms to create an electoral advantage, each within their own ethnic party subsystem. While it is reasonable to expect mostly free and fair elections in the future, these will be contested on an increasingly uneven playing field. To revitalize democratization in BiH domestic and foreign actors will need to look beyond elections and national institutions. They will need to focus on subnational politics and deep-rooted power structures that blend executive dominance with economic power and informal party networks.

Notes

1. In this paper, I use the term autocratization when referring to BiH for reasons elaborated by Lührmann and Lindberg (2019).
2. In the Sejdić and Finci case, the European Court of Human Rights found that BiH's constitution discriminated against certain groups of citizens and violated the European Convention on Human Rights (Hodžić and Stojanović 2011).
3. The fourth, multiethnic playing field partially overlaps with the Bosniak one and is bound by the same degree of openness.
4. The following search strings were used to identify articles: <protesti OR prosvjedi +Dragičević+'Banja Luka'>; <politički+utjecaj+mediji+RTRS OR BHT OR RTVFBIH>; <javna+preduzeća+izbori+SDA OR SNSD OR HDZ>; from Al Jazeera Balkans (http://balkans.aljazeera.net, 24 June 2019), Buka magazin (https://6yka.com, 24 June 2019), Dnevni avaz (https://avaz.ba, 26 June 2019), Klix (https://www.klix.ba, 25 June 2019), Nezavisne novine (https://www.nezavisne.com, 25 June 2019), Radio slobodna Evropa (https://www.slobodnaevropa.org, 24 June 2019), Radio televizija Republike Srpske (https://www.rtrs.tv, 26 June 2019).
5. Personal interview #2 with journalist, Banja Luka, April 2019.
6. Personal interview #14 with academic, Sarajevo, February 2019.
7. Personal interview #8 with member of civil society, Sarajevo, March 2019.
8. Personal interview #8 with member of civil society, Sarajevo, March 2019.
9. In local language: Pravda za Davida.
10. Personal interview #11 with academic, Banja Luka, March 2019.
11. Personal interview #1 with journalist, Banja Luka, March 2019.
12. Personal interview #6 with member of civil society, Banja Luka, March 2019.
13. Personal interview #2 with journalist, Banja Luka, April 2019.
14. Personal interview #11 with academic, Banja Luka, March 2019.
15. Personal interview #11 with academic, Banja Luka, March 2019.
16. Personal interview #11 with academic, Banja Luka, March 2019 and personal interview #2 with journalist, Banja Luka, April 2019.
17. Personal interview #3 with journalist, Sarajevo, February 2019.
18. Personal interview #7 with member of civil society, Banja Luka, March 2019.
19. Personal interview #1 with journalist, Banja Luka, March 2019.

20. Personal interview #15 with academic, Sarajevo, April 2019.
21. Even though there are reported cases of occasional voter intimidation, vote buying, and mail voting fraud (Pod lupom 2018).
22. Personal interview #10 with member of civil society, Mostar, April 2019. *Štela* is a colloquial expression for personal connections with the potential to produce benefits.
23. The report concludes that 'BiH governments forego up to 3.0 percent of GDP in potential income per year through inefficiencies' in SOEs (Parodi and Cegar 2019, 23).
24. Research on interest groups shows ethnic party dominance that results in a bifurcated system with three separate interest group subsystems (Kapidžić 2019).
25. Personal interview #17 with a member of a Serb political party, Banja Luka, March 2019.
26. Personal interview #19 with member of a Bosniak political party, Sarajevo, March 2019.
27. Personal interview #3 with journalist, Sarajevo, February 2019.
28. There are also variations among cantons within FBiH but such inquiry is beyond the scope of this paper.

Disclosure statement

No potential conflict of interest was reported by the author.

ORCID

Damir Kapidžić http://orcid.org/0000-0002-8619-3530

References

Behrend, J., and L. Whitehead, eds. 2016a. *Illiberal practices: Territorial variance within large federal democracies*. Baltimore: Johns Hopkins University Press.
Behrend, J., and L. Whitehead. 2016b. The struggle for subnational democracy. *Journal of Democracy* 27(2): 155–169. doi:10.1353/jod.2016.0023.
Bermeo, N. 2016. On democratic backsliding. *Journal of Democracy* 27(1): 5–19. doi:10.1353/jod.2016.0012.
Bertelsmann Stiftung. 2018. Bertelsmann transformation index 2018. https://www.bti-project.org/en/data/.
Bieber, F. 2006. *Post-war Bosnia*. Basingstoke: Palgrave Macmillan.
Bieber, F. 2018. Patterns of competitive authoritarianism in the Western Balkans. *East European Politics* 34(3): 337–354. doi:10.1080/21599165.2018.1490272.
Blagovcanin, S., and B. Divjak. 2015. *How Bosnia's political economy holds it back and what to do about it*. Washington, DC: Center for Transatlantic Relations. https://ti-bih.org/wp-content/uploads/2015/10/How_Bosnias_Political_Economy_Holds_It_Back_And_What_to_Do_About_It.pdf.

Bojičić-Dželilović, V. 2006. *Peace on whose terms? war veterans' associations in bosnia and herzegovina.* In Challenges to peacebuilding: Managing spoilers during conflict resolution, edited by E. Newman and O. Richmond, 200–218. Tokyo: United Nations University Press.

Bojičić-Dželilović, V. 2013. Decentralization and Regionalization in Bosnia-Herzegovina: Context, model and implementation challenges. In *Decentralization and local development in South East Europe. Studies in economic transition*, edited by W. Bartlett, S. Maleković, and V. Monastiriotis, 83–99. London: Palgrave Macmillan.

Bose, S. 2002. *Bosnia after Dayton. Nationalist partition and international intervention.* New York: Oxford University Press.

Centar za istraživačko novinarstvo. 2018. Upravljanje javnim preduzećima: Stranka prije struke. https://www.cin.ba/upravljanje-javnim-preduzecima-stranka-prije-struke/.

Center for Insights in Survey Research. 2018. Bosnia and Herzegovina: Understanding perceptions of violent extremism and foreign influence. http://www.iri.org/sites/default/files/march_28-april_12_2018_bih_poll.pdf.

Chandler, D. 2000. *Bosnia: Faking democracy after Dayton.* London: Pluto.

Communications Regulatory Agency. 2018. Overview of imposed executive measures for February 2018. https://rak.ba/en/news/565.

Coppedge, M., J. Gerring, C.H. Knutsen, S.I. Lindberg, J. Teorell, D. Altman, M. Bernhard, et al. 2019. V-Dem [Country-Year/Country-Date] Dataset v9. *Varieties of Democracy (V-Dem) Project.* doi:10.23696/vdemcy19.

Cvjetićanin, T., E. Zulejhić, D. Brkan, and B. Livančić-Milić. 2019. *Disinformation in the online sphere: The case of BiH.* Sarajevo: Citizens' Association 'Why Not'.

Dahl, R. 1989. *Democracy and its critics.* New Haven: Yale Univ. Press.

Dolenec, D. 2013. *Democratic institutions and authoritarian rule in Southeast Europe.* Colchester, UK: ECPR Press.

Džankić, J. 2018. Capturing contested states: Structural mechanisms of power reproduction in Bosnia and Herzegovina, Macedonia and Montenegro. *Southeastern Europe* 42, no. 1: 83–106. doi:10.1163/18763332-04201005

EU Delegation to BiH. 2019. For an effective and credible rule of law in BiH. https://europa.ba/?p=62701.

Foreign Policy Initiative BH. 2008. *Governance structures in BiH. Capacity, ownership, EU integration, functioning state.* Sarajevo: Foreign Policy Initiative BH.

Freedom in the World. 2018. *Freedom house.* https://freedomhouse.org/sites/default/files/FreedomintheWorld2018COMPLETEBOOK.pdf.

Gans-Morse, J., S. Mazzuca, and S. Nichter. 2014. Varieties of clientelism: Machine politics during elections. *American Journal of Political Science* 58(2): 415–32. doi:10.1111/ajps.2014.58.issue-2.

Gibson, E. 2005. Boundary control: Subnational authoritarianism in democratic countries. *World Politics* 58(1): 101–32. doi:10.1353/wp.2006.0018.

Gibson, E. 2012. *Boundary control: Subnational authoritarianism in federal democracies.* Cambridge: Cambridge University Press.

Gilbert, A., and J. Mujanović. 2015. Dayton at twenty: Towards new politics in Bosnia-Herzegovina. *Southeast European and Black Sea Studies* 15(4): 605–610. doi:10.1080/14683857.2015.1130359.

Gordy, E., and A. Efendic, eds. 2019. *Meaningful reform in the Western Balkans.* Bern: Peter Lang.

Günay, C., and V. Dzihic. 2016. Decoding the authoritarian code: Exercising 'legitimate' power politics through the ruling parties in Turkey, Macedonia and Serbia. *Southeast European and Black Sea Studies* 16(4): 529–49. doi:10.1080/14683857.2016.1242872.

Hodžić, E., and N. Stojanović. 2011. *New/old constitutional engineering? Challenges and implications of the European court of human rights decision in the case of Sejdic and Finci v. BiH.* Sarajevo: Analitika - Centre for Social Research.

Horowitz, D.L. 1985. *Ethnic groups in conflict.* Berkeley: University of California Press.

Hulsey, J. 2015. Electoral accountability in Bosnia and Herzegovina under the Dayton framework agreement. *International Peacekeeping* 22(5): 511–25. doi:10.1080/13533312.2015.1100081

Hulsey, J., and D. Stjepanović. 2017. Bosnia and Herzegovina: An archetypical example of an ethnocracy. In *Regional and national elections in Eastern Europe*, edited by A. Schakel, 35–58. London: Palgrave Macmillan.

Kapidžić, D. 2017. Segmentirani stranački sustav Bosne i Hercegovine. *Političke Perspektive* 7(1–2): 7–23. doi:10.20901/pp.7.1-2.01

Kapidžić, D. 2019. A mirror of the ethnic divide: Interest group pillarization and elite dominance in Bosnia and Herzegovina. *Journal of Public Affairs* 19: e1720. doi:10.1002/pa.1720.

Kapidžić, D. 2020. The rise of illiberal politics in Southeast Europe. *Southeast European and Black Sea Studies* 20(1) (forthcoming).

Kasapović, M. 2005. *Bosna i Hercegovina: Podijeljeno društvo i nestabilna država*. Zagreb: Politička Kultura.

Keil, S. 2016. *Multinational federalism in Bosnia and Herzegovina*. London: Routledge.

Kmezić, M., and F. Bieber, eds. 2017. The crisis of democracy in the Western Balkans. An Anatomy of Stabilitocracy and the Limits of EU Democracy Promotion. Balkans in Europe Policy Advisory Group. https://biepag.eu/wp content/uploads/2017/05/final.pdf.

Levitsky, S., and L.A. Way. 2010. *Competitive authoritarianism: Hybrid regimes after the cold war*. Cambridge: Cambridge University Press.

Lijphart, A. 1999. *Patterns of democracy: Government forms and performance in thirty-six countries*. New Haven, CT: Yale University Press.

Lührmann, A., and S. Lindberg. 2019. A third wave of autocratization is here: What is new about it? *Democratization* 26(7): 1095–113. doi:10.1080/13510347.2019.1582029.

Marković, G. 2012. *Bosanskohercegovacki federalizam*. Sarajevo: University Press.

McCulloch, A., and J. McGarry, eds. 2017. *Power-sharing: Empirical and normative challenges*. New York: Routledge.

McGill, P., 2019. Can EU ambitions power a harmonious future for Bosnia-Herzegovina? *The Banker*, April 1. https://www.thebanker.com/World/Central-Eastern-Europe/Bosnia-Herzegovina/Can-EU-ambitions-power-a-harmonious-future-for-Bosnia-Herzegovina/(language)/eng-GB.

Merdzanovic, A. 2018. From international statebuilding to domestic political clientelism: The failures of postwar liberalization in Bosnia and Herzegovina. In *Illiberal and authoritarian tendencies in central, Southeastern and Eastern Europe*, edited by M. Solska, F. Bieber, and D. Taleski, 225–243. Bern: Peter Lang.

Mujanović, J. 2017. *Hunger and fury: The crisis of democracy in the Balkans*. New York: Oxford University Press.

Norris, P., and M. Grömping. 2019. Perceptions of electoral integrity, (PEI-7.0). *Harvard Dataverse*. doi:10.7910/DVN/PDYRWL.

O'Donnell, G. 1993. On the state, democratization and some conceptual problems: A Latin American view with glances at some postcommunist countries. *World Development* 21(8): 1355–69. doi:10.1016/0305-750X(93)90048-E.

OSCE. 2019. *Bosnia and Herzegovina general elections (7 October 2018): ODIHR election observation mission final report*. Warsaw: OSCE-ODIHR. https://www.osce.org/odihr/elections/bih/409905.

Parodi, F., and B. Cegar. 2019. State-owned enterprises in Bosnia and Herzegovina: Assessing performance and oversight. IMF Working Paper No. 19/201.

Perry, V. 2015. Constitutional reform processes in Bosnia and Herzegovina: Top- down failure, bottom-up potential, continued stalemate. In *State-building and democratization in Bosnia and Herzegovina*, edited by S. Keil and V. Perry. London: Routledge, 15–40.

Pod lupom. 2018. Opšti izbori 2018. http://podlupom.org/v2/bs/clanak/opsti-izbori-2018/361.

Popovikj, M., B. Gjuzelov, and J. Bliznakovski. 2019. How to sustainably decrease clientelism and ensure fair political competition in the WB?. In *Meaningful reform in the Western Balkans*, edited by E. Gordy and A. Efendic. Bern: Peter Lang, 103–115.

Reuters. 2018. Bosnians demand resignation of interior minister over student's death. December 30. https://www.reuters.com/article/us-bosnia-protests/bosnians-demand-resignation-of-interior-minister-over-students-death-idUSKCN1OT0L0.

Solska, M., F. Bieber, and D. Taleski, eds. 2018. *Illiberal and authoritarian tendencies in central, Southeastern and Eastern Europe.* Bern: Peter Lang.

Sorguc, A., and H. Rovcanin. 2019 Rise in Bosnian defamation cases raises censorship fears. *Balkan Insight*, June 20. https://balkaninsight.com/2019/06/20/rise-in-bosnian-defamation-cases-raises -censorship-fears/.

Stokes, S., T Dunning, M. Nazareno, and V. Brusco. 2013. *Brokers, voters, and clientelism: The puzzle of distributive politics.* Cambridge: Cambridge University Press.

Tilly, C., and S. Tarrow. 2007. *Contentious politics.* Boulder: Paradigm.

Touquet, H. 2012. The Republika Srpska as a strong nationalizing state and the consequences for postethnic activism. *Nationalities Papers* 40(2): 203–20. doi:10.1080/00905992.2011.652609.

Turčilo, L., and B. Buljubašić. 2017. *Media and shrinking space in Bosnia and Herzegovina.* Sarajevo: Heinrich Böll Foundation.

Zakošek, N. 1997. Pravna država i demokracija u postsocijalizmu. *Politička Misao* 34(4): 78–85.

Zdeb, A. 2019. When the state turns against its own citizens, resistance becomes duty? *New Eastern Europe* 38(5): 85–89.

Soft competitive authoritarianism and negative stability in Kosovo: statebuilding from UNMIK to EULEX and beyond

Adem Beha and Arben Hajrullahu

ABSTRACT
After 1999, democratization, normalization and Europeanization were the key processes through which Kosovo's final political status was expected to take shape. All three processes, however, were guided by the stability paradigm. Though Kosovo cannot be categorized as a typical authoritarian state, its political leaders have openly displayed illiberal tendencies, governing in an unaccountable manner and utilizing public assets for their private gain. In the period from 1999 to 2008, while UNMIK's approach was based on maintaining stability instead of democratization, a *soft competitive authoritarianism* began to emerge incrementally. In its first decade of independence, Kosovo's statehood remained internationally disputed, whereas its governance culture was characterized by a lack of internal accountability, which is a key component of the soft competitive authoritarianism in the country. Thus, the negative trajectory of political developments did not change even after the deployment of EULEX and the 2008 declaration of independence. This article analyses the development of authoritarian and illiberal tendencies in Kosovo and suggests that the democratization and Europeanization discourses served to conceal soft competitive authoritarian practices in Kosovo.

1. Introduction

With the 1999 international intervention and the United Nations Interim Mission in Kosovo (hereafter UNMIK), a new, irreversible political momentum was created that would be later formulated in the Balkan Contact Group[1] maxim 'there is no turning back', meaning that Kosovo could not return to Serbia's rule. UN Security Resolution 1244[2] left Kosovo's political status to be determined in the future. The international community built transitional institutions and, while rhetorically supporting the new democracy in Kosovo, it was largely led by the idea of keeping the situation under control in the country until a final decision over its political status was reached. To maintain peace and stability in Kosovo, as a test for the success of the intervention and statebuilding, UNMIK took a lenient approach to corruption and cronyism. Taking advantage of this, Kosovar leaders moved to strengthen their clientelist and patrimonial networks. These were mainly driven by the Democratic Party of Kosovo (PDK)[3] formed by former Kosovo Liberation Army (KLA)[4] commanders, and the Democratic League of

Kosovo (LDK),[5] the party that during the 1990s under the leadership of Ibrahim Rugova sought independence by peaceful means.

In 2007, after nearly two years of negotiations led by the UN Secretary General's Special Envoy Martti Ahtisaari, the Comprehensive Proposal for Kosovo Status Settlement (hereafter the Ahtisaari Proposal) recommended supervised independence for Kosovo with enhanced rights for the Serbian community in Kosovo (D'aspremont 2007; Kostovicova 2008; Ker-Lindsay 2009; Papadimitriou and Petrov 2012). Kosovo declared its independence on 17 February 2008. However, its statehood remains contested internationally because its sovereignty is not recognized by all countries, including two (Russia and China) of the five permanent members of the UN Security Council. The International Civilian Office (hereafter ICO), an international body, was authorized to monitor the implementation of the Ahtisaari Proposal. Almost at the same time, the European Rule of Law Mission in Kosovo (hereafter EULEX) was deployed with the aim of strengthening the capacity of Kosovo institutions in the area of rule of law. UNMIK remained in place, but with practically no governance competencies.

To date, more than half of the UN member states recognize Kosovo as an independent state. Five EU member states (Cyprus, Greece, Spain, Slovakia and Romania) have not yet recognized Kosovo. Following the 22 July 2010 International Court of Justice (hereafter ICJ) ruling that the declaration of Kosovo's independence did not contradict international law, Serbia and Kosovo have been required to engage in an EU-facilitated dialogue process aiming to overcome their disputes. Meanwhile, the governing 'manipulative political elites' in Kosovo (Hajrullahu 2011) have used the narrative of 'Euro-Atlantic integration' to avoid accountability, transparency, and responsibility towards their voters and to hide failures in the country's governance. This strategy of repeatedly engaging the narrative of 'Euro-Atlantic integration' while camouflaging governance failures has provided conditions for the emergence of a soft competitive authoritarian regime. By gaining international legitimacy and capitalizing on the real or supposed role as a factor for domestic and regional stability, the political elites have continued to enhance their clientelist networks, share wealth and power among narrow groups of people, while the majority faces high unemployment rates and endemic corrupt governing practices.

The narrative that continues to 'legitimize' the political elites in Kosovo is the abstract process of Europeanization and integration of Kosovo into the Euro-Atlantic structures. Since 1999 the Kosovar political elite has gained and legitimized its power based on the narrative that it is working to meet these goals. Nonetheless, it has narrowed the space of democratic transition in the country by reproducing clientelist networks that serve their interests. Instead of achieving these integration and developmental goals, a *soft competitive authoritarianism* has been incrementally installed, in which the state is partially used to serve party interests to distribute economic resources to companies close to the ruling parties. The absence of political elites governing in the general public interest has compromised democratic accountability. The specificity of soft competitive authoritarianism in Kosovo, unlike the cases of competitive authoritarianism raised by Levitsky and Way (2002), lies in the fact that the international military and civil presence in Kosovo, KFOR, UNMIK, and EULEX, has hindered efforts by any political party to put the whole country's economy, society, politics, and the media under a single centralized control. Moreover, in contrast to competitive authoritarianism regimes, in Kosovo political opponents are not imprisoned and most of the local and general elections have been held in relatively fair conditions.

The remainder of this article is structured in four sections. The first section outlines a theoretical framework for how illiberal democracy and soft competitive authoritarianism interacts with statebuilding. The second section analyses how the democratization rhetoric has been misused to enable the establishment of soft competitive authoritarianism in the country. The third and fourth sections analyse the way the post 1999 normalization and Europeanization rhetoric have been used to enable the emergence of soft competitive authoritarianism in Kosovo, followed by a conclusion. Through analysis of local political developments in Kosovo, this article both contributes to a better scholarly understanding and challenges the internationally and domestically proclaimed objective of establishing a functional democratic governing system based on rule of law in post 1999 Kosovo.

2. Illiberal democracy and soft competitive authoritarianism meet statebuilding

The fall of the 'Iron Curtain' has been symbolically followed by the rise of an 'Authoritarian Curtain'. Partially authoritarian regimes are now considered an obstacle to the fulfilment of the Fukuyamian eschatology, which foresaw the worldwide spread of liberal democracy. Many countries that have made the transition from authoritarianism to democracy, from Southeast Europe, Latin America to Asia, are within a grey zone and classified as neither democratic nor authoritarian regimes. They 'are located in the middle of a continuum anchored by democracies at one pole and dictatorship at the other', combining the elements of both political regimes, thus resulting in hybrid regimes (Bunce and Mcfaul 2010, viii). These regimes have slowly begun to stabilize. The premise of transitologists that over time they will move towards consolidated democracy is now regarded with scepticism. Scholars have used different adjectives to describe such regimes, such as pseudo-democracy, illiberal democracy, semi-democracy, semi-authoritarian regimes, competitive authoritarianism, sultanist regimes, and so on (Chehabi and Linz 1998; Collier and Levitsky 1997; Zakaria 1997; Schedler 2002; Ottaway 2003; Levitsky and Way 2010). The political elites in many transitional countries have imitated institutional forms of democracy to re-legitimize their power. As Damir Kapidžić argues in the introduction to this volume, countries in Southeast Europe 'are not experiencing a sudden democratic reversal. Rather, structural deficiencies centred around a strong executive, weak checks and balances and institutionalized informality are exploited by political parties to tilt the playing field through the use of illiberal governing practices' (Kapidžić 2020).

The expectation that, after the collapse of communism, liberal democracy would become an inevitable governing form for all countries remains illusory. Different political systems have used the formal notion of democracy to instal government practices that have nothing or very little to do with liberal democracy. Zakaria (1997, 30) makes an essential distinction between constitutional liberalism and democracy. For him, 'constitutional liberalism is about the limitation of power, democracy about its accumulation and use.'

Steven Levitsky and Lucan A. Way argued that transition does not necessarily end in democracy. The post Cold War world is characterized by the spread of numerous hybrid political regimes. To describe these regimes, these scholars developed and invented the term 'competitive authoritarianims' as a hybrid regime that is neither fully authoritarian nor democratic. According to them, 'competitive authoritarian regimes are civilian regimes in which formal democratic institutions exist and are widely viewed as the primary means of gaining power, but in which the incumbents' abuse of the state places them at a significant advantage vis-a-vis their opponents. Such regimes are competitive in that opposition parties use democratic institutions to contest seriously for power, but they are not democratic because the playing field is heavily skewed in favour of incumbents. Competition is so real but unfair' (2002, 5–6). In such regimes, political elites see democratic institutions as a means to gain power and violate these institutions as soon as they come to power. These regimes do not meet the minimum democratic criteria. Though elections are held in these regimes, they are not free, but are characterized by electoral fraud, in which incumbents use state resources for private interests, while opposition candidates and journalists are threatened (Levitsky and Way 2002, 53).

Competitive authoritarian regimes are widespread throughout Eastern Europe, Latin America, and Asia. The legitimizing narrative of authoritarian elites in these political systems is that political transition, openness to democracy, and liberalism can be dangerous for certain social groups, especially for the business elite and the military. According to Jon C. Pevehouse, business elites fear that democracy could populist to power that might jeopardize their property and financial interests, whereas military elites are afraid to lose their privileges and be subject to civilian control. Thus, both groups resist the opening up and liberalization of the political system. 'Ideally, authoritarian leaders hope to expand their power through limited change – increasing legitimacy and forestalling calls for further reform' (Pevehouse 2002, 521). According to Pevehouse membership in international organizations can contribute to the democratization of authoritarian regimes due to pressure placed on them to undertake reforms accompanied with sanctions. At the same time, membership in international organizations can reduce their fears, as they perceive that an external guarantor will take care of their interests. He argues that 'organizations with a higher democratic density are more likely to be associated with democratic transitions. Democratic "density" refers to the percentage of permanent members in the organization that are already considered democratic' (2002, 525).

The 1999 international military intervention did not resolve the issue of the political status of Kosovo, 'that is the root of the conflict: the zero-sum contest over the territory' (Yannis 2009, 162). Kosovo's political status remained ambiguous in the international system, and 'since 1999 Kosovo has thus existed in a certain political limbo, officially a part of the state of Serbia and Montenegro, but in reality largely independent of any influence from Belgrade and administered primarily by the UN mission' (Tansey 2007, 133). Since Kosovo's institutions had no democratic and little institutional legacy, the process of democratization was predominantly exogenous, led by OSCE administrators and experts as one of the pillars of UNMIK. The institutional architecture of Kosovo built after the war of 1999 – – the Constitutional Framework for Provisional Self-Government in Kosovo and other UNMIK regulations – – was aimed at establishing a democratic political culture through which the radical forces among the Albanian and Serb political elites would be marginalized.

In the years following 1999 UNMIK enjoyed full powers. However, by the time of Kosovo's declaration of independence in 2008 the authority of the mission was reduced and now more than one decade on, the mission is considered obsolete by Kosovo's institutions. According to UN Resolution 1244 (1999) UNMIK was in charge of creating and supervising the provisional democratic institutions in Kosovo, the incremental transfer of competences to these institutions, and the facilitation of the political process that would define the future status of Kosovo. UNMIK was supposed to establish an omnipotent judiciary, executive, and legislative branch. However, there was no effective instance of UNMIK holding the local elites accountable. As a result of its democratic deficit and the lack of accountability mechanisms, Chesterman (2004, 75) has classified UNMIK as a 'benevolent autocracy', while Veton Surroi considered it a 'new postmodern neo-colonial power' (quoted in Judah 2008, 97). Although over the last two decades, two international missions, a UN mission (UNMIK) and the other an EU mission (EULEX), have ruled Kosovo, the country has not yet succeeded in building a consolidated democracy.

Why is it that despite the massive investments in building a democratic society, Kosovo is still not a full democracy? The main reason behind the failure to instal democracy and hold the local political elite to account is, perhaps, to be found in the lack of a sustainable diplomatic solution for Kosovo. The international community was focused on ending the violence and ethnic motivated atrocities, and not on finding sustainable political solutions for the countries in the region. King and Mason argue that a form of conditioned independence for Kosovo should have been offered even in 1999, an independence that was conditioned upon fulfiling the rule of law and the rights of minorities criteria (King and Mason 2006, 257). Following Kosovo's declaration of independence in 2008, Kosovo faced two risks: first, due to the Serbia's failure to recognize Kosovo's independence the lack of full recognition and consolidation of its international statehood; and, second, state capture by its own political elite resulting in weak democratic and the absence of cultures of good governance.

Independent Kosovo is a hybrid regime. The political elite has controlled the transition and slowed down the process of democratization, whenever this process jeopardized their interests. Kosovo's political elites rhetorically accept democratic rules but, in practice, operate with methods of authoritarian governance, including control over the legislative agenda and interference in the justice system. We have named this type of regime here soft competitive authoritarianism.

3. Methodological constraints

Ahram and Goode (2016, 834) have identified three methodological challenges in the study of authoritarianism: first, access to data and timing; second, data validity; and third, integrity and ethical issues. The first challenge relates to limited access to data (*data collection*) in authoritarian regimes. The second challenge relates to the quality and validity of the data (*research security*), considering the fact that authoritarian regimes provide data and information, much of which reflects regime propaganda and is not necessarily valid data. The third challenge relates to the ethical dilemma (*subjective safety*) of how researchers should treat information received from their sources based on the fact that any information brought to them by the public may be associated with a risk to their lives.

However, the above constraints notwithstanding the challenge of conducting research in Kosovo is mitigated by the following three factors: the political regime is relatively open; media and civil society are relatively free; and, third, the country remains, to some extent, under civil international supervision accompanied by the military presence of

KFOR. These three circumstances make the task of research in Kosovo less precarious than in a fully authoritarian regime.

This study draws on and analyses the following sources: independent domestic and international media and organizations reports (*Insajder, Preportr, Jeta në Kosovë, KCSS, ICG, UNDP*), as well as academic studies in its consideration of the applicability of contemporary theories on authoritarian and illiberal regimes to Kosovo. Partisan news and reports issued by political party controlled local media, such as *Epoka e Re* (PDK) and *Bota Sot* (LDK) were not used. In addition, between November 2018 and March 2019 the authors conducted ten semi-structured interviews with scholars and civil society activists in Kosovo.

Since Kosovo is a unique example of a country which, on one hand, has had an international military and civil supervisory presence, whilst, on the other hand being internally ruled by an unaccountable political elite, repeatedly operating in a grim and lawless area, with authoritarian tendencies and therefore it is treated as an individual case study. This is consistent with Florian Bieber's recent claim that '[t]he fact that much of competitive authoritarian rule takes place informally, not through laws and formal decisions, means that the comparative rankings are misleading' (2018, 340). Having this in mind, we have analysed the case of *soft competitive authoritarianism* in Kosovo through context analysis, by emphasizing specific features and practices of state capture phenomenon.

4. Democratization rhetoric as an enabler of soft competitive authoritarianism

During the period of UNMIK's international administration 1999–2008, the only legitimate political discourse was that of democratization. In order to gain *de jure* international acceptance as well as *de facto* domestic legitimacy, politicians competing for political power employed a formal democratization discourse in public. However, this democratization rhetoric served more as a facade than as an actual institutional and cultural tool to affect a transition from the authoritarian legacy of the Serb-dominated regime to an inclusive democratic society. Kosovo was confronted with an internationally blessed local political elite, which repeatedly used a democratization discourse and at the very same time engaged in establishing and strengthening soft authoritarian governance.

The roots of soft competitive authoritarianism in Kosovo can be traced back to the beginning of international civilian administration, which aimed to build order, peace, security and domestic democratic institutions. When UNMIK, the civilian presence, and KFOR, the military force, were deployed in Kosovo in June 1999 and Serbian forces had to withdraw, an institutional vacuum emerged in the country. The former leaders of the KLA who later established political parties as well as the strong men of the LDK, which operated as the main Kosovar political party in 1990s very soon filled this institutional vacuum. Thus, 'Kosovo was the epitome of collapsing state institutions, which were easily countervailed by powerful patronage networks. Soon enough established patronage networks, that carried the stench of the conflict, were structured into hierarchical parties and rallied around a "super patron"' (Tadić and Elbasani 2018, 5).

Kosovo's political parties are not guided by ideological programmes, but by a clientelistic, patronage, and patrimonial logic. One of the paramount misconceptions in UNMIK's approach was that Kosovo's political parties were 'treated as if they resembled their Western counterparts – a group of civic minded people bound together by a shared commitment to certain ideological principles. In reality, they were personally driven patronage networks, some of them rooted in the KLA' (King and Mason 2006, 244). UNMIK established a local administration in Kosovo accommodating mainly the interests of the two largest parties, the LDK and the PDK. The legitimacy of the former political group derived from the parallel system and the peaceful civil resistance of the 1990s, 'while the latter one, consisting mainly of warlords, benefited from their military legitimacy and reputation of national heroes, on their way to becoming the new state-makers' (Hoxha et al. 2016, 82). UNMIK would have difficulties with maintaining the situation under control if it had excluded the members of these two parties. As Democracy for Development (D4D), a local think-tank in Kosovo, observed the UNMIK co-optation policy, primarily aimed at preserving peace, prioritized a power-sharing arrangement between major power-holders and individual promotion through group membership. (D4D 2013, 30).

The majority of the political elite after the war, regardless of their KLA or LDK back-ground, had no experience in democratic governance, and the sole political experience they knew was 'the politics of opposition, which is about blaming the authorities rather than taking responsibility – a world of declarations, gestures, and in-fighting, rather than policy initiatives, legislation and management' (King and Mason 2006, 60). In the first phase of political transition 1999–2002, the political elites coming from the KLA, from which two political parties emerged, namely the PDK and the Alliance for the Future of Kosovo (AAK),[6] were considered as potential spoilers that could not be trusted with executive power, given the Serbian community fear of revenge from these elites and the promise of the international community to build an inclusive and multi-ethnic society and institutions. Thus, as Oisin Tansey noted (2009, 117), 'in both the pre- and post-election periods in UNMIK's tenure, international authorities have intervened in the competition between local political elites and parties, and sought to shape political outcomes, with an explicit aim of minimizing the prospects of political dominance by any one political party or commu-nity, and promoting inclusive and moderate politics in Kosovo'.

However, not co-opting these elites into the governments was considered a potentially bigger threat for the stability of the country. Therefore, between 1999 and 2008, UNMIK's unaccountability to the local population resulted in the maintenance of the status quo and stability by co-opting the so-called radical and moderate Kosovo-Albanian and -Serbian political elites into a joint institutional structure of governance. This co-optation of the elites came at a high price, namely the lack of virtually any accountability of these elites towards Kosovo citizens. The politics of UNMIK's coopera-tion with only one group of political party leaders, who were loyal to the international administration agenda, encouraged authoritarian practices within Kosovo's political parties, which considered international legitimacy more important than national elec-toral legitimacy. 'This has inevitably encouraged authoritarian practices within political parties and made external legitimacy more important than local legitimacy. This complex entanglement of power and legitimacy reduces opportunities for positive social change, increases nepotism and patronage relations, and suppresses any critical voice that seeks to challenge this figuration' (Visoka and Richmond 2016, 8).

The process of democratization can lead to the establishment of a political society of free and equal citizens governed by fair laws. Such a society has not yet been established in Kosovo. Governing a post-conflict society whose political status remained unresolved, UNMIK in co-operation with KFOR managed to prevent large-scale outbreaks of violence and inter-ethnic revenge in Kosovo. Although this goal was achieved relatively successfully, this was not enough for the Kosovo-Albanian political elite, whose demands converged on a lowest common denominator, namely independence for Kosovo. In the absence of an exit strategy and a concrete offer for the Kosovo-Albanian elite, UNMIK traded status and stability that came at a high cost for the country's (non-) functional democracy. The local and international political elite implicitly agreed on maintaining stability in Kosovo, disregarding good practice in democracy and the rule of law. Thus the local political elite begun to engage in corrupt and clientelist practices. UNMIK and later EULEX closed their eyes to these practices, as long as the elite was contributing to maintaining stability albeit without accountability and democracy. This had produced the model of 'stabilitocracy', or what Beha and Selaci have referred to as 'negative stability' (2018), that is toleration of corrupt and criminal practices by Kosovo's political elite in exchange for maintaining stability, preventing inter-ethnic violence and upholding the status quo until a decision on the final status of Kosovo has been reached. As King and Mason argue (2006, 60), 'in the name of "stability" the mission betrayed many of the brightest, most idealistic people in Kosovo in favour of the most thuggish.'

This negative trajectory did not change much after the deployment of EULEX and the 2008 declaration of independence. Kosovo was put under EU supervision with the aiming of ensuring the fulfilment of the obligations deriving from the Ahtisaari Plan and of preventing state capture by local political elites. Andrea Capussela has argued that 'without external intervention, both the economy and the political system were likely to fall under the tight control of the elite because Kosovo lacked efficiently large, effective and organized social forces to act as a counterpoise to the political, economic and military power of the dominant coalition' (Capussela 2015, 93).

The new constitution that entered into force in June 2008 defines Kosovo as a democratic, parliamentary republic based on the separation of powers. Though the Kosovo Assembly is supposed to be a body that supervises the Government in fact, it is the Government that controls the agenda and debates in the Parliament. As a result of the proportional electoral system in a single electoral zone, and the lack of internal party democracy, members of the parliament from the governing parties do not behave as accountable to their voters but rather they serve only as a 'rubber stamp' of the Government. The political career of Members of Parliament depends on their unconditional loyalty to party leaders, while the latter are 'true patriots' who draft lists with their obedient 'clients' within the party of Members of Parliament, Ministers, Deputy ministers and other posts based on the 'patron-client' logic. In this way, the Assembly does not fulfil its key role of being a supervisory body, and consequently the governance system has turned into a 'prime ministerial republic', a neologism coined by Gëzim Selaci to describe the functioning of Kosovo's political system in which the head of government rules in an autocratic way undermining the authority of the Parliament (Selaci 2017, 44). International organizations that have closely followed the process of state building in Kosovo pointed out that the country 'suffers from the widespread impression that it is run by a lawless political elite in control of every aspect of society' (ICG 2010, 1).

Following the declaration of independence, a number of strong men who had fought in the KLA, won mandates in the Parliament. Although EULEX suggested a narrative that it would investigate high-profile cases of corruption, under the 'umbrella' of the parliamentary immunity and other public posts the 'strong men' protected themselves from prosecution. The European Parliament Rapporteur for Kosovo Ulrike Lunacek requested that Members of Parliament, who were under investigation, resign from their positions and not hide behind claims of immunity (Gashi 2011). This situation was clarified in 2011 after a decision by the Constitutional Court of Kosovo, which stipulates that members of Parliament of Kosovo enjoy only functional immunity, and that they could be prosecuted for penal acts outside Parliament (Constitutional Court 2011).

Following this ruling by the Constitutional Court, in November 2012 EULEX arrested the Minister of Transport and Telecommunication Fatmir Limaj, a KLA ex-commander from the Malisheva region, for organized crime, abuse of official position, bribe taking, and failure to declare the financial support received for his electoral campaign (EULEX Press Release 2014). Before and during his mandate as minister in one of the ministries with the highest allocated budget, Limaj was deputy-leader of the PDK, and the second highest vote-winner in the party. Thus, he was considered the main rival to the party leader, Hashim Thaçi, whose intent was to leave the party in the hands of Kadri Veseli, the Head of the Kosovo Information Service (SHIK),[7] an infamous former underground intelligence organization linked to the KLA. Limaj publically declared that the charges against him were politically motivated. He subsequently left the PDK and in 2014 set up a new party known as NISMA for Kosovo[8] (Leposhtica 2015). In November 2017, Limaj was acquitted of corruption charges (Insajder 2018). This represented a classic case reflecting the incompetence or lack of professionalism of EULEX judges, and direct interference in the justice system for the purpose of hounding political rivals. In an article in The Guardian, Andrea Capusella noted that 'EULEX has become a symbol of incompetence, not of European values, and a costly veil that hides the shenanigans of the elite from the eyes of Kosovo's citizens' (Capusela 2011).

The absence of any convictions on charges of corruption and illegal gain has become a politically and societally normalized phenomenon in Kosovo. For instance, between 2016 and 2018 no high-level political officials were sentenced with a decisive court verdict or effective conviction. Institutions, such as the Assembly, the Government and the state agencies often serve as refuges for Members of Parliament. Ministers and Directors, who have become millionaires and have not been able to justify their wealth against their publicly earned incomes. The law requires that politicians report their wealth to the Kosovo Anti-Corruption Agency but are not bound to provide any proof of its origin. Kosovo has failed to build a justice system that can fight high-profile corruption with integrity. The justice system remains vulnerable to political interference. Neither local nor European institutions of justice have produced tangible results in fighting corruption. In spite of the existence of multiple institutions, agencies and laws with the purpose of fighting corruption, the effectiveness and willingness of these institutions, as well as the boldness of judges and prosecutors remain low. As a result, citizens' trust in local and international institutions of justice also remains low. Public opinions surveys indicate that only 27.2% of citizens trust the courts, and 31% of them trust the institution of State Prosecutor in Kosovo. The negative trends in citizens' trust in judicial institutions is linked to the fact that the fight against corruption among high-profile politicians degenerated into empty rhetoric which was not translated into tangible action. In addition, less than a quarter of citizens have trust in the EULEX mission (KCSS 2018).

In light of the fact that international missions in Kosovo have remained more focused on internal and regional stability rather than a thorough reform of the governance culture, Kosovo has been prone to state capture and misuse of public resources for the private interests of its own political elite. A leaked phone conversation in 2016 provided evidence of state capture by the leaders of PDK, known as 'Pronto-Affair'. In a Don Corleone 'I'll make him an offer he can't refuse' style, the head of the PDK parliamentary group, Adem Grabovci, referring to himself as 'the chief of chiefs' and answering phone calls with 'Pronto', in conversation with other party members, is heard compiling lists for the appointment of judges, civil servants, chiefs of Police, and members of public companies' boards, independent state agencies and other public institutions. Regarding himself as an executioner of orders coming from heads of the party, Grabovci is heard to offer public positions to persons close to the PDK, positions which they could not refuse as the party 'needed its own men in those positions'. In the leaked conversations, one member of the PDK is heard to say that he did not even formally apply for the position for a member of a board in a public company for which he was recommended. However, Grabovci informed him that he was, nonetheless, chosen for that position (Kajtazi 2016). The PDK driven 'Pronto-Affair' is only one illustrative example of state capture in internationally supervised Kosovo.

5. Normalization rhetoric as an enabler of soft competitive authoritarianism

The Kosovo-Albanian political elite viewed independence as a political goal from the moment the international administration and military force were deployed in Kosovo in 1999. Although Kosovo declared independence on 17 February 2008, its statehood remains internationally disputed. The international community has, however, initiated a dialogue to lead to the normalization of relations between the governments of Serbia and Kosovo. This EU-led dialogue process, though indispensible for Kosovo to gain further international support, has re-legitimized the very same political elite that have been misruling Kosovo since 1999. Two normalization stages are explored here. First, by normalization we are referring to the post-conflict phase during which parties have addressed the causes of the conflict, which in Johan Galtung's terms can be defined as a 'positive peace' (Galtung 2012). After 1999, the term normalization meant the mollification of inter-ethnic relations within Kosovo. Second, in the post-2008 period this term refers to the realization of good and peaceful neighbourhood relations between Kosovo and Serbia, which would eventually imply the latter's recognition of the former.

During the period of UNMIK-led governance up to the declaration of independence, normalization in Kosovo involved a process of domestic dialogue and the creation of conditions for peaceful inter-ethnic coexistence between the majority and the non-majority communities in Kosovo. In summer 2002, the Head of UNMIK, the Special Representative of the Secretary General (SRSG), inaugurated the policy 'Standards for Kosovo', as a prelude to opening final status negotiations. According to Dominik Zaum 'UNMIK's original strategy envisaged the use of governance benchmarks and progress in the resolution of the status question to manage the transition of authority to local institutions' (2009, 201). This politics of conditioning was aimed at keeping political elites focused on building 'a multi-ethnic society where there is democracy, tolerance, freedom of movement and equal access to justice for all people in Kosovo, regardless of their ethnic background' (UNMIK 2003). According to this document, Kosovo's political elite was required to meet eight standards of good governance, including the functioning of democratic institutions, rule of law, freedom of movement, sustainable return of displaced persons, protection of minority rights, protection of property rights, protection of cultural heritage, conducting a dialogue with Serbia to address the issues of missing persons, energy, and transport. The political elite in Kosovo considered these standards 'as unrealistically ambitious and unachievable in the short term' (UNSC S/2004/932, 15). The results of this policy were mixed and some of the standards were never met, either because Kosovo had no institutional capacities, or because the local political elite were unwilling to build a multi-ethnic society, before Kosovo's final status had been settled. As stated at that time in an ICG report:

> It is, however, a mistake to link it directly with the resolution of status, understood as the relationship with Serbia. Given the low level of development and the institutional exclusion of Kosovo's Albanian majority throughout the 1990s that led to a lack of local capacity, the achievement of standards in many areas is bound to be slow. On the other hand, the absence of clarity over Kosovo's future relationship with Serbia is a basic factor complicating relations between the Albanian majority and the Serb minority in the province (2003, 4).

Some Kosovo Serbs fearing possible retaliation from Albanians for what has happened in the 1990s fled to Serbia. Many others were concentrated in enclaves throughout Kosovo, especially in the northern municipalities where they practically found themselves under the government of Serbia instead of being administered by UNMIK and the Provisional Institutions of Self-Government in Kosovo. Serbs in these enclaves built parallel institutions, thus opposing the UNSC Resolution 1244 (1999) (OSCE 2003). The parallel education, healthcare, and justice institutions were financed by Serbia. Over time informality, the grey economy and insecurity grew among the Serbs. In effect, the northern municipalities of Kosovo split and Kosovo and UNMIK institutions did not exercise any effective authority in the area.

Building a multi-ethnic society implied the functional and effective inclusion of the Kosovo Serb community and other non-majority communities in Kosovo institutions, a goal that was only weakly realized. For decades the Kosovo Albanian and Serbian political leaders had been more interested in appearing as 'true representatives' of their ethnic groups whose votes they counted on than in addressing issues of multi-ethnicity. Leaders from both communities used ethnicity as a political tool to avoid taking responsibility for their political failures in building effective and democratic governance structures in Kosovo. Agon Hamza observed that ethnicity was used as an ideology to hide the real political and economic problems of the country. According to him,

> the moment you talk about economic exploitation, corruption as a constitutive element of the State power in Kosovo, political injustice, and so forth, multi-ethnicity is brought up as a counter-argument, which is, an effective force of censorship. A couple of years ago, KFOR's agitprop unit for popular brain washing issued the infamous billboard, all around Kosovo, in which a dog and a cat were hugging, followed by a message: 'If they can do it, why can't you?' This stands as the pure example of racism par excellence: leaving aside the disgusting treatment of Albanians and Serbs as animals, liberal multicultural tolerance, as portrayed in KFOR posters, is here advertised as possible as a 'natural' co-existence between the cat and a dog (Žižek and Hamza 2013, 88–89).

Dialogue with Serbia was one of the eight standards that Kosovo had to meet as a precondition for opening status negotiations. The purpose of the dialogue was to build stability in Kosovo and the broader region. The participation of Kosovo and Serbia 'in bilateral and multilateral arrangements to benefit stability in the region', was considered one of the aims of the normalization of the relationship between the two parties (UNMIK

2003, 14). However, the Kosovo-Albanian political elite was not interested in entering into direct dialogue with Serbia, especially in the period of postwar trauma during which the dominant discourse in Kosovo was that of 'traitors and heroes'. Ibrahim Rugova of the LDK, who enjoyed uncontested legitimacy due to his victory in the first two elections (local and general) after the war, hesitated to engage in direct dialogue with Serbia. Being taken hostage and forced to shake hands with Slobodan Milošević during the war in 1999 – – a meeting propagated as 'national treason' by the Political Directorate of the KLA headed by Hashim Thaçi – – was initially thought to have shaken Kosovars' belief in Rugova's leadership. However, the results of postwar elections proved the contrary. On one hand, Hashim Thaçi's PDK refused to participate in the dialogue, given the bitter rivalry between these two parties. Some eminent LDK members were assassinated in the immediate period after the war for which the party blamed the forces that emerged from the KLA, particularly the PDK and its illegal intelligence service SHIK. On the other hand, the PDK accused the LDK of undertaking policies that ran counter to national interests, because by insisting on its peaceful resistance policy it did not directly support the KLA war.

Given the political context in postwar Kosovo, the participation of the Kosovo political elite in the June 2003 European Council and the EU – Western Balkans Thessaloniki Summit was considered a reward for starting the dialogue between Serbia and Kosovo. The Head of UNMIK persuaded the leaders of the PDK and the LDK to participate by promising a European agenda for Kosovo and direct participation in the Thessaloniki Summit alongside the UNMIK delegation but on the condition that they commenced a process of dialogue with Serbia (King and Mason 2006, 170).

After February 2008, the Kosovo Serbs living in northern municipalities contested the legitimacy of the Kosovo authorities even more strongly than before. Meanwhile, EULEX failed to deploy personnel in the northern municipalities until December 2008. Under the direct control of Serbia, Kosovo Serbs burned down Kosovo custom facilities at two border crossings in the northern municipalities and took the railway under their power. Moreover, several Kosovo Serb police officers were forced to resign from their positions in the Kosovo Police Service. In this way, the parallel Serb structures were strengthened (ICG 2008, 3). The political elites that represented these structures were directly legitimized by Serbia, with no need for internal legitimacy from and accountability to the local Kosovo Serbs. Between 2000 and 2012 Serbia spent about half a million euro a day to finance these structures. In 2012 and 2013 alone, Serbia paid 634 million euro from its state budget to finance parallel structures in Kosovo. An investigation by B92 TV station found that although these funds were supposed to be devoted to building roads, bridges, buildings and to paying salaries for Kosovo Serbs, a sizable proportion of these funds was misused and 'almost none of this money actually reached those to whom it was assigned and for whom it was really needed' (Andric 2014). The Serbian political elite was directly involved in the manipulation of these funds. Since Serbia was interested in instrumentalising Kosovo Serbs, it did not hold their political elite to account. Similarly to the Kosovo Albanian political elite, Serbia has built its clientelist networks without addressing the essential needs of the local Kosovo Serbs.

The objective of the EU-facilitated 'dialogue for normalisation of relations' has been to solve the conflict between Kosovo and Serbia. Normalization as a process implies different things for different parties. For Kosovo, the process of normalization implies the integration of the northern municipalities under Kosovo's jurisdiction, the dismantling of parallel structures and the expectation that the latter will recognize the state of Kosovo. For Serbia, Kosovo remains both an issue of domestic and foreign policy. The Constitution of Serbia considers Kosovo as an integral part of Serbia, whereas it deals with Kosovo as a foreign policy concern through its 'Office for Kosovo and Metohija'. Normalization means the derecognition of Kosovo's independence, preventing Kosovo's membership in international organizations and the maintenance of frozen conflict, in particular in the northern municipalities dominated by Serbs and controlled by Belgrade (ICG 2013, 5; Obradović-Wochnik and Wochnik 2012). In fact, Serbia's position on normalization implies normalization of the status quo, keeping the conflict alive, and the normalization of the discourse that the political status of Kosovo remains an unsettled issue. For the EU, the process of normalization implies moving Kosovo and Serbia closer to the EU as an opportunity to overcome disagreements and guarantee regional stability.

In October 2012, a meeting between prime ministers Hashim Thaçi and Ivica Dačić, launched the dialogue at the political level and after ten rounds of talks mediated by the High Representative of the Union for Foreign and Security Policy Catherine Ashton, on 19 April 2013, Kosovo and Serbia signed The First Agreement of Principles Governing the Normalization of Relations. The agreement aimed, *inter alia*, at accommodating the interests of Kosovo-Serbs, dismantling the parallel structures, establishing an association/community of Serb majority municipalities and organizing elections in the northern municipalities (Beha 2015). The representatives of Kosovo argued that through this agreement Serbia was *de facto* recognizing Kosovo as a state, whereas representatives of the opposition in Kosovo argued that the agreement challenged the functionality and the multi-ethnic character of Kosovo. The agreements were written in an ambiguous language, which meant that each party would be able to (mis-) interpret it according to its own political interests.

The 2018 EU Strategy on the Western Balkan countries urged an effective and comprehensive normalization of Belgrade-Pristina relations through the EU-facilitated dialogue stressing that a 'comprehensive, legally binding normalisation agreement is urgent and crucial so that Serbia and Kosovo can advance on their respective European paths' (EC 2018, 7). Kosovo and Serbia, however, have not yet reached a final and legally binding agreement. Although the Kosovo-Albanian political elite seeks recognition from the government of Serbia, the latter has not only categorically rejected this, but it has also made a sustained effort to thwart Kosovo's membership in any international organizations and lobbied to withdraw Kosovo's recognition by other states as well as to prevent new recognitions. With no positive prospects in sight, political elites from both Kosovo and Serbia benefit from the normalization discourse that gives them legitimacy to act as agents of their respective peoples. External recognition as their country's key negotiators allows them to mask authoritarian practices at home. While the dispute between Serbia and Kosovo is kept alive, authoritarian governing tendencies thrive in both countries.

6. Europeanization rhetoric as an enabler of soft competitive authoritarianism

The overwhelming majority of Kosovo's political elite has built a political career capitalizing on the empty rhetoric of 'Euro-Atlantic integration'. In the last decade, three post-independence prime ministers who came from three different political parties, the PDK, LDK, and AAK, have promised visa liberalization for Kosovo citizens. Only one year after the declaration of independence, leaders of all political parties in Kosovo pledged free movement in the Schengen area, at a time when Kosovo had not even accepted a roadmap regarding the visa liberalization process. In 2019 Kosovo's citizens remain the most isolated people in Europe even though visa liberalization for Kosovo's citizens has remained a key electoral promise across all political parties.

Political elites have used the visa liberalization card as one of the methods for attracting votes, even though the process is not dependent only on Kosovo's institutions, but also on those of the EU and EU member states. The Kosovar political elite has manipulated the visa liberalization discourse representing it to the public as a 'historical event' towards European integration rather than as a very first step in a long process of democratizing reforms together with the eradication of irrelevant and authoritarian ruling practices.

The 2003 Thessaloniki Declaration offered a European perspective to all governments in the Western Balkans. By omitting a decision on Kosovo's political status, the international community's stated policy goal was that political status should be resolved within 'the European perspective', a euphemism that could not be refused by Serbia or by Kosovo. This euphemism of the 'European solution' for Kosovo did not actually imply a solution in view of its continued international interim administration. Kosovo did not fulfil the basic criteria for aspiring members to join the EU: a democratic sovereign state, underpinned by the rule of law and with a free market economic system. Therefore, the so-called European solution did not imply reaching a positive outcome in terms of the status itself, but ensuring that when the status issues were settled, both Pristina and Belgrade would be closer to the European Union than before, and have moved in the right direction' (Yannis 2009, 164). Sixteen years on, Kosovo is not progressing in terms of its EU integration process. Despite the fact that EU countries remain divided over Kosovo's statehood, the EU has continued to play a crucial role in the country enabling Kosovo to reach a Stabilization and Association Agreement (hereafter SAA) in 2016 and leading the dialogue with Serbia. However, it is not clear whether the EU presence in Kosovo is leading to the construction of a future EU sovereign member state or whether the EU is negotiating forms through which a non-sovereign state can join (Hajrullahu 2019, 116). Although the SAA is the first important agreement Kosovo has signed with the EU, Kosovo is not treated as a state. Gëzim Visoka argues that:

> Kosovo has negotiated the SAA under self-defeating conditions and under the pressure from the EU. Like any legal or political document, the SAA is written by the EU and accepted by Kosovo almost completely without any change. The most painful part of this agreement, which has never been sufficiently discussed in Kosovo, is the acceptance of a clause mentioning that no part of the SAA should be understood as recognition of Kosovo by EU institutions and member states (Visoka 2019).

The progress of Serbia and Kosovo towards European integration is inextricably linked to the process of normalization between the two countries. In Resolution 64/298 of the UN General Assembly through which the EU was authorized to facilitate the dialogue between Serbia and Kosovo, it is underlined that the 'dialogue would be to promote cooperation, achieve progress on the path to the European Union and improve the lives of the people' (UNGA 2010). Given that the issue of a final agreement between Kosovo and Serbia is considered by the EU as the key to bringing peace to the region, for the Kosovo political elite international legitimacy takes primacy over the internal legitimacy. These elites have constantly misused the rhetoric of 'international friends' of Kosovo and often have justified their policies using the discourse of 'requirements coming from international friends.'

Armed with external legitimacy from the EU and the US, the 'reformist' political elites in Kosovo have not been reluctant to harshly criticize either the opposition or civil society for their alleged 'anti-European or anti-American' approach. This approach has results in attacks on opposition forces and civil society, which have an interest in improving governance within the country or improving the Government of Kosovo's negotiating position with Serbia. For instance, in September 2018 in an interview for Klan Kosova TV the leader of the PDK and the speaker of Kosovo Assembly Kadri Veseli emphasized that 'pro-Russians and pro-Serbians are all those who try to divide the people of Kosovo, and who promote ideas that put in doubt our partnership with the international community, specifically with the United States of America' (Klan Kosova TV 2018). Consequently, all those political and social forces that criticize any proposal of Kosovo's 'international friends' can be potentially tagged as 'pro-Russians' and pro-Serbs'.

Prime Minister Ramush Haradinaj employed the same discourse against the Special Prosecutor Elez Blakaj, by accusing him of being willing to leave Kosovo out of the Schengen visa liberalization. Blakaj was conducting investigations as part of the so-called Veterans case in which many people are alleged to have falsely obtained the status of KLA war veterans. The Kosovo government published a report identifying 46,230 individuals who had obtained certificates as war veterans. Blakaj's investigations suggested that 19,060 veterans had been added to the list falsely, thus causing Kosovo's budget a loss of 38.8 million euros annually. Blakaj investigated these names along with some of the KLA war leaders who had enabled this practice. Prime Minister Haradinaj had set a limit of 30 days for Blakaj's investigation and asked him to report findings to his office, an unlawful practice breaching the constitutional principle of separation of judicial and executive powers. In August 2018, Prosecutor Blakaj resigned and fled Kosovo on the grounds that he had been put under direct pressure from the state prosecutor and some powerful politicians in Kosovo concerning his investigations into the case of veterans. Blakaj was also one of the prosecutors investigating the 'Pronto case', which exposed evidence of state capture by the PDK's political elite (KLI 2018). This was a clear-cut case of political interference in the justice system. These practices prevent Kosovo from meeting the rule of law standards required by the EU.

From Kosovo's internal perspective, the EU has for a long time ignored the fact that local elites govern in an undemocratic way. Only in its November 2016 Communication on enlargement did the European Commission explicitly mention 'clear symptoms and varying degrees of state capture' (EC 2016). Similarly the 2018 EU Strategy on the Western Balkans states that all Western Balkan 'countries show clear elements of state capture, including links with organized crime and corruption at all levels of government and administration, as well as a strong entanglement of public and private interests' (EC 2018, 3). The promise of EU membership for the Western Balkan countries appears to be the only effective driver of further economic and political reforms.

From a regional perspective, the European conditionality of 'normalization before integration' seeks to use the carrot of advancement towards integration into the EU as a means of solving the conflict between Kosovo and Serbia. The 2018 EU Enlargement Strategy underlines the fact that without full and comprehensive normalization, lasting stability in the region cannot be achieved (EC 2018). However, Kosovo's progress towards potential EU membership remains conditioned by several factors. First, Kosovo's independence is not recognized by five EU member states. Second, Kosovo's governing capacity to implement meaningful reforms remains limited. Third, the political climate in the EU is not favourable for the EU's enlargement, due to the uncontrolled migration into the EU area and the rise of radical right-wing political forces with their more isolationist policy positions (USAID 2017).

In spite of the hopeful promise that the Europeanization process would resolve the dispute between Kosovo and Serbia and help to stimulate the democratization of both countries, this promise remains unmet. On one hand, Kosovo has failed to 'Europeanize' its domestic politics and to institutionalize the formal and informal norms and values of democracy. In addition, its foreign policy has been reduced to normalizing relations with Serbia. On the other hand, Serbia has failed to 'Europeanize' its foreign policy in relation to Kosovo as it continues to insist that Kosovo is an integral part of Serbia. A peace agreement between the two countries could open up a new peace chapter in the region and also increase EU pressure for substantive democratic reforms in both countries and beyond as well as possibly changing the autocratic practices of political elites. But this still appears to be a distant prospect.

7. Conclusions

Since the 1999 international intervention, Kosovo has experienced several concomitant multi-layered transitions. The political elites, in particular those emerging from the Kosovo war who enjoyed the rewards for liberating the country, have successfully stabilized their clientelist networks, while impeding and controlling the economic and political transition to a functioning democratic system based on a market economy and the rule of law. In the absence of full clarity over the country's future status, elites have exploited the UNMIK agenda of ensuring stability to put themselves in a position where they have access to power and public resources. In spite of massive international investment in the rebuilding of the post-1999 Kosovo, this did not fundamentally change the governance culture, which is characterized by the use of public resources for private gain and unaccountability to the people. By (mis-) using the macro-politics of the 'final political status settlement', 'the finalization of statehood', and finally the empty and vague rhetoric of 'Euro-Atlantic integration' the very same political entrepreneurs have managed since 1999 to successfully gain *internal power* and *external legitimacy*.

The political elites in Kosovo presented themselves as being 'Reformist and Europeanisers' well placed to maintain internal stability and contribute to regional stability. The results of their soft competitive authoritarian (un-)democratic governance and their real contribution to maintain the negative stability could not be glorified. During UNMIK's administration, the corrupt practices of the political elites in Kosovo – – though with limited scope due to their limited power – – were tolerated as long as they did not confront the objectives of the international administration of maintaining the status quo, rhetorically approving the politics of multi-ethnicity and the pursuit of the 'wait and see' policy, until the decision about the final political status of the country had been agreed. Thus, political elite cycles in post 1999 Kosovo have incrementally built their clientelist networks. After the 2008 independence, when those elite cycles took charge of the state institutions, though with a continuing EULEX presence and the ICO as a temporary international supervisory body, they managed to establish and enhance their clientelist networks. This resulted in a captured state as demonstrated in the exemplary 2016 PDK-led 'Pronto-Affair'. After 2008 the political elite began to extend its influence by capturing and (mis-) using a number of state institutions, independent agencies and public companies for their own private gain. The same elite that controls wealth distribution successfully prevents the Parliament from exercising its supervisory role over the government, and result in the increment establishment of what we have named here as *soft competitive authoritarianism*.

The international euphemistic promise of a 'European perspective' and the local empty rhetoric of 'Euro-Atlantic integration' have not resulted in a fair democratic and socially just system based on the rule of law in Kosovo. By effectively making external legitimacy more important than local legitimacy the international community silenced potential agents of the democratization and Europeanization processes in Kosovo and beyond. Furthermore, the prospect of being socialized in an extractive system has prevented the emergence of a 'new generation' of political elites who can build functional and accountable democratic governing structures based on the values of inclusive governance, rule of law, and the increased accountability of local elites to public opinion. The above conclusions suggest that the EU ought to pursue a more proactive and results-based approach to Kosovo's institutions as part of its EU integration process and cease to legitimize authoritarian governing practices for the sake of maintaining stability.

Notes

1. The Balkan Contact Group was established in London on 25 April 1994 and composed of: United States of America, Great Britain, France, Germany, Italy and the Russian Federation. The aim of the Balkan Contact Group was to create a coordinated Balkan policy for the states represented in this forum.
2. United Nations Security Council (UNSC). 1999. Resolution 1244 (1999). https://undocs.org/S/RES/1244(1999).
3. Partia Demokratike e Kosovës (PDK).
4. Ushtria Çlirimtare e Kosovës (UÇK).
5. Lidhja Demokratike e Kosovës (LDK).
6. Aleanca për Ardhmërinë e Kosovës (AAK).
7. Shërbimi Informativ i Kosovës (SHIK).
8. NISMA për Kosovën.

Disclosure statement

No potential conflict of interest was reported by the authors.

ORCID

Arben Hajrullahu (iD) http://orcid.org/0000-0002-7435-435X

References

Ahram, I.A., and J.P. Goode. 2016. Researching authoritarianism in the discipline of democracy. *Social Science Quarterly* 97, no. 4: 834–49. doi: 10.1111/ssqu.12340.

Andric, G. 2014. Millions earmarked for Kosovo Serbs 'Wasted'. *BalkanInsight*, September 23. http://www.balkaninsight.com/en/article/serbia-misspends-millions-aimed-to-help-kosovo/1589/54.

Beha, A. 2015. Disputes over the 15-point agreement on normalisation of relations between Kosovo and Serbia. *Nationalities Papers: the Journal of Nationalism and Ethnicity* 43, no. 1: 102–21. doi: 10.1080/00905992.2014.990367.

Beha, A., and G. Selaci. 2018. Statebuilding without exit strategy in Kosovo: Stability, clientelism, and corruption. *Region: Regional Studies of Russia, Eastern Europe, and Central Asia* 7, no. 2: 97–123. doi: 10.1353/reg.2018.0018.

Bieber, F. 2018. Patterns of competitive authoritarianism in the Western Balkans. *East European Politics* 34, no. 3: 337–54. doi: 10.1080/21599165.2018.1490272.

Bunce, V., and M. Mcfaul, eds. 2010. *Democracy and authoritarianism in the post-communist world*. Cambridge: Cambridge University Press.

Capusela, A. 2011. Eulex in Kosovo: A shining symbol of incompetence. *The Guardian*, April 9. https://www.theguardian.com/commentisfree/2011/apr/09/eulex-kosovo-eu-mission.

Capussela, A. 2015. *State-building in Kosovo: Democracy, corruption and the EU in the Balkans*. London: I B. Tauris.

Chehabi, H., and J. Linz, eds. 1998. *Sultanistic regimes*. Baltimore: Johns Hopkins University Press.

Chesterman, S. 2004. *You, the people: The United Nations, transitional administration, and state-building*. Oxford: Oxford University Press.

Collier, D., and S. Levitsky. 1997. Democracy with adjectives: Conceptual innovation in comparative research. *World Politics* 49, no. 3: 430–51. doi: 10.1353/wp.1997.0009.

Constitutional Court of Kosovo. 2011. Aktgjykim lidhur me imunitetin e deputetëve të Kuvendit të Republikës së Kosovës, Presidentit të Republikës së Kosovës, dhe anëtarëve të Qeverisë së Republikës së Kosovës. http://gjk-ks.org/wp-content/uploads/vendimet/KO98-11_SHQ_AKTGJYKIM.pdf.

D'aspremont, J. 2007. Regulating statehood: The Kosovo status settlement. *Leiden Journal of International Law* 20, no. 3: 649–68. doi: 10.1017/S092215650700430X.

Democracy for Development (D4D). 2013. *A Class of its Own: Patronage and its impact on Social Mobility in Kosovo*. Pristina: Democracy for Development Institute. http://d4d-ks.org/wp-content/uploads/2013/05/D4D_PI_2_ENG_WEB.pdf.

EULEX. 2014. Vendimi i Gjykatës së Apelit për rastin 'MTPT 1'. Press Release. http://www.eulex-kosovo.eu/al/pressreleases/0571.php.

European Commission (EC). 2016. *Kosovo 2016 report*. Brussels: European Commission. https://ec.europa.eu/neighbourhood-enlargement/sites/near/files/pdf/key_documents/2016/20161109_report_kosovo.pdf.

European Commission (EC). 2018. *European Commission, Communication from the Commission to the European Parliament, the Council, the European Economic and Social Committee and the Committee of the Regions. A credible enlargement perspective for and enhanced EU engagement with the Western Balkans*. 65 final, Strasbourg. https://ec.europa.eu/commission/sites/beta-political/files/communication-credible-enlargement-perspective-western-balkans_en.pdf.

Galtung, J. 2012. *Peace, positive and negative. The encyclopedia of peace psychology*. 1st ed. Edited by D.J. Christie. Oxford: Blackwell Publishing Ltd.

Gashi, Z. 2011. Qeveria i drejtohet Kushtetueses. Radio Evropa e Lirë. https://www.evropaelire.org/a/24271091.html.

Hajrullahu, A. 2011. The missing 'Functional elites' and the challenge of democratisation. In *20 years after the collapse of communism. Expectations, achievements and disillusions of 1989*, ed. N. Hayoz, L. Jesien, and D. Koleva, 167–76. Bern: Peter Lang.

Hajrullahu, A. 2019. The Serbia Kosovo dispute and the European integration perspective. *European Foreign Affairs Review* 24, no. 1: 101–20.

Hoxha, A., D. Milovanović, and Y. Buzhala. 2016. Historical and socio-economic context of informal relations between political and economic actors in Kosovo. In *Informal power networks, political patronage and clientelism in Serbia and Kosovo*, ed. S. Cvejic, 77–86. Belgrade: SecCons.

Insajder. 2018. Fatmir Limaj dy herë u lirua nga akuzat për krime lufte, tash lirohet edhe nga akuzat për korrupsion. https://insajderi.com/fatmir-limaj-dy-u-lirua-nga-akuzat-per-krime-lufte-tash-lirohet-edhe-nga-akuzat-per-korrupsion/.

International Crisis Group (ICG). 2003. *Thessaloniki and after: The EU and Serbia, Montenegro and Kosovo*. Sarajevo/Brussels: International Crisis Group (ICG).

International Crisis Group (ICG). 2008. *Kosovo's fragile transition*. Europe Report, no. 196. Pristina/Brussels: International Crisis Group (ICG).

International Crisis Group (ICG). 2010. *The rule of law in independent Kosovo*. Pristina: Europe Report no. 204.

International Crisis Group (ICG). 2013. *Serbia and Kosovo: The path to normalisation*. Pristina: Europe Report no. 223. Pristina.

Judah, T. 2008. *Kosovo: What everyone needs to know*. Oxford: Oxford University Press.

Kajtazi, V. 2016. Dosja e shefave: Shteti në dorë të nëntokës. https://Insajderi.Com/Hulumtime/Dosja-E-Shefave-Shteti-Ne-Dore-Te-Nentokes/.

Kapidžić, D. 2020. The rise of illiberal politics in Southeast Europe. *Southeast European and Black Sea Studies* 20, no. 1: xx.

Ker-Lindsay, J. 2009. The emergence of 'Meditration' in international peacemaking. *Ethnopolitics: Formerly Global Review of Ethnopolitics* 8, no. 2: 223–33. doi: 10.1080/17449050902894995.

King, I., and W. Mason. 2006. *Peace at any price: How the world failed Kosovo*. New York: Cornell University Press.

Klan Kosova TV. 2018. Veseli tregon cilët sipas tij janë pro-rusë dhe pro-serbë. September 3. https://www.youtube.com/watch?v=FIGMmLIIQDg.

Kosovar Center for Security Studies (KCSS). 2018. *Kosovo security barometer*. 8th ed. Pristina: Kosovar Centre for Security Studies (KCSS).

Kosovo Law Institute (KLI). 2018. *Political interferences in the politicized prosecutorial system, alarm for the need of vetting in the police, prosecution and courts*. Pristina: KLI.

Kostovicova, D. 2008. Legitimacy and international administration: The Ahtisaari settlement for Kosovo from a human security perspective. *International Peacekeeping* 15, no. 5: 631–47. doi: 10.1080/13533310802396160.

Leposhtica, L. 2015. Prokurori në Rastin Limaj: Korrupsioni Kancer që Dëmton Kosovën. Kallxo.com. https://kallxo.com/prokurori-ne-rastin-limaj-korrupsioni-kancer-qe-demton-kosoven/.

Levitsky, S., and L.A. Way. 2002. Elections Without Democracy: The rise of competitive authoritarianism. *Journal of Democracy* 13, no. 2: 51–65. doi: 10.1353/jod.2002.0026.

Levitsky, S., and L.A. Way. 2010. *Competitive authoritarianism: Hybrid regimes after the Cold War.* Cambridge: Cambridge University Press.

Obradović-Wochnik, J., and A. Wochnik. 2012. Europeanising the 'Kosovo Question': Serbia's policies in the context of EU integration. *West European Politics* 35, no. 5: 1158–81. doi: 10.1080/01402382.2012.706415.

Organization for Security and Co-operation in Europe (OSCE). 2003. *Parallel structures in Kosovo.* Pristina: Organization for Security and Co-operation in Europe (OSCE), Mission in Kosovo.

Ottaway, M. 2003. *Democracy challenged: The rise of semi-authoritarianism.* Washington DC: Carnegie Endowment For International Peace.

Papadimitriou, D., and P. Petrov. 2012. Whose rule, whose law? Contested statehood, external leverage and the European Union's rule of law mission in Kosovo. *Journal of Common Market Studies* 50, no. 5: 746–63. doi: 10.1111/j.1468-5965.2012.02257.x.

Pevehouse, C.J. 2002. Democracy from the outside-in? International organizations and democratization. *International Organization* 56, no. 3: 515–49. doi: 10.1162/002081802760199872.

Schedler, A. 2002. The nested game of democratization by elections. *International Political Science Review* 23, no. 1: 103–22. doi: 10.1177/0192512102023001006.

Selaci, G. 2017. *Republika në Udhëkryq: Kosova në dekadën e parë të pavarësisë.* Skopje: Logos-A.

Tadić, K., and A. Elbasani. 2018. State-building and patronage networks: How political parties embezzled the bureaucracy in post-war Kosovo. *Southeast European and Black Sea Studies* 18, no. 2: 1–18. doi: 10.1080/14683857.2018.1474551.

Tansey, O. 2007. Democratization without a state: Democratic regime-building in Kosovo. *Democratization* 14, no. 1: 129–50. doi: 10.1080/13510340601024355.

Tansey, O. 2009. *Regime-building: Democratization and international administration.* Oxford: Oxford University Press.

United Nations General Assembly (UNGA). 2010. Resolution adopted by the General Assembly: 64/298. Request for an advisory opinion of the International Court of Justice on whether the unilateral declaration of independence of Kosovo is in accordance with international law. A/RES/64/298. https://www.securitycouncilreport.org/wp-content/uploads/ROL%20A%20RES64%20298.pdf.

United Nations Interim Mission in Kosovo (UNMIK). 2003. Standards For Kosovo. Pristina. http://www.securitycouncilreport.org/atf/cf/%7B65BFCF9B-6D27-4E9C-8CD3-CF6E4FF96FF9%7D/Kos%20Standards.pdf.

United Nations Security Council (UNSC). 2004. United Nations Security Council Letter Dated 17 November 2004 from the Secretary-General addressed to the President of the Security Council. S/2004/932.

United States Agency for International Development (USAID). 2017. *Kosovo Political Economy Analysis. Final Report.* Pristina.

Visoka, G. 2019. Monologu Politik mes BE-së dhe Kosovës. https://sbunker.net/osf-alumni/89833/monologu-politik-mes-be-se-dhe-kosoves/.

Visoka, G., and O. Richmond. 2016. After liberal peace? From failed state-building to an emancipatory peace in Kosovo. *International Studies Perspectives* 1, no. 20: 1–20.

Yannis, A. 2009. The politics and geopolitics of the status of Kosovo: The circle is never round. *Southeast European and Black Sea Studies* 9, no. 2: 161–70. doi: 10.1080/14683850902723470.

Zakaria, F. 1997. The rise of illiberal democracy. *Foreign Affairs* 76, no. 6: 22–43. doi: 10.2307/20048274.

Zaum, D. 2009. The norms and politics of exit: Ending postconflict transitional administrations. *Carnegie Council for Ethics in International Affairs* 23, no. 2: 189–208. doi: 10.1111/j.1747-7093.2009.00206.x.

Žižek, S., and A. Hamza. 2013. *From myth to symptom: The case of Kosovo.* Pristina: Kolektivi Materializmi Dialektik.

Influencing votes, winning elections: clientelist practices and private funding of electoral campaigns in Albania

Gentiana Kera [iD] and Armanda Hysa [iD]

ABSTRACT
The present article is part of a broader effort to understand and analyse the relationship between formal and informal norms and institutions in the Balkans. Free and fair elections are a central component of any functioning democracy and, in the case of Albania, an essential element of its EU accession process. Elections can also be affected by political clientelism, which puts their outcomes' credibility into question. Political clientelism is a principal sector of informal relations and practices and informal and/or illegal funding of electoral campaigns are identified as its key mechanisms. This article addresses a number of issues related to clientelist practices and private funding of electoral campaigns, focusing on the general parliamentary elections of June 2017. The main research question investigates the ways in which private funding of electoral campaigns works in practice. Based on data gathered through ethnographic fieldwork, interviews, reports on the electoral process, and other secondary sources, we argue that informal clientelist practices permeating private funding of electoral campaigns enable political parties to further and strengthen clientelist relations and to influence the electoral result.

1. Introduction

The conduct of free and fair elections as a central component of a functional democracy remains an essential element in Albania's EU accession process. The pre-election period of the last general parliamentary elections in Albania (February–May 2017) was tense, with the main opposition party boycotting the parliament and blocking the EU-related reform on justice over serious concerns that the subsequent June elections would involve fraud by the governing Socialist Party. This decision was based on the opposition's claims that the local elections held on 11 September 2016 in Dibra (region in north-eastern Albania) were undermined by informal practices in procuring votes as well as by clientelism, vote buying, and other illegal activities and practices. The Democratic Party announced its boycott on 18 February 2017, and a protest tent was erected in front of the government building. All opposition parties, as well as coalition parties were invited to join. Their primary demand was the resignation of PM Edi Rama, and the formation of a technical government that would take action against informal and illegal practices undermining local elections, thus paving the way for genuinely free and fair elections. After three months of failed talks, negotiations led by the US State Department representative, Hoyt Brian Yee, produced a deal on May 18th, marking the end of the parliamentary boycott by the DP. General parliamentary elections took place on 24 June 2017.[1]The Albanian electoral code has been regularly modified and refined just before elections until 2015. The last two general parliamentary elections (2013, 2017) were deemed free and fair from a formal point of view, yet scepticism remains. On the one hand, the EU requests evidence that reforms in the political and judicial fields are sustainable and not merely formal adoptions of EU standards, including elections. On the other hand, many local actors indicate that such reforms, especially electoral ones, are undermined despite their formal compliance with rules and procedures.

Campaign funding is a crucial issue in all elections. Political parties and candidates are increasingly relying on donations for effective campaigns, which raises concerns about dubious financial sources offering funds in exchange of favouritism, resulting in corrupt practices and misuse of influence through state institutions. Money fuels the main mechanisms of the clientelist system.

Our main research question concerns the ways in which private funding of electoral campaign takes place. What are the donation procedures, what are the donors' expectations, and how do informal or illegal practices of private funding impact the state of democracy, especially free and fair elections? Based on ethnographic fieldwork data gathered between February and November 2017, including 23 semi structured interviews and 12 non-structured conversations, as well as reports on the electoral process and other secondary sources we argue that informal clientelist practices permeating private funding of electoral campaigns enable political parties to strengthen clientelist relations and to influence electoral results. In discussing private funding we do not imply that it is always a source for clientelist ties between businesses or individuals and political parties, but we argue that undeclared informal private funds used for electoral purposes, which are often impossible to track, can distort elections, and they constitute a key mechanism of electoral and political clientelism. When all such mechanisms are considered together the electoral process and its outcome may be said to be negatively affected, thus casting doubts on the fairness of political completion.

In the following section we introduce the theoretical model developed by the INFORM project research team,[2] which seeks to explain not only the ways in which formal and informal rules, institutions, and practices are interconnected but also the gaps between rules and regulations and how things are done in practice. Such gaps undermine various reforms necessary for the EU integration process, and this article constitutes an effort to grasp one of these gaps.

The third section deals with legal norms regulating the organizing of private funding, and the importance of financial transparency for the outcome of elections. The data analyses in the fourth section address concerns with the lack of transparency as reported by various monitoring bodies. Data gathered from informants, insiders of three main party structures, and other sources indicate the disproportion between actual and declared costs of electoral campaigns, and the reasons involved. The final section concludes that undeclared private money or services during election campaigns augment the risk of future political favours for actors involved.

2. Theoretical considerations and methodology

Our analysis is developed within the INFORM project theoretical model (Figure 1). In the broader picture of informal relations and practices, political clientelism constitutes a principal sector, while informal and/or illegal funding of electoral campaigns are considered as key mechanisms within political clientelism.

Our project's key research question was to what extent does the transposition of EU rules and regulations into national legal, political, and economic systems lead to substantive changes in practices and procedures, or do they remain 'empty shells' with little influence in social life (Gordy and Efendic 2019, 8). A starting premise for the analysis was that the problem is not informality *per se*, rather, '*the gap between formal legal resolutions and informal practices in the everyday life*' (Gordy and Efendic 2019, 8). According to Gordy and Efendic (2019, 10–11) such gaps represent unregulated spaces in the system where politicians and individuals in a position of power take advantage of public resources, goods, and services for personal gain.

Figure 1. A theoretical model of interconnection between formal and informal relations.[3]

This theoretical frame aims to transcend approaches that either condemn or celebrate informality. A key effort to overcome this dualism was made by Helmke and Levitsky (2004), but as Gordy and Efendić note they still maintain the dualism of good and bad informality, and 'the preference for state-based solutions that characterized the literature that precedes it' (2019, 12).

Our theoretical model views formal constraints as products of adopting formal rules, which are based on the EU *acquis communautaire*. Examples of laws passed in accordance with the EU *acquis communautaire* but not entirely implemented in the Western Balkans indicate that regulations–both formal and informal–do not automatically become constraints. Rather, to become effective in practice they must pass through what we call an 'enforcement belt' – the process of interpretation, designing mechanisms of implementation, and positive and negative sanctions that enable their effectiveness. The upper part of the figure represents 'the formal' and the lower part 'the informal'. The enforcement belt therefore implies not only the complexity of formal institutional mechanisms of interpretation and execution, but also the complexity of informal mechanisms, such as face to face a/symmetrical relationships and a set of networks that translate informal norms into informal practices/institutions. The continuum at the middle represents the space where formal and informal mechanisms of interpretation and implementation interfere, thereby creating gaps between the ways in which 'things ought to be done' and 'how they are actually done.'

There is a shared agreement that political clientelism is a long-lasting, dyadic, and face to face relationship between a patron and a client (Hilgers 2011, 567–588). It is defined by 'reciprocity, voluntarism, exploitation, domination and asymmetry ... beneficial for both patron and client' (Kitschelt 2000, 849). Apart from its 'populist appeal', political clientelism has been considered a mode of vertical inclusion. Yet, it differs from populism (Auyero 2012, 97) in being a particular form of party-voter linkage (Tomsa and Ufen 2013, 4; Auyero 2012, 97), whereby holders of political offices distribute public resources, direct payments, access to jobs, goods, and services (otherwise unavailable for those without contacts) in the form of favours, in exchange for political support at the polls (Kitschelt and Wilkinson 2007; Auyero 2012, 97; Wantchekon 2003, 400).

Political clientelism is then a set of informal practices and relations implemented by informal mechanisms through non-official channels, but also through formal ones, especially in cases when public resources are used for electoral purposes. Bliznakovski et al. (2017, 6) have identified inducements (including vote-buying, employment, and selective distribution of social benefits), and enforcement mechanisms (carousel voting, photographing the ballot, and compiling lists of 'guaranteed voters') that transform clientelist practices into informal constrains in Western Balkans societies.

Electoral political competition may be seen as a set of formal mechanisms within the enforcement belt, which transform the rules and regulations defining a democratic and pluralistic system into institutions (the upper part of the model). Clientelist informal practices that permeate this set of mechanisms (elections) affect the essence of such transformation, and therefore use the implementation belt to transform these formal rules into formal institutions modelled by political clientelism (lower part of the model).

Within the electoral process, the private funding of electoral campaigns constitutes a mechanism that enables such political institutions (parties) to reach the voters without however guaranteeing success, election victories, etc. The electoral code is the formal rule that regulates the way in which this mechanism should operate (upper part of the model). Informal/illegal funding of electoral campaigns can thus be identified as an implementing informal mechanism that transforms informal deals into informal constrains (post electoral clientelist partnerships – lower part of the model). Political parties obtain through such a mechanism the capital to buy votes (short term clientelism), promise fiscal (or other) favours, and secure business partners loyal to the party after landing a position in public offices (long term clientelism) that are capable of influencing voters (e.g., employees). By influencing the election outcome they affect the very concept of political representativeness which is essential to a fair and competitive process, thereby deepening the gap between normative and actual elections.

For our empirical research on clientelist electoral practices we rely on data gathered through ethnographic fieldwork between February and November 2017. When using political ethnography we have in mind its potential to provide insights into the relations between political institutions, their sets of practices, and day-to-day interactions between political actors and citizens (see Baiocchi and Connor 2008, 140; Auyero 2006, 257–259; Adler-Nissen 2016, 13). In the case of political clientelism, it is difficult to find evidence through documents or quantitative methods, therefore ethnography provides us with unique insights from both citizens and activists of political parties, who sometimes act as brokers in those relations.

The data were gathered through ethnographic fieldwork, as well as semi-structured, in-depth interviews and conversations with voters. We conducted five semi-structured interviews with active members of local structures of three main political parties in Albania, eighteen semi-structured interviews with individuals on their decision to vote, before and after elections, as well as twelve non-structured conversations with individuals on their voting intentions. The interviewees were from Tirana, Kavaja, Tropoja, Erseka, Korça, and Elbasan. All interviews were conducted in confidentiality, and the names of the interviewees are not disclosed. Other primary sources include media and monitoring reports on elections, published by both national and international organizations. In support of the analyses we also rely on two interviews with Albanian experts of the European Integration process, conducted as part of a wider research within INFORM, in addition to quantitative data from the survey conducted in the framework of the INFORM project which included 919 respondents in Albania.[4]

3. Legal regulations on electoral campaign funding in Albania – the formal rule

The financing of political parties has received considerable attention by scholars as the political completion between parties and individual politicians plays a central role in the functioning of democracy. The relation between money and politics is analysed in a volume edited by Burnell and Ware (2017), which investigates the funding of political competition among parties and politicians in new or emerging democracies, comparing their experience with the formative years of democratization in several established democracies of North America and Western Europe. Burnell argues that 'the ways in which political finance impact on how parties and politicians involve the party membership, connect with affiliated bodies, and relate to voters and the general public are also matters of profound importance to the quality of democracy' (Burnell 2017, 8–9). Although the impact of political finance on democracy does not represent the greatest threat, given that the political parties' effectiveness can weaken for many other reasons, it can be more difficult to enforce legal controls on political finance in new democracies where the rule of law is weak or the governance capabilities are limited (Burnell 2017, 10).

According to the Albanian Electoral Code, electoral campaigns are supported through public funds released by the State Budget to political parties registered as electoral subjects; through income generated by the electoral subject itself as per the legislation in force; through gifts in monetary value, goods, or services rendered; and loans taken by the political parties.[5] About 95% of the electoral campaign fund is distributed, as per the Parliament's decision, among the political parties registered as electoral subjects that received no less than 0.5% of the valid votes in the previous elections[6]. The remaining 5% is distributed among the rest of the subjects. The Central Election Committee is responsible for distributing the electoral campaign budget based on the number of votes they received in previous elections.

The enhancement of campaign financing transparency has been a key OSCE/ODIHR recommendation in all previous election reports. On 22 May 2017, various amendments were adopted into the law of Political Parties, the Law on Audio-visual Media, and the Criminal Code, which introduced new regulations on campaign finance, campaigning, political advertising in broadcast media, new electoral offences, while increasing sanctions for existing ones. Changes in the Law on Political Parties, for example, required political parties to submit campaign donations and spending records within 60 days after the election, and placed limits on campaign spending. Amendments to the Criminal Code and Law on Political Parties stiffened penalties, including imprisonment, for vote buying and selling, and other criminal electoral conduct. New criminal offences in the Criminal Code included abuse of public functions for electoral activities, and misuse of other individuals' identification documents. In addition, more detailed prohibitions on vote buying and selling were introduced (OSCE/ODIHR 2017, 5).

There are various legal prohibitions regarding public and private funding of political parties. Article 88 of the Electoral Code specifically prohibits any use of resources of any central or local public institution for campaign purposes, as well as the recruitment, dismissal, release, movement or transfer in duty in public institutions or entities during electoral campaigns. Following the agreement of 18 May 2017, the abuse of public function for electoral purposes was included as an offence in the Criminal Code.

The political scene during the transition period has been dominated by the Socialist and Democratic Parties, which has polarized the Albanian political scene and divided the Albanian society. Kajsiu has argued that the ideological and political differences between the two parties has been fading away and that 'the two major parties have increasingly relied on institutional arrangement, clientelistic networks, and polarizing political discourses in order to continue dominating the Albanian political scene' (Kajsiu 2016, 11). Gërxhani and Schram (2009) have argued that the country's cultural and geographical diversity has led to a political environment where clientelistic practices reinforce society's polarization thereby affecting voting behaviour. A possible explanation of the role of clientelism is seen in the fact that formal governmental institutions are still underdeveloped, which enables informal institutions to fill the vacuum.

The largest political parties currently are the Socialist Party, the Democratic Party, and the Socialist Movement for Integration. The 2013 parliamentary elections resulted in a government led by the Socialist Party (SP), bringing about a power shift from the previous government led by the Democratic Party (DP). The left-wing Socialist Party has been in government since 2013, while the Democratic Party and the Socialist Movement for Integration are the main opposition parties. The Albanian parliament has 140 members, elected for a four-year term through a closed list proportional representation system in 12 multi-member electoral districts. In the 2017 elections, the Socialist Party received 74 seats, while the two main opposition parties, the Democratic Party and the Socialist Movement for Integration received 43 and 19 seats, respectively. Other parties with members in the parliament include the Party for Justice, Integration and Unity (three seats), and the Social Democratic Party (one seat).

4. Clientelism and private funding of electoral campaigns – formal and informal practices

While abuse of public resources may be easier to track due to visibility in media and in public documents, private funding of political parties is a much more complicated issue. The electoral code states that private funding of the campaign should not exceed 1,000,000 ALL (Albanian *Lek*) per donor, and the donation must be deposited in the beneficiary party's bank account, opened for this purpose. Companies that have received public funds in excess of 10,000,000 ALL in the two years prior to the election or have participated in more than one public project are not eligible to donate to political parties.[7]

The campaign expenditures of a political party must not be over ten times greater than the highest amount in public funds received by a contestant. However, monitoring and auditing reports of party finances indicate that while political parties never report campaign expenditures higher than this legal limit there are serious concerns that political parties do not declare their income, costs, and campaign expenses. Monitoring reports of certified audits on political parties campaign finances published on the Central Election Commission homepage reflect various problems, including lack of contracts for electoral offices, lack of detailed bills for electoral events and other activities, lack of lobbying contracts, failure to declare electoral meeting expenses, incomplete billing of services related to electoral meetings, and lack of transparency on the number and location of electoral offices (Hysa et al. 2018, 27–28).

The monitoring of electoral campaign expenses would be an important method to enhance political parties' funding transparency. Despite legal improvements, resources for auditing campaign expenditures are limited. For the June 25th parliamentary elections, the Central Elections Committee appointed financial experts to monitor campaign spending. One such expert reports that they faced numerous problems that hindered the monitoring:

> We were appointed for monitoring with delay, just two weeks before the elections. Municipalities divulged electoral office locations with delay. Political parties did not give official written answers about the list of electoral activities planned, which made the monitoring difficult (Manjani 2017).

While arguing that this electoral campaign was more positive than the previous one, political scientist Afrim Krasniqi emphasized that progress in reducing electoral expenses, more accurate financial declarations by political parties or the compromise about less advertising are minimal in comparison with the complex problems of high informality within political parties:

The main electoral funding comes from three sources: direct funding outside of political lines by 'strong' groups in the electoral district, immeasurable funding in goods by different companies or public resources, and international lobbying in hundreds of millions of ALL carried out before the campaign (Manjani 2017).

A newspaper report from November 2017 revealed that the Democratic Party had signed a contract for 675,000 USD with an American lobbying company, which was not declared in the Party's financial statement. The Party also contracted another lobbying company for 150,000 USD. The Socialist Party and the Socialist Movement for Integration also had lobbying contracts in high amounts (Likmeta 2017). According to the Democratic Party financial statement, there were consulting contracts totalling only 16,602,878 ALL (Hysa et al. 2018, 29), approximately 155,000 US dollars. Following the report, the Tirana prosecutor's office announced in December 2017 that it had started a criminal investigation against the Democratic Party on charges of fraud, withholding or falsifying the income declaration (Binjaku 2017).

One of our interviewed experts on European Integration process who was asked to identify informal practices in his field of expertise (politics) stated the following:

> One of the good principles of governance is financial transparency which is anchored in the Constitution and is mandatory for every institution. Today it is impossible to obtain detailed information on expenses and incomes in every sector. This is especially true for electoral campaigns and political parties in violation of Article 9 of the Constitution and the obligations of Albania towards the Council of Europe of Venice Commission.[8]

Asked about the financial transparency of political parties he answered:

> Out of the three main financial sources, namely donations, membership fees, and money from the state budget, only the last one is easily verifiable and transparent. The two other sources that account for about 70% of the financing are informal, thus making the whole representative structure informal. Every time we have elections we spend a year discussing the effects of informality in the electoral process.[9]

Jano has argued that party financing for both Democratic Party and Socialist Party relies heavily on the state budget, and public funding constitutes 88% to 99% of total party revenues. Membership fees are negligible, accounting at best for only 6% of the total party financing. The most significant contributors are those working in public offices (Jano 2016, 25).

Understanding how private funding of political parties functions in practice was a central research question for our fieldwork. In the course of interviews with members of main political parties during and shortly after the campaign, the interviewees were asked about campaign funding, donors, donation procedures, and their perceptions of eventual expectations of donors. While our interviewees were often reluctant to discuss electoral campaign financial issues, or stated that they had no information on how funding worked and who was involved, we were able to receive information on how things work in practice during electoral campaigns.When asked how the funding of the electoral campaign functions, our Democratic Party interviewee explained:

> Part of the funding comes from the Party. Another part comes from donors within the electoral district. In our sector we have three persons with small and medium size businesses who give money according to their capacities. We cover the phone bills ourselves, while receptions and coffees during electoral meetings were paid in part by our candidate who told us that she has three sponsors. However, we as Party structure

members do not know their names. Albanian parties are generally funded by big business-men, while small and medium sponsors of any activity keep a low profile. The Democratic Party lacks sponsors.[10]

When asked why small businesses sponsor campaign activities, he replied:

> If you have a small or medium size business and you have sponsored a party which then wins the elections, you have the right contacts in the future administration. For example, if you have problems with the tax office, e.g., you have not paid a fine or a specific tax, or you have more workers than you actually declared, then it is enough for you to call your contact person and remind him that you have sponsored the campaign. Tax officers will leave you in peace. This is how it works with both Socialist and Democratic Party.[11]

Our Democratic Party interviewee's answers show that on the one hand opposition parties can receive less private funding as compared to those in power, and on the other hand they imply the more precarious situation of small and medium donors who donate but hide their political involvement in case the party they supported does not win. The perception among politically active individuals that business owners' funding of electoral campaigns is a means to procure advantages or avoid problems with the future state administration was also stressed by another interviewee, active within the Socialist Movement for Integration, who told us that, 'We hear of businessmen sponsoring all parties with small sums, so that they can be in good terms with everyone.'[12]

When asked about whether he knew of private sponsors funding the deputy candidates' electoral campaign, one of our interviewees who is a member of the Socialist Party active in the electoral campaign said:

> Not that I know of. It is the party that provides funding for the campaign in that district. I mean the main expenses, such as posters, advertising, and so on, while technical matters, such as who pays for the hotel and travel expenses are solved chiefly through sponsors. For example, you can lodge at the hotel of a supporter, and someone else pays for lunch. There have been cases when candidates have stayed even one month in the district, and this is something that is always solved differently. It is not always the same solution. The main funding for the elections comes from the party.[13]

Asked how party funding by private subjects has changed over the years, this Socialist Party representative commented: 'I do not have any information. It looks like it has increased, but I am not convinced that it is a substantial increase. There have been many individual donors during these elections, but the sums have not necessarily been larger.'[14] His comment on the motivation for funding a political party was: 'I believe that a type of influence, real or purported, on politics, a kind of favour they hope to obtain is the main reason.'[15]

The evolving relationship between parties and donors over time is an important aspect in identifying any trends. When asked whether he thought the relationship between party and business has increased or decreased, our interviewee from the Democratic Party explained:

> I think it is a stable situation. I do not think there will be any weakening because party conjunctures are dependent on business. Albanian political parties are financed by big businesses, and this is not going to change any time soon. Party structures depend on the business ties they manage to create. Take electoral campaign activities for instance, and try to compare the funds that the political parties get from the state with the real costs. You will see that those funds are so small that they cannot cover most of the expenses needed. Let me

give you my example. When I was involved with the youth structure of the party, I participated in eight parties organized for the youth in Tirana. Hundreds of people participated. I alone consumed six drinks, which cost a medium of 2500 ALL per party. What about the rest? Remember that such parties were organized all over Albania. What about other electoral activities?[16]

Such remarks draw attention to one of the in-kind forms of donations for political parties. The question is who pays for the entertainment parties or rallies and other electoral meetings organized across the country by political parties? According to Petersen and Kamolli, 'parties do not (want to) report the in-kind donations and the law does not provide sufficient information on their reporting. Failure to disclose in-kind donations affects transparency directly because it has become a widespread practice in the country that a large proportion of spending during campaigns is made not by parties but by third parties (e.g., businesses or private individuals) on their behalf' (Petersen and Kamolli 2018, 4).

Such has been the case not only during the 2017 general parliamentary elections. A survey conducted by Transparency International Albania in 2012 showed that while reporting by political parties was considered reliable there was a general perception that certain private donations (especially in-kind) are left out of their financial reports. The respondents had a strong perception that the biggest donors do not want to be disclosed because their real motivation is to promote future favours by the government (Transparency International Albania 2013, 17–18).

According to Smilov, 'the size of a country and the existence of oligarchs have an important influence on political finance. Wealthy entrepreneurs can affect domestic politics regardless of the type of political finance regulation, which suggests the ineffectiveness of such regulation. The phenomenon of "oligarchic parties", or parties set up by wealthy individuals, is quite widespread in many of the countries discussed' (Smilov 2014, 182). He further argues that 'entrepreneurial political projects become problematic when they are the result of, or aim to achieve, illegitimate links between power and money or when they result in governmental favouritism vis-a-vis specific economic interests' (Smilov 2014, 182).

A common pre-election practice during Albania's transition period has been the approval of extensive public works by central governments or local institutions. Contracts for public works are signed with companies after calls for tenders, which are not always transparent for the public or are rarely made through direct public procurements. During the 11 September 2016 partial local elections for Dibra Municipality, the Democratic Party candidate stated that the mayor appointed in Dibra had approved 34 contracts to private companies for public works from July to August 2016, and that public financing for August alone was higher than for the previous three years combined. He also stated that two of the largest public works contracts were made to a company close to the Socialist Party and the money the company paid in advance was used to buy votes (Shehu 2016). Despite such allegations and many similar cases made public during the last years, there were no concrete measurements by the judiciary. This fact makes it impossible to reach any conclusions on the truthfulness of such allegations and therefore complicates any further analysis of the impact such practices can have on a fair and competitive election process.

Another interviewee, a journalist who followed closely the electoral campaign in a small municipality in Central Albania, told us:

> Almost all the companies working with public money fund the campaign of the party in power. They are required to do so if they want to keep doing business in the field of public works and investments. They also feel obliged to do so, because they received money through tenders and concessions. Of course, such sums are not donated formally, through bank accounts. They withdraw cash from bank accounts, part of which they deliver to the party in power, and they use the remainder for vote buying. For example, in the municipality where I followed the campaign two big construction companies manage all public work related to construction and infrastructure in the region. These companies not only financed the campaign of Socialist Party, but they led that campaign in the region. Some of their employees were involved in vote buying with company money. The municipality also puts pressure on companies for future construction permits (not connected to public works), so that they can continue sponsoring the campaign.[17]

This last information brings our attention to the misbalance of political influence created by such clientelist relations. Our interviewee also told us that the Democratic Party has faced great difficulties to find strong sponsors in these elections:

> Businessmen are not so much concerned with seeing the party they sympathize getting in power, and then benefiting from it. They are more concerned to know in advance that they will get tenders and concessions, so they sponsor, based on intuition, the Party that they feel is stronger.[18]

Indications that campaign financial reports delivered by the political parties often do not disclose all donations and expenses raise serious concerns about potential undue influence on politics, especially by large companies. There are regular reports on Albanian media regarding possible corruption cases in public procurement procedures, and preferred treatment for companies close to the ruling party.

Albania has a regional proportional electoral system. MP candidates are chosen from a list compiled by political leaders. While they must be people of a certain reputation and influence in the electoral district who must be proposed by the local party organizations, there are cases when the candidates are completely unknown to party structures and membership, with no participation in party activities. In such cases, our interviewee from Democratic Party said:

> I know from conversations within the party but also with individuals who were active in other parties and organisations that in order to become a deputy candidate when one has not been promoted by the base and is unknown to party structures, one has to donate 350 to 400 thousand euros. I know of one such case but I cannot disclose the name.[19]

The very fact that potential party candidates must find financially powerful sponsors through an informal mechanism of sponsorship as the one described above makes it clear that vote-buying as a form of short term clientelism would be impossible to organize without it. In our sub-sample of 18 qualitative semi-structured interviews, four interviewees admitted to having been offered favours (long term solutions for such problems such as employment, legalization of informal dwellings, etc.). In four cases they were offered money, mobile phones (for a whole neighbourhood), sacks of wheat flour (for the interviewee's entire village), and relief from taxation in exchange for their vote. If within such a small sample, chosen *randomly*, almost half of the votes were casted in exchange of money, in kind, or other longer term favours, we can only start to imagine the degree in which this mechanism transforms the formal multi-party democratic system into a political clientelist one using elections as an instrument.

Such examples indicate a perception among politically engaged individuals that the private donors' main expectation in return for their support is greater access to state institutions if the party they supported wins. The potential risks that wealthy individuals and business can gain undue influence over the political system through private donations are relevant beyond the Albanian case. As Ohman has argued, 'in many countries there is a fear that politicians may give preferential treatment to corporations that have supported them. This may have a negative influence on public procurement and development initiatives, and may hurt not only a democracy, but also the effectiveness of administration and governance' (Ohman 2013, 3).

Besides advantages in receiving public money and contracts, the most frequent reason for businesses funding political parties was to avoid problems or solve eventual issues with the state administration, especially the fiscal sector. A 28 years old businessman who managed his own shop in Tirana said that the rationale behind his vote in the last elections was the promise made to him for tax relief for his business, and that this was his only expectation from voting for the party he chose.[20]

A 20-year-old student from Tropoja who voted for the Democratic Party admitted that she was offered travel expenses from Tirana to Tropoja in order to vote. When asked who paid for this, she answered:

> There was a close friend of the MP candidate who financed minibuses transporting students from Tirana to Tropoja, and paid for their travel expenses. Many were businessmen who benefitted through tax reductions, tenders, and annulment of late payment fees.[21]

Evidence gathered through interviews is further corroborated by data from the INFORM survey indicating that business owners and private sector employees are vulnerable to the potential abuse of state resources, especially through tax offices and state institutions' discriminatory stances towards businesses. The question 'Have you ever been offered money or a favour in exchange for your vote in elections?' was answered in the affirmative by 19.6% of the survey respondents. Since the question was general, the answers should not be deemed valid only for the 2017 parliamentary election. The analysis of answers to the abovementioned question according to the respondent's economic status shows higher percentages of answers in the affirmative among those employed in the private sector. Only 7.5% of those employed full time in state sectors answered affirmatively, as opposed to 36.4% of those employed part-time. Among those formally employed full-time in the private sector 20.1% answered yes, while 28.3% of the self-employed answered yes. Percentages of affirmative answers were also high among the informally employed, students, and pensioners, reflecting the higher vulnerability of persons who were offered money or favours in exchange for their vote (Hysa et al. 2018, 33).

Among those who affirmed that they had turned to a party official/influential for help, the largest proportion (22.7%) were self-employed, followed by formally full time employed in the private sector (18.2%). About 11.4% of 'yes' answers came from people employed in the public sector. Persons employed full time in the private sector constituted the largest proportion of people admitting to have been asked by their manager/boss to participate in activities of a certain party, at 31.5% (Hysa et al. 2018, 33–34). Such data indicate a considerable impact of political clientelism in the private sector, which needs legal framework improvements and the implementation of existing regulations on party finances.

Our data show that although private funding is not the only source for electoral campaigns, it is an important element in the transparency and fairness of elections and political completion as a basis for democratic representativeness. While legal framework amendments have been continuously approved by the parliament, the implementation of legal provisions on party and electoral finances has often been problematic. Undeclared private funding for political parties raises serious questions on the reasons for financial support by individuals and/or businesses, their expectations in return for their support, and the rationale behind voting. Voting in return for eventual favours by the winning party turns voters into party clients and fuels political clientelism, thereby distorting the free and fair electoral competition.

Our ethnographic and survey data demonstrate that voter expectations from parties are often directly related to concrete favours in exchange for their vote. It can be assumed that large companies that contribute to political parties have higher expectations from the winning parties, and that they have a privileged position and better access to public work contracts and state institutions. The abuse of public resources by governing parties for electoral purposes is not addressed in this article, but it is clearly a related issue because preferential treatment of businesses in public works and contracts is a form of abuse with state resources, which distorts fair competition and increases the risk of creating monopolies for businesses close to those in power. This in turn creates a favourable position for incumbent parties prior to and during the elections.

5. Concluding remarks

Free and fair elections constitute an important pillar of democracy. A fair political competition needs transparency of campaign finances and in general of money in politics. The enhancement of campaign funding transparency has been an important issue of public debates in Albania during its transition. While eventual abuse of public resources has received greater attention and can be easier to track due to visibility in media and in public documents, private funding of political parties and electoral campaigns is a much more complicated issue in which private and public interest intertwine.

Our research explored electoral campaign private funding based on evidence gathered through interviews and survey data. The aim was to analyse how private funding works in practice and what are the expectations of donors. We argue that undeclared private funding can be a source for political clientelism.

The main findings show that electoral campaign finances in Albania, especially in-kind donations are not entirely transparent. Informal contributions to parties and their campaigns are difficult to track, despite the legal framework and limitations. Widespread use of clientelist practices contribute to favour incumbent parties during elections, and it distorts elections because they are used to solve everyday problems in exchange for votes, as means of intimidation, or preferred treatment of voters.

Private funding can be an important source for the establishment of long-term clientelist relations between businesses and political parties. Legal limits on contributions to political parties by individuals and businesses aim to reduce possible undue influence by individuals and businesses on political decisions. While in the case of Albania such limitations formally exist, evidence shows that there are discrepancies between legal regulations and practice, which can affect the quality of elections and governance. There are serious concerns that political parties do not declare their income and expenses in full, especially in-kind donations. Expenditure monitoring during electoral campaigns would be an efficient method to enhance political party funding transparency. Despite legal improvements pertaining to political parties' finances, resources for electoral campaign expenditures audits during campaigns are limited.

Political clientelism is detrimental to democracy because it distorts fair competition during elections and provides certain groups of interest–usually those that contribute to party finances–with easier access to state resources. Preferential treatment by politicians for large businesses can negatively influence public procurement procedures, damage democracy, and undermine the effectiveness of governance. Qualitative and quantitative data analyses indicate that an electoral playing field is created in Albania, which favours incumbents, although all three larger parties seem to practice similar mechanisms on securing private funds. Since political parties often use the election campaign period to grant favours for votes, the governing parties have more playing ground and resources to offer. Our ethnographic research indicates the perception that the higher the funding for the political parties, the greater the future chances of profit by public resources for the donors. Private funding as such is not a problem *per se*, but doubts about the unregulated and undeclared nature of political parties' funding raises serious concerns about the eventual misuse of public resources, especially by parties in power.

Notes

1. By then, our data gathering process for the Horizon 2020 project 'INFORM: Closing the Gap between Formal and Informal Institutions in the Balkans' had already started. As part of INFORM research team we decided to focus our ethnographic research on elections, in order to investigate how political clientelist ties affect and are in turn affected by the electoral process.
2. The Horizon 2020 research project INFORM, 'Closing the gap between formal and informal institutions in the Balkans,' was carried out by a consortium of over forty researchers from nine institutions in nine countries, including the six Western Balkans (WB) states that are currently at various stages in the process of EU accession. Launched in March 2016, the three-year research project was carried out in the framework of the EU's Horizon 2020 research and innovation programme under grant agreement No. 693,537.
3. Eric Gordy, Alena Ledeneva, and Predrag Cvetičanin, eds., Forthcoming. *The Gap Between Rules and Practices: Informality in Southeast Europe*. London: UCL Press.
4. The survey database conducted in the framework of the INFORM project has not been published yet. The survey data are used to corroborate findings from the interviews in this article.
5. Article 87/1§ Financing sources for the electoral campaign. The Electoral Code of the Republic of Albania. (Approved by Law no. 10 019, dated 29 December 2008, amended by Law no. 74/2012, dated 19 July 2012 and Law no. 31/2015, dated 2 April 2015), 48. https://www.osce.org/albania/159501?download=true.

6. Article 87/2§ State Budget funds for the electoral campaign. The Electoral Code of the Republic of Albania (see endnote 5).
7. 1,000,000 ALL are approximately 8,200 EUR according to the InforEuro exchange rate in September 2019, 10,000,000 ALL are approximately 82,000 EUR according to the same source.

   1. Electoral subjects may receive funds for the purposes of their electoral campaigns only from domestic natural or legal persons. For the purposes of this Code, an Albanian citizen who resides outside the territory of the Republic of Albania shall also be considered a domestic natural person.
   2. The amount that each natural or legal person may give to an electoral subject may not exceed one million ALL or the equivalent thereof in kind or services.
   3. Donation of funds by a legal person or any of its shareholders is prohibited if one of the following conditions applies: (a) has received public funds, public contracts or concessions in the last two years, exceeding ten million ALL; (b) exercises media activity; (c) has been a partner with public funds in different projects; (d) has monetary obligations towards the State Budget or any public institution. This obligation is not applicable if the shareholder owns these shares as a result of a public offer. Available at The Electoral Code of the Republic of Albania (see endnote 5).

8. Interview with EU integration expert, Tirana, May 2018.
9. Interview with EU integration expert, Tirana, May 2018.
10. Interview with Democratic Party member, Tirana, July 2017.
11. Interview with Democratic Party member, Tirana, July 2017.
12. Interview with Socialist Movement for Integration member, Tirana, February 2018.
13. Interview with Socialist Party member, Tirana, January 2018.
14. Interview with Socialist Party member, Tirana, January 2018.
15. Interview with Socialist Party member, Tirana, January 2018.
16. Interview with Democratic Party member, Tirana, July 2017.
17. Interview with journalist, Tirana, June 2017.
18. Interview with journalist, Tirana, June 2017.
19. Interview with Democratic Party member, Tirana, July 2017.
20. Interview with small business owner, Tirana, October 2017.
21. Interview with student, Tirana, November 2017.

Acknowledgments

We would like to thank both editors of the special issue and the anonymous reviewers for their valuable comments and suggestions that helped substantially improve this article.

Disclosure statement

No potential conflict of interest was reported by the authors.

Funding

This article is based on findings of the ethnographic report 'Informal and clientelist political practices in Albania: The case of the 2017 general elections' (Armanda Hysa, Gentiana Kera, and Enriketa Pandelejmoni), in the framework of research project INFORM: Closing the gap between formal and informal institutions in the Balkans, Horizon 2020, Grant agreement no 693537. Available at:

ORCID

Gentiana Kera (iD) http://orcid.org/0000-0003-3221-070X
Armanda Hysa (iD) http://orcid.org/0000-0002-8552-3921

References

Adler-Nissen, R. 2016. Towards a practice turn in EU studies: The everyday of European integration. *Journal of Common Market Studies* 54(1): 87–103.

Auyero, J. 2006. Introductory note to politics under the microscope: Special issue on political ethnography I. *Qualitative Sociology* 29: 257–59. doi: 10.1007/s11133-006-9028-7

Auyero, J. 2012. Poor people's lives and politics: The things a political ethnographer knows (and does not know) after 15 years of fieldwork. *New Perspectives on Turkey* 46: 95–127. doi: 10.1017/S0896634600001527

Baiocchi, G., and T.B. Connor. 2008. The ethnos on the polis: Political ethnography as a mode of inquiry. *Sociology Compass* 2(1): 139–55. doi: 10.1111/j.1751-9020.2007.00053.x.

Binjaku, F., 2017. Ekspertët mbeten skeptikë për hetimet mbi financat e partive politike. *Reporter*, December 4. https://www.reporter.al/ekspertet-mbeten-skeptike-per-hetimet-mbi-financat -e-partive-politike.

Bliznakovski, J., B. Gjuzelov, and M. Popovikj. 2017. The informal life of political parties in the Western Balkan societies. Report in the framework of research project INFORM: Closing the gap between formal and informal institutions in the Balkans, Horizon 2020, Grant agreement no 693537. https://www.ucl.ac.uk/ssees/sites/ssees/files/idscs-informal_life_of_political_parties -report-27092017.pdf.

Burnell, P. 2017. Introduction: Money and politics in emerging democracies. In *Funding demo-cratization*, ed. P. Burnell and A. Ware, 2–21. New York: Routledge.

Burnell, P., and A. Ware, eds. 2017. *Funding democratization*. New York: Routledge.

Gërxhani, K., and A. Schram. 2009. Clientelism and polarized voting: Empirical evidence. *Public Choice* 141: 305–17. doi: 10.1007/s11127-009-9453-8

Gordy, E., and A. Efendic. 2019. Engaging policy to address gaps between formality and inform-ality in the Western Balkans. In *Meaningful reform in the Western Balkans. Between formal institutions and informal practices*, ed. E. Gordy and A. Efendic, 7–20. Bern: Peter Lang.

Gordy, E., A. Ledeneva, and P. Cvetičanin, eds. Forthcoming. *The gap between rules and practices: Informality in Southeast Europe*. London: UCL Press.

Helmke, G., and S. Levitsky. 2004. Informal institutions and comparative politics: A research agenda. *Perspectives on Politics* 2(4): 725–40. doi: 10.1017/S1537592704040472.

Hilgers, T. 2011. Clientelism and conceptual stretching: Differentiating among concepts and among analytical levels. *Theory and Society* 40(5): 567–88. doi: 10.1007/s11186-011-9152-6.

Hysa, A., G. Kera, and E. Pandelejmoni. 2018. Informal and clientelist political practices in Albania: The case of the 2017 general elections. Report in the framework of research project INFORM: Closing the gap between formal and informal institutions in the Balkans, Horizon 2020, Grant agreement no. 693537. https://www.ucl.ac.uk/ssees/sites/ssees/files/ethnographic_report_informal_and_client.case_of_the_2017_general_elections.pdf.

Jano, D. 2016. Organizations of political parties in Albania. In *Organizational structures of political parties in Central and Eastern European Countries*, ed. K. Sobolewska-Myślik, B. Kosowska-Gaştoł, and P. Borowiec, 21–39. Krakow: Jagiellonian University Press.

Kajsiu, B. 2016. Polarization without radicalization: Political radicalism in Albania in a comparative perspective. *Journal of Contemporary European Studies* 24(2): 1–21. doi: 10.1080/14782804.2016.1159545.

Kitschelt, H. 2000. Linkages between citizens and politicians in democratic polities. *Comparative Political Studies* 33(6–7): 845–79. doi: 10.1177/001041400003300607.

Kitschelt, H., and S.I. Wilkinson. 2007. Citizen-politician linkages: An introduction. In *Patron, clients, and policies: Patterns of democratic accountability and political competition*, ed. H. Kitschelt and S.I. Wilkinson, 1–49. Cambridge: Cambridge University Press.

Likmeta, B. 2017. Kontrata e fshehtë e PD me lobistin amerikan, transferta milionëshe përmes kompanisë 'offshore'. *Reporter*, November 22. https://www.reporter.al/kontrata-e-fshehte-e-pd-me-lobistin-amerikan-transferta-milioneshe-permes-kompanise-ofshore/.

Manjani, O. 2017. Maja e ajsbergut: Partitë politike fshehën shpenzimet e fushatës nga ekspertët e KQZ. *Reporter*, December 4. https://www.reporter.al/maja-e-ajsbergut-partite-politike-fshehen-shpenzimet-e-fushates-nga-ekspertet-e-kqz/.

Ohman, M., 2013. Controlling money in politics: An introduction. https://www.ifes.org/sites/default/files/a_brief_introduction_to_money_in_politics_final_magnus_ohman.pdf.

OSCE/ODIHR. 2017. Final report: Parliamentary elections 25 June 2017 Republic of Albania. *Election Observation Mission*. http://www.osce.org/odihr/elections/albania/346661?download=true.

Petersen, A., and M. Kamolli. 2018. The importance of regulation and enforcement for political party financial transparency in Albania. *Law Journal* 6: 1–10.

Shehu, S. 2016. Numrat e Dibrës. http://www.panorama.com.al/numrat-e-dibres/.

Smilov, D. 2014. Eastern, Central and South-eastern Europe and Central Asia. In *Funding of political parties and election campaigns. A Handbook on political finance*, ed. E. Falguera, S. Jones, and M. Ohman, 173–205. Stockholm: International IDEA.

Tomsa, D., and A. Ufen, eds. 2013. *Party politics in Southeast Asia: Clientelism and electoral competition in Indonesia, Thailand and Philippines*. Oxon: Routledge.

Transparency International Albania. 2013. Buying influence: Money and political parties in Albania. https://www.transparency.org/files/content/feature/2013_CRINIS_Albania_EN.pdf.

Wantchekon, L. 2003. Clientelism and voting behavior: Evidence from a field experiment in Benin. *World Politics* 55(3): 399–422. doi: 10.1353/wp.2003.0018.

Structural weaknesses and the role of the dominant political party: democratic backsliding in Croatia since EU accession

Dario Čepo

ABSTRACT

Croatia is regarded as a success story of the EU's enlargement policy. However, this narrative conflicts with the situation on the ground and with expert surveys, which depict incremental, yet persistent democratic backsliding in recent years. A shift towards illiberal practices, primarily focused on the liberal part of the liberal-democratic nexus, is taking place. This research aims to explore the prevalence and causes for the re-emergence of illiberal practices in Croatia by employing an interpretive method to evidence gathered from media articles and research reports published 2013–2019. The use of illiberal policies by the governing Croatian Democratic Union (HDZ) in three areas of the political system – the capture of independent agencies, control of the judiciary, and the weakening of independent media – is found to be the driver of democratic backsliding. Causes are found in structural reasons linked to the dominant party. Without either internal power-sharing constraints or external EU conditionality pressure, the HDZ has been able to take advantage of structural weaknesses of the system it built and shaped during the 1990s.

1. Introduction

Ever since the conclusion of Croatia's negotiation with the European Union in 2011, and especially at the time of Croatia's accession in 2013, a narrative of Croatia as a success story of the EU's enlargement policy has been pushed by both domestic elites and their European counterparts. Hence, Croatia should serve as a poster child for other countries wanting to join the EU, especially to those in Southeast Europe. It was a change from just a couple of decades ago, when Croatia was more or less isolated internationally, while it internally suffered from the rise in autocratic tendencies of then-president Franjo Tudman.

Croatia's political system during the 1990s can be categorized as a semi-authoritarian regime (Zakošek and Čular 2004), a competitive authoritarian regime (Levitsky and Way 2010), an illiberal democracy (Dolenec 2008) or an authoritarian democracy (Čular 2000). During the early 1990s, the newly established 'regime emerged as the result of institutionalization of the HDZ movement into a political regime, with two distinct characteristics: a) in terms of substance, the regime was an authoritarian regime; b) the regime acquired its legitimacy through reasonably free and fair democratic procedures' (Čular 2000, 30).

Croatia has started its democratization path towards liberal democracy only after the dominant political party, the Croatian Democratic Union (HDZ), lost power both at the presidential and parliamentary elections in 2000. The next decade saw democratic consolidation, assisted by accession negotiations and the conditionality principle championed by the European Union. There was a strong insistence on introducing new and strengthening existing independent institutions and actors, media freedom, the anti-corruption parliamentary committee, and even overhauling the judiciary as a whole. The European Commission reports showed slow but steady improvement in all these areas. Hence, 'societal dynamics and those of the party system have experienced the strengthening of pluralist democratic values' (Dolenec 2013, 41). Consolidation was expected to continue after the accession process, helped by the membership in the European Union.

Another critical element to maintaining Croatia's democratic consolidation was cohabitation between an HDZ-dominated government and an opposition candidate as President. During the decade when the most significant strides towards democratic consolidation occurred, HDZ was either in opposition or governed but did not control the office of the President of the Republic. The institution of the President became largely ceremonial after constitutional changes in 2000 and 2001, albeit still stronger than in other parliamentary systems. The President shared power with the government over the security apparatus, i.e., secret service, an important actor in maintaining the rule of law.

However, since 2013, Croatia has experienced partial democratic backsliding. Looking at the development of Croatia's transition to democracy from 2009 to 2018 the decline occurred in areas of national-level democratic governance, independent media, and judicial framework (Freedom House 2018). If we focus on the 2013–2018 period, since the accession of Croatia to the European Union, the decline is even more evident with backsliding in the fight against corruption joining the previous three. Similar conclusions can be found in v-dem reports, as the introductory article by Kapidžić (2020) shows.

Historical institutionalism is a particularly helpful theoretical framework to understand this decline, with its 'emphasis on how institutions emerge from and are embedded in concrete temporal processes' (Thelen 1999, 369), as well as the insistence on path dependency. In Croatia, democratic consolidation can be linked to periods of challenged HDZ dominance, while elements necessary for democratic backsliding resumed its path-dependent course once HDZ regained the monopoly of power and no external actor was present to serve as a pressure point.

Institutionalism of rational choice can help show that institutions and actors are interlinked, with actors forming not only institutions themselves but also the rules under which these institutions function, (mis)behave, and influence the system at large (Shepsle 2006). It helps explain how seemingly identical institutions can function as enablers of democracy in one period, while undermining democracy in another, with the only difference in the party interpreting and applying institutional rules and procedures.

Adopting an interpretive method allows us to focus on actors' perspectives, ascribed meanings of events, language used in written material by individuals, groups, and institutions to build a dominant narrative, and on subtle changes in context (Bayard de Volo 2015), that would otherwise be missed if our focus was solely on quantifiable evidence. This way, we can see what societal actors, media, representatives of state institutions, and the political elite did in the observed period, how they explained their activities, and how those explanations can be interpreted to understand the observed backsliding that occurred in Croatia.

By combining historical institutionalism and institutionalism of rational choice with the interpretive method, the focus of this paper is on crucial institutions that were weakened, captured, or marginalized with the aim either to reduce the ruling elite's accountability or to use resources for the benefit of the party in power. It was especially important to scrutinize the government's activities towards judicial and media independence, as well as towards autonomous and independent institutions, which serve as proxies for understanding the decline in the level of national democratic governance.

Within the analytical and methodological framework set by the introductory article (Kapidžić 2020), the goal of this paper is to explore the underlying factors in the political system of Croatia that made the rise of illiberal politics possible. The main research questions ask how widespread are illiberal practices in Croatia; and what are the reasons for democratic backsliding since 2013, and especially since 2015.

Data were gathered through Boolean search queries in Google with a focus on HDZ, democracy, and areas the Freedom House report indicated as declining – media, judiciary, and democratic governance – (e.g., HDZ AND demokracij* AND sloboda medija; HDZ AND pravosude OR sudska vlast). For the variable of 'national-level democratic governance', proxies were used (e.g., HDZ AND sukob interesa AND povjerenstv*; HDZ AND pravobranitelj*). The data focused on the post-accession period, after 2013, but was expanded further into the past in order to capture any structural reason for the dysfunction of the analysed institution, actor, or an area of the political system. In this way, a sample of Croatian language online articles, documents, and reports was identified for further analysis.

The next section focuses on the development of the party system and examines the link between the major political actors in Croatia and dominant contentious issues that divide society at large. Following sections analyse how democracy has been weakened through concrete examples of institutions, actors, and agencies that have been captured or marginalized and their resources misused. Finally, I discuss the reasons for the democratic backsliding of Croatia.

2. Political actors and contentious issues in croatia

The HDZ was, and still is, the dominant political actor in Croatia. Although the major centre-left and strongest opposition party, the Social Democratic Party (SDP), has managed to come to power on two occasions, it only secured the wins after major internal crises in HDZ and with backing of almost all relevant opposition forces. In the 1990s, the semi-presidential system of government, favoured by Tudman and the HDZ during Croatia's wartime/transitional period 'provided an appropriate institutional framework for authoritarian regressions in the processes of political decision-making and in the context of political decisions' (Kasapović 2000, 3). At the same time, the party system was 'characterized by a combination of two negative characteristics: absence of alternation in power, and a mixed-party system constellation' (Dolenec 2013, 85).

Despite this, the party system of Croatia has been very stable in the three decades since independence. After 2015 there have been some signs of disintegration, with SDP in the weakest position since 2000, and the HDZ losing voters to newly formed right-radical parties, but still maintaining dominance. The rapid rise of anti-establishment, anti-system, or populist parties, however, has proved to be a significant influence on the destabilization of the Croatian party system. Some of the newly established parties display confusing agendas as they 'criticize political elite for being incompetent and corrupt, while at the same time advocating alliance with this same elite in order to implement reforms and bring prosperity to Croatian society' (Grbeša and Šalaj 2017, 7).

There are also several influential veto actors that share an ideological point of view in which 'the world is divided into good, nation-building Croats, HDZ voters, and the communists, alleged opponents of the formation of an independent Croatian state' (Cipek 2017, 155). The most influential are the Catholic Church and veterans' organizations. They make use of HDZ's rule to direct government resources to their particular aims and are in turn used by the HDZ when in opposition to advance conservative and nationalistic political agendas. In recent years, conservative civil society organizations and religious-political social movement that are sometimes antagonists, but mostly allies of the HDZ, have joined them. Their influence cannot be underestimated due to 'the continued strengthening of illiberal groups, which Croatia's government and president have tolerated or even encouraged' (Freedom House 2018).

It is notoriously hard to come by the correct number, but some sources indicate that Croatia has around 500,000 registered veterans (Dolenec 2017; Bagić and Kardov 2018). In the mid-1990s they started organizing into influential organizations. 'Partly in response to this mobilization, from 1994 onwards, HDZ governments created a comprehensive institutional architecture of entitlements for veterans, instituting durable material linkages alongside symbolic ties to this population' (Dolenec 2017, 55). As the party in government during the Homeland War, it is logical that HDZ influences, and is influenced by, veterans' groups. Predominantly, veterans ideologically lean to the right in higher numbers, and they are more inclined to vote for right-wing parties (Bagić and Kardov 2018). Their strength is most evident in their power to demand action by the government, either by calling for boycotts, law changes, or disregard of constitutional and legal obligations, especially on public issues salient to the ideological right. These political taboos include 'the Croatian nation-state and consequently definition of *a proper* Croatian national identity, or who are *the real* Croats, and the Homeland War as one of the constitutive processes for the creation of nation-state and identity' (Blanuša 2017, 176).

Similarly, close links between HDZ and the Catholic Church need to be taken into account. The influence of the Church on Croatian politics is significant, yet this institution is analysed rarely as a political actor. Such omission is glaring given the growing political power of the Church and its establishment as a veto actor during the 1990s. A watershed moment was the 1997–1998 agreements between Croatia and the Holy See (Marinović and Markešić 2012). These agreements helped consolidate the dominant position of the Church in Croatian society (Zrinščak 1998), but were also used to prop up the national position and international reputation of the beleaguered HDZ regime (Lušić 2002). Since then, the Church has been a dominant veto player. Church officials started to appear in public as engaged political actors, tactically using the language of constitutionally guaranteed normative and procedural protections, while at the same time undermining democratic consolidation by constantly inciting culture wars (Petković 2013).

Finally, the influence of conservative civil society organizations should be mentioned. An example is the rise and success of In the Name of the Family, a civil society organization and citizens' initiative with a right-wing-leaning political agenda. 'Political nature of the movement manifests itself through multiple attempts to scrap the legislation and practices of both state and private institutions that are contradicting the value system of the Christian (Catholic) majority. The religious-political nexus of the movement is confirmed by its continuous involvement in policy-making' (Petričušić et al. 2017, 61). It is necessary to view them as important political actors, due to their involvement in defining, expanding, and influencing the trajectory of contentious policies and politics on gender and minority rights, particularly in the period since 2013.

There is robust cooperation between the Church and civil society organizations focused on mobilizing the conservative population, which depicts themselves as representing a moral majority (Petković 2013). The Church-linked institutions used their political influence to voice their positions on significant policies (e.g., education reform), to bemoan media reporting on the Church's position, and to complain about lacking response by government institutions (HBK 2014). This has a negative impact on liberal elements of democracy leading to democratic backsliding.

Contentious political issues in Croatia are predominantly linked to the left-right ideological cleavage and focus on the cultural arena of politics. These are issues of education reform, LGBTIQ* rights, World War II remembrance, rights of national minorities, and more recently immigration policy. The latter has become an ideological conflict between the liberal left and the nationalist right and is linked to a myriad of other questions such as demographic prospects of Croatian society, high levels of emigration, a diminishing welfare state, and labour market stability.

The most salient issue is the cultural trauma and collective memory of both World War II and the 1990s Croatia's war of independence, also called the Homeland War. The two main elements within this issue are the Bleiburg commemoration for World War II Ustaše regime soldiers and the *Za dom spremni* Ustaše salute. Both are linked to (re) interpretations of World War II atrocities and controversial aspects of the 1995 war campaigns on Croatian territory, institutionalized through the Victory and Homeland Thanksgiving Day. The Bleiburg commemoration remains 'a central point of political contestation within the Croatian memory landscape' (Pavlaković et al. 2018, 29), with parts of society not willing to accept different interpretations or new historiographical concepts linked to it (Grahek Ravančić 2018). Distinct segments of Croatian society 'have opposed versions of past events, opposed evaluations, and hence opposed streams of memories in the present. Croatian society is riven to the point that we live parallel histories' (Cvijanović 2018, 141). The positions of different actors towards Bleiburg 'often had very little to do with the massacre itself, but instead served as a powerful symbolic platform to promote certain political or strategic agendas and to vilify – or at the very least marginalize – others' (Tokić 2018, 86). In this case, nationalist faction of HDZ and their allies portray others as disloyal or outright enemies opposed to an independent Croatia. These 'others' are most often the Serb minority as well as left-liberal politicians, activists, civil society organizations, and political parties. All of this is used by political elites to control the society by fomenting a narrative of conflict and struggle against an external Other.

Additional salient contentious issues are linked to reproductive rights, including the right to abortion, as well as domestic violence protection of women and children, manifested in the ratification process of the Istanbul Convention in the Croatian parliament. Religious-political social movement, conservative civil society organizations, and the Catholic Church used the ratification issue to push for a rollback of women's rights. This has also been used by the HDZ to attack the opposition and their dissidents (Puljić-Šego 2018), as bringing into question the survival of the nation, which is threatened by negative demographic trends. By signalling willingness to impose severe restrictions on abortion procedures, expanding the notion of conscientious objection, or introducing official statements that reinterpret the Istanbul Convention, the pro-European wing of HDZ tries to accommodate more conservative and nationalist segments within the party. These compromises in turn empower the Church, conservative civil society organizations, and illiberal political actors, depicting their causes as just, and normalizing their discourse of struggle against a liberal onslaught on Croatian culture. All of this helps destabilize liberal democracy in Croatia and opens doors for further democratic backsliding.

The most recent contentious issue of immigration policy is linked to European Union membership. As an emigration country for the past two centuries, Croatian society has difficulties in portraying the country as an immigrants' goal. Regardless of readiness to help specific groups of immigrants over others (refugees vs. economic migrants) (Medlobi and Čepo 2018) and of positive media narratives on migrants during the 2015–2016 period (Čepo et al. forthcoming), Croatian society has profoundly negative attitudes towards immigration. HDZ uses this attitude to turn the narrative from the humanitarian to securitizing. This helps the government legitimize itself in the eyes of the European Union, as a good guardian of EU external borders, while receiving support from a migrant-sceptic public. At the same time, HDZ used the migrant crisis to attack SDP as weak on national security, while alluding to demographic and cultural threats.

3. Electoral practices

The current electoral law, adopted in 1999, proved to be one of the most stable elements of the political system as a whole. However, as some criticisms show, it favours the largest political parties, does not reflect the demos due to unnatural electoral units, and over-represents some areas while underrepresenting other. There are even accusations of electoral engineering (Podolnjak 2013). All of these criticisms can, and have been, discussed and analysed (see, e.g., Kasapović 2017), with an almost universal conclusion that there is no will among political actors to change the electoral law, despite some activities in this regard. Two citizens' initiatives focused on changing electoral law failed to gather enough signatures to proceed to the referendum stage (HINA 2014), a recommendation by the State Electoral Committee (D. D. 2019) was dead on arrival, as was the proposal by smaller parliamentary parties (HINA 2019a). There were even some informal proposals (Markovina 2019) by the governing HDZ that would award the relative winner with additional mandates. It seems, though, that even the worst criticisms – those regarding uneven electoral units – have negligible influence (Čular 2018) on the outcome of elections, and hence, the will of the people.

The only major issue that has some influence on the legitimacy, if not the legality of the electoral process, has been the issue of the electoral registry. Due to the lack of a single electoral registry in the last two decades, legitimacy issues have tainted all elections in Croatia. The main criticisms are linked to the number of people on voter rolls. Some argued that there are more voters in Croatia than inhabitants (Bago 2009), while others found that many people on electoral rolls lack any form of identification and live at non-existent addresses (Trajković 2013), and even deceased have been found voting on some electoral rolls (N1 Hrvatska 2016).

While the electoral law on the national level has not been changed much, the same cannot be said for laws on local and regional elections. First, there was the change to elect local and regional executives directly. This significantly weakened the position of local legislatures with respect to their executives (Koprić and Škarica 2017). The HDZ-led government then further changed the law to strengthen the position of local and regional chiefs of the executive, effectively transforming them into undisputed local rulers, who are all but guaranteed to stay in power even if legislatures reject their policies and citizens act against them (Koprić 2017). This, according to some analysts, unconstitutional move (Jurasić 2018), was aimed at securing HDZ's control over local politics. The capture of cities, municipalities, and regions, was used then for public funds' extraction. However, it was also a form of local political patronage focused on helping smaller parties that prop up HDZ's national government.

All this leaves Croatian citizens with a lack of trust in the electoral system, which further breeds apathy. This is particularly pronounced among youth (Čepo 2019), who increasingly exhibit 'anti-elite, anti-systemic attitudes – as well as authoritarianism and a few right-wing political attitudes – with the strong leader preference' (Derado et al. 2016, 141). Their 'selective acceptance of liberal-democratic values suggests an insufficient understanding of democratic principles and rules' and leads them to show 'the highest level of trust in repressive institutions (armed forces and the police)' (Gvozdanović et al. 2019, 45).

4. Independent media

Regarding the freedom of expression and alternative sources of information, the situation is much bleaker. While the governing party tries to maintain the veneer of respecting democratic norms and obligations stemming from the European Union membership, according to the Freedom House, this area is one of the most significant contributors to the recent democratic backsliding of Croatia (Prelec 2018).

The process of weakening of media freedoms in Croatia was achieved through two distinct approaches. One is led by the HDZ and involves using the normative framework to capture the institutions necessary for controlling the critical voice of media. Another is led by HDZ's allies in the civil society helped by conservative and right-wing parties and involves outright attacks on media through judicial harassment, misuse of media law, and personal attacks on 'ideologically impure' individuals within the media system.

The crucial issues of historical revisionism regarding World War II remembrance are nowhere more vivid than on local TV stations (Arbutina and Opačić 2016). One of the most influential journalists espousing a revisionist narrative, Velimir Bujanec, was even invited as a guest at the inauguration of the Croatian president, the HDZ candidate Kolinda Grabar Kitarović. His anti-minority, ultranationalist TV show, Bujica, is often a target of ethics complaints by the Agency for Electronic Media (AEM), an independent regulatory body. The Agency, formed in 2009 with a mission of enhancing media pluralism and media freedom, is appointed by Parliament to whom it is accountable. Practically, however, the executive has principal influence due to the dominance of the government over the parliamentary majority.

After a decision to suspend the licence of Z1 TV station that carried the Bujica TV show in 2016, Velimir Bujanec and his allies led protests against the Agency, but especially personal attacks against its then head, Mirjana Rakić, one of the most accomplished and well-respected journalists in Croatia. She was depicted as an enemy of the Croatian society, as a Serb (the worst insult in the eyes of Croatian ultranationalists), and as bent on thwarting the freedom of expression (G. D. 2016). The HDZ-led government did not defend the Agency or its head (Marić et al. 2016), and following pressure for her removal from the then nationalist minister of culture, Rakić resigned (Puljiz 2016). She was replaced by Josip Popovac, a manager of Croatia's public broadcaster, who led that institution during the previous HDZ government of Ivo Sanader, who was later charged for corruption. This assured to the current HDZ government that the Agency would not create too much trouble for the party's allies and proxies.

With the capture of the Agency, HDZ not only removed a robust independent body that could thwart its intention of subduing public media but also got the opportunity to dispense money from the fund supporting media pluralism and diversity. This was already evident in 2017 when the fund dispensed grants to many more right-wing and conservative media, including the Z1 TV station (S. S. 2017), that only a year earlier temporarily lost licence due to hate speech of their prime journalist.

However, the most vivid example of HDZ's capture of media is the complete subjugation of the Croatian National Television (HRT), a public broadcaster with a national reach. Instrumentalization of the public broadcaster into a mouthpiece of the government/party has been one of the central policies of the HDZ during the 1990s. During the accession negotiation, the European Union insisted on complete independence of HRT, which was, more or less successful. After Croatia became an EU member, the situation once again reversed. The HDZ decided that the capture of the national broadcaster with four TV programmes and several radio channels is vital for their grip on power. They were aided by the previous left-liberal government's decision to change the law on HRT and to give parliament the right to appoint the broadcaster's director (Despot 2016). Hence, the HDZ acted according to democratic procedure but with an aim to limit freedom of expression (Forum.tm 2016). The following examples confirm this intention. After the party installed their preferred candidate as director, a nationalist and conservative former editor and journalist (Rožman 2016), they began with personnel purges (Grozdanić 2016), cancelling established and popular programmes critical of ruling elites (Pavić 2017), and even filed lawsuits against their own employees, other news organizations, and civil society organizations (Klarić 2019). Although it initially seemed that the HDZ-government did the same thing as their SDP predecessors in choosing the head of HRT, the process within the institution that occurred afterwards was very different. This process of purges, dismissals, and lawsuits meant to stifle dissent shows the intent of the

HDZ to change the nature of the public broadcaster and turn it back into an instrument of the regime, as it was during the 1990s.

This did not fully materialize due to competition from other broadcasters with national reach (Kovačević 2017), cable news channels, and the changing media landscape. In response, HDZ adopted different tactics towards critical journalists, organizations, and media houses. Although there were no cases of government trying to either limit political messages on private broadcasting or suppress critical voices by denying licences for critical media channels, it did try to keep some critical and independent media marginalized. This was the case with the regional TV station N1, an affiliate of CNN. Although an official decision was never adopted, for several years since coming to power, all government officials, including the HDZ ministers, were forbidden to appear on N1 news shows[1]. This silent boycott by the government was a retaliation for N1's often-critical portrayal of policy blunders and scandals of HDZ politicians.

Media institutions that the HDZ and its allies could not capture, they tried either to marginalize by establishing parallel institutions (Pilsel 2015) or to bring down through bureaucratic and judicial harassment. An example is the Croatian Journalists' Association (HND). The association, its president, and many of its members have been sued, either by right-wing activists, politicians, captured institutions, or other actors (HINA 2019b). Their Association's president, a journalist working for HRT, was fired under dubious circumstances after taking over the Association (HINA 2018). A parallel institution, Croatian Journalists and Publicists, was established, which embraced views that regularly support right-wing issues and actors.

The return of HDZ to power saw an increase in physical attack on journalists, as well as legal harassment through lawsuits. Judicial harassment, through misuse of libel laws, has become endemic, with some sources reporting that, as of February 2019, there are over one thousand ongoing lawsuits opened against journalists and media organizations in Croatia (Danas.hr 2019). Since 2016 there has been a rise in attacks and threats against journalists where many of these cases never get resolved, nor do the journalist get justice through the legal system (tportal 2017).

In conclusion, while there is no outright government censorship, owner-influenced, editor-influenced, as well as self-censorship is high in Croatian media. Critical stances, especially towards the government, are low to non-existent among the most-watched and most-read media. There are taboo topics, including the veteran groups' collective rights and the power of the Catholic Church. All of this weakens media freedom and hence, democratic consolidation in Croatia.

5. Horizontal accountability and institutional oversight

The professionalization of public administration was an important benchmark Croatia needed to attain during the accession process. The European Commission kept issuing reports noting that significant progress was needed for a coherent legislative framework and its implementation (Lalić Novak 2010). The European Union insisted on adoption of policies aimed at full administrative reform in Croatia, funded through generous European grants, projects, and technical assistance (Koprić 2014). However, there was no interest to depoliticize and professionalize administration; the changes were cosmetic, with both politicians and bureaucracy avoiding meaningful reforms at all costs (Koprić

2016). Both national and local administrative apparatuses loathe openness and transparency, even 'when those standards are legally prescribed. They are inclined to disclose light information, which is not politically loaded and have no direct connection to the accountability mechanism' (Musa et al. 2015, 415). While normative obligations are followed (such as putting law proposals up for public consultations), the actual willingness of the authorities to implement proposed reforms and changes is lacking (Đurman 2016), which makes citizens disinterested and prone to apathy.

To fight against the misuse of public administration by the government, the European Union put much emphasis on establishing and strengthening independent agencies and regulatory bodies. Knowing that 'the agency's autonomy and agency control depend not only on the agency design but also on the capabilities of relevant actors, such as parliaments, governments or ministries, of controlling their agencies' (Musa 2013, 392), the EU assumed that imbuing the agencies and regulatory bodies with normative independence would be enough to insulate them from political meddling. While formally these bodies in Croatia show autonomy in their functioning, contextual factors (such as the attitude of the political actors) need to be taken into account (Musa 2019) to see if they are working as independently as the law and the reforms intended.

This is not the case because a similar capture to the one happening in media occurred here as well. The most visible example is the institution of the Information Commissioner. Its first head, an academic and right-to-information expert, built the agency from the ground up and gave it weight (notably in regards to forcing the government to be more transparent). Once her term ended, the candidate who, during the nomination process, tried to hide his long-time HDZ membership succeeded her. He also insisted that the institution should not get more power to punish public bodies who breach freedom-of-information obligations (Lukić 2018c).

Another captured institution is the Ombudsman for Children, a constant target of religious-political social movements and conservative civil society organizations during the term in office of Ivana Milas Klarić, a family law expert. Once the HDZ government came to power, they changed the law, stipulating that the new law also requires the selection of a new ombudsman. The candidate that was finally appointed gave public transphobic statements and supported removing references to gender from legal acts, including the Istanbul Convention (Sarkotić 2017).

One more independent agency that HDZ managed to capture was the National Foundation for Civil Society Development. This was accomplished in order to tap into the resources of the Foundation for patronage and to award position to party members as a reward for their loyalty (Brakus 2018). The abundant funds, coming partially from national lottery earnings, were used to reward party allies, including organizations that are part of the religious-political social movement (Gabrić 2018) and that were previously critical of the foundation (Telegram 2017). The foundation was even found giving financial assistance to the organizations whose members are, or were, members of government themselves (Vidov 2018).

6. Independent judiciary

Although constitutionally designed as independent and equal, the judiciary, in practice, never had an autonomous or institutionally separate role in the Croatian political system.

The latest polls show it to be one of the least trusted institution among the citizens (S. D. M. 2017). The public perceives the system corrupt, unjust, and under the influence of politics. Legal experts perceive many judges, especially those in lower courts, as inadequate for the positions they occupy. All of this is the result of the HDZ dismantling the judicial system in the early 1990s and ultimately capturing it in subsequent years. The HDZ's control over firing, appointing, and financing made judges reluctant to show their independence (Ravlić 2017). Judges who were not 'capable to understand their role in fulfiling national interests and using the law in a flexible way that supports the high goals of the governing parties and president Tuđman' (cf. Uzelac 2001), were deemed either remnants of the Communist regime or Serbs disloyal to the new state, and hence had to be removed from office. Loyal party cadres appointed in their place often lacked experience and legal knowledge but had an abundance of support for their party.

Particularly destructive for the fairness of the judicial system was Tuđman's tendency of unrestrained rule through executive orders. Some of the longest-serving executive orders were those regarding the organization and functioning of the judiciary (Uzelac 2001). All this made the judiciary one of the first parts of the political system to be captured, which sanctioned HDZ's unrestrained rule. The situation did not change much even after regime change in 2000, nor was the EU accession process any more successful in reforming the judiciary. Two institutions are the main reasons for the intransigence of judges, and the judiciary as a whole – the Constitutional Court and the State Judicial Council.

The Constitutional Court is a peculiar institution in Croatia. It is a judicial institution but is not part of the judicial (sub)system. Rather, it is part of the political system, although many vehemently oppose the notion that it is a political institution. According to some (Crnić 2001), the institution is outside of the system of separation of powers, a separate constitutional category that rules on laws but cannot be ruled by law. This made it into a final arbiter whose decisions cannot be even questioned, let alone overruled or changed. This juristocracy is very dangerous for liberal democracy due to the lack of democratic legitimacy of the Court. During the 1990s, it seemed that the Constitutional Court was the only bulwark against complete dominance of the HDZ in the judicial sphere. The court ruled against several major initiatives intended to capture the judicial system, but as the years passed and the war in Croatia continued, even the judges of the Constitutional Court felt reluctant to oppose Tuđman and his government directly. The relative autonomy of the Court all but ended in 1999 when HDZ used their majority in the parliament to appoint five prominent party members as new judges, with the opposition accepting two spots for 'their' members (Uzelac 2001). Hence, the politicization of the Constitutional Court was complete and HDZ's grip over it was fortified and used in subsequent years, especially during the years when the party was in opposition. Today, the Constitutional Court is formally independent, yet politicized.

The Constitutional Court is not the most problematic institution in the judicial system. The State Judicial Council (DSV) is primarily responsible for dysfunction in the judiciary and is also one of the most notorious bodies in the entire judicial branch (Uzelac 2001). It was established as a way for judges to influence appointments themselves without any external, primarily political, influence. However, HDZ governments in the 1990s decided to nominate almost all members of the Council according to loyalty and not expertise. This perverted the idea that Council membership should be based on merit and, instead, created a body that neither had expertise, legitimacy nor was democratically elected (Uzelac 2001).

Notwithstanding democratic changes in 2000, the decade of accession negotiation that followed, and finally membership in the European Union, the deficiencies the HDZ government created in the judicial sector have thoroughly undermined that part of the governing system. These deficiencies have especially remained in the DSV, a profoundly flawed institution whose defects have been amplified by the weaknesses of post-2000 governments and frozen by insistence of the EU for full independence of judicial institutions. This allowed the DSV to consider itself untouchable even concerning other judicial institutions such as the Constitutional Court. Therefore, it does not come as a surprise that the DSV ignored the rulings of the Constitutional Court (Lukić 2018a), and made controversial judicial appointments (Lukić 2018b). The HDZ government has continued to politicize the institution by, among others, nominating politicians with legal background and almost no judicial legitimacy as DSV members (Romić 2017).

7. Discussion

Taking into account the question of how widespread illiberal practices are in Croatia, the analysis showed that since 2013 – but especially since 2015 – they were spreading to ever more policy areas and to essential institutions within the political system. These practices are still on a much smaller scale compared to Poland or Hungary, let alone other countries of Southeast Europe. In addition, the spread of illiberal practices seems to be focused on the liberal part of the liberal-democratic nexus, particularly targeting media freedoms, independent institutions, and the judiciary. The democratic part, represented through electoral practices, is more or less stable and largely respected by the political elite.

Despite this partial spread of illiberal practices, there is a fear that the contagion would spread to other areas, including electoral practices. The main reason for such fear is the steady rise in the number of institutions, actors, and policies affected by illiberal practices. To give an example we can look at media freedoms and independence of media. One of the first acts of the newly elected HDZ-led government in 2015 was sacking the head of the national public broadcaster and installing a loyalist instead. Soon afterwards, the Agency for Electronic Media, a media watchdog, was overtaken, after its head resigned due to pressure by right-wing actors and organizations allied with HDZ. The new head allowed the agency to become marginalized by not pursuing action against even the most blatant examples of ethics violations. At the same time, the Ministry of Culture halted public funding for non-profit media, many of which were critical of HDZ and their allies. In order to weaken the criticism by long-established professional organizations (like the Croatian Journalists' Association), media figures close to the HDZ and right-wing political forces organized parallel association. This, in turn, was used to prove that the media sector in Croatia functions, while the criticisms are a product of 'Soros mercenaries' in left-wing media and their intent to vilify the HDZ government in the international arena. The latest wave of attacks on media independence is linked to intimidation, arrests, and lawsuits against journalists, editors, and outlets, usually for 'insulting the moral sentiment of the public', 'psychological injury' or for libel. Restrictive media laws allow this to happen with backing of the judiciary. This example shows how incremental undermining of norms and rules which are vital for safeguarding liberal democracy works cumulatively, piling new instances of violation of liberal-democratic norms on top of those already in place. Hence, such practices become accepted, and the normalization of illiberal policies and politics continues with detrimental repercussions.

The re-emergence of democratic backsliding since 2013 is linked to a combination of internal structural factors and diminished external pressures for democratization. Internal structural factors are linked to institutional weaknesses of the political system of Croatia, which were inherited from the 1990s. The Croatian political system was built and moulded during the war and by the undisputed power of the HDZ and its then leader F. Tuđman. The aim of the system was either to maximize the power of the HDZ or to stymie the power of opposition forces. A second internal issue is the cohabitation or power sharing between HDZ and the opposition forces. Between 2000 and 2015, HDZ was either in opposition (2000–03 and 2011–15) or held only one of two institutions of power (the government 2003–11, and the presidency 2014–15). This way the HDZ lacked a monopoly of power, while opposition actors were able to, more or less successfully, keep it in check.

The success of opposition forces in keeping the HDZ in check was aided by external factors, especially the negotiation process for EU accession. In addition, the pro-European wing of HDZ – the one in power between 2000 and 2012 – had an interest to be a good pupil and accept necessary reforms. It allowed for brief yet critical period of democratic advancement and consolidation in Croatia.

These two factors – external control and internal power sharing – effectively disappeared in 2013 and 2015, respectively. Once Croatia became a member of the EU, stick part of the 'stick-and-carrot' policy of conditionality disappeared. With it, any possibility to put pressure on the government by EU institutions and actors also faded. This freed the HDZ government to act in their interest without fear of reprisal. Once the HDZ secured a monopoly of power, winning both the 2014 presidential and 2015 (and 2016) parliamentary elections, nothing stood in their way. The illiberal politics of the 1990s were once again resumed. Most evident was the uptick of corruption practices and the capture of institutions and organizations with significant power of the purse, now even more critical due to funds opened to Croatia from cohesion, structural, and other common EU policies.

8. Conclusion

The conditionality principle was supposed to be the tool the European Union used to consolidate democracy in candidate countries of Central and Eastern Europe, bringing about the Europeanization of those polities. Once the democratic capacity of a candidate state becomes sufficient, and democracy becomes stronger, the reward of European Union membership will follow. This was supposed to happen in the case of Croatia.

What happened instead? Since the 2013 accession of Croatia to the European Union, and especially since the HDZ re-established a monopoly of power in 2015, we witnessed democratic stagnation, weakening, and in some cases, even backsliding in an ever-growing number of segments of the Croatian political system. The liberal component of democracy is more affected than the electoral, although there are issues in the latter as well. Hence, the focus of this paper was primarily on the backsliding that affects factors relevant to the liberal component of democracy.

Backsliding was visible in many vital sectors, including media independence, the judicial framework, and among independent and autonomous institutions. The examples given in this paper, backed up by evidence from media and research reports, support the trends displayed in both v-dem and Nations in Transit data. Since 2015, Croatia displayed an accelerated weakening of autonomous spheres, a monopolization and abuse of power, capture of public resources, and a marginalization of critical institutions and actors. The acceleration in democratic decline was shadowed by incremental executive encroachment and the accumulation of illiberal policies. This, in turn, can lead to a normalization of backsliding in the eyes of the public.

The primary source of this backsliding is the historical legacy of the Croatian institutional framework – overarching structural weaknesses built into the system by the HDZ during the 1990s. Forces that acted as a break on HDZ's abuse of the political system between 2000 and 2013 disappeared in recent years with no indication that they will return any time soon. In addition, the changing nature of the European Union itself does not leave much room for optimism. The dominance of the EPP, a Christian Democratic/conservative party family, shows us that as long as the stability of the (economic/security) system is maintained and as long as the centre-right conservative forces hold power in member states, the EU will turn the blind eye towards democratic backsliding on the national level. Internal forces in the form of cohabitation does not seem likely. HDZ, a member of the EPP, as the dominant party in the Croatian political system, will be able to navigate between abusing the liberal component while respecting the electoral component of democracy. As long as democracy is not the only game in town the dominant party will not be punished either by domestic or international actors. In the long run, this does not bode well for the consolidation of the liberal component of democracy and can endanger the electoral component as well.

While Croatia has not returned to the competitive authoritarianism of the 1990s, it is a defective democracy (Merkel 2011; Boban 2016), with a weak and captured institutional framework, both on national and especially on the local level (GONG 2017). The use of illiberal policies is on the rise, but its effects are overall still restrained compared to other countries in Southeast Europe. While some policy areas have been captured by actors propagating illiberal views, there are many others which still function, albeit imperfectly, as liberal institutions. This paper identified issues and policy areas that might further derail the consolidation of democracy and that would then tip Croatia, a member state of the European Union, towards a hybrid (democratic) regime, or even competitive authoritarianism.

Note

1. Personal conversation with N1 editors and journalists.

Acknowledgements

The author would like to thank the two anonymous reviewers for their insightful comments, as well as Vera Stojarova and Damir Kapidžić for the excellent editorial work.

Disclosure statement

No potential conflict of interest was reported by the author.

Funding

The research for this paper was funded by the University of Zagreb—Faculty of Law 2019 grant, as a part of the 'New Croatian Legal System' project.

References

Arbutina, P., and T. Opačić. 2016. Lokalne fašistovizije. *Novosti*, December 24. https://www.portalnovosti.com/lokalne-fasistovizije.

Bagić, D., and K. Kardov. 2018. Politička participacija i stranačke preferencije ratnih veterana u Hrvatskoj. *Politička misao* 55, no. 3: 82–103. doi:10.20901/pm.55.3.03

Bago, M. 2009. Jedinstveni u Europi, više birača nego stanovnika. *Dnevnik.hr*, April 17. https://dnevnik.hr/vijesti/hrvatska/hrvatska-ima-vise-biraca-nego-stanovnika.html.

Bayard de Volo, L. 2015. Comparative politics. In *Routledge handbook of interpretive political science*, ed. M. Bevir and R.A.W. Rhodes, 241–55. New York: Routledge.

Blanuša, N. 2017. Trauma and taboo: Forbidden political questions in Croatia. *Politička misao* 54, no. 1–2: 170–96.

Boban, D. 2016. Promjene u sustavu vlasti i konsolidacija demokracije: usporedba uloge predsjednika države u Hrvatskoj i Slovačkoj. *Studia lexicographica* 10, no. 1: 151–72.

Brakus, A. 2018. Mladunčad HDZ-a. *Novosti*, February 23. https://www.portalnovosti.com/mladuncad-hdz-a.

Čepo, D. ed. 2019. *Odredište EU: budućnost mladih u Hrvatskoj*. Zagreb: Centar za demokraciju i pravo Miko Tripalo.

Čepo, D. M. Čehulić, and S. Zrinščak. forthcoming. What difference a time makes? Framing media discourse on refugees and migrants in Croatia in two time periods (2015–2016 and 2018). *Hrvatska i komparativna javna uprava*.

Cipek, T. 2017. The spectre of communism is haunting Croatia. The Croatian right's image of the enemy. *Politička misa* 54, no. 1–2: 150–69.

Crnić, J. 2001. Ustavni sud Republike Hrvatske: iskustva i perspektive. *Politička misao* 38, no. 4: 126–45.

Čular, G. 2000. Political development in Croatia 1990–2000: Fast transition – postponed consolidation. *Politička misao* 37, no. 5: 30–46.

Čular, G. 2018. Metodološki izazovi ustavnog sudovanja: učinci podjele na izborne jedinice na rezultate izbora u Hrvatskoj 2000–2016. *Anali Hrvatskog politološkog društva* 15, no. 1: 7–28. doi:10.20901/an.15.01

Cvijanović, H. 2018. On memory politics and memory wars: A critical analysis of the Croatian dialogue document. *Politička misao* 55, no. 4: 109–46. doi:10.20901/pm.55.4.05

D. D. 2019. DIP izradio jedinstveni izborni zakon, evo koje promjene predlažu. *Dalmacija Danas*, February 2. https://www.dalmacijadanas.hr/dip-izradio-jedinstveni-izborni-zakon-evo-koje-promjene-predlazu

Danas.hr. 2019. Završio novinarski prosvjed: 'Hrvatska je rekorder po broju sudskih tužbi protiv medija, a HRT vodi križarski rat'. *Net.hr*, March 2. https://net.hr/danas/hrvatska/uzivo-poceo-je-novinarski-prosvjed-okupilo-se-vise-stotina-ljudi-oteli-ste-medije-novinarstvo-ne-damo/

Derado, A., V. Dergić, and V. Međugorac. 2016. Croatian youth and populism: A mixed methods analysis of the populism 'Breeding Ground' among the youth in the City of Zagreb. *Revija Za Sociologiju* 46, no. 2: 141–73. doi:10.5613/rzs.46.2.2

Despot, S., 2016. SDP-ova koalicija omogućila HDZ-u preuzimanje javne televizije. Faktograf.hr, February 17. https://faktograf.hr/2016/02/17/1526/

Dolenec, D. 2008. Europeanization as a democratising force in post-communist Europe: Croatia in comparative perspective. *Politička Misao* 45, no. 5: 23–46.

Dolenec, D. 2013. *Democratic institutions and authoritarian rule in Southeast Europe*. Colchester, UK: European Consortium for Political Research.

Dolenec, D. 2017. A soldier's state? Veterans and the welfare regime in Croatia. *Anali Hrvatskog politološkog društva* 14, no. 1: 55–76. doi:10.20901/an.14.03

Đurman, P. 2016. Europeizacija javne uprave i načelo otvorenosti. *Godišnjak Akademije pravnih znanosti Hrvatske* 7, no. 1: 342–73.

Forum.tm. 2016. Preuzimanje HRT-a u najboljoj maniri državnih udara. March 3. http://www.forum.tm/vijesti/preuzimanje-hrt-u-najboljoj-maniri-drzavnih-udara-4270

Freedom House. 2018. *Nations in transit 2018*. Washington DC: Freedom House. https://freedomhouse.org/report/nations-transit/nations-transit-2018

G. D. 2016. Napadi na Rakić i Violić podsjećaju na Miloševićevu fašističku politiku. *Tportal.hr*, January 28. https://www.tportal.hr/vijesti/clanak/napadi-na-rakic-i-violic-podsjecaju-na-milosevicevu-fasisticku-politiku-20160128

Gabrić, T., 2018. Premijer Plenković i njegovi vragovi. *H-alter.org*, March 13. https://www.h-alter.org/vijesti/premijer-plenkovic-i-njegovi-vragovi

GONG. 2017. *Naša zarobljena mista. Istraživački izvještaj studija kvalitete lokalnog javnog upravljanja u Hrvatsko*. Zagreb: GONG.

Grahek Ravančić, M. 2018. The historiography of bleiburg and the death marches since croatian independence. *Politička misao* 55, no. 2: 133–44. doi:10.20901/pm.55.2.07

Grbeša, M., and B. Šalaj. 2017. Populism in Croatia: The curious case of the bridge (Most). *Anali Hrvatskog politološkog društva* 14, no. 1: 7–30. doi:10.20901/an.14.01

Grozdanić, D., 2016. Kovačićevih sedamdeset. *Novosti*, May 5. https://www.portalnovosti.com/kovaievih-sedamdeset.

Gvozdanović, A., V. Ilišin, M. Adamović, D. Potočnik, N. Baketa, and M. Kovačić. 2019. *Youth study Croatia 2018/2019*. Berlin: Friedrich-Ebert-Stiftung e. V.

HBK. 2014. Priopćenje s 49. plenarnog zasjedanja Sabora HBK. *Hbk.hr*, October 23. http://hbk.hr/priopcenje-s-49-plenarnog-zasjedanja-sabora-hbk/.

HINA. 2014. Ustavni sud: Nedovoljno potpisa za referendum o izboru zastupnika 'imenom i prezimenom'. *Novi list*, December 11. http://www.novilist.hr/Vijesti/Hrvatska/Ustavni-sud-Nedovoljno-potpisa-za-referendum-o-izboru-zastupnika-imenom-i-prezimenom.

HINA. 2018. HRT otpustio urednika i novinara Hrvoja Zovka: Kao razlog za izvanredni otkaz naveli i Istanbulsku, oglasio se i HND. *Net.hr*, September 25. https://net.hr/danas/hrvatska/hrt-otpustio-urednika-i-novinara-hrvoja-zovka-kao-razlog-za-izvanredni-otkaz-naveli-i-istanbulsku-konvenciju/.

HINA. 2019a. Most predlaže promjene izbornog zakona: Maksimalno 120 zastupnika, 3 preferencijska glasa, *Vijesti.hr*, January 10. https://vijesti.rtl.hr/novosti/hrvatska/3318891/most-predlaze-promjene-izbornog-zakona-maksimalno-120-zastupnika-3-preferencijska-glasa/

HINA. 2019b. EFJ, IFJ call on HRT to withdraw lawsuits against journalists. *Euractiv.jutarnji.eu*, January 23. https://euractiv.jutarnji.hr/en/politics-and-society/legislation/efj-ifj-call-on-hrt-to-withdraw-lawsuits-against-journalists/8302409/.

Jurasić, M., 2018. Ivan Koprić: Lex šerif je neustavan. *Večernji list*, March 1. https://www.vecernji. hr/vijesti/ivan-kopric-lex-serif-zakon-o-lokalnoj-i-podrucnoj-samoupravi-1229502.

Kapidžić, D.2020. The Rise of Illiberal Politics in Southeast Europe. *Southeast European and Black Sea Studies* 20, no. 1. (forthcoming)

Kasapović, M. 2000. Electoral politics in Croatia 1990–2000. *Politička misao* 37, no. 5: 3–20.

Kasapović, M. 2017. Jesu li izborni sustavi sredstva dramatična utjecaja na sudbine zemalja? *Političke Analize* 8, no. 32: 17–21.

Klarić, J., 2019. HND ima zgodan brojač kojim mjere za koliko novca HRT tuži novinare; danas su na 2,14 milijuna kuna. *Telegram.hr*, January 31. https://www.telegram.hr/politika-kriminal /hnd-ima-zgodan-brojac-kojim-mjere-za-koliko-novca-hrt-tuzi-novinare-danas-su-na-214-milijuna-kuna/.

Koprić, I. 2014. Prilagodbe hrvatske javne uprave europskim standardima. *Godišnjak Akademije pravnih znanosti Hrvatske* 5, no. 1: 8–39.

Koprić, I. 2016. Reforma javne uprave u Hrvatskoj: ni bolni rezovi ni postupne promjene–Nužna je nova upravna paradigma. *Političke analize* 7, no. 26: 3–12.

Koprić, I., 2017. 'Lex šerif': To je zakon za moćnike, a protiv građana. *Express*, December 28. https://www.express.hr/top-news/lex-serif-to-je-zakon-za-mocnike-a-protiv-gra-ana-13519.

Koprić, I., and M. Škarica. 2017. Evaluacija neposrednog izbora načelnika i župana u Hrvatskoj nakon dva mandata: korak naprijed, dva nazad. In *Zbornik radova 7. međunarodne konferencije 'Razvoj javne uprave'*, ed. S. Gongeta and M. Smoljić, 156–72. Vukovar: Veleučilište 'Lavoslav Ružička'.

Kovačević, B., 2017. Vlada je shvatila da preuzimanje HRT-a nije dovoljno pa angažiraju PR-a; u što bi nas on trebao uvjeriti? *Telegram.hr*, November 15. https://www.telegram.hr/price/vlada-je-shvatila-da-potpuno-preuzimanje-hrt-a-nije-dovoljno-pa-angaziraju-pr-a-u-sto-bi-nas-on-trebao-uvjeriti/.

Lalić Novak, G. 2010. Hrvatska uprava u izvješćima Europske komisije i SIGME 2010: Ograničen napredak u reformi javne uprave. *Hrvatska i komparativna javna uprava* 10, no. 4: 927–40.

Levitsky, S., and L.A. Way. 2010. *Competitive authoritarianism*. Cambridge: Cambridge University Press.

Lukić, S., 2018a. DSV ipak zaposlio ženu čije je imenovanje već poništio Ustavni sud. *Jutarnji list*, July 27. https://www.jutarnji.hr/vijesti/hrvatska/dsv-ipak-zaposlio-zenu-cije-je-imenovanje-vec -ponistio-ustavni-sud/7659129/.

Lukić, S., 2018b. Od sedam sudaca u DSV-u jedino Neven Cambj želi još jedan mandate. Splitski sudac, koji je tužeći medije dobio 180.000 kuna, ima šanse ostati u DSV-u. *Jutarnji list*, November 19. https://www.jutarnji.hr/vijesti/hrvatska/od-sedam-sudaca-u-dsv-u-jedino-neven-cambj-zeli-jos-jedan-mandat-splitski-sudac-koji-je-tuzeci-medije-dobio-180000-kuna-ima-sanse-ostati-u-dsv-u/8072579/.

Lukić, S., 2018c. Pičuljan iz životopisa izbacio podatak da je bio član HDZ-a. *Jutarnji list*, November 14. https://www.jutarnji.hr/vijesti/hrvatska/piculjan-iz-zivotopisa-izbacio-podatak-da-je-bio-clan-hdz-a/8054369/.

Lušić, T., 2002. Ugovori između Svete stolice i Republike Hrvatske, Thesis, Diplomatic Academy. http://www.mvep.hr/custompages/static/hrv/files/lusic_tajana.pdf.

Marić, J., S. Pavić, and Z. Duka. 2016. Nakon Radmana, Mirjana Rakić: Vijeće za elektroničke medije iduća meta Vlade. *Novi list*, March 10. http://www.novilist.hr/Vijesti/Hrvatska/Nakon-Radmana-Mirjana-Rakic-Vijece-za-elektronicke-medije-iduca-meta-Vlade?meta_refresh= true.

Marinović, A., and I. Markešić. 2012. Vjerske zajednice u Hrvatskoj pred europskim izazovima. In *Hrvatska u EU: Kako dalje?* ed. V. Puljiz, S. Ravlić, and V. Visković, 349–72. Zagreb: Centar za demokraciju i parvo Miko Tripalo.

Markovina, D., 2019. Zašto je ideja koju spominje HDZ, da po novom zakonu pobjednik izbora dobije i bonus zastupnike, ozbiljno opasna. *Telegram.hr*, January 12. https://www.telegram.hr/ price/zasto-je-ideja-koju-spominju-u-hdz-u-da-po-novom-zakonu-pobjednik-izbora-dobije -i-bonus-zastupnike-ozbiljno-opasna/.

Medlobi, M., and D. Čepo. 2018. Stavovi korisnika društvenih mreža o izbjeglicama i tražiteljima azila: post festum tzv. izbjegličke krize. *Političke perspektive* 8, no. 1–2: 41–69. doi:10.20901/pp.8.1-2.02

Merkel, W. 2011. *Transformacija političkih sustava*. Zagreb: Biblioteka Politička misao.

Musa, A. 2013. Agencies in Croatia: Something old or something new?. *Hrvatska i komparativna javna uprava* 13, no. 2: 353–98.

Musa, A. 2019. Kontrola nad upravom u kontekstu europeizacije: neovisna kontrolna tijela u Hrvatskoj kao čuvari integriteta. *Zbornik radova Pravnog fakulteta u Splitu* 56, no. 1: 179–208. doi:10.31141/zrpfs.2019.56.131.179

Musa, A., D. Bebić, and P. Đurman. 2015. Transparency and openness in local governance: A case of Croatian cities. *Hrvatska i komparativna javna uprava* 15, no. 2: 415–50.

N1 Hrvatska. 2016. Misteriji hrvatske politike - kad mrtvi glasaju. *N1*, August 10, http://hr.n1info.com/Vijesti/a142740/Misteriji-hrvatske-politike-kad-mrtvi-glasaju.html.

Pavić, S., 2017. PREVIŠE POLITIKE? HRT ukida 'Hrvatsku uživo' zbog emisije o gastronomiji i – 'modernoj psihologiji'. *Novi list*, September 11. http://www.novilist.hr/Vijesti/Hrvatska/PREVISE-POLITIKE-HRT-ukida-Hrvatsku-uzivo-zbog-emisije-o-gastronomiji-i-modernoj-psihologiji.

Pavlaković, V., D. Brentin, and D. Pauković. 2018. The controversial commemoration: Transnational approaches to remembering bleiburg. *Politička Misao* 55, no. 2: 7–32. doi:10.20901/pm.55.2.01

Petković, K. 2013. Politike moralnosti – politička slika kulturnih ratova u Hrvatskoj. *Političke analize* 4, no. 16: 3–13.

Petričušić, A., M. Čehulić, and D. Čepo. 2017. Gaining Political power by utilizing opportunity structures: An analysis of the conservative religious-political movement in Croatia. *Politička misao* 54, no. 4: 61–84.

Pilsel, D., 2015. Društvo po mjeri Bujanca. *Autograf.hr*, July, 6. https://www.autograf.hr/drustvo-po-mjeri-bujanca/.

Podolnjak, R. 2013. Suvremeni hrvatski izborni inženjering kao sofisticirani oblik izborne manipulacije. *Zbornik Pravnog fakulteta u Zagrebu* 63, no. 1: 155–87.

Prelec, T. 2018. Croatia. In *Freedom house. 2018. Nations in transit 2018*. Washington DC: Freedom House. https://freedomhouse.org/report/nations-transit/2018/Croatia

Puljić-Šego, I., 2018. HDZ odgovorio Milinoviću: 'Šampion abortusa poziva se na Istanbulsku'. *Večernji list*, September 6. https://www.vecernji.hr/vijesti/hdz-odgovorio-milinovicu-sampion-abortusa-poziva-se-na-istanbulsku-1268381.

Puljiz, H., 2016. Mirjana Rakić podnijela ostavku: Ostali smo sami! *Tportal.hr*, March 18. https://www.tportal.hr/vijesti/clanak/mirjana-rakic-podnijela-ostavku-ostali-smo-sami-20160318.

Ravlić, S. 2017. *Liberalna demokracija*. Zagreb: Plejada.

Romić, T., 2017. Državno sudbeno vijeće važno je političko tijelo, tu moraju biti neovisni ljudi. *Večernji list*, July 9. https://www.vecernji.hr/vijesti/drzavno-sudbeno-vijece-vazno-je-politicko-tijelo-tu-moraju-biti-neovisni-ljudi-1181509.

Rožman, K., 2016. Tko je Siniša Kovačić. Na HRT-u je već 20 godina, bio je šef udruge HNIP, smijenili su ga iz Dnevnika 3 koji je pokrenuo s Dijanom Čuljak i Togonalom. *Jutarnji list*, March, 3. https://www.jutarnji.hr/vijesti/hrvatska/tko-je-sinisa-kovacic-na-hrt-u-je-vec-20-godina-bio-je-sef-udruge-hnip-smijenili-su-ga-iz-dnevnika-3-koji-je-pokrenuo-s-dijanom-culjak-i-togonalom/27310/.

S. D. M. 2017. Ekskluzivno: Imaju li građani povjerenja u pravosuđe? *Dnevnik.hr*, July 17. https://dnevnik.hr/vijesti/hrvatska/ekskluzivno-istrazivanje-dnevnika-nove-tv-o-povjerenju-gradjana-u-pravosudje—483093.html.

S. S. 2017. Evo koji su mediji dobili novac od Grada Zagreba i VEM-a. *Tportal.hr*, June 12. https://www.tportal.hr/vijesti/clanak/evo-koji-su-mediji-dobili-potpore-od-grada-zagreba-i-vijeca-za-elektronicke-medije-20170612.

Sarkotić, G., 2017. Tko je Helenca Pirnat Dragičević – Nova pravobraniteljica za djecu. *Narod.hr*, November 17. https://narod.hr/hrvatska/tko-helenca-pirnat-dragicevic-nova-pravobraniteljica-djecu

Shepsle, K.A. 2006. Rational choice institutionalism. In *The Oxford handbook of political institutions*, ed. R.A.W. Rhodes, S.A. Binder, and B.A. Rockman, 23–38. Oxford: Oxford University Press.

Telegram. 2017. Ovo je dosta zabavno; U ime obitelji dobili su novac od Zaklade koju su napadali da financra samo podobne udruge. *Telegram.hr*, December 27. https://www.telegram.hr/politika-kriminal/ovo-je-dosta-zabavno-u-ime-obitelji-dobila-je-novac-od-zaklade-koju-su-napadali-da-financira-samo-podobne-udruge/.

Thelen, K. 1999. Historical institutionalism in comparative politics. *Annual Review of Political Science* 2, no. 1: 369–404. doi:10.1146/annurev.polisci.2.1.369

Tokić, M.N. 2018. Avengers of Bleiburg: Émigré Politics, Discourses of Victimhood and Radical Separatism during the Cold War. *Politička misao* 55, no. 2: 71–88. doi:10.20901/pm.55.2.04

Tportal.hr. 2017. Medijska 2016. u znaku kaosa i devastacije HRT-a. *tportal.hr*, January 12. https://www.tportal.hr/vijesti/clanak/medijska-2016-u-znaku-kaosa-i-devastacije-hrt-a.

Trajković, S , 2013. Strašna istina o biračkim popisima. Čak 340.000 birača nema osobnu i živi na nepostojećoj adresi! *Jutarnji list*, January 7. https://www.jutarnji.hr/vijesti/hrvatska/strasna-istina-o-birackim-popisima-cak-340.000-biraca-nema-osobnu-i-zivi-na-nepostojecoj-adresi/1184087/.

Uzelac, A. 2001. Hrvatsko pravosuđe u devedesetima: od državne nezavisnosti do institucionalne krize. *Politička misao* 38, no. 2: 3–41.

Vidov, P., 2018. Državna zaklada dala 130 tisuća kuna udruzi u čijem predsjedništvu sjedi Plenković. *Faktograf*, January 19. https://faktograf.hr/2018/01/19/drzavna-zaklada-dala-130-tisuca-kuna-udruzi-u-cijem-predsjednistvu-sjedi-plenkovic/.

Zakošek, N. and G. Čular. 2004. Croatia. In *The handbook of political change in Eastern Europe*, ed. F.H. Aarebrot, S. Berglund, and J. Ekman, 451–92. Northampton: Edward Elgar.

Zrinščak, S. 1998. Crkva i država: Europski kontekst i postkomunističko iskustvo. *Revija za sociologiju* 29, no. 1–2: 15–26.

Media in the Western Balkans: who controls the past controls the future

Věra Stojarová

ABSTRACT

The contribution assesses the role of the media in respect to democratization and EU accession in the countries of the Western Balkans (WB) and the development of press freedom over the long run. The author closely analyses the legislative framework and its implementation in practice and focuses in particular on the economic and political pressure on the media in the region. The article offers three arguments to explain the bad shape of media freedom in the Balkans: structural factors (state advertisements as the main source of income, economic tycoons close to incumbents as media owners), proximate or external factors (the deteriorating level of media freedom in some EU countries and the whole WB region, with an accent on stability rather than democracy) and political-societal dynamics (defamation and libel as means to punish journalists, verbal and physical assaults on journalists). The media in the WB region do not serve as the watchdog of democracy but are instead used as a means to reinforce illiberal regimes.

Introduction

In 2018, the European Commission released a new enlargement strategy for the Western Balkan states offering them a credible enlargement perspective and setting 2025 as a possible enlargement date. Nevertheless, the progress of all Western Balkan states towards membership has thus far been very slow. Furthermore, we have seen clear democratic backsliding in the last ten years in the region, so the optimism about upcoming membership seems to be premature as all of the EU aspirants would have to change their track and deliver difficult and key reforms in democratic development in order to reach the goal of liberal democracy (c.f. e.g. Kmezić and Bieber 2017; Guasti and Mansfeldová 2018).

As Levitsky and Way stress, four arenas are of particular importance in the contest between liberal democracy and authoritarian regimes: 1) the electoral arena; 2) the legislature; 3) the judiciary; and 4) the media. (Levitsky and Way 2002). The media in ripe autocracies are entirely controlled by the government and no opposition voices are allowed. In liberal democracies, the media function as a watchdog who monitors and holds those in power accountable. The media has been regarded as the fourth estate, supplementing the three branches of government by providing checks and balances. They also serve as the basic source of information, and quality information constitutes one of the cornerstones of genuine democracy, since 'a broadly and equitably informed citizenry helps assure a democracy that is both responsive and responsible' (Delli Carpini and Keeter 1996, 1). Democracy is strengthened and its integrity ensured by the free flow of information and competition among public and private media articulating a variety of political viewpoints to educate the public and allow it to make informed choices, particularly at election time (Gunther and Mughan 2000, 5). Free media, its quality and independence, is essential and one of the cornerstones of liberal democracy.

In the grey zone in-between, in illiberal democracies, we find media controlled by the government but also independent media that serve as a mouthpiece for opposition forces. Those in power in illiberal democracies seek subtler mechanisms of repression than those in authoritarian regimes. These techniques embrace the selective allocation of state advertising, bribery, manipulation of debts and taxes owed by media outlets, the fomentation of conflicts among stockholders, and restrictive press laws that facilitate the prosecution of independent and opposition journalists usually via extensive use of libel laws to harass or persecute independent newspapers legally (Levitsky and Way 2002). They might also deny the opposition adequate media coverage, harass opposition candidates and their supporters or use governmentally controlled media as a mouthpiece of propaganda and glorification of the regime in order to skew the playing field in favour of incumbents so the competition is real but not fair (Levitsky and Way 2010, 5). The regime might also empower the regulatory bodies to overlook the audio-visual arena in order to provide 'balanced' coverage, with the definition of balance determined by the regulatory body. Other (vague) terms such as 'human dignity' or 'good faith' and 'fairness' might be misused and restricted, so the media arena creates a self-censorship culture in which journalists are under immense pressure to conform to the ruling political agenda.

Existing scholarly accounts of freedom of the media in the Balkans suggest that Balkan media freedom becomes an oxymoron. Of greatest concern in the last decade have been the links between the media and politicians, dependence of media on the governing party and physical and verbal assaults on journalists (Abazi undated; ANEM 2015; Belgrade Centre for Human Rights 2012, 2018; Bieber and Kmezic 2015; Blazeva et al. 2015; Blazeva and Mukoska 2018; Brunwasser et al. 2016; Fetoshi 2017; Jusić and Irion 2018; Kolozova and Georgijev 2018; Lani and Cupi 2002; Petković et al. 2014; Vladisavljević 2019; Vogel 2015). Some are only case studies; many of the existing comparative analyses are either outdated or do not include Croatia, assessments and comparisons of the contemporary situation in North Macedonia, or omit the link between the quality of the media and the quality of democracy.

Our text tries to fill this gap. The aim of this text is to examine the media and its impact on the quality of democracy in the Balkan region via simple comparison. The countries examined in this text are those of the Western Balkans – Albania, Bosnia and Herzegovina (BiH), Kosovo, North Macedonia, Montenegro and Serbia. Although Croatia can no longer be called a Western Balkan country since its integration into the EU, it does share many patterns with its neighbours in terms of media control. It was thus included, as a comparison between it, as an EU member state, and the aspirants for EU membership is valuable. We look at the legislative framework and how it is implemented in practice, accompanied by a close overview of media ownership and many of the possible constraints media face. The text does not omit the physical and verbal assaults on journalists and so presents a unique, comprehensive analysis of the media in the region. The constitutions and primary legislation dealing with the media were used as the primary source, and several country analyses by different authors were used as the secondary source. Several semi-structured interviews (3–6 from each country) with journalists, media scholars, and members of civil society from the Western Balkan region were undertaken to give better understanding of the issue. The focus was on the link between the quality of the media and the quality of democracy in respective countries.

In this article, we argue that the countries of the Western Balkans have not gone through sudden democratic reversal in terms of media freedom. What we can observe is the continuous misuse of power in the last decade by the extremely strong executive slowly usurping supremacy and control over the media. The control is mostly indirect and subtle in order to preserve the image of democracy. Nevertheless, in many instances we see killings, physical attacks and threats as the direct abuse of power towards media. The author offers three arguments to illuminate the poor quality of media freedom in the Balkans: structural factors (dependency on state advertisements, economic tycoons close to the incumbents as media owners), proximate or external factors (deteriorating level of media freedom in some EU countries and stability coming before democracy) and political-societal dynamics (defamation and libel as means to punish journalists, verbal and physical assaults on journalists as the norm). Media are used as a means to reinforce the illiberal regimes and history has taught us whoever controls the past, controls the future. Control over the media is one of the essential pieces of the puzzle in the illiberal picture that provides legitimacy to the authoritarian leaders and helps to bolster the regimes.

The paper's structure is as follows: The first part presents an overview of the main broadcasting and print media use in the region. This is followed by an analysis of the legislative framework and the role of the regulatory bodies involved; issues of libel and defamation are discussed. The third part looks at media ownership and economic pressure, followed by a section dealing with political pressure and censorship. The last part focuses on the intimidation of journalists, and the physical and verbal assaults they face. The conclusion then outlines the paper's main findings and broader implications for the region.

Overview of the media sector in the Western Balkans

Balkan countries share similar patterns in the use of media – the main source of information remains state TV in all of the countries under our scrutiny; 50–60% use TV as the main source of information (c.f. BBC 2017, 2017a, 2018; Flanders Investment and Trade 2016; Be in Kosovo undated; Cvetanoski 2016). Virtually all households have a TV set and the public broadcasters are viewed as the main source of information; private broadcasters have comparable and sometimes higher audience ratings but are viewed as entertainment. Daily newspapers have experienced the biggest decline in overall consumption in the first decade of the 21st century so all of the daily newspapers in the region moved to the internet and in most cases there is a strong convergence between online and offline newspaper component.

As the Table 1 shows, the media sector in all of our Balkan countries can be characterized as very fragmented. In Albania, a country of less than three million people, there are around 21 daily newspapers, one national public TV station and three national privately owned TV stations, three radio stations and scores of local TV and radio stations. In North Macedonia, the number of TV and radio stations per capita is even higher: there are over 60 commercial TV channels and over 80 radio stations. This fragmentation in North Macedonia could be attributed to the reflection of the multi-lingual structure of the society, airing in Macedonian and Albanian and, on the local level, also in Romany and the Serbian/Croatian/Bosnian languages (Šopar 2008, 120). The Montenegrin media sector is also very fragmented with a relatively high number of media outlets. We could also observe huge polarization of the media in Montenegro, as the sector is divided between the pro-government media and those critical of the government (Kerševan Smokvina et al. 2017, 17). In Serbia, the market is probably least fragmented in terms of population size: there are more than 200 TV channels, six private TV stations are licenced to broadcast nationally and over 200 have regional licences. In Croatia, the public broadcaster HRT dominates the arena, although it faces competition from private networks including the leading national station Nova TV.

Table 1. Media sector in the Western Balkans. Social media platforms counted according to their traffic generation capabilities i.e. the amount of traffic they refer to other websites (Statcounter Global Stats 2019). Sources: TV, Radio (BBC 2017) Population (Worldometers 2019), Social media (Statcounter Global Stats 2019), Number of dailies (Chartsbin.com), other info not found in the above-mentioned sources (BIRN/Reporters without borders 2017; Vukanović 2016; www.irex.org).

	Population	TV national public/ national private/ regional and local	Radio national public/ national private/ regional and local	Daily newspapers/circulation of dailies	Internet access	Top social media platform
Albania	2.9 mil.	1/3/over 60	1/2/over 60	21/est. 70 000 max. copies sold	2 mil.	FB (61%), Pinterest 18%
BiH	3.5 mil.	3/mainly on entity level/ over 200	3/over 200 entity/ regional/ local	7/N/A reach of dailies between 1.4% and 8.4%	2.6 mil.	FB (99%,) Twitter (0.3%)
Croatia	4.1 mil.	1/7/over 20	1/3/over 150	13/300 000 copies sold	3.8 mil.	FB (82%) Pinterest (10.1%)
Kosovo	1.8 mil	1/4/over 20	1/6/over 80	9/12 000 copies sold	1.6 mil.	FB (N/A) Instagram (N/A)
Montenegro	629 thous.	1/4/over 10	1/6/over 50	4/14 300 copies sold	398 thousand	FB (92.5%) Pinterest (2.9%)
N. Macedonia	2.1 mil.	1/5/over 60	1/3/over 80	10/34 100 printed	1.5 mil.	FB (93.4%), Pinterest 2.75%
Serbia	8.7 mil.	1/6/over 200	1/1/more than 300	12/1.5 mil. copies	4.7 mil.	FB (89.8%), Pinterest 3.4%

Ethnic and state divisions in Bosnia and Herzegovina shape the media in the country, as outlets run by the entities are more popular than the state-wide ones. Public Service Broadcasting (PSB) in Bosnia and Herzegovina is a reflection of the country's complex political and constitutional arrangements. Considering the linguistic similarities between the three official languages (Bosnian, Serbian, and Croatian), lawmakers have established a unique Public Service Broadcasting System consisting of three broadcasters: a state-level broadcaster (*BHRT*) and the two entity-level broadcasters (*RTRS* and *RTVFBiH*) (Jusić and Džihana 2008, 82). In Kosovo, again the ethnic division shapes the media outlets, as we have the media for the Albanians and the media aimed at Serbs. Although they are all based in Kosovo, they have strong competition from popular networks based in Albania and Serbia similarly to BiH, where the local broadcasters face competition from Croatia and Serbia.

The way Balkan citizens access their media has seen important changes in the last few years as the internet has gained in popularity. Approximately 70% of the population in all of the countries is online (the highest is probably Kosovo with 80% of internet users). Access to the internet is not only high, but is also without restrictions. Facebook is the top social media resource in the Balkans; the second position varies according to the country, with Pinterest gaining popularity over previously hailed YouTube. A significant portion of the general population has access to the internet and it has become the second most important medium for obtaining information; the share of internet increases at the expense of TV (BBC 2017, 2017a; Kyrke – Smith undated; Fetoshi 2017; Macedonian Institute for Media 2015; Turčilo in Turčilo et al. 2017).

One of the main paradoxes of the media in ex-Yugoslavian countries is that while it did have periods of governmental control, the media in these countries all share a liberal tradition stemming from the high decentralization of the media during the communist regime (Tunnard 2003, 103). Being aware of the methodological, conceptual and other problems with measuring media freedom (see e.g. Behmer 2009; Schneider 2014), when looking at the 2017 media freedom ratings by Freedom House (Graph 1), the worst ranked Western Balkan country was North Macedonia, while the best WB country was Croatia. The scores also reflect deteriorating media freedom in all of the countries under our scrutiny, except one, Kosovo, where the slight improvement is justified by the improvement in the way authorities handle threats against journalists. What is intriguing is that Croatia has fallen steadily; the drop was not only due to the misuse of the concept of hate speech aimed at the closure of Serbian minority media launched by the Croatian nationalists in their 2016/17 campaign but also due to the fact that journalists investigating corruption, organized crime or war crimes are often subject to intimidation campaigns and that the government kept interfering in the Croatian public broadcasting company HRT (Freedom House 2017).

Legislative framework and the regulatory bodies

The legislation of the Western Balkan countries in terms of media is very well developed according to the EU standards. The accession process and subsequent Europeanization is pivotal in the shaping of countries' legislation as the EU´s political commitment to media pluralism and freedom is generally high, since they are both considered to be fundamental elements for the democratization of the enlargement countries (Brogi et al. 2014).

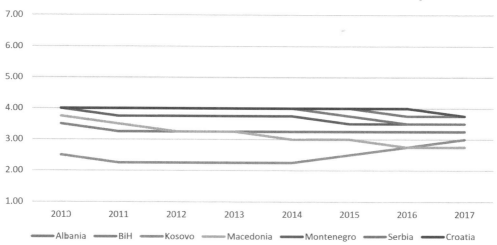

Graph 1. Independent Media Score 2010–2017. (Data taken from Freedom House 2010–17).

All countries with the exception of Kosovo are, as members of the Council of Europe, signatories of the European Convention on Human Rights, which is then part of their legislation (sometimes it is even recalled in the constitution itself) and guarantees the freedom of expression. Kosovo, not having signed the Convention, guarantees the freedom of expression in the Kosovo Constitution (de Hert and Korenica 2016). Media freedom and plurality is guaranteed and censorship prohibited by all of the constitutions in the region (c.f. Constitutions in respective countries). The right to information is guaranteed only by some of the Constitutions (Kosovo, Albania, Montenegro, Croatia, and North Macedonia). Nevertheless, the legal regulations are not necessarily observed - even though the right to access information is guaranteed in the Montenegrin constitution, the government quite often denies access to information that would uncover corruption. According to the European Union (EU), in 2014, 1,007 of 4,058 initial requests for access to public information were denied, amounting to a non-compliance rate of 25 percent (Freedom House Montenegro 2016). The research from IREX shows that journalists find it difficult to request and obtain information from the government in the whole region (www.irex.com).

The regulatory bodies are generally perceived as being weak, unprofessional, biased and dependent on the political powers (Erichsen et al. 2013). Furthermore, they are usually elected with a simple parliamentary majority, and are thus closely related to the ruling party. The countries' media regulators are, in most of the cases, not financially independent, sometimes have inadequate monitoring capacity or are seen as highly politicized.

In most of the countries, defamation was decriminalized so that it is no longer punishable by imprisonment, but remains punishable by fines[1]. The decriminalization of libel and defamation is generally welcomed; but it is also criticized, as the accompanying fines could be extremely high compared to the regular wages of journalists. The reputations of investigative journalists can be easily destroyed and the damages imposed by the courts for alleged psychological trauma can threaten the very existence of the media. Defamation laws and lawsuits can very easily lead to self-censorship and thus threaten investigative journalism in the countries. The problem also remains how judges determine emotional distress and what standards they use, let alone that the judiciary system is quite often under political control.

Table 2 show, that in Albania, Serbia and Croatia, defamation is still a criminal offence, but considered a misdemeanour and punishable by fine. In Croatia, it is not considered a criminal act of defamation if a claim is truthful and publicized for the sake of public interest or for some other justified reason. However, the law gives plenty of space for interpretation of what information is of public interest so it is left to the court to interpret case by case, which has resulted in many controversial court rulings. In the last few years, there has been an increase in lawsuits against media outlets for defamation, instigated by members of parliament, the government, the legal system, civil society groups and other media. There have been many cases in which the media were sanctioned with a fine although the published content about e.g. a politician occupying a public function was proven to be true (c.f. Leka 2018; Freedom House 2016). Criminal law remains a significant potential pressure mechanism on the media. Open-ended methods such as incitement to hatred or security-related standards are common, and examples of this practice are numerous (Bieber and Kmezić 2015, 11). Public figures can (and do) use these methods as means to punish journalists, and this curtails the plurality of the media and induces fear among journalists. Croatia and Montenegro have the harshest laws on insulting the national symbols (emblem, national anthem, flag, and republic) – mocking these is punishable by up to one year in prison. In Albania and Serbia, the punishment such behaviour is a fine or imprisonment up to three months, while in North Macedonia, it is only a fine. Montenegro and North Macedonia are the only countries that penalize blasphemy or insult to religion. Looking at the available statistics dealing with the lawsuits against journalists, the leading countries are both Croatia and Serbia.

Media ownership and working under economic pressure

Television, radio, and newspapers are operated both by state-owned and private corporations. The public broadcasters are usually financed through a taxes, licence fees, budget allocations, advertising, and sale of programmes, sponsorships or their own production and they are overseen by the regulatory bodies described earlier. Throughout the regions, the public broadcasters are financially dependent on the state and quite often show a strong pro-government bias. Most of the media in the region are privately owned by locals while foreign ownership of the media is rather limited, which could have also contributed to the lack of growth of media professionalization. The media landscape is highly fragmented and saturated, but instead of bringing more diversity, the outcome is low profitability and undermining of economic sustainability (Brogi et al. 2014).

In many countries, local media are often financed and subsidized largely by local governments. For this reason, these media are often criticized for being mouthpieces of local government. The surveys of BIRN and Belgrade Centre for Human Rights showed

Table 2. Defamation in the WB countries (Trpevska et al 2018:37; Çollaku 2018).

	Defamation and libel	Insult of Public officials	Insult of state and National symbols	Defamation of head of the state	Defamation of foreign head of state/symbols	Blasphemy/insult of religion
Albania	Criminal Law. Fine from 50.000 to 1.500 000 Lek. No official statistics.	Insult of judges – fine or imprisonment up to three months	Flag, emblem – fine or imprisonment up to 3 months	-	-	-
BiH	Decriminalized. Protective public officials – prison between three months and three years. Large numbers of lawsuits have been filed against journalists (since 2003, around 100 per year). In September 2016 there were 173 active cases in the courts.	-	-	-	-	-
Croatia	Criminal Law. Insult – fine up to 90 times daily rate. Shaming – up to 180 times daily rate. Defamation – up to 360 times daily rate. Over 500 lawsuits per year.	-	Imprisonment up to one year	-	Imprisonment up to one year	-
Kosovo	Decriminalized. Fine. Over 20 ongoing lawsuits against journalists	-	-	-	-	-
Montenegro	Decriminalized. Offence punished by fine of 3.000–10.000 euro. Relates also to mocking nations and ethnics. No official statistics.	-	Imprisonment up to one year	-	States and symbols fine 3.000 to 10.000 euro	Mocking religion – Prison one to eight years
N. Macedonia	Decriminalized. Around 35–40 lawsuits against journalists.	-	Fine	-	State and symbols – fine	Mocking religious symbols – imprisonment 1–5 years
Serbia	Criminal Code. Fine ranging from 40.000 to 200 000 Serbian dinars. Large number of lawsuits against journalists (over 400 per year)	-	Fine or imprisonment up to three months	-	Mocking symbols fine or imprisonment up to three months	-

that 8 out of 15 Serbian media outlets in the sample were owned or under the control of individuals well known for their affiliation with politicians in power and the real owners of 18 out of the 30 most influential outlets in Serbia remain unknown (Belgrade Centre for Human Rights 2012; BIRN/Reporters without borders 2017; Mirovni Institute 2004; Kerševan Smokvina et al. 2017; Kmezić 2019, 102). In Montenegro, despite the legal requirements to inform the regulator about the ownership structure, there is no practice to inform the public about media ownership and consequently the public is familiar only with the illusory owners of certain media. Consequently, Petros Stathis, a Greek entrepreneur closely related to the governing party in Montenegro, owns several national media outlets, but as there is no central publicly available register containing all the information regarding media ownership, there are allegations that he is only a fictive owner (Čađenović and Radulović 2017).

The main sources of private media revenues are advertising, in-house programming production, budget subsidies and revenues from copies sold. However, revenues are scarce, the advertising market has been consistently shrinking and, throughout the region, the state remains the main advertiser, which raises questions of media independence. Financial crises in the public service media were quite often used as the basis for imposing political influence. In North Macedonia, after winning the elections in 2006, the VMRO-DPMNE led government took steps to consolidate Macedonian Radio-Television's organizational and financial crisis, imposing its political control over the new management and supervisory bodies. In order to achieve these goals, several amendments to the 2005 Broadcasting Law were adopted over the following years and the over-exposure of the government's work and the public service broadcaster's obedience to the ruling party were omnipresent (Trpevska and Micevski 2017). In Montenegro, there is a perception that the Government's interference is higher when it comes to the work of the public broadcaster, but the biggest commercial TV stations are considered to be excessively pro-governmental as well (Čađenović and Radulović 2017; Brogi et al. 2014; Brkić 2015). Governments also act selectively when it comes to non-tax payers – e.g. the Montenegrin *TV Vijesti* (accused, by the way, by the government media of unprofessional and illegal behaviour) blamed unfair media conditions when the Montenegrin government blocked its bank accounts for nearly two months for failure to make a regular tax payment; this resulted in enormous financial losses and the company brought the issue to the Courts. The latest decision in this regard is that of the Government of Montenegro of 2 March 2017 to call off debts of broadcasters in the amount of €1,847,189; this represents 36 monthly invoices to 53 broadcasters (13 local public radio stations, 3 local public television stations, 31 commercial radio stations and 6 commercial television stations). This support is expected to continue in the coming years, for a total amount of €1,597,052 for the years 2017–2021. There is multiple and cumulative evidence that these funding mechanisms are used to support 'pro-government media' (Nikolić 2019).

Economic pressure is also used selectively by the governments. A typical example of this is when, in 2008, the Croatian government blocked the bank accounts of the Croatian satirical magazine *Feral Tribune* (which was highly critical of the government) because of their VAT debt, which led to the suspension of publication. A similar situation occurred in Montenegro in 2015, when the account of the *TV Vijesti* was blocked because of tax debts. In Serbia, in 2018, the Serbian website *Južne vesti* accused the country's tax authority of deliberately subjecting it to prolonged and undue financial inspections because of its critical reports aimed at the government (www.safejournalists.net). Editorial independence is also threatened by the fact that some media outlets rely on revenues from their owners' other businesses.

The state has become one of the major sources of revenue in the media sector in the region, be it in the form of subsidies or indirectly through state advertising. The state remains the major advertiser in all of the cases, which positions it to condition advertising contracts with editorial loyalty. It is estimated that 25 percent of the annual Serbian state advertising budget is spent in the media sector, while in North Macedonia the state was among the top five advertisers for several consecutive years (Bieber and Kmezić 2015, 18). The interviewed scholars from North Macedonia agree that the state of affairs has changed there: since 2017, the state is no longer the main advertiser and it no longer promotes its ideas and ideology (Kolozova 2018). In Montenegro, some newspapers receive an important amount of state advertising, while others receive almost none. Several stakeholders revealed that they do not receive state advertising even when they offer to publish this advertising free of charge. State advertising is not managed in a transparent manner and the allocation of this advertising discriminates between media outlets. Similarly, in neighbouring Albania, opposition media rarely have state advertisements (Nikolić 2019; Kondi 2018).

Advertising is also a tool used to silence the media, and the state chooses only government-friendly media to advertise government-controlled public companies. Government-friendly media also seem to be favoured in the case of subsidies; the direct financing of media from the state budget, usually on the local level, also remains a problem. Many of the interviewed journalists and experts stated that low salaries also remain one of the major challenges. As the level of journalists' salaries remains low, some journalists supplement their low wages with other sources of income, which can potentially lead to conflicts of interest in their reporting. The underpaid journalists tend to self-censorship in order to keep their job, which underpins the illiberal regimes.

Working under political pressure, censorship and self-censorship

Political control can be manifested in various ways. The first example is parliamentary control of the public broadcasters and its potential misuse. HDZ-led Government interference in the Croatian public broadcasting company HRT in 2016 challenged media independence in the country. HRT's director general (appointed by the Social Democratic Party led Parliament) was fired before the elections and a new interim director, Siniša Kovačić, was appointed. Kovačić then embarked on a massive round of staff restructuring and approximately 70 journalists were reassigned or replaced; critics saw this as an ideologically driven purge. Journalists experience political interference from time to time – for example, government officials tried to discredit journalist Danka Derifaj after she reported about alleged nepotism in the town of Jastrebarsko in 2014. One recent example is that of former Minister of Finance Martina Dalić who admitted to having personally stopped the publication of information about state intervention in the retail enterprise *Agrokor* in 2017 (Vozab 2019). Journalists and civil society groups describe an atmosphere in which certain politicians have deliberately fostered mistrust in critical media, regulatory bodies and human rights defenders so as to undercut the credibility of these institutions. Frequently, this is manifested in verbal attacks on 'leftist media" that display insufficient 'patriotism', with journalists smeared as 'traitors', 'anti-Croats' or equated with members of groups such as the Četniks. Saša Leković, president of the Croatian Journalists' Association (HND), commented on the current atmosphere for media in Croatia: 'Once a country is an EU member, nobody cares anymore' (Griffin 2016; Matić 2018).

In Bosnia and Herzegovina, it is very common for media owners and managers to be very closely related to the incumbents, and consequently they develop mutually beneficial relations (media funding in return for expecting media support and propaganda). The media in the country depend on the interests of their owners, and their editorial policies reflect the preferred political option (Brogi et al. 2014). The independent researchers in Bosnia and Herzegovina stress the control the editorial board has over *Radio Televizija Republike Srpske*. As a public station, and the most watched broadcasting service in the Republika Srpska (RS), it is able to shape public discourse, putting up strong barriers against changes in regulation (Hasić and Karabegović 2018, 7). In Bosnia and Herzegovina, a good example of this is the case of *klix.ba*. In 2014, the popular website published an audio recording of the former prime minister of Republika Srpska, Željka Cvijanović, implicating her in a corruption scandal; soon afterwards, klix.ba reporters were subject to police interrogation and pressures involving threats of criminal charges for publishing unauthorized material. Tanja Topić, an independent journalist now working for the Fridrich Ebert Stiftung regional office in Banja Luka, stressed that the pressure on the media in Republika Srpska became stronger in 2006 when Milorad Dodik became Prime Minister: 'Firstly, they started to put pressure on those based in Sarajevo, then they hindered the opposition media to press conferences, and stopped the journalist accreditations to the critical ones which followed with the verbal attacks on the journalists either on the ethnic basis or on the sexual or gender basis' (Topić 2018).

In Serbia, the political pressure on the media is mainly related to the former prime minister and current president Aleksandar Vučić who launched a war with the critical media. This sent a strong message about unwelcomed investigative journalism. As one of the journalists recalled for the Slavko Ćuruvija Foundation, 'a news programme used to be politics, politics, sport and weather and now it is Vučić, Vučić, Vučić, sport and weather' (Fondacija Slavko Ćurivija 2018; Škoro 2016). Pro-government newspapers lead smear campaigns against independent news outlets or NGOs critical of the government. State officials fail to condemn threats and hate speech made against journalists or even use them to promote assaults on media, and therefore condone the attacks on journalists. Quite prominent in this respect is Aleksandar Vučić calling journalists liars, traitors, enemies and foreign spies. The survey conducted by BIRN jointly with Reporters Without Borders found that three quarters of surveyed journalists (74%) negatively assessed the state of media freedom in Serbia in 2017. Half of them (50%) believe that serious obstacles exist to the practical attainment of media freedoms and the rights of journalists, while a quarter (24%) believe that in practice there are no conditions at all to attain media freedoms. When asked 'Who is the main source of control of the media content in Serbia today?', 58% answered that it was the political establishment, while 9% said it was the owners and management jointly (BIRN/Reporters without borders 2017, 14).

In Montenegro, politically motivated changes in the national broadcaster RTCG, and putting it under the control of the government and ruling party, raises serious concern. The government has initiated changes in the Law on Public Broadcasting Services of Montenegro that restrict its independence. According to experts of the Council of Europe, some solutions that deal with finance, management structure and the RTCG Council are very problematic and undermine the professional independence of national broadcasters. The Council of Europe pointed out that resisting the law is much better and in accordance with international standards. Representatives of the major printed media have expressed fears that changes 'were being made' to discipline the independent media rather than to legally regulate that area (Nikolić 2019).

One North Macedonian media advocate says that 'the pressure on the media is never explicit and what we see is an indirect pressure. The situation in North Macedonia has changed for the better as now we see open criticism of the government, which was not before. However, the government still kept the all mechanisms and style regarding the media. What we see is a state capture' (Kolozova 2018). In North Macedonia, media advocates complain about over-legislation, which is stuck in the old mechanisms asking for too detailed provisions for the broadcasters, which puts them too easily under political pressure, and for a small technical mistake they can very easily go bankrupt (Shishovski and Lechevska 2015). The number of court cases related to media and journalists generally induces fear, fuels self-censorship and discourages investigative journalism. The democracy watchdogs in North Macedonia also complain about the new amendments to the Electoral code, which legalize political advertising in the commercial media during election campaigns that are paid for with public money and overseen by the State Election Commission. They fear the politicization of the commission and of once again losing the freedom of media reporting (Association of Journalists of Macedonia (AJM) 2018).

In Albania, the media outlets typically take an editorial line that suits the interest of their owners, who are often involved in politics and thus self-censorship remains a big challenge, and bias is especially visible during the election periods. Editorial independence and protection of the journalistic profession are victims of economic and political priorities that are interwoven within the media system. Often sandwiched between business and politics, journalists routinely resort to self-censorship, preferring to keep and advance their job (Freedom House Albania 2015; Albanian Media Institute 2018). The Albanian media institute published a survey related to the pressure on the media; the editors and journalists named political parties (39%), central and local organs of executive power (27.8%) and the media owners (21.7%,) as the sources of greatest pressure exerted on their media, followed by private advertisers (14.8%) and equal pressure by the judiciary and criminal circles (at 7.8% each), while 24.3%, the third biggest group, preferred not to answer or claimed to not be able to make an assessment at this issue (Albanian Media Institute 2018). Similarly to the neighbouring countries, the country is living through an era of exacerbated political rhetoric against the media, with the Prime Minister offending and insulting journalists on live TV as primus inter pares. Idavet Sharifi stressed in the interview that in Albania the government has started to aggressively use social media to distribute government propaganda in an attempt to offer an alternative to the free media in distributing news to its citizens. ERTV is a 'brutal example of this' (Sherifi 2018).

In Kosovo, the main journalists' association, AGK, claims that government officials use verbal threats against journalists, and that journalists who criticize public officials are often denounced as traitors or Serbian sympathizers. The editors' self-censorship remains and the stories critical of the government are barred from being published or broadcast. When critical, the media outlets are subject to intimidation through tax investigations or blocked from accessing public information (Freedom House 2016). The lack of investigative journalism, the presence of political bias, extensive coverage of the ruling party and minimal coverage of opposition parties predominate the media sector in Kosovo.

The survey of Regional Cooperation Council Balkan Barometer 2018[2] shows (Graph 2) that 64% of the respondents totally disagree (32%) or tend to disagree (32%) with the statement that the media are independent of political influence, while only 5% totally agree and 22% of the respondents tend to agree with the statement. The biggest scepticism towards the independence of the media seems to be in Bosnia and Herzegovina, and Montenegro, quite surprisingly, fares the best in this survey in terms of perception of media independence.

Intimidation, physical assault, assassination of journalists

The last decade of the 20th century was not very pleasant for journalists in the Balkans: over 80 journalists were killed, abducted, went missing or died under suspicious circumstances during the wars in the 1990s (Borissova 2014). A couple of cases provoked international outrage and condemnation. In Serbia, it was the murder of Slavko Čuruvija in 1999. According to the indictment, an 'unknown person' ordered the killing

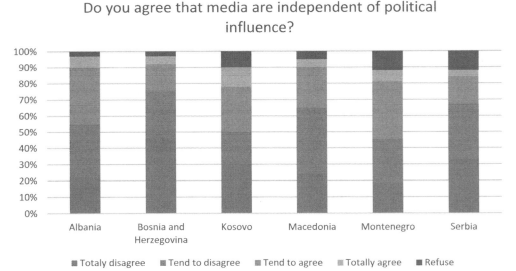

Graph 2. Independence of media. (Data from the survey of Regional Cooperation Council 2018)

and the former head of Serbian State Security Radomir Marković abetted the crime, while three former security service officers took part in the organization and execution of the murder. It is basically the same situation with the proceedings related to the murder of the editor-in-chief of the Montenegrin newspaper *Dan*, Duško Jovanović, who was killed in 2004; the culprit is still unknown.

Episodes of physical aggression seem to be on rise since 2014. Verbal and physical attacks by both political representatives and pro-government media against journalists happen on a daily basis, the worst situation in this respect seems to be in Serbia, Croatia and Bosnia and Herzegovina; both Montenegro and Serbia report one death of a journalist (Table 3). Olivera Lakić, a Montenegrin journalist involved in investigating cigarette smuggling and its link to politics, was threatened, attacked, beaten and even shot. We can recall the smear campaign from 2014 in Montenegro against Vanja Čalović, the executive director of the Montenegrin watchdog Network for Affirmation of the NGO Sector (MANS), in which the government controlled daily newspaper *Informer* and state-owned *Pobjeda* were involved. Most recently (2018), there is the case from Croatia, when Ivan Djakić, the son of MP Josip Djakić, threatened journalist Ivan Žada, first in public and then on Facebook. The Croatian Journalist Association stresses that the number of attacks against journalists is rising and political leaders remain silent (HND 2018). The journalists who criticized the nationalist tone embodied in the presence of controversial nationalist singer Marko Perković Thompson at the World Cup celebrations were put on a black list compiled by right wing supporters; this black list of allegedly unpatriotic reporters circulated on social networks for a while.

Most of the attacks on journalists remain unsolved; the report by Human Rights Action in Montenegro states that 2/3 of the 55 cases of attacks on journalists in Montenegro in the 2004–2016 period remain unsolved (Radović et al. 2016). In the 2006–2015 period, there were close to 400 cases of violations of freedom of speech and the rights of journalists, while criminal charges were pursued in only nine of those cases (Bieber and Kmezić 2015).

The politicians contribute to the image of journalists as charlatans and openly lead smear campaigns against them, calling them traitors or public enemies. The verbal assaults on journalists then become normalized through the political narrative and become part of daily political and social life. The journalists are afraid to investigate any organized crime or corruption that lead to politicians and their links with criminal groups; the media no longer can play the role of watchdogs of democracy and so the position of the incumbents is fostered. The European Union can no longer rebuke countries in the region for illiberal practices. Keeping in mind the situation in

Table 3. Media freedom 2014–2018 (Source: Index on censorship 2019).

	Deaths	Physical assaults	Arrests and Detentions	Intimidation	Criminal charges	Total reports(including other)
Albania	0	10	1	9	0	31
BiH	0	15	4	47	1	118
Croatia	0	21	1	41	0	132
Kosovo	0	13	4	17	0	38
Montenegro	1	7	3	19	4	46
N. Macedonia	0	14	9	31	3	112
Serbia	1	26	8	40	4	153

Hungary, Viktor Orbán has become a great example to follow, and Vučić and others only follow in his footsteps. Stability comes before democracy so the result is stable and illiberal politics in the Western Balkan region.

Conclusion

The article offered three arguments to explain the bad shape of media freedom in the Balkans: structural factors (state advertisements as the main source of income, economic tycoons close to incumbents as media owners), proximate or external factors (deteriorating level of media freedom in some EU countries and accent on stability rather than democracy) and political-societal dynamics (defamation and libel as means to punish journalists, verbal and physical assaults on journalists).

The structural factors are determinant for the overall picture: the media ownership structures are blurred, quite often openly or allegedly linked to the political scene. The state remains one of the main advertisers in the media and thus it is the main source of revenues; this is used quite often by the states as an efficient weapon against non-obedient journalists. Low salaries also belong among the main challenges for media freedom in the Balkans – journalists seek other jobs and might end up in a conflict of interest, or simply fearing to lose their jobs refrain from investigative journalism. Governments also quite arbitrarily punish the non-obedient media outlets by freezing their bank assets or putting them under harsh financial control. Most of the funding then goes to pro-government media and the critical and non-obedient outlets receive an insignificant portion. State funding for the media is non-transparent and not regulated and far from fulfiling the European standards (public interest driven and based on non-discriminatory criteria) and is often transformed into a means of controlling the media.

The external factors cannot be omitted in case of the Western Balkans. The European Union is no longer as appealing and its carrot and stick approach is not as effective, especially with so many players interested in the region – Russia, Turkey, the United States, China and Saudi Arabia above all. What's more, the WB countries are aware of the double standards and can easily relate themselves to EU member Hungary rather than to any other member with high quality of media freedom. Disunity and too many different voices and claims in the European Union mean that the only demand the EU can have and prefer is stability. As those in glass houses shouldn't throw stones, Western Balkans receives the message that stability comes before democracy, so there is no need to make efforts to protect media independence.

Vis à vis the political-societal dynamics, in all of the countries, some media outlets are very close to the government and are used by the government to attack both independent media and civil society. They also quite often offer little criticism of governmental politics and give little or no space to governmental critics. Even though censorship officially does not exist, self-censorship is widely applied due to subtle political and economic pressures. Journalists quite often face physical or verbal assaults, and it is very common to be verbally attacked by politicians or smeared by pro-governmental media. It seems that while there is a stable situation in media freedom vis à vis the politicians in the Federation of BIH (FBH), Kosovo and Montenegro, there has been a slight improvement in North Macedonia, large scale deterioration in Republika Srpska and Serbia and slight aggravation in Albania and Croatia. Nevertheless, the score of the all countries is pretty bad compared to established democracies. The countries use defamation and other potential pressure mechanisms on the media through open-ended methods such as security related standards or incitement to hatred.

Although we do have some democracy in terms of plurality of the media, the reality is that the media are afraid to function as a watchdog monitoring those in power; they are constantly under political and economic pressure, so the accountability of politicians becomes obsolete (Table 4). Citizens obtain twisted or distorted information, which helps the ruling parties and leaders to stay in power. The citizens, provided with warped information, make decisions and elect the same leaders who provide them with the twisted information. The illiberal regimes are then strengthened or cemented, so we have seen the same faces in Balkan politics over the last thirty years: most prominently Milo Djukanović in Montenegro and Milorad Dodik in Republika Srpska. The democracy in Serbia seems to have declined sharply since the 2014 inauguration of Alexandar Vučić as Prime Minister and it is also noteworthy that we see slight aggravation in Croatia, an EU country where journalists, especially those covering organized crime, war crimes and corruption, continue to face harassment. Croatia also is on the top of the list of total reports of incidents against journalists, along with Serbia, BiH and North Macedonia. The legitimacy of the media depends on the idea that they are trustworthy, but in a system where a large proportion of the population does not trust the media, the whole system is paralysed and there is no light at the end of the tunnel.

Despite all of that, there are still many journalists who stand against the discrimination and raise their voices and concern. The voices, however, are often targeted at and ask for aid from the European Union; the majority of the declarations or media ratings stemming from the region appear only in English and never in local languages. Many of the journalists then face verbal and physical assaults, which are overlooked, and the state institutions are not interested in investigating or punishing the aggressors. The

Table 4. Media pluralism in the WB – main features.

	Legislative framework	Economic pressure	Political pressure
Albania	Well developed	State advertising	Verbal attacks on journalists by politicians common
BiH	Well developed Intimidation and assaults on journalists one of the highest in the region	State advertising	Verbal attacks on journalists by politicians common
Croatia	Well developed Leader in lawsuits against journalists Imprisonment up to one year for insult of the state Intimidation and assaults on journalists one of the highest in the region	State advertising Opposition media under attack	Verbal attacks on journalists by politicians common
Kosovo	Well developed	State advertising	Pro-government bias
Montenegro	Well developed Imprisonment up to one year for insult of the state	State advertising Opposition media under attack	Verbal attacks on journalists by politicians common
N. Macedonia	Well developed	State advertising	Pressure on media indirect
Serbia	Well developed Leader in lawsuits against journalists Imprisonment up to one year for insult of the state Intimidation and assaults on journalists one of the highest in the region	State advertising Opposition media under attack	Verbal attacks on journalists by politicians common

dichotomy between the approved legislation and the implementation in practice remains a challenge for the Western Balkan countries. What's more, as the case of Croatia shows, is that membership in the EU does not resolve all of the problems. It is far more difficult to fight democracy when being in the EU club; being in the EU does not necessarily secure living in a liberal democracy.

The fact that the democratic façade remains and that the pressure mechanisms on the media contribute to the erosion of democracy is intriguing. The Balkan states seem to be captured by a strong executive, and a society based on networks helps to foster the supremacy of the executive, which seems to penetrate into the everyday lives of citizens. Control over the media is essential for illiberal regimes, as they provide twisted information in the form of Potemkin villages, reinforcing and sublimating the merits of the ruling elite and also covering up the bad deeds of the incumbents. Governmental propaganda is crucial for the regime to be preserved; the media lose their function as a watchdog of democracy; and the incumbents are no longer accountable to the citizens. The legitimacy of the media lies in their trustworthiness, but when a large proportion of the citizens do not trust the media, they lose their function as the fourth power in democracy and instead provide legitimacy to authoritarian leaders.

The role of the media is crucial in democracy as it contributes to the society with active and well-informed citizens. In the Balkans, on the contrary, media are used as means to cement illiberal regimes. The case of North Macedonia shows us that in order to change the situation more must be done. Merely changing the ruling elite is not enough, as the deficits are more structurally related. As media do remain the fourth power even in 21st century, we must not overlook their crucial role for democracy. When overlooked, Western Balkans will continue to dance in the vicious circle of illiberal politics.

Notes

1. For comparison of defamation laws see OSCE (2017). Out of 28 EU counties, 25 treat defamation as a criminal offence. Of those 25, 21 impose imprisonment as a sanction. In the vast majority of those 21 countries, imprisonment is imposed on the offender when the defamed person is a public figure. The paradox is then that the EU asks for decriminalization of defamation, but in most of its countries, defamation has not been decriminalized and can be punishable by imprisonment (Spaic et al. 2016).
2. Balkan Barometer is annual public opinion survey commissioned by the Regional Cooperation Council to gather and interpret data spanning a number of thematic areas and topics.

Disclosure statement

No potential conflict of interest was reported by the author.

Funding

This work was supported by the research project: 'Current Issues in Political Science III' undertaken at the Department of Political Science, Faculty of Social Studies, Masaryk University.

References

Albanian Media Institute. 2018. *Albanian media scene vs. European standards. Report based on council of Europe's indicators for media in democracy*. Tirana. http://www.institutemedia.org/Documents/PDF/Albanian%20Media%20Scene%20vs%20European%20Standards.pdf

ANEM. 2015. "Pravni monitoring medijske scene u Srbiji. Publikacija XII." http://anem.org.rs/sr/aktivnostiAnema/monitoring/story/17828/DVANAESTA+MONITORING+PUBLIKACIJA+ANEMA.html

Association of Journalists of Macedonia (AJM). 2018. "Amendments to the electoral code jeopardize the work and freedom of the media." AJM, Independent Union of Journalists and Media Workers (SSNM) and Council of Media Ethics of Macedonia. July 28. http://znm.org.mk/измените-на-изборниот-законик-ги-загр/?lang=en

BBC. 2017. "Albania profile-media." https://www.bbc.co.uk/news/world-europe-17680734

BBC. 2017a. "Croatia profile – Media." https://www.bbc.co.uk/news/world-europe-17217826

BBC. 2018. "Kosovo profile – Media." https://www.bbc.co.uk/news/world-europe-18328868

Behmer, M.. 2009. "Measuring media freedom: Approaches of international comparison." In *Press freedom and pluralism in Europe: Concepts and conditions*, ed. A. Czepek, M. Hellwig, and E. Nowak, 23–34. Bristol: European Communication Research and Education Association.

Belgrade Centre for Human Rights. 2012. "Human rights in Serbia 2011. Legal provisions and practice compared to international human rights standards." http://www.bgcentar.org.rs/bgcentar/eng-lat/wp-content/uploads/2013/04/Human-Rights-in-Serbia-A-Comprehensive-Report-for-2011-in-Serbian-and-English-2012.pdf

Belgrade Centre for Human Rights. 2018. "Human rights in Serbia 2017." http://www.bgcentar.org.rs/bgcentar/eng-lat/wp-content/uploads/2018/03/Human-rights-in-Serbia-2017.pdf

Bieber, F. and M. Kmezić. 2015. "Media freedom in the Western Balkans." Biepag. http://www.biepag.eu/publications/media-freedom-in-the-western-balkans/

BIRN/Reporters without borders. 2017. *Media ownership monitor*. Srbija. http://serbia.mom-rsf.org/rs/

Blazeva, A., V. Borovska, K. Lechevska, and J. Shishovski. 2015. *Freedom of expression, association and entrepreneurship in a captured state: Macedonia in 2015*. Skopje: Institute of Social Sciences and Humanities.

Blazeva, A. and A. Mukoska. 2018. *Policy document concerning the public policy on the effects of existing regulation of editorial/media freedom*. Skopje: Institute of Social Sciences and Humanities.

Borissova, T., 2014. "Unresolved journalist murder cases continue to plague Balkans." Osservatorio Balcani e caucaso transeuropa, February 26. https://www.balcanicaucaso.org/eng/Areas/Serbia/Unresolved-journalist-murder-cases-continue-to-plague-Balkans

Brkić, D., 2015. "Media integrity report: Media ownership and financing in Montenegro." Agency for Electronic Media. http://mediaobservatory.net/sites/default/files/Media%20Ownership%20and%20Finances%20in%20Montenegro.pdf

Brogi, E., A. Dobreva, and P.L. Parcu. 2014. "Freedom of media in the Western Balkans." Directorate-General for external policies of the union. EU. Brussels. http://www.europarl.europa.eu/RegData/etudes/STUD/2014/534982/EXPO_STU(2014)534982_EN.pdf

Brunwasser, M., L. Turčilo, and D. Marko. 2016. *Monitoring and evaluation support activity (measure-BiH). Assessment of the media sector in Bosnia and Herzegovina.* Sarajevo: USAID. http://www.measurebih.com/uimages/Assessment%20of%20the%20Media%20Sector%20in%20B&H.pdf

Čađenović, I. and M. Radulović. 2017. *Montenegro: Double standards in regulating media concentration.* Podgorica: Osservatorio balcani e caucasus transeuropa. https://www.balcanicaucaso.org/eng/Areas/Montenegro/Montenegro-double-standards-in-regulating-media-concentration-179589

Çollaku, P. 2018. *Kosovo. Indicators on level of media freedom and journalists' safety.* Pristina: Association of Journalists of Kosovo.

Curuvija, F.S. 2018. "Svedočejne novinara o pritiscima: Medije kontrolišu političari i urednici." http://www.slavkocuruvijafondacija.rs/svedocenja-novinara-o-pritiscima-medije-kontrolisu-politicari-i-urednici/

Cvetanoski, I. 2016. "Macedonia: The media struggle." https://www.balcanicaucaso.org/eng/Areas/Macedonia/Macedonia-the-media-struggle-171312

de Hert, P. and F. Korenica. 2016. "The New Kosovo constitution and its relationship with the European convention on human rights: Constitutionalization 'Without' ratification in post-conflict societies." Max-Planck-Institut für ausländisches öffentliches Recht und Völkerrecht. http://www.zaoerv.de/76_2016/76_2016_1_a_143_166.pdf

Delli Carpini, M.X. and S. Keeter. 1996. *What Americans know about politics and why it matters.* New Haven, CT: Yale University Press.

Erichsen, B.,, R. Naseniece, D. Reljić, G. Seufert, A. Tomanić, and I. Uribe. 2013. "Western Balkans and Turkey. Media and freedom of expression fact-finding and scoping study." European Commission. https://www.rcmediafreedom.eu/Publications/Reports/Western-Balkans-and-Turkey.-Media-and-freedom-of-expression-fact-finding-and-scoping-study

Fetoshi, A. 2017. "The role of media in European integration process: Kosovo Case." Journal of Mass Communication & Journalism. https://www.omicsonline.org/open-access/the-role-of-media-in-european-integration-process-kosovo-case-2165-7912-1000338.pdf

Flanders Investment and Trade. 2016. *The broadcasting sector in Croatia.* Zagreb/Brussels. https://www.flandersinvestmentandtrade.com/export/sites/trade/files/market_studies/2016-Croatia-Broadcasting-sector.pdf

Freedom House. 2015. "Albania." https://freedomhouse.org/report/freedom-press/2015/albania

Freedom House. 2016. "Freedom of the Press Kosovo 2016." https://freedomhouse.org/report/freedom-press/2016/kosovo

Freedom House. 2017. "Freedom house index 2017." https://freedomhouse.org/report/freedom-world/freedom-world-2017

Griffen, S., 2016. "Croatia: Media freedom in turbulent times." Report on the June 2016 Joint International Mission. https://ipi.media/wp-content/uploads/2016/08/Croatia-Report-IntlMission-PDF-2.pdf

Guasti, P. and Z. Mansfeldová, eds. 2018. *Democracy under stress. Changing perspectives on democracy, governance and their measurement.* Prague: Czech Academy of Sciences.

Gunther, R.,and A. Mughan. 2000. *Democracy and the media. Comparative perspective.* Cambridge: Cambridge University Press.

Hasić, J.,, and D. Karabegović. 2018. "Elite responses to contentious politics on the subnational level: The 2014 Bosnian protests." *Southeast European and Black Sea Studies* 18: 367–80. doi:10.1080/14683857.2018.1489609.

HND. 2018. "Otac i sin Đakić prijetili i psovali novinara." 16 October. https://www.hnd.hr/otac-i-sin-dakic-prijetili-i-psovali-novinara

Index on censorship. 2019. "Mapping media freedom." https://www.indexoncensorship.org/wp-content/uploads/2019/02/index-report-2018-v6-FINAL-29January2019v6.pdf

Jusić, T. and A. Džihana. 2008. "Bosnia and Herzegovina." In *Divided they fall. Public service broadcasting in multiethnic societies*, ed. S. Bašić Hrvatin, M. Thompson, and T. Jusić, 81–119. Sarajevo: Medijacentar.

Jusić, T. and K. Irion. 2018. *Media constrained by context. International assistance democratic media transition in the Western Balkans.* Budapest: CEU Press.

Krševan Smokvina, T., J.F. Furnémont, M. Janssen, D. Mijatović, J. Surčulija Milojević, and S. Trpevska, ed. 2017. *Montenegro edia sector inquiry with recommendations for harmonisation with the Council of Europe and European Union standards.* https://rm.coe.int/montenegro-media-sector-inquiry-with-the-council-of-europe-and-europea/16807b4dd0

Kmezić, M. 2019. "EU role of law conditionality: Democracy or stabilitocracy promotion in the Western Balkans?" In *The Europeanisation of the Western Balkans. A failure of EU conditionality?* ed. J. Dzankic, S. Keil, and M. Kmezić, 87–109. Basingstoke: Palgrave Macmillan.

Kmezić, M., and F. Bieber, eds. 2017. *The crisis of democracy in the Western Balkans. An anatomy of stabilitocracy and the limits of EU democracy promotion.* Graz: BIEPAG.

Kolozova, K., 2018. "Interview." Institute of Social Sciences and Humanities. Skopje. October 17.

Kolozova, K. and G. Georgijev. 2018. *Deliberation: The path of dismantling the #statecapture in Macedonia.* Skopje: Institute of Social Sciences and Humanities.

Kondi, G., 2018. "Interview and questionnaire via email." Journalist in Shqiptarja, November 5.

Lani, R. and F. Cupi. 2002. "The difficult road to the independent media: Is the post-communist transition over?" *Southeast European and Black Sea Studies* 2, no. 1: 75–89. doi:10.1080/14683850208454673.

Leka, A. 2018. "Defamation law and practice in the age of internet in Albania." *European Journal of Interdisciplinary Studies* 4:3. http://journals.euser.org/files/articles/ejis_v4_i3_18/Leka.pdf

Levitsky, S. and L.A. Way. 2002. "Elections without democracy. The rise of competitive authoritarianism." *Journal of Democracy* 12, no. 2: 51–65. doi:10.1353/jod.2002.0026.

Levitsky, S. and L.A. Way. 2010. *Competitive authoritarianism: Hybrid regimes after the cold war.* Cambridge: Cambridge University Press.

Macedonian Institute for Media. 2015. *Analysis. 2015. Macedonia in the digital age – Between the rights and responsibilities while communicating on internet.* Skopje. http://www.mim.org.mk/attachments/article/853/Macedonia%20in%20the%20digital%20age%20–%20between%20the%20rights%20and%20responsibilities%20while%20communicating%20on%20Internet.pdf

Matić, J. 2018. *Kontrola i sloboda medija. Svedočenje novinara.* Beograd: Fondacija Slavko Čuruvija/BIRN/NUNS/EU. http://www.slavkocuruvijafondacija.rs/wp-content/uploads/2018/02/Kontrola-i-sloboda-medija-Kljucni-nalazi-Slavko-Curuvija-fondacija.pdf

Mirovni institut. 2004. "Concentration of media ownership and its impact on media pluralism and freedom." In *Conference proceedings Bled.* http://www2.mirovni-institut.si/media_ownership/index.htm

Nikolić, O., 2019. "Interview and questionnaire via email." Director of the Institut za medije Crne Gore. January 10.

OSCE. 2017. "Defamation and insult laws in the OSCE region: A comparative study." https://www.osce.org/fom/303181?download=true

Petković, B., S. Bašić Hrvatin, and S. Hodžić. 2014. *Značaj medijskog integriteta: Vraćanje medija i novinarstva u službu javnosti Regionalni pregled i istraživački izvještaj o medijskom integritetu u Bosni i Hercegovini.* Sarajevo: Medijacentar.

Radović, M., T. Bulatović, and T.G. Prelević. 2016. *Prosecution of attacks on journalists in Montenegro.* Podgorica: Human Rights Action.

Regional Cooperation Council. 2018. "Balkan Barometer 2018: Public opinion survey." https://www.rcc.int/pubs/66/balkan-barometer-2018-public-opinion-survey

Schneider, L. 2014. *Media freedom indices. What they tell us and what they don´t.* Bonn: DW Akademie.

Sherifi, I., 2018. "Interview and questionnaire via email." Academic expert based in Epoka University and European University in Tirana. November 23.

Shishovski, J. and K. Lechevska. 2015. *Technology of state capture. Overregulation in Macedonian media and academia.* Skopje: Institute of Social Sciences and Humanities.

Škoro, S. 2016. *Vučić i cenzura.* Belgrade: Tercija.

Šopar, V. 2008. "Macedonia." In *Divided they fall. Public service broadcasting in multiethnic societies,* ed. S. Bašić Hrvatin and M.J. Thompson, 119–59. Sarajevo: Medijacentar.

Spaic, A., C. Nolasco, and M. Novovic. 2016. "Decriminalization of defamation – The Balkans case a temporary remedy or a long term solution?" *International Journal of Law, Crime and Justice* 47: 21–30. doi:10.1016/j.ijlcj.2016.05.002.

Statcounter Global Stats. 2019. "Social media stats." http://gs.statcounter.com/social-media-stats/

Topić, T., 2018. "Interview." Independent journalist currently working for Friedrich Ebert Stiftung. Banja Luka, October 30.

Trpevska et al. 2018. *Indicators on the level of media freedom and journalists' safety in the Western Balkans.* Belgrade: NUNS. http://safejournalists.net/wp-content/uploads/2018/12/indicators_on_the_level_of_media_freedom_WB_2018.pdf

Trpevska, S. and I. Micevski. 2017. "The development and future of PSB in Macedonia: Towards the construction of a participatory PSB model." Analitika Sarajevo. http://www.analitika.ba/sites/default/files/publikacije/PSB%20Macedonia.pdf

Tunnard, C.R. 2003. "From state-controlled media to the 'Anarchy' of the internet: The changing influence of communications and information in Serbia in the 1990s." *Southeast European and Black Sea Studies* 3, no. 2: 97–120. doi:10.1080/713999348.

Turčilo, L., A. Osmić, and J. Žiga. 2017. *Mladi, politika i mediji. Priručnik za razvijanje političke i medijske pismenosti mladih.* Sarajevo: Friedrich Ebert Stiftung.

Vladisavljević, N. 2019. "Media discourse and the quality of democracy in Serbia after Milošević." *Europe-Asia Studies*:1–25. doi:10.1080/09668136.2019.1669534.

Vogel, T., 2015. "Media freedom and the integrity in the Western Balkans. Recent developments." European Fund for the Balkans. http://www.balkanfund.org/publib/other/Media-freedom-and-integrity-in-the-Western-Balkans-Recent-developments.pdf

Vozab, D., 2019. "Interview and questionnaire via email." Academic expert based at the University of Zagreb. January 28.

Vukanović, Z. 2016. *Foreign direct investment inflows into the South East European media market. Towards a hybrid business model.* Cham, Switzerland: Springer.

Worldometers. 2019. "Population." https://www.worldometers.info/

∂ OPEN ACCESS

Rule of law and democracy in the Western Balkans: addressing the gap between policies and practice

Marko Kmezić

ABSTRACT
Three decades since the beginning of democratization processes, the Western Balkan countries have built a democratic façade by holding elections, by promulgating legal acts guaranteeing freedom of expression, or by constitutionally declaring a strict system of checks and balances. In reality, however, political elites rely on informal structures, clientelism, and control of the media to undermine democracy. Given that formal democratic freedoms are effective only to the extent that political elites are bound by the effective rule of law, the core argument of this study is that the structural weaknesses of democratic institutions are purposefully exploited by domestic regimes, which are able to misuse these fragile institutions to their advantage.

1. Introduction

As famously suggested by Francis Fukuyama in 1992 – only three decades ago – after the fall of the Berlin Wall it seemed that the Western ideals of liberal democracy, the rule of law and individual rights would be spread undisturbed throughout the world, leading to 'the end of history.' Indeed, the end of the Cold War saw the collapse of single-party and military dictatorships throughout Central and Eastern Europe, most of Asia and Latin America. But not all of the countries caught up in that time's changes succeeded in transforming themselves into fully-fledged democracies. As global economic crisis, an array of nationalistic, ethnic, and religious conflicts, terrorist acts and the war on terror dissolved the 'triumphalist confidence of the 1990s' (Tamanaha 2004), the academic world gradually discovered a more 'nuanced' (Bieber 2018a) understanding of democratization processes: one that acknowledged different shades of political systems, ranging from fully-fledged liberal democracy to outright authoritarian regimes.

Seen from this angle, the Western Balkan countries (WB) – Albania, Bosnia and Herzegovina (BiH), Kosovo, North Macedonia, Montenegro and Serbia – constitute an ideal playing field for political scientists interested in gradations of democracy. Since the introduction of multi-party political systems in the early 1990s, the WB have experienced a variety of 'hybrid regimes' (Collier and Levitsky 1997) falling in the wide spectrum between consolidated democracies and autocracies, yet never reaching the standing of fully consolidated liberal democracies.

This is an Open Access article distributed under the terms of the Creative Commons Attribution-NonCommercial-NoDerivatives License (http://creativecommons.org/licenses/by-nc-nd/4.0/), which permits non-commercial re-use, distribution, and reproduction in any medium, provided the original work is properly cited, and is not altered, transformed, or built upon in any way.

The situation on the ground vindicates those who warned that Western Balkan political regimes should not be considered just a passing malfunction or a crisis of democracy, but rather a discrete and stable type of regime. Indeed, three decades since embarking on their democratization processes, the WB are positioned at the bottom of a political continuum from liberal democracy to outright authoritarianism. Conceptually, these regimes are best defined as competitive authoritarian systems, as first described by Levitsky and Way (2010, 5), meaning

> civilian regimes in which formal democratic institutions exist and are widely viewed as the primary means of gaining power, but in which incumbents' abuse of the state places them at a significant advantage vis-à-vis their opponents. Such regimes are competitive in that opposition parties use democratic institutions to contest seriously for power, but they are not democratic because the playing field is heavily skewed in favor of incumbents.

Enduring problems regarding the rule of law in the Western Balkans have already been pointed out by the latest Freedom House (2016) *Freedom in the World* report that observes an absence of the rule of law and an increase in patronage networks and clientelism, which threaten democratic institutions in the region. Similarly, in its 2018 Communication on a credible enlargement perspective for the region, the European Commission (2018) departed from its usual technocratic account of the state of the rule of law and straightforwardly declared that the countries show 'clear elements of state capture, including links with organised crime and corruption at all levels of government and administration, as well as a strong entanglement of public and private interests.'

Prominent explanations of the rule of law and democratization nexus in the WB are offered by the academic literature which observes that political elites rely on informal structures and clientelism and control of the media (Keil 2018), and even the regular manufacture of crises to undermine democracy and the rule of law (Kmezić and Bieber 2017). Similarly, by factoring informal domestic politics Richter and Wunsch (2019) have provided fresh evidence on how widespread state capture prevents governments in the region from pursuing effective democratic transformation.

This article puts forward a comprehensive theoretical argument that the apparent absence of the democratic rule of law profoundly impacts politics in the WB by acting as a break to democratic impulses, and by creating the regime-centred legal setting allowing for utter arbitrariness and violence of the ruling elites. Given that formal democratic freedoms are effective only to the extent that political elites are bound by the rule of law, the core argument of this study is that the structural weaknesses of democratic institutions are purposefully exploited by domestic competitive authoritarian regimes, which are able to misuse these fragile institutions to their advantage.

Starting from the premise that the key dimension of democratic substance that is missing in the region is the democratic rule of law, this study closely scrutinizes the dynamics at play in the WB in terms of trends, patterns and paradoxes beyond the procedural nexus of democracy, authoritarianism and the rule of law.

Bringing together the study of rule of law and democratization and approaches from comparative politics, this study argues that without a functional rule of law there are no institutional safeguards left, neither for *real* democracy nor for mere *electoralism* or *formal democracy*, presupposing: (1) elected officials; (2) free, fair and frequent elections; (3) freedom of expression; (4) alternative sources of information; (5)

associational autonomy; (6) inclusive citizenship (Dahl 2005, 188). Corresponding to the above mentioned constituent elements of formal democracy, this study offers an in depth analysis of elections, media, and patterns of clientelism, aiming to a) advance evidence for new patterns of illiberal politics in the WB by means of abuse of the weak state institutions in order to maintain a status quo of hollowing democratization, b) determine which legitimation tools are used by domestic elites and c) suggest how to prevent further democratic backsliding in the WB and revitalize the democratic processes in the region.

2. Theoretical argument: the lack of the functional rule of law

Observing the frequent violations of rule of law that characterized many *formally* democratic countries in the early 2000s, in the Balkans but also in Latin America, Africa and Asia, democracy scholars began to understand that it is precisely the degree to which the democratic rule of law exists in a given society that reflects the democratic quality of the entire regime (Linz and Stepan 1996; Magen and Morlino 2008). Before proceeding with the study's main research question, it is necessary to clarify the meaning of the term 'functioning rule of law'.

Both the democracy and the rule of law principles have a long common tradition in most influential legal orders, but they have not been precisely defined by any of them. The definition of the rule of law and democracy remains legitimately open-ended, and there-fore academics and practitioners alike are at liberty to formulate what attributes must be included in their definition. Yet, it is of interest for this study to observe that the rule of law and democracy are in fact interlinked and mutually reinforcing concepts. When considered not solely an instrument of the government but as a rule to which the entire society, including the government, is bound, the rule of law is fundamental in advancing democracy. Conversely, O'Donnell (2004) claims that the system of the rule of law within a democratic framework ensures mechanisms of political accountability, which in turn ensures the equality of all citizens and constrains potential abuses of state power. Hence, the rule of law should be understood as the 'foundation upon which every other dimen-sion of democratic quality ultimately rests' (Magen and Morlino 2008, 7).

This brings us to conclude that the key function of the functional rule of law is the ability to control the conferral of wide and unguided powers of the political and economic elites. No doubt, this is area in which the doctrine of the separation of powers serves the ends of the rule of law, yet neither of the two principles alone are not able to answer the trends of state capture and the crisis of constitutionalism in which (non-) elected clientelistic elites are given the power to legislate, govern and impact on state institutions, including the judiciary. More precisely, most of the regimes in the WB, as a result of the high party discipline, strong control over the parliamentary majority, and legitimized corrupt elites (Richter and Wunsch 2019) have been able to create the legal basis for their contentious actions and practices. Accordingly, there is a common mantra under which every conduct and action, no matter how controversial, is at least formally in agreement with positive legal order. In this sense, it is clear that it is more material aspects of the rule of law incorporating such elements as an effective electoral system, guarantees for a strong civil society, and protection of the effective performance of the various state agencies from potential obstructions and intimidation by powerful State actors,- that are necessary requirements for the existence of the functional rule of law.

Thus, establishing a lasting and effective rule of law requires not only the presence of (independent) state institutions, but also a widely shared identification with the law in society – citizens and political and economic elites alike. Accordingly, in a political system that upholds the rule of law, the legal system is fair, competent and efficient, while the government is embedded in a legal framework that is accepted by officials.

This is not currently the case in the WB where political elites have been successful in building a democratic façade; but this, of course, is not enough to make democracy effective. Formal democracy has been established by holding regular elections (or *premature* elections, which is often the case in Serbia, for example), by means of promulgating legal acts guaranteeing freedom of expression, or by constitutionally declaring a strict system of checks and balances. But in reality, elites are obstructing citizens' political and individual rights by violating the rule of law.

Starting from this basic argument, this study sets out to explain the seemingly enduring obstacles to establishing liberal democracy and a functioning rule of law in the Western Balkans. First, the WB emerged from authoritarian regimes in the classical sense, where there is only one political party serving to provide a veil of legitimacy to an illegitimate government. Building on this legacy, regime change acquired a 'new morphology through a process of concentration' (Dolenec 2013, 20), whereby the executive established dominance over the parliamentary and judicial branches of power. In addition, Zakošek (1997) observed that non-institutional actors frequently proliferated around the executive office, thus further weakening the state institutions' capacity to prevent abuses by other public agencies and high-ranking individuals. Second, economic liberalization was abused for economic gain, thus transforming political into economic elites. This happened via the privatization of state-owned companies and through state intervention in the enterprise sector. Abusing their access to 'privileged information [and] privileged loan terms' (Ramet and Wagner 2010, 22), political party affiliates built private fortunes and media empires overnight. In a second step, that economic power was used to wield political influence, leading to 'inside state capture' (Dolenec 2013, 21). Finally, the sidelining of formal institutions and legal instruments led to competing networks of clients, further entrenching state capture, practices of clientelism, patronage, corruption and abuse of office.

The three processes described above profoundly distorted the path of political development in WB. As a result, despite legal and constitutional provisions guaranteeing multi-party elections, the separation of power, media pluralism, and so on, the long-standing practice of the concentration of power unconstrained by the rule of law successfully adapted to new circumstances, strengthening competitive authoritarian rule in the region.

In the following two sections I will demonstrate how the above-mentioned processes are manifested in two rule of law-related sub-fields, namely in the case studies of electoral processes and freedom of expression.

3. Elections

Free and fair elections are a cornerstone of democratic rule. In the absence of either of these two legitimizing factors, elections are meaningless as they fail to meet their original purpose: to provide citizens a genuine opportunity to challenge the incumbent elites in the electoral arena. Thus far, elections in the Western Balkans have contributed to the political transformation of the region. Through their regularity, they have given legitimacy to the democratic process in all the countries of the region. However, on the other hand, many elections in the Western Balkans have been 'divisive, fraudulent, boycotted by some parties, contested on various occasions and linked with excessive spending or corrupt party financing' (Anastasakis 2014, 15).

Democratic consolidation in the region is hampered by the fact that those who hold political power also control public and private resources, and are thus in a privileged position to solidify their dominance through the voting process. Citizens recognize that the election dynamic is tilted towards the elites in power, which results in a low level of trust in electoral processes across the region. Citizens' trust in the election process is lowest in BiH, at only 11% (Centar za Izborne Studije 2017). This in turn leads to a vicious circle whereby those very same citizens are more inclined to take part in the clientelistic chain offered by the system rather than confront it. Hence in Serbia, for example, the ruling SNS has roughly 750,000 party members: 200,000 more than the party membership of Germany's ruling Christian Democratic Union, and even 600,000 more party affiliates than the UK's Conservative Party.[1] In order to process this information one must keep in mind that Serbia's population is just above seven million people, in comparison to Germany's 83 million or the UK's 66 million citizens.

In light of this observation, the analysis of the quality of the election processes will not focus on the voting process itself. Instead, it will closely consider four key sectors capable of affecting the electoral process, with potentially grave consequences for the rule of law, namely (1) Exploitation of public resources; (2) Media dominance; (3) Electoral register; and (4) Voter fraud and vote coercion.

Exploitation of public resources

The exploitation of public resources in election campaigns creates a major corruptive force in the electoral process, as it introduces or exacerbates power inequalities and provides unfair leverage for the elected incumbent or political parties via patterns of clientelism, party patronage, corruption, and nepotism. It erodes the quality of democracy, as incumbent elites can take advantage of a civil service, public contractors, government communications, public media, and even private companies and privately owned media which are part of the established clientelistic chain. After the elections, powerful voted officials can *pay back* the services rendered during the campaign by securing well-paid positions in the public sector for their supporters, providing access to privileged information, granting favourable procurement contracts, and so on. This system of *paying back* was best described by the former Serbian President Tomislav Nikolic (2008), who openly shared his understanding of the reason for participating in politics: 'to be able to provide jobs or hospital treatment to [his] friends.' The fact that none of the Western Balkan countries' legislators have precisely defined the notion of public resources, or enumerated activities that can be introduced under election campaign costs, leaves vast space for manipulation.

For the most part, the abuse of state resources follows the line of 'relational clientelism,' (Nichter 2018), that is, the relationships between the incumbent political parties and voters. Hence, political parties are acting as providers of jobs, lucrative public procurement contracts or favourable credits in return for secured votes, or in the worst cases even punish their non-voters. It is striking how as of lately described abuses of public resources often takes place in plain sight, or even under the spotlight of news cameras, as for example in the case of the Bosnian Serb member of the tripartite BiH Presidency, Milorad Dodik, who openly threatened 'to fire on the spot' (TV1. 2018) those who vote against him, or alternatively the President of the Jagodina City Assmebly in Serbia, Dragan Marković Palma who is regularly handing out public money to Jagodina citiznes without any political supervision or fiscal accountability thus directly feeding into the clientelistic chain between himself and the voters.[2] Promises made during election campaigns regularly include an increase of salaries in the public sector or the creation of new public institutions as a way of creating new public positions. More frequent, however, are cases of indirect clientelism whereby political parties provide 'targeted help to specific groups' (Prelec 2019), for example, through farming subsidies or by directing social workers to households in need.

On the other hand, the incumbents' misuse of administrative resources – state events and/or financial/technical resources – for campaign purposes is present in all countries in question. In practice, varieties of this problem range from pressure exerted on civil servants and public employees to the use of state events and resources during the electoral campaign, for example via the public officials' visits to companies, schools, hospitals, factories, or construction sites. In Kosovo alone, misuse of public office was observed in 96 out of the 655 electoral campaigning activities scrutinized during the 2017 Kosovo elections (Prelec 2019).

One specific problem area of the misuse of public office is the blurring of the lines between party and state. These include, for example, identifying local infrastructure projects that could be carried out in the pre-election period to create incentives to vote for a specific incumbent; disproportionate spending of parts of the budget during the pre-election phase; using public property for campaign advertising; using public funds for campaigning purposes. Blurring the line between the party and the state is particularly common in Serbia and the Republic Srpska, where, for example, municipal officials organize concerts by popular folk singers in the municipal premises as a 'gift' to citizens, while in fact promoting specific electoral lists (Alo 2018), or provide public transport buses for the SNS campaign (Nikolić 2017). The boundaries between the state and party have also been blurred by involving teachers and pupils in campaign events – sometimes even during school holidays (Andrić 2019) – or by civil servants campaigning during office hours or carrying out official duties, such as doctors providing medical advice in a political campaign (JugMedia 2016).

Media dominance

Considering their performance with regard to upholding the freedom of expression, media should adhere to the principles of fairness, balance and impartiality. This goes not only for their coverage of election campaigns, but also for programming that does not explicitly relate to elections, including news, interviews, and political talk shows. Although the situation regarding the incumbent political parties' media dominance varies across the Western Balkans, the general conclusion is that balance and impartiality in reporting remain serious concerns.

Media bias is most visible in public broadcasting services that are financially dependent on the parliament, and thus susceptible to political influence. The media dominance of the incumbent political parties in public broadcasting services is significant and well recorded in Kosovo and Serbia. Serbian President Aleksandar Vučić, for example, had four times more presence in public media than the next-placed candidate during the 2017 presidential elections (Gavrilović et al. 2017). At the time of the elections Vučić was acting as Prime Minister, and this added to his media presence as a candidate meant that he accounted for a whopping 61.2% per cent of the media presence of all election candidates, more than nine times the next-placed candidate, who received only 6.4% (Novi Sad School of Journalism 2017). In BiH the situation follows the political division within the country: Republika Srpska's public broadcaster, Radio Television Republika Srpska (RTRS), is extremely politicized, while the influence is less outright in the Federation's Federalna Televizija (FTV) (Ibid). Similarly, in major print media, the Serbian incumbent Aleksandar Vučić featured on 147 front pages during the election campaign, of which 118 were positive. The next-placed candidate featured on 79 pages, of which 39 were negative (Gavrilović et al. 2017). Parts of the privately-owned media with a wide reach – especially TV stations with national broadcasting licences and high circulation tabloids – frequently take part in vicious smear campaigns against political opponents, as described in more detail in section 4 of this article.

Free political advertising exists in all the Western Balkan countries, although it does not always meet the requirement of proportional access. More worrisome, however, is that political contestants are not able to ensure the fairness of the electoral process, even through paid advertising. In North Macedonia the public media are not allowed to broadcast paid political advertising at all, while in Kosovo the Election Law (Article 49.12) allows private broadcasters the right not to air paid political advertising time. In other countries of the region there are no restrictions on paid political advertisement, although in Montenegro some parties reported significantly lower costs for media advertising than that offered in the official price lists, raising suspicion of covert deals (Prelec 2019).

Electoral register

So far, none of the Western Balkan countries have created credible and electronically accessible electoral registers. Irregularities in the electoral registry distort the outcome of the voting process or, in the worst cases, can be misused for election fraud. Problems with the electoral registry, particularly a significant presence of deceased or emigrated voters, are a common occurrence across the region.

For example, in BiH the electoral register contains 3,345,486 voters (Central Election Commission 2016), while only 3,531,159 people are estimated to still live in the country, making the electoral register implausible (Agency for Statistics of Bosnia and Herzegovina 2013). In the city of Tuzla the Electoral Commission even registered more voters than then there are registered residents. The situation is similar in Serbia (Ilić 2017) and North Macedonia (Bieber 2018b), and even worse in Kosovo, where, at present, there are more voters on the electoral register than citizens in the country (Prelec 2019).

The lack of appropriate legal frameworks on the transmission of data regarding the recently deceased, and the high level of emigration from the WB countries – which is significantly higher than the official statistics suggest (Vračić 2018) – are among the biggest logistical hurdles to updating the electoral registers. But the main problem in tackling the issue of cleaning the electoral registers is the persistent lack of political will to act on this matter. This is perhaps best observed in the context of the 2012 Serbian general elections, which were overshadowed by the opposition SNS's accusations that the ruling Democrats had instrumentalised the voter registry. After the two sides had swapped power following the elections, the SNS completely downplayed these accusations and continued to organize elections without making any modifications to the election register.[3]

Recent evidence of outright political manipulation through the misuse of electoral registers in North Macedonia explains the political will to maintain flawed electoral registers. The 2015 leaked tapes revealed how the Macedonian government took advantage of inaccuracies in the electoral register by creating fake identities for *phantom voters* and bringing people from outside the country to the polls during the 2013 local elections (Prelec 2019).

Voter fraud and vote coercion

Illegal interference in the process of an election – either by increasing the vote share of the favoured candidate, depressing the vote share of the rival candidates, or both – is still fairly widespread in the Western Balkans. While the bulk of irregularities are estimated to take place before the opening and after the closure of the polling stations, problems which have been observed during election day include pressure on voters, for example through the presence of supporters outside polling stations telling people not to vote (Prelec 2019), the presence of supporters inside (Ibid) or outside polling stations (Nedeljnik 2018) taking photos and writing down the names of those who voted,[4] etc.

Another method of confusing people into voting for a candidate other than the one they intended to vote for is to create political parties with names or symbols similar to those of existing candidates or parties. In the 2018 local election in Belgrade, for example, the list of the previously unknown *Enough is Enough of Robbery, Corruption and Thievery – Radulović Milorad* drew the public's attention due to its striking similarity to a previously announced list *Enough is Enough and – For these ones to go, and for them not to return* (CRTA 2018). In addition, the aforementioned manipulations of the electoral register and the postal vote have become potential sources of pre-election voter fraud. The registration of fake voters from Croatia for postal voting is a well-documented issue of pre-electoral voter fraud in the 2018 elections in BiH (Prelec 2019).

4. Media freedom

Freedom of expression is a fundamental right of every human being. Media freedom is often seen as a corollary of the general right to freedom of expression (Amos et al. 2012). This comes as no surprise, since a diverse and impartial media is in fact a crucial promoter, but also a protector, of freedom of expression. In addition to media freedom, freedom of expression includes a range of other aspects, focusing notably on holding, receiving and imparting ideas or information. Thus, freedom of expression includes other less formal channels of communication, ranging from discussions and debates in public spaces to social media. However, traditional media remains at the core of freedom of expression.

Recent assessments of the situation concerning media freedom in the Western Balkans have been sobering. The region is brewing with incidents of media freedom violations, attacking not just the basic right to freedom of expression, but also the state of democracy as such. Harlem Désir, the Organization for Cooperation and Security in Europe (OSCE) Representative for Freedom of the Media, recently stated that due to the lack of 'strong political will to support and protect the media and their diversity [...] there is still a long road ahead' (2018) for the Western Balkan countries to reach satisfying levels of media freedom.

This assessment is in line with the findings of other authoritative sources of information regarding global media freedom, which highlight deterioration across the board in the region. According to Freedom House's annual Freedom Press Report, the media in these countries is considered only partly free (Freedom House 2016). The Media Sustainability Index, produced by the IREX, reports on the 'collapse of law, ethics, professionalism, and social norms' (Reporters without Borders 2018) which marked the previous year in the media field in the Western Balkans. The Reporters Without Borders World Press Freedom Index ranks Bosnia and Herzegovina as 62nd and North Macedonia as 109th out of the 180 countries considered in its latest report (Reporters without Borders 2018) – the highest- and lowest-ranked Western Balkan country respectively. In absolute numbers, the latest Reporters Without Borders index demonstrates a slight rise in the region's ranking, but this is the result of an overall deterioration in media freedom in Europe and the rest of the world rather than any improvement of the media scene in the Western Balkans. Overall, each of the aforementioned sources implies a decline in regional press freedom, with setbacks registered in the legal, political and economic environment.

The Western Balkan media landscape can best be explained by observing the features of 'hybrid media systems' (Voltmer 2013): the mixture of, on the one hand, liberal ideas of a free and de-regulated press, the sudden liberalization of the media market, and the flourishing of various commercial audio-visual outlets, with, on the other hand, the legacy of the communist past, post-conflict and contextual local factors such as the high level of clientelism, and the backsliding of democracy. This section describes features of Western Balkan hybrid media systems by tracing (1) the legacies of the authoritarian past, (2) the abuse of the media system for media control, and (3) methods of indirect and (4) direct pressure on media.

Legacies

Before proceeding with an analysis of specific cases, I will take a broader historical perspective into account. This will affirm that backsliding in media freedom in the Balkans is not a recent trend nor an exception, but rather the rule. Following 60 years of communist rule marked by the absolute control of media (Jović 2008), the press gradually acquired limited freedom in the 1980s, only for this to be curtailed by the nationalist and authoritarian politics that emerged towards the end of the decade. The introduction of a multi-party political system in the following years resulted in the evaporation of single party control over the media, but this did not mean the end of political interference. By abusing the power of the media to influence public opinion, public authorities in Yugoslav successor states made the press an essential tool in igniting the wars of the 1990s (Thompson 1999). This media landscape presented a picture that was formally pluralist, but remained government-controlled. Even after the second democratic revolution in 2000, governments in the region were more oriented towards political reform and lacked wide-ranging control over the media, but they continued to use the control mechanisms of their authoritarian predecessors. Furthermore, independent journalists' economic vulnerability provided an opportunity for economic interference in the media, including influence exercised by the representatives of foreign capital.

Abuse of the legal system for media control

The new legislative framework which aims to improve access to information about public affairs, has largely failed to break the clientelistic chain and prevent political influence on the media. First, the law completely omits the regulation of state advertising, while at the same time it allows for the co-financing of media projects of common interest as a permissible form of state aid. These categories, therefore, remain unregulated and non-transparent across the region, and as such they are potential tools for creating clientelistic relations between state bodies and the media. According to a study prepared by the Balkan Investigative Reporting Network (BIRN) in 2012 and 2013, the Serbian government, its specialized agencies and public companies have spent approximately 12.5 million EUR on media. Half of this sum was shared between only four media outlets, while the other half was divided among 500 other recipients (Maksić 2015). In addition, the pressure on media comes from marketing agencies that are connected to the ruling elite (Tadić Mijović and Šajkaš. 2016). In Serbia, for example, after the change of power in the 2012 elections the Mediapool marketing agency, run by Goran Veselinović, former employer of the current Serbian President Aleksandar Vučić, became the most influential actor in the advertising business despite having a relatively low profile until then (Georgiev and Đorđević 2014).

Media regulatory institutions are nominally independent of government bodies, both functionally and financially. However, their employees are still included in the corps of civil servants, and as such they are subjected to governmental oversight. Although the governments of the region took no visible actions that could qualify as interference in the independence of the broadcasting regulators, continuous manipulation by informal, rather than direct, political influences still exists across the WB according to Matić (2016).

Particularly worrisome is the trend of abusing state bodies in order to limit the scope or prevent the work of journalists.[5] The most illustrative example of such practice was the secret police's unauthorized surveillance of journalists in North Macedonia in 2015, which caused both political crisis and media controversy in the country, contributing to a growing atmosphere of caution and self-censorship among Macedonian journalists (Vangelov 2019). As seen in the case of *Zrenjaninske novine* in Serbia, the government uses its tax policies selectively so that critical media may be shot down as a reprisal for

ILLIBERAL POLITICS IN SOUTHEAST EUROPE

their critical journalism, while loyal media, such as *TV Pink*, are allegedly allowed to owe millions of euros in unpaid taxes (Barlovac 2015).

Recent years have seen a positive development with regard to the decriminalization of libel and the confinement of journalists' responsibility for defamation to civil procedure and monetary compensation, measures which are expected to have a positive impact on investigative journalism. Nonetheless, criminal law still remains a significant potential pressure mechanism on the media, particularly through the selective interpretation of open-ended concepts such as public disturbance, incitement to hatred or security-related standards. In addition, judges remain partially unaccustomed to key international legal documents on freedom of speech and the practice developed by the European Court of Human Rights (Kmezić 2018). As a result it occurs that, as in the case of Stojan Marković, journalists are held legally responsible even for satirical articles about public officials.

Informal pressure on media

Despite the fact that the media market in the Western Balkans includes numerous registered outlets – for example, there are 2,072 registered media in the Serbian Business Registers Agency, of which 216 are TV stations (IREX 2018) – social and political diversity are still not adequately reflected in media content. The majority of regional media outlets are closely connected with the centres of political and economic power, as confirmed in reports like the World Press Freedom Index (Reporters without Borders 2018). However, unlike the explicit political pressure and censorship of the past, influences on media today are much more subtle and covert. This does not necessarily diminish their efficiency, but it does make their identification much more difficult. In the words of Veran Matić, former director of the Belgrade-based *B92* radio station that withstood numerous attacks by Slobodan Milošević's authoritarian regime in the 1990s, today there are 'more ways to restrict freedom, and as they get more sophisticated, it is impossible to pick up on them at once' (Matić 2009). Even though there have been important steps towards a more free and independent media in recent decades, political pressure and attempts to control the media have remained in place, supplemented by growing economic pressure on media outlets and the emergence of private media controlled by political and economic elites. The political pressures that lead to self-censorship are facilitated by the fact that a great number of journalists continue to work in informal conditions, lacking both individual and collective work contracts. These negative tendencies are additionally cultivated by the lack of general political and social transparency and the weakness of the underdeveloped media market in rural parts of the region.

Furthermore, the ongoing privatization of the media is marked by numerous controversies, including the purchasing of media by party cronies. Political influence over the media is exerted through the media owners' direct involvement in politics, hidden shares, or owners' affiliations with particular politicians. An example is the case of the privatization of Niška Television, where Vladan Gašić, son of a senior member of the ruling Serbian Progressive Party (SNS), has become one of the owners (Dobrašinović 2016). On several occasions privatization has been implemented by a legal entity wholly or partly financed from public funds (Dobrašinović 2016). Thus, political influence and control of the media has survived the transformation of ownership, only to reappear in a new shape.

Direct pressure against the media

Government officials regularly put direct pressure on the media. Matić (2016) establishes that pressures on the editors-in-chief are more powerful than any legal pressure to respect the rights of others. In such cases, the editors serve as brokers in the clientelistic chain. Their dependency is based on the previously established pattern of the politically-driven appointment of chief editors in the remnants of the state-owned media, and their low incomes under private ownership. In addition, there are no formal arrangements to guarantee editorial independence for editors and journalists (Londo 2018). The existing work contracts cover merely administrative matters and do not contain anything like a conscience clause, thus enabling the top-down continuation of the clientelistic chain in media.

Even the highest-ranking public officials, such as the President of the Republic of Serbia Aleksandar Vučić, are involved in such pressure. Vučić repeatedly engages in transparent confrontations with journalists and media outlets in his near-daily public addresses, accusing some of working for foreign governments or the CIA (Balkan Insight 2015). His Montenegrin counterpart Milo Djukanović did not hesitate to accuse the *Vijesti* media group of promoting 'fascist ideas' and 'wanting to overthrow power at any cost' (Vijesti 2018). Such smear campaigns against independent news outlets and investigative journalists are backed up by the remnants of publicly-owned media and the mushrooming tabloid journals. Their sole aim is to personally discredit disloyal journalists by fabricating unfounded stories labelling them as, for example, 'sado-masochistic French spies' (Informer 2016) or accusing them of 'bestiality' (Tomović 2014).

Particularly worrisome are political influences on public media broadcasters. In most of the Western Balkan countries, public service broadcasters are either used for political purposes or commercialized, or both, failing to provide either impartial news or quality programming due to 'political colonisation and instrumentalisation' (Marko 2016). Moreover, as a consequence of non-transparent and occasionally illicit financial management, public service braodcasters are used as a means of transferring public resources (such as well-paid positions and funds dedicated to programme production and advertising) to party clients (Bajomi-Lazar 2016). In such a context, regulatory frameworks and legislative protection of public media broadcasters' independence are ineffective against populist and increasingly authoritarian elites who 'adjust laws as they wish, in order to turn [public service broadcasters] into instruments of political power' (Marko 2016). The most illustrative example of political influence on public media service is the dismissal of the entire editorial team and several journalists at Radio Television Vojvodina (RTV), which coincided with a change in power in the northern Serbian region following the most recent provincial elections. In an open letter, 77 journalists and editors from RTV condemned the wave of dismissals and demanded an explanation as to whether they were politically motivated (Dragojlo 2015). Most recently, in March 2019 protestors in Belgrade stormed the Serbian public broadcaster Radio Television Serbia (RTS) to denounce its reporting bias. Amidst the growing tensions, Pauline Adès-Méval, head of the influential media watch organization Reporters Without Borders, called on the RTS to fulfil its task as a public service media outlet.

5. Discussion and conclusions

This article noted that the rule of law, a functioning prerequisite for the region's convergence to liberal democracy, is absent. It further argues that democracy needs to be analysed not just at the level of political regime, but also in relation to the state and governance. In other words, the framing of the depicted democratic backsliding across the board in WB in terms of the democratic rule of law, reflect awareness of an empirical reality in which what is absent from supposedly democratic regimes are not formal democratic constitutions or procedures, but the more elusive qualities that characterize real democracies. Hence, by juxtaposing the constitutive elements of formal democracy against the functioning rule of law, this study maintains that the WB lack the substance not just of liberal, but also of formal democracy.

Along these lines the study established how since the start of the democratic transition in the 1990s, voters have freely expressed their political preferences in more or less regular election cycles, but nonetheless these elections have been frequently plagued by various irregularities that secured the triumph of the incumbent candidate or the ruling party. Second, it showed how the control of media has become political *loot*, as public and private media alike are continuously (mis)used to provoke popular mobilization, thus putting the incumbents at a significant advantage over their opponents. In other words, this study was able to confirm that political systems in the Western Balkans have provided for electoral competitions, but have largely failed to ensure the conditions for their fairness according to the rule of law. The institutialisation and viability of democracy in the region has failed, meaning that, thirty years since the start of the democratization process, the political systems in the Western Balkans should still be considered mere competitive authoritarian regimes.

Before proceeding to specific explanations of the regional problems described, it must be said that they are not unique to the geographical area of the Western Balkans. The reversal of democracy and the rule of law occurs today even in long-standing democracies like the United States, where it is principally linked with the growing prevalence of neoliberal governmentality, which allows for the persistent weakness of the state and institutions. It is in this regard that Cavatorta rightly emphasizes that both democratic and authoritarian regimes seem to be moving towards a common system of governance where 'real policy-making power is concentrated in a few hands' (2010, 218).

But what makes the WB case so distinct is the inherent lack of internal capacities to eliminate the conditions preventing its countries from moving beyond the category of *electoral* to *liberal* democracies. How can the implementation of democratic laws be ensured, and how can the independence of state institutions and media be secured in order to substantively enhance the chances for democratic consolidation? Success in this matter rests upon the precondition of eradicating the root causes of the Western Balkans' un-rule-of-law-embedded political systems. The key remains to unlock a new party dynamics that would enable these countries to break away from their established patterns of clientelism, informal networks and strong party control over media and state institutions. In other words, liberal structures must be strengthened in order to persistently challenge illiberal power structures and norms. If this does not happen, the prevalence of these patterns will cement the democratic smokescreens behind which *business as usual* shall continue in decades to come.

Machiavelli knew enough to say the following: 'There is nothing more difficult to carry out, nor more doubtful of success, nor more dangerous to handle, than to initiate a new order of things' (1532, 19). This is precisely the task for the WB if they are to move away from the current competitive authoritarian political order – not simply to achieve a change of elites, but to initiate a completely new order of things.

The good – albeit conditional – news is that there seems to be a way out of the vicious circle of the Western Balkans' state capture. This was recently seen in North Macedonia, where, against all the odds, the country's authoritarian leader, Nikola Gruevski, was defeated in the 2016 general elections. The realization of the *Macedonian scenario*, as it is pejoratively called by the neighbouring countries' authoritarian leaders, was not easy to achieve. It required an honest political settlement by all parliamentary parties over the issues guaranteeing the fairness of the electoral process, massive bottom-up pressure from local civil society and grassroots groups, and decisive top-down pressure applied by the EU, which included robust international supervision with strong oversight mechanisms, including on media reporting. Yet ensuring a more enduring political transformation requires not simply a change of government, but a change of everyday practice, retreating from informal and fast fixes, ensuring independent and accountable institutions and promoting a meritocratic system. On the success of the *Macedonian scenario*, meaning the eventual transition from competitive authoritarianism to democracy, as well as on the result of the WB6 democratic transition, the jury is still out.

Notes

1. Interview with a high-ranking politician, Belgrade, January 2019.
2. Interview with a political analyst, Belgrade, June 2019.
3. Interview with an NGO activist, Belgrade, January 2019.
4. Interview with an election observer, Podgorica, May 2019.
5. Interview with a journalist, Skopje, January 2019.

Disclosure statement

No potential conflict of interest was reported by the author.

References

Agency for Statistics of Bosnia and Herzegovina. 2013. *Preliminary results of the 2013 census of population, households and Dwellings in Bosnia and Herzegovina.* http://www.bhas.ba/obavjes tenja/Preliminarni_rezultati_bos.pdf.

Alo. 2018. Šaban Šaulić žestoko odgovorio Đilasu! January 28. https://www.alo.rs/vip/estrada/ saban-saulic-zestoko-odgovorio-draganu-dilasu/143126/vest.

Amos, M. J. Harrison, and L. Woods, eds. 2012. *Freedom of expression and the media.* Brill: Nijhoff.

Anastasakis, O. 2014. Election consolidation in the post-communist Balkans. Progress and obstacles. *Caucasus International* 4, no. 4: 15–25.

Andrić, V., 2019. Šta će đaci u školi na raspustu? *Danas*, February 26.

Bajomi-Lazar, P., 2016. Public service television in the Western Balkans: A Mission Impossible. *LSE Media Policy Project Blog*. https://blogs.lse.ac.uk/mediapolicyproject/2016/12/08/public-service-television-in-the-western-balkans-a-mission-impossible/.

Balkan Insight. 2015. Serbian PM Slams EU, Alleging BIRN Lies. January 10. https://balkaninsight.com/2015/01/10/serbia-pm-slams-eu-alleging-birn-lies/.

Barlovac, B. 2015. Media integrity report: State-media financial relations in Serbia. *Southeast European Media Observatory*.

Bieber, F. 2018a. Patterns of competitive authoritarianism in the Western Balkans. *East European Politics* 34: 337–54.

Bieber, F. 2018b. For Macedonia, is joining NATO and the EU worth the trouble? *Foreign Policy*. https://foreignpolicy.com/2018/09/13/for-macedonia-is-joining-nato-and-the-eu-worth-the-trouble/.

Cavatorta, F. 2010. The convergence of governance. Upgrading authoritarianism in the Arab World and downgrading democracy elsewhere? *Middle East Critique* 19: 217–32.

Centar za Izborne Studije. 2017. *Iskustva i preporuke NVO sektora za unapredjenje kvalitete izbornog procesa u Bosni i Herzegovini*. Sarajevo: Heinrich Boell Stiftung.

Central Election Commission of Bosnia and Herzegovina. 2016. *Decision on the number of voters in Bosnia*. May 4.

Collier, D. and S. Levitsky. 1997. Democracy with adjectives: Conceptual innovation in comparative research. *World Politics* 49: 430–51.

CRTA Election Observation Mission. 2018. *Belgrade Elections 2018 – Final Report*. https://crta.rs/en/belgrade-elections-2018-final-report/.

Dahl, R. 2005. What political institutions does large-scale democracy require? *Political Science Quarterly* 120: 187–97.

Désir, H.J.P. 2018. EU-Western Balkans media days. Keynote speech of the OSCE Representative on Freedom of the Media. September 17. https://www.osce.org/representative-on-freedom-of-media/396089?download=true.

Dobrašinović, D. ed. 2016. *Citizens' supervision of media privatization in Serbia*. Prokuplje: Toplica Center for Democracy and Human Rights.

Dolenec, D. 2013. *Democratic institutions and authoritarian rule in Southeast Europe*. Colchester: ECPR Press.

Dragojlo, S. 2015. Serbia tells state media to prepare for sale. BIRN, June 18. http://www.balkaninsight.com/en/article/serbia-tells-state-media-to-prepare-for-sale.

European Commission. 2018. A credible enlargement perspective for and enhanced EU engagement with the Western Balkans: COM(2018) 65 final. Strasbourg, February 6.

Freedom House. 2016. Back Where we started in the Balkans. Freedom at Issue Blog. https://freedomhouse.org/blog/back-where-we-started-balkans.

Fukuyama, F. 1992. *The end of history and the last man*. New York: Avon Books.

Gavrilović, Z., M. Mijatović, and D. Pavlica. 2017. *Mediji, javnost i izbori*. Biro za društvena istraživanja.

Georgiev, S., and A. Đorđević. 2014. Oglašavanje kao privatni posao vlasti, *BIRN*, March 27. https://javno.rs/istrazivanja/oglasavanje-kao-privatni-posao-vlasti.

Ilić, V., 2017. Nevolje sa biračkim spiskom. *Peščanik*, April 15. https://pescanik.net/nevolje-sa-birackim-spiskom/.

Informer. 2016. Sado-maso French Spy: Who is actually KRIK's chief editor? March 18.

Jović, D. 2008. *Yugoslavia: The State that Withered Away*. West Lafayette: Purdue University Press.

JugMedia. 2016. Lekari iz SNS-a merili pritisak i šećer po mesnim zajednicama. June 6. https://jugmedia.rs/lekari-iz-sns-a-merili-pritisak-i-secer-po-mesnim-zajednicama/.

Keil, S. 2018. The Business of State Capture and the Rise of Authritarianism in Kosovo, Macedonia, Montenegro and Serbia. *Southeastern Europe* 42: 59–82.

Kmezić, M. 2018. Captured media: Limitations and structural hindrances to media freedom in Serbia. *Review of Central and East European Law* 43: 457–82.

Kmezić, M., and F. Bieber. 2017. *The crisis of democracy in the Western Balkans: An autonomy of stabilitocracy and the limits of the EU democracy promotion*. Belgrade: Balkans in Europe Policy Advisory Group.

Levitsky, S., and L.A. Way. 2010. *Competitive authoritarianism. Hybrid regimes after the cold war.* Cambridge: Cambridge University Press.

Linz, J., and A. Stepan. 1996. *Problems of democratic transition and consolidation: Southern Europe, South America, and post-communist Europe.* Baltimore: The John Hopkins University Press.

Londo, I. 2018. *Albanian media scene vs. European standards.* Tirana: Albanian Media Institute.

Machiavelli, N. 1532. *The prince.* London: Penguin Classics.

Magen, A., and L. Morlino. 2008. *International actors, democratization and the rule of law.* London: Routledge.

Maksić, T. 2015. *Media reform stalled in the slow lane.* Paris: World Association of Newspapers and News Publishers.

Marko, D. 2016. *The future of public service broadcasting in the Western Balkans: The need for a new paradigm.* Sarajevo: Analitika.

Matić, J., 2016. Editors in Serbia: Closer to owners than to journalists. *Southeast European Media Observatory.*

Matić, V. 2009. B92 twenty years later. *Vreme,* May 22.

Nedeljnik. 2018. Privođenja, napadi, paralelni spiskovi: Kako je protekao izborni dan u Lučanima. December 16.

Nichter, S. 2018. *Votes for survival: Relational clientelism in Latin America.* Cambridge: Cambridge University Press.

Nikolić, M., 2017. GSP prevoz za miting SNS – Tako izgleda kad grad prihoduje. *N1,* March 25. http://rs.n1info.com/Vesti/a237650/GSP-autobusi-za-miting-SNS.html.

Nikolic, T., 2008. Speech at the central state administration of the Serbian radical party meeting. Belgrade. September 12. https://www.youtube.com/watch?v=uhUX4WpoXro.

Novosadska novinarska škola. 2017. Medijska (ne)zavisnost. http://www.novinarska-skola.org.rs/sr/wp-content/uploads/2019/03/Istrazivanje-Medijska-nezavisnost-u-2017.pdf.

O'Donnell, G. 2004. The quality of democracy: Why the rule of Law matters. Guillermo O'Donnell. *Journal of Democracy* 15, no. 4: 32–46.

Prelec, T. 2019. Rule of law and elections: How to tackle systemic problems. In *Strengthening the rule of law in the Western Balkans: Call for a revolution against particularism,* J. Marović, T. Prelec, and M. Kmezić. ed., 27–43. Belgrade: Balkans in Europe Policy Advisory Group.

Ramet, S.P., and P. Wagner. 2010. Post-socialist models of rule in central and Southeast Europe. In *Central and Southeast European politics since 1989,* ed. S.P. Ramet, 9–36. Cambridge: Cambridge University Press.

Reporters without Borders. 2018. World press freedom index. https://rsf.org/en/ranking/2018%2C.

Richter, S., and N. Wunsch. 2019. Money, power, glory: The linkages between EU conditionality and state capture in the Western Balkans. *Journal of European Public Policy* 27, no. 1: 41–62.

Tadić Mijović, M., and M. Šajkaš. 2016. *Captured news media: Bosnia and Herzegovina, Serbia, and Montenegro.* Washington DC: Centre for International Media Assistance.

Tamanaha, B. 2004. *On the rule of law: history, politics and theory.* Cambridge: Cambridge University Press.

Thompson, M. 1999. *Forging war: The media in Serbia, Croatia and Bosnia-Herzegovina.* Luton: University of Luton Press.

Tomović, D. 2014. Montenegro rights activist sex claims spark outrage. *BIRN,* June 24. https://balkaninsight.com/2014/06/24/montenegro-rights-activist-sex-claims-spark-outrage/.

TV1. 2018, Dodik prijeti otkazima, mora se glasati za njega. September 27. https://tv1.ba/vijesti/bih/dodik-prijeti-otkazima-mora-se-glasati-za-njega/.

Vangelov, O. 2019. The primordialism of ethnic nationalism in macedonia. *Europe-Asia Studies* 71: 2013–24.

Vijesti. 2018. Djukanović: Vijesti promovišu fašističke ideje. April 11.

Voltmer, K. 2013. *The media in transitional democracies.* Cambridge: Polity Press.

Vračić, A. 2018. The way back: Brain drain and prosperity in the Western Balkans, policy brief. *European Council on Foreign Relations.*

Zakošek, N. 1997. Pravna država i demokracija u post-socijalizmu. *Politička Misao* 4: 78–85.

Big dreams and small steps: comparative perspectives on the social movement struggle for democracy in Serbia and North Macedonia

Gazela Pudar Draško ⓘ, Irena Fiket ⓘ and Jelena Vasiljević ⓘ

ABSTRACT
This paper provides a comparative analysis of social movements' characteristics and capacities to struggle against illiberal tendencies and incite political change in Serbia and North Macedonia. First, we discuss the illiberal elements of political regimes in the countries in question, Serbia and North Macedonia. Then, we provide a comprehensive overview of progressive social movements in the two countries, formed and organized as a response to different authoritarian and non-democratic tendencies. Finally, we point to some differences in their organizing, coalition-forging and issue-defining principles, which, we believe, may help to explain the relative success of social movements in North Macedonia in producing relevant political outcomes, compared to the weak political impact of social movements in Serbia. Empirical data were collected during the summer of 2018 through in-depth interviews with members of social movements in North Macedonia and Serbia.

1. Introduction

Serbia and North Macedonia[1] are the focus of this study because of similarities in their current or recent political regimes, which have exhibited many features of illiberal politics. The two countries offer two compatible yet different socio-political scenarios, reflecting and encompassing many diverse elements of democratic crisis, experienced in other southeast European countries as well. However, after the regime change in N. Macedonia in 2017, the two countries seem to be heading in opposite directions, with N. Macedonia consolidating its democratic course, while Serbia is exhibiting ever-stronger autocratic tendencies. The role of social movements in democratization is becoming ever more important: their active involvement in protests has led to regime change in N. Macedonia, and their increased visibility and presence is fuelling the growing resistance to the ruling regime in Serbia. The main goal of this paper is to comparatively analyse these social movements' capacities to produce political outcomes, that is, to bring about political, or outright regime change in the two countries (Bosi et al. 2016).

Recent regime change in N. Macedonia was arguably the result of a joint effort by multiple actors struggling against the illiberal politics of the former Prime Minister, Nikola Gruevski. Namely, after the December 2016 elections and a turbulent political process, the Social Democratic Union of Macedonia (SDSM), led by Zoran Zaev, managed to form a coalition government in May 2017. This moment has been praised for breaking with the authoritarian regime of Nikola Gruevski. More importantly for our study, it came about as a result of a significant degree of coordinated cooperation between social movements and the political opposition. The synergy of political and civil society actors has been impressive, and this coalition of democratizing forces has proven to be a major agent of democratic political change in this country (Schenkkan et al. 2018).

Contrary to the case of N. Macedonia, autocratic tendencies in Serbia still have not produced consolidated and substantial cooperation among different political and civil society actors, despite an overall consensus that democratic freedoms are severely threatened. The most recent Freedom House report (2019) placed Serbia among partially free states, recording a substantial decline over the past 4 years in terms of political rights and civil liberties. Only quite recently, with the launching of the *#1od5Milliona* [one in five million] protests, has the regime faced an organized form of dissent[2]. Although taking place every Saturday since late 2018, the protests' concrete effects and potentials to mobilize different social actors are yet to be seen.

Social and protest movements have received renewed and heightened attention since the economic crisis of 2008 (Della Porta 2014, 2015; Della Porta et al. 2017). However, the region of southeast Europe is still understudied in this respect, in spite of the series of movements and short-term initiatives that have spread across the region – from the 2012–2013 Slovenian protests, the Croatian *Right to the city* movement, the eruption of *Citizens' plenums* in Bosnia and Herzegovina in 2014, several scattered movements and locally focused protests in Serbia, to the so-called Colourful revolution in N. Macedonia.[3] Building on very few studies in this domain (Horvat and Štiks 2015; Fagan and Sircar 2017; Bieber and Brentin 2018; Bieber 2018a; Mujanović 2018), this article offers the first qualitative comparison between social movements in two Western Balkan countries, with seemingly very different political impact. The aim of our research is to understand the characteristics of the movements in Serbia and North Macedonia, and to try to explain the relation between the observed differences between them and the (different) political outcomes they produced.

Our analysis of the social movements of Serbia and N. Macedonia is primarily based on empirical findings obtained through semi-structured in-depth interviews conducted during the summer of 2018.[4] However, given the almost complete lack of data on specific social movements in these countries, we have also drawn upon other sources, helping us to better understand the context in which the movements have emerged and elaborate in more detail the comparative ground of our analysis. Our empirical research therefore also relies on participant observation of the 2017 protest waves in Serbia, interviews with key informants of the 2014 mass protests in N. Macedonia (the so-called Colourful Revolution), as well as analyses of the social movements' programmes, press releases and articles when available. We provide new empirical evidence and use it to support the view – up until recently somewhat neglected in the literature – which links democratization and social movements. Our initial premise is that given the blockade of other channels of political action within the context of captured states (Bieber 2018b), social movements in Serbia and N. Macedonia should be seen as relevant and necessary actors of democratization. However, it should be noted that the democratization literature focuses mainly on institutional actors that pursue democracy as a goal, overlooking social movements or perceiving them mainly as potential threats to democracy (Tarrow 1995; Bermeo 1997). On the other hand, the literature on social movements mainly focuses on democratic countries of Western Europe, where the opportunities for social movements to organize and act were qualitatively and quantitatively bigger, therefore seeing democracy as a prerequisite for social movements. Only recently have the social sciences recognized the importance of social movements for democratization of authoritarian societies (Della Porta 2014; Trejo 2012; Almeida and Cordero Ulate 2015).

Relying on the thesis that progressive social movements play an important role in pursuing and strengthening democratic values, we focused our comparative analysis on detecting and understanding the role of those values in the analysed social movements' agendas and various spheres of action. Our empirical analysis, therefore, focuses on 1) the movements' organization, motivation and proclaimed goals, 2) wider beliefs and ideas that guide the movements' actions, and 3) their internal structure and organization. We put particular emphasis on the comparative perspective, looking at both similarities and differences in the approaches of the Serbian and N. Macedonian movements, with the aim to assess their overall potential to challenge illiberal political tendencies.

2. Explaining the context: challenges to democracy and decline of political trust in Serbia and N. Macedonia

The countries of the Western Balkans are seemingly reliving competitive authoritarianism that characterized much of the region in the 1990s. However, the ruling regimes of today are structurally different from those of the 1990s (Bieber 2018a), and they reflect both local specificities of the democratization process in the region and the global rise in illiberal political trends. These trends connect formal democratic procedures with authoritarian tendencies and ruling parties' and figures' (institutional and extra-institutional) efforts to remain in power indefinitely. Authoritarian leaders have learned to become more effective in manipulating democratic institutes of elections, parties and legislature to enhance power-prolonging effects (Kendall-Taylor and Frantz 2014). 'Toxic leaders' have various instruments at their disposal to build and preserve dependence of different actors by providing advantages such as clientelism and patronage (Džihić and Hayoz 2016, 7). 'Captured institutions' and widespread clientelism are major indicators of illiberal and autocratic tendencies, and as Cengiz Günay and Džihić (2016) have shown ruling parties in both Serbia and N. Macedonia primarily act as machine parties, central to gaining and maintaining power with the aim to (ab)use state resources. The overall situation is largely supported by the indefinitely delayed accession to the European Union and preference of its leaders for *stabilocracy*, rather than liberal democratic development in the region (Kmezić and Bieber 2017).

After initial success in improving the state of democracy, evidenced in increased freedom of elections and press, paving the road towards joining the EU, the illiberal trend can be said to have begun in the late 2000s. The process of the Europeanization implied aligning national policies with EU standards and acquis, in general, inspired by liberal democratic discourses and neoliberal economic concepts (Cengiz Günay and Džihić 2016; Lazić 2011). However, progress has slowed down. Symptomatic changes came in different forms for different countries in the Western Balkans: political instabilities in Serbia revealed themselves most dramatically with the assassination of the Prime Minister Zoran Đinđić in 2003; in N. Macedonia, the instalment of the populist government of Nikola Gruevski marked a new political turn for this country (Bieber and Ristić 2012). In 2010, both countries were below the cut-off point of $6000 GDP per capita – the level of economic development that contributes positively to democratic survival and development. With $5056 and $4201, respectively, Serbia and N. Macedonia joined Albania as the only 3 of the 13 post-communist countries below the threshold (Dolenec 2013, 59).

At the time, the Global Democracy Ranking placed both countries among those with medium scores, with N. Macedonia as a country with significant decline in ranking over the previous few years (Democracy Ranking 2016). Similarly, the World Press Freedom Index (2014) evaluated the freedom of press in N. Macedonia as the worst in the region placing it 123rd (out of 180) with slow improvement until 2018 (109th place). According to the same source, the Serbian media freedom had been slowly deteriorating in the past years, from 63rd place in 2013 to 76th in 2018.

Both countries have open 'identity' issues, manipulation of which enables even more manoeuvring space for ruling elites to suppress freedoms and pluralist values. In Serbia, the ongoing disputes about Kosovo and its unresolved status provide fertile ground for emotional mobilization of citizenry and effective discursive tool for diverting public attention from socio-economic problems. The name issue in North Macedonia has gained peculiar momentum through 'antiquisation' of identity and claims to heritage of ancient Macedonia, causing the dispute with Greece. The ruling elites have been using the state of the 'ethnic condominium' of ethnic Macedonians and Albanians to further suppress liberal values and democracy (Crowther 2017). This is especially emphasized through political competition within ethnic blocs, and the absence of a party that would break across ethnic lines – something the present ruling party is trying to counter (for more, see Daskalovski and Trajkovski 2017). Additionally, as a result of 'EU enlargement fatigue' and slow integration process, which are causing popular dissatisfaction, the ruling parties in both countries increasingly use nationalism to distract the voters from growing economic problems.

In explaining the context in which social movements became active on the political scene of N. Macedonia and Serbia, one should equally take into account the differences between the two countries' political landscapes. In Serbia, change in political power in 2012 led to the dissipation of the previously ruling coalition: at present, the ruling party is on one side, with many small and weak parties on the other. N. Macedonia is a different case, as a country with a strong two-party system – or four-party system, if we take into account the two major Albanian parties. The Social Democratic Union of Macedonia (SDSM), which prior to 2017 was the key opposition party, engaged heavily with social movements and supported citizens' street protests before coming to power in 2017. The Serbian opposition scene is scattered and has been unable, until recently, to mobilize citizens' deep dissatisfactions with pervasive and authoritarian ruling structures. Unlike in N. Macedonia, the social movement and protest organizers in Serbia have so far refused to enter into coalition with political parties, indicating a lack of trust in political organizations and existing parties.

Another important element of the general socio-political context contributing to growing relevance of social movements is the issue of *mistrust*, i.e., the growing distance of citizens from political institutions, which are perceived as corrupt and solely in service of politicians' interests. Trust in political parties and non-governmental organizations is very low in Serbia. In 2010, only 17.6% of citizens trusted political parties, while NGOs enjoyed the trust of 22.2% of the population. With the exception of the (ICTY) Hague tribunal and NATO, parties and NGOs were the least trusted institutions in Serbia (Bešić 2011, 125). More recently, CESID (Centre for Free Elections and Democracy, Serbia) polls show even further deterioration of trust in political and non-governmental organizations, with findings that only 11% of citizens trust political parties and 16% trust NGOs (Centar za Slobodne Izbore i Demokratiju (CeSID) 2017, 35). A recent study (Fiket et al. 2017) emphasized that citizens' attitudes and feelings towards politics and politicians in Serbia are most accurately described as *loathing* and *contempt*. Parties are seen as organizations whose sole function is to serve the interest of the corrupted elite, with no distinct ideology or values. Having such attitudes towards politics and politicians, and largely perceiving the whole political system as malfunctioning, citizens often choose not to participate in formal political arenas.

N. Macedonian citizens, in general, showed similar levels of mistrust in their political organizations and institutions. Two N. Macedonian institutions in which citizens had very little trust in March 2017 were the State Commission for the Prevention of Corruption (trusted by 15% of the people), and political parties (at 16%) of recorded trusting citizens (Macedonia National Public Opinion Poll 2017). The erosion of trust in political parties is evident when compared to 2010, when 23.3% of citizens trusted parties (Klekovski et al. 2010). The context of overall mistrust is evident also among 65% of citizens stating that their country is moving in the wrong direction (National Democratic Institute (NDI) 2017). However, in 2010, compared to Serbia, N. Macedonian citizens exhibited a much higher degree of trust in non-governmental organizations – 42.5%. The highest trust was recorded among students (55.1%) and young people aged 18 to 29 (50.5%) – comprising the majority of active citizens engaged in protests and social movements in N. Macedonia. Although we lack more recent hard data on N. Macedonia, indirectly we can draw some conclusions and say that citizens in N. Macedonia are more trusting and politically efficient as the RCC (Regional Cooperation Council) polls reveal that almost half (47%) of N. Macedonian citizens believed that citizens' and civil society organizations could effectively scrutinize the government and make it accountable to citizens (compared to only 35% in Serbia; RCC 2017, 128).

Such general political mistrust (as in the Serbian case) can be an indicator of a crisis of democracy; but it can also serve, to a certain degree, as a protective mechanism for the interest and values of the civil society (Rosanvallon 2006, 9). Della Porta (2012) notes that social movements often attract critical, mistrustful citizens, who challenge institutions and build new spaces for articulation of social trust.

Finally, an important factor in understanding the social movements' role in channelling mistrust of political organizations towards trust of other forms of organizing is the possibility of citizens to participate effectively in local political arenas. This is especially relevant for Serbia, as it is larger and more highly centralized than N. Macedonia. Citizens are marginalized and their capacity to influence local institutions, even as envisaged by the law, is reduced to consultations without decision-making powers, therefore contributing additionally to citizens' alienation and mistrust (Đorđević 2006). In addition, the electoral system is structured in such a way that political representatives of local communities are almost entirely dependent on political parties, instead of being responsible to their local electorate (Đorđević 2011). At the same time, opposition democratic parties in Serbia seem to be failing at building connections with the populace and at formulating creative, authentic and realistic responses to problems faced by the population. This has opened the opportunity for local civic initiatives and movements to fill the 'trust gap' and position themselves as new political actors responding to tangible, local needs of citizens.

3. The contentious political arenas and progressive social movements in Serbia and N. Macedonia

The lack of trust in institutional political arenas and political parties' inability to channel and manage citizens' discontent has opened the space for the creation of the non-institutional political arenas; namely citizens became actively engaged in different forms of contentious politics, most notably through new waves of mass protests and the emergence of new social movements.[5]

The first mass protests since the overthrow of Slobodan Milošević happened in Serbia in 2017.[6] The protests were apparently non-organized and were rather a spontaneous reaction to the usurpation of political power, conveniently embodied in Aleksandar Vučić's shift from one position of power (prime minister) to another (president). Protestors claimed that the elections were not fair, free and regular in many aspects, especially regarding the media space that Vučić took during the campaign. The protest was known in public as a 'Protest against Dictatorship', the title of the Facebook page functioning as the main communication channel while the protests were taking place. Some organized groups, such as the police and army unions, also joined.[7] The principal common denominator was disillusionment with the political elite and political institutions. Among the demands of protesters were: abolishing the 'dictatorship' and the complete removal of the political elite headed by Aleksandar Vučić, fair and free elections, free media, de-capturing the state, decentralization, shift in priorities of economic and social policies, protection of labour rights and improved status of all workers, protection of living standards and entirely publicly financed educational and health system (Babović et al. 2017; Petrović and Petrović 2017; Fridman and Hercigonja 2016). Protestors claimed to be apolitical underlining that they did not want leaders or a specific political party to lead them (although three presidential candidates and most opposition parties stated their support for the demonstrations; Pešić 2017). From Belgrade, the protests spread to other cities such as Novi Sad, Niš and Kragujevac, Subotica, Sombor, Kraljevo, Kruševac, Zrenjanin, Leskovac, Požarevac and Bor, primarily via social media. The lack of any kind of substantial coordination disabled the protesters from connecting the various protest sites to include populations from other urban centres and from rural areas, which would have possibly have allowed the protests to grow and sharpen. Further, the heterogeneity of the participants holding different ideological and political preferences also prevented the protests from growing and becoming more articulate. Consistently ignored by the authorities and lacking a clear and coherent agenda, they slowly died out after 2 months without becoming a movement. The most active protestors faced charges in February 2018 for organizing unauthorized gatherings.[8] All other protests that have taken place in Serbia, since the power shift in 2012, were local – city – initiatives led by movements that are included in this research study.

The N. Macedonian arena of contentious politics opened in 2014 with student protests (followed shortly by the professors' protests) against the reform of the university enrolments politics and for greater university autonomy (Pollozhani 2016). Soon afterwards, the smaller protests grew into a massive protest movement 'Protestiram' (I protest), after citizens' strong reactions to president Ivanov's decision to pardon high government officials accused of corruption and abuses of power (see Milan 2017; Stefanovski 2016).[9] Protests were organized every day in several N. Macedonian cities contributing to the feeling of greater political efficacy among citizens from day-to-day. After paint bombs were thrown at different buildings built as part of the project 'Skopje 2014', to express citizen rage in a peaceful way, the protest movement became known as the 'Colourful Revolution' (Reef 2017). The dissatisfaction in N. Macedonia was channelled towards the urban €600 million project – Skopje 2014, whose objective was to make Skopje more 'ancient' (Dimitrov et al. 2016).[10] Unlike in Serbia where protests organized by local movements and 'Protest against Dictatorship' demanded the removal of all visible signs of political parties, the protest organizers in N. Macedonia cooperated closely not only among themselves but also with the main opposition party SDSM.

In the following sections, we will more closely examine, through a comparative perspective, progressive social movements as the main actors of contentious political arenas in Serbia and N. Macedonia. In selecting the sample, we followed Snow et al.'s (2004) definition of social movements that focuses on collectives acting 1) with some degree of organization and continuity[11] 2) outside of institutional channels, for the purpose of 3) challenging or defending extant institutionally based authority, and adding the criterion of 4) universal inclusiveness. Movements included in this research are the following ones: Studentski plenum (Student Plenum), Solidarnost (the leftist movement, Solidarity), Protestiram (I protest) and Ecoguerilla from N. Macedonia, and Ne davimo Beograd (Don't let Belgrade d(r)own), Združena akcija za Krov nad glavom (United action: roof over head), Studentski pokret Novi Sad (Student movement from Novi Sad), Inicijativa za Požegu (Initiative for Požega), Lokalni front Kraljevo (Local front Kraljevo), Zrenjaninski socijalni forum (Zrenjanin social forum), Tvrđava Smederevo (Smederevo fortress), Udruženi pokret slobodnih stanara (United movement of free tenants) and Odbranimo reke Stare planine (Defend the rivers of Mt. Stara Planina) from Serbia.[12]

4. Commonalities and shared characteristics between the social movements in Serbia and N. Macedonia

When asked about the reasons for their activism or events that have triggered the formation of their movements, our interviewees mostly stated concrete and specific events. For instance, in N. Macedonia those were: police brutality and the President's acquitting corrupt politicians (Protestiram), proposed changes to the law on higher education and imposition of rigorous state exams (Studentski plenum), extreme pollution in the city of Tetovo (Ecoguerilla).

In Serbia, some of the issues that triggered the movements to organize were: sudden and unexplained removal of the director of the Cultural Centre of Kraljevo (Lokalni front Kraljevo), the urban rejuvenation project Belgrade Waterfront followed by illegal demolition on Hercegovačka Street in Belgrade executed to clear up space for the project (Ne davimo Beograd), the local municipality's decision to purchase a piece of real estate co-owned by the spouse of the president of the Municipal Assembly at price of 100,000 € (Inicijativa za Požegu), a plan to build mini hydroelectric power plants that would endanger the rivers in eastern Serbia (Odbranimo reke Stare planine).

As mentioned in the introduction, we start from the thesis that social movements play an important role in pursuing and strengthening democratic values. More precisely, we focused our analysis on detecting those values in 1) movement organization motivation and stated goals, 2) beliefs and ideas that guide their actions, and 3) their internal structure and organization.

4.1. The movement organizations' motivation and stated goals

One of the most common characteristics of the analysed movements was that they were largely established in response to a concrete event or political act by the governing elites, deemed undemocratic and illegitimate. The types of reactions and events in questions largely shaped the initial goals and *raisons d' être* of the movements. Thus, at least when discussing their initial phase, most of the analysed movements could be called single-issue (Jacobsson 2015).[13] However, the movement members, when discussing these concrete, single political issues, described them as 'the tip of the iceberg', as evoking and symbolizing wider issues, like widespread corruption, captured institutions, regime pressure on society, controlled media, or undemocratic decision-making: 'It is the drop that overfilled the glass (...) so before that, we have first of all a wider context of the state, so everything that happens to us is so much corruption, so much impoverishment and so much humiliation of the citizens;'[14] 'Our focus is [more democratic and efficient] local government. But in the wider sense, it is precisely that we need citizens within the political arena where they must see themselves as participants and not spectators.'[15]

> In the public discourse there was only information from the media (...) completely controlled by the ruling party (...) and the ruling party was not accepting anything different from what they imagined. (...) Society was completely apathetic. A depression from which there was no escape. Probably that was the reason why so many people who previously protested against the government decided to join under one goal.[16]

Even though initially formed as a direct reaction to specific issue and related undemocratic conduct of the governing elites, the need to engage politically was very often articulated by the representatives of the movements. This need in the narratives of the activists is strongly associated with urgency to find solutions to social problems in a less authoritarian way, contrary to what governments do. A common theme was the call for more democracy through inclusion of citizens into the political arena, especially when it came to the goals of the movements, whether stated in their official documents or given in interviews by their activists.[17] In this regard, the dominant vision of democracy is a kind of social democracy with a strong participatory element: 'And here [in our goals] we come to socialism, democratization in decision-making on the management of public goods, especially those affecting all citizens or at least a large number of citizens.'[18]

> Our movement fought against state exams that were seriously undermining the autonomy of the university. Besides that, we were fighting against the undemocratic rule of the VMRO-DPMNE because they tried to shrink the political space.[19]

4.2. General beliefs and ideas that stand behind the movements' actions

Along with the movements' motivations and goals, most often mentioned in the narratives of the activists were the principles that guided their actions: equality of all under the law, freedom of speech and media, government responsive to citizens, a strong welfare state. In the words of one of the activists:

> A good society [for which we are fighting] is a society where people can freely manifest their freedom, satisfaction, dissatisfaction, (...) (where citizens) have knowledge of how to organize and lead debates (...) where there are no big economic and social divisions (...) based on solidarity (...) which treats all members of society equally and there is justice for everybody. A society where there is good education, good health system, social system and a society where the citizens are active (...) inclusion of the people in the process of creation of politics.[20]

The democratic ideal that could be drawn from the movements' motivations and goals is extended to the deliberative model of democracy (Fishkin 1991; Habermas 1996; Dryzek 2000), stressing here the importance of equality of participation and the value of debate: 'Every voice [must be] heard and respected (...) we have social responsibility to be active members of society. That means to debate, to emancipate, to mobilize people;'[21] 'We lack a culture of debate. A culture of presenting arguments, listening to the other side and then drawing conclusions [making decisions].'[22]

However, the movements here explored do not convey an elaborate critique of representative democracy and strong advocacy of deliberative models, which is characteristic of many contemporary social movements belonging to, say, 'real democracy' movements (Roos and Oikonomakis 2014).

4.3. Internal structure and organization of the movements

The relevance of the deliberative model of democracy for the movements here considered is additionally confirmed through their reflections and internal debate on 'the most democratic way to organize' and attempts to respect deliberative standards in their decision-making procedures as well as their modes of communicating their messages to other citizens.

Every single participant in the research underlined the importance of inclusion of all movement members in taking decisions. Being, on the other hand, aware that this goal cannot be reached in larger communities, most of them defined flexible ways in which decisions could be made and would allow modifications, thus providing the opportunity to change in specific situations.

Still, no matter how specific ways of decision-making across the movements were (such as, for example, working groups dedicated to specific issues or areas that facilitate decision-making by framing the issues to be debated by the all members of the movement), they all insisted on horizontality, openness and most importantly debate. They avoided the aggregative model of decision-making (Benhabib 1996; Knight and Johnson 1994), so the voting procedure was used very rarely. Instead, their main modus operandi was discussion among equals where argumentations and not numbers count. It should be noted, however, that the activists are highly aware that sometimes the price to pay for such demanding procedure is efficacy.

Finally, inclusivity and dialogue also guided their communication with other citizens. Their messages and public announcements were crafted with competence and time resources of citizens in mind: terms they use are quite simple and quotidian. Very often, these movements operate inventively, involving a public action that is inviting for citizens and therefore opening the possibility for others to join: 'We insist on versatility in our performance, messages should never be sent only through one person, because we need a different approach for different target groups.'[23]

5. Mapping the differences between social movements in N. Macedonia and Serbia

At first glance, the difference between the role and engagement of social movements in challenging illiberal regimes in N. Macedonia and Serbia is more than obvious. Street protestors, student movement, 'novice' activists, as well as civil society veterans, all joined forces with opposition parties and gave their share in toppling Gruevski's regime in N. Macedonia. Doubtlessly, EU's change of policy played a part as well (Dimitrov et al. 2016). All in all, relatively peaceful regime change, overwhelming international support for the new government's course, and the new composition of the Parliament (Sobranie) – now comprising several MPs coming from the ranks of the activist movements[24] – are good reasons to consider the N. Macedonian social movements' struggle a success. On the other hand, Serbia's President and absolute holder of all power in the country, Vučić, still seems to be leading the game, despite the on-going weekly protests in several Serbian towns (the protests started in December 2018). Social movements are scattered, their cooperation seems to be only in the inception phase, while cooperation with opposition parties is very loose and weak, resembling the state of those parties themselves – still looking for a way to consolidate and coordinate their tactics against the regime.

However, to look at the differences in outcomes, or trajectories of social struggles in the two countries, only through their social movements' capacities to engage and cooperate would, of course, be overly simplistic. Internal political constellations, history and dynamics of the two countries are very different. This is not to mention the role of external factors, especially the EU, whose politics of supporting *stabilocracy* in the region had its own rationale in supporting change of Zaev, and conversely, to refuse to deny support to Vučić (CIRSD 2018). Additionally, there is the timeframe that puts another caveat on any comparative perspective: challenging Gruevski's regime in a coordinated and strategic manner started some time ago, and time itself may have been the factor contributing to success; similar struggles against Vučić's regime have only just begun.

Having said all that, we still believe that juxtaposing the two contexts, mapping the scene of active movements in N. Macedonia and Serbia, and finally drawing some comparative conclusions, may help us better understand conditions, potentials and constrains to bottom-up civic engagement for democratization in the Western Balkans.

5.1. Transcending the constraints of 'single-issue oriented' struggles

As already observed, the majority of movements from both countries were formed around concrete events that served as a 'trigger' not only for the creation of movements but also for our interviewees' desire to become engaged and 'do something'. These events, thus, often described as 'tip of the iceberg' also had an *indexical* significance, appearing as a tangible manifestation of larger, deeper, systemic and pervasive political and societal problems, compelling them to collective (re)action: unlawful acquittal of politicians accused of corruption by the President of the Republic ('a slap in the face to the Macedonian public'); extreme pollution in the city of Tetovo; imposing rigorous state exams on students; building mini hydroelectric power plants endangering the rivers in eastern Serbia; corruptive deals made with the local assembly to buy illegal real-estate owned by the spouse of the President of the Assembly, etc.[25]

For Macedonian activists, there seemed no difficulties in relating the initial, 'activating' problems with what later (or in parallel) evolved into a joint struggle against Gruevski's regime: 'Our movement was fighting against the state exams which were seriously undermining the autonomy of the university. Besides that, we were fighting the undemocratic rule of the VMRO-DPMNE.'[26]

Statements like this one were often found in narratives of N. Macedonian activists, emphasizing at the same time a concrete issue, a bigger issue and a single, unifying frame of struggle. Serbian activists, on the other hand, despite making similar claims about direct links between 'initiating issues' and the 'bigger picture' (and despite effectively addressing, through their activism, multiple issues at once) often reflected in the interviews on the problem of how to transcend the initial cause and how to stream it into a larger (coalitional) struggle against the regime:

> The fact is, despite everything, we still are a single issue movement, we are perceived as such ... We were established as a reaction to something, and we're lacking a plan about where we are going and why ... it's mainly responsive, not proactive.[27]

Some initiatives from Serbia had been formed around concrete issues, which have become over time either obsolete or resolved, forcing them to change focus on their own. Zrenjanin Social Forum, for example, was established as a platform for the struggle of Jugoremedija factory workers. After the factory went completely bankrupt, the Forum started reorienting itself towards connecting different workers' struggles into a broader coalition. The United Movement of Free Tenants initially grew out of the struggle over heating prices in Niš, which now seems to be resolved. But the Movement has continued to exist and has even become one of the most vocal opponents of the regime, without changing its name. Sometimes it is difficult for the external observer to connect and interrelate such movements' formative periods, events that happened in the meantime, and presently occurring reorientations towards a more general anti-regime stance.

5.2. Legacy or burden of previous protests

The history of protest activities – that is, what took place prior to the analysed movements – goes hand in hand and overlaps with the previous issue of (overcoming) the initiating moment. Because, as it turns out, it is not only the triggering event that forms a movement: equally important is the history of different activisms.

Almost all N. Macedonian activists talked about their movements as building on previous waves of protests: 'against police brutality' (the case of Martin Neskovski),[28] 'AMAN', 'tax raise for intermittent contracts of employment', etc. These not only helped pave the way to consolidation of movements, but also served as initial grounds for forging alliances between activists, NGOs and opposition parties, something that would later prove to be of the utmost importance.

Serbian activists told a somewhat different story, which had two important elements. One is that no similar collective protests shaped the recent history of movement forging: struggles were dispersed, local, and were never able to capture the wider interest, let alone forging broader coalitions (up until the very present moment). Second – and this is an important peculiarity of the Serbian case – the type of past activism most often mentioned, as sort of a specific legacy, was involvement in anti-Milošević protests from the 1990s: 'I was beaten by police as early as 1991, it is then that I started my war, so to speak.'[29]

Activists of Local front from Kraljevo had been active in the anti-Milošević youth organization Otpor! (Resist!), and had been at the time often derogatorily described in public as Otporaši (resisters). Such experiences from 1990s Serbia, as an illustration of past activism, is of course very different from the N. Macedonian case. This is primarily because they refer to a different type of civic activism, one that took place in a very different social and political context. And second, because younger generations of activists (mostly belonging to the left) are very critical of 1990s citizens' engagement against Milošević, seeing it as having been too narrow, naively focused on liberal democracy instead of on social and economic rights, etc. This generation gap then additionally burdens the possibility for common visions and joint struggle of activists from different generations. Sometimes, the older generation look at the present regime as repetition, an unresolved problem of autocracy that already existed in Milošević's 1990s. On the other hand, the younger generation is more prone to look at the present situation as a local manifestation of the global trend of crisis of democracy and authoritarian tendencies.

5.3. Orientation towards external factors, most notably the EU and NATO

Probably the biggest and most striking difference – partly expected – between the movements in N. Macedonia and Serbia, can be found in their activists' attitudes towards the EU and NATO. A round of questions in the interviews aimed at our interviewees' attitudes and reflections on several international players, among which the EU and NATO were perceived to be crucial. In general, for activists in N. Macedonia, the two organizations mostly received positive qualifications and were often described as necessary consolidators in the region. Critical voices were moderate and few. For instance, an activist from the leftist movement stated: 'Small countries like Macedonia in the current economic and political constellation will always be on the periphery . . . I perceive the EU as a tall wall and although I know this wall is difficult to change, it is better to be inside then outside.'[30]

Other critical voices note that it was the EU who supported Gruevski for a long time, stressing its hypocritical role. NATO is mostly seen as a security safeguard, as a guarantor of peace in the region.

The narratives of Serbian activists reveal more ambivalence and sharper criticism. The attitudes towards the EU vary significantly – from describing the Union in terms of 'solidarity and good quality life', 'good potential', to 'too much bureaucracy', and simple responses like 'oh, not good', 'oh, no' – to more elaborate, yet still negative characterizations like 'coalition of neoliberal capital exponents'. Similar ambivalence and mistrust is observable in attitudes towards the enlargement politics and the so-called Berlin process. However, unanimously negative attitudes were expressed towards NATO. Even though not all interviews held reflections on the 1999 NATO military campaign and bombing of FR Yugoslavia, it stands to reason to associate the explicitly negative views of our respondents ('even worse horror [than the EU] . . . alliance of bullies . . . empire . . . wars') with the general negative assessment of NATO by Serbian citizens that has been recorded in surveys for a longer period (Beogradski centar za bezbedonosnu politiku (BCSP) 2017).

We believe this observation to be indicative of broader differences between the situations in which the movements of the two countries find themselves. Cooperation with political parties, civil society organizations (CSOs) and external actors are much more likely to happen if some crucial political agendas, which have been shaping the whole region of the Western Balkans, have not previously provoked polarizations and strong emotional responses among citizens. The case of Serbia seems to open some problems in this respect, given not only highly ambivalent attitudes towards the EU and strong negative emotional responses to NATO, but also due to many 'open' questions, suitable for 'emotional exploitation' and thus political manipulation – like the status of Kosovo and thus state borders and sovereignty – all of which potentially obstruct the consolidation of any anti-regime coalition. Contrary to this, the relative congruence of attitudes towards EU and NATO in N. Macedonia seems to solidify a coherent narrative about the need for 'westernization' or Euro-Atlantic integration of the country, which acts as a powerful driver for political change.

5.4. Other differences regarding internal organization and positioning in relation to other movements

As noted in the previous section, one of the most salient features of all analysed movements in both countries, or at least the most frequently mentioned characteristic by their activists, is the movements' radically democratic internal organization. Some movements insist on their horizontal structure (described by some as 'the movement's biggest value and achievement'), organized around 'working groups' of equal importance, while others emphasized leaderlessness, consensual decision-making, high degrees of openness, inclusivity, etc. Naturally, a few disclaimers also followed these statements consisting of admittance that some individuals act or feel as belonging closer to the 'core group' of the movement, or that such non-hierarchical structure poses an obstacle in some situations. Observable in the N. Macedonian narratives is contemplation and critique of internal disagreements, mostly around principled decisions, like whom to support in elections, whether to join the parties or not, and how to delegate members. These issues seem to belong entirely to a set of problems observed among horizontally organized movements in general (Sitrin 2016; Maeckelbergh 2011).

For Serbian activists, the problem of 'structurelessness' and proclaimed radical equality of members opened different problems to ponder: 'It is a gang of friends who have known each other for a long time ... sometimes it's an advantage ... but these strong social connections prevent us from getting things done, because responsibility is only presupposed, but then never upheld.'[31]

The phrase non-hierarchical organization is here connected with intimacy, close friendship and similar world-views. It reveals much needed *personal trust* among activists, but potentially stands in the way of transforming a movement into an effective and reliable political actor that would deserve political trust of citizens. The fact that these stories are more prominent among the movements in Serbia could imply that they are simply 'younger' than N. Macedonian ones, not in terms of their inception date, but in terms of their involvement in continuous and cooperative struggle against the regime. Also, when asked about their movements' greatest achievements, N. Macedonian activists mostly enumerated their concrete victories, including, of course, the regime change. In Serbian activists' narratives, real, tangible successes are mostly mentioned second (if at all) – with the exception of the organization A Roof Over Our Heads, whose activists did underscore successful preventions of evictions. Mentioned first were: 'the change of atmosphere', 'affecting other people', 'making them become activists themselves', and building togetherness and new forms of movements. All this seems to further imply that the social movement struggle in Serbia is only in its inception phase against illiberal politics – not only due to concrete political factors but also in terms of the 'maturity' and efficacy of movements themselves.

An oft-mentioned topic in discussions about the regime change in N. Macedonia has been the intimate cooperation (not always without problems) between the movements and civil society organizations (CSOs). In Serbia, the situation is somewhat different, despite the fact that some of the activists also work in the NGO sector, and despite some occasional cooperation. The predominant attitudes of our interviewees towards CSO actors reveal (critical) distance, cautiousness and sometimes mistrust. Like in the case of attitudes towards external political actors, this may be connected to growing distance Serbian citizens are expressing generally towards both the politicians and CSO actors.

6. Concluding discussion

This article has sought to comprehensively map one important part of the nascent activist scene in the Western Balkans – through a comparative perspective of both similarities and differences between social movements in Serbia and N. Macedonia. In this concluding chapter we wish to further discuss some of the main factors contributing to the achievement of relevant political outcomes in N. Macedonia compared to, so far, weak political impact of social movements in Serbia. By focusing on the social movements active in the period from 2014 to 2017, prior to the demise of Nikola Gruevski, we have been able to capture retrospective reflections of the N. Macedonian movements' activists regarding the struggles that led to political change in the country, and compare their narratives to those of the activists from Serbia presently struggling to achieve similar political effects.[32]

The movements' representatives in both countries emphasized similar goals and values, like social justice and rule of law. They also expressed commitment to 'bringing citizens back into politics' and to practicing and promoting deliberative democracy – through attempts to respect deliberative standards in their own decision-making processes. Such arenas that have been developed within movements represent significant experimental sites that could feed participatory values into institutions. However, it remains to be seen to what extent transfer of human capital from movements to institutions that happened in N. Macedonia (and potentially could happen in Serbia) indeed produces systemic democratic change in the political arena.

When we look at the differences, our major finding is that the movements in N. Macedonia acted as part of a wider network of political actors, collaborating closely with opposition parties, which enabled the articulation of demands on a larger scale and opened space for a unifying frame of struggle. Activists from social movements in Serbia, on the other hand, are still struggling to find a way of streaming their diverse sites and issues of struggle into a larger (coalitional) front against the regime – despite effectively addressing different issues at once, and articulating direct links between 'initiating issues' and the 'bigger picture'. Only recently some local movements in Serbia have started to collaborate with each other and to insist on broader alliances.

Two issues should be taken into consideration when reflecting on the incapacity of social movements in Serbia to build coalitions with other oppositional political actors. Both are related to the context of historical legacy and levels of trust in political institutions and organizations. First, an important factor for opening/limiting manoeuvring space for social movements in N. Macedonia and Serbia to forge and strengthen alliances with other relevant political actors is the (recent) legacy of social movement activism. N. Macedonian movements were building on previous, but fairly recent waves of protest that not only provided relevant political experience but also promoted alliances between movements, political parties, NGOs and other political actors. This has not been the case in Serbia, which has not experienced any major political outcomes of the movements' mobilizations since the fall of Milošević.

Another factor hampering the potential of social movements in Serbia from joining forces with other political actors and becoming a relevant political actor is the mentioned overall mistrust in politics, often described by citizens as 'a dirty business where no one can act and stay credible' (Fiket et al. 2017). Some of this rhetoric has been appropriated by the movement members themselves, leading to a situation where many social movements are hesitant about getting involved in politics proper. They are balancing between *acting* in a political arena and wanting to be recognized as *non-political or a-political actors*. This can be effectively observed in the current wave of protests in Serbia, where a majority of the analysed social movements mostly stand aside, restrained from active and visible participation in the protests. The social movement scene in Serbia is, thus, characterized by very low levels of trust in established political actors (parties), and by building interpersonal trust among the movements' members instead. However, the move from interpersonal trust, closed in the movements' core circles, to building trustworthy mass movements that could articulate political demands is very slow. Lack of professionalization and weak cooperation between different movements in Serbia potentially stand in way of transforming the movements into influential political actors. For similar reasons, it is hard to expect that they will provide a pool of human resources for weak opposition parties, as was the case in N. Macedonia.

Further, recent political history in Serbia is such that the overall political culture is permeated with mistrust towards international players and institutions, most notably the European Union and NATO. This compounds the difficulty of forging coherent narratives and ideological stances among different political actors (institutional and non-institutional), and, additionally, may have enduring consequences for external recognition of social movements in Serbia as trustful partners deserving of support.

In N. Macedonia, a variety of movements at one period of time, synergistically streamed into a single movement against Gruevski's regime. In Serbia, strong mistrust in political actors, combined with a weak opposition scene stands in the way of building stronger political coalitions. The struggle of social movements against illiberal politics in Serbia seems to be only in its inception phase. It seems as though this process, still very much in the making, will much more likely lead to the emergence of a new political actor than to a coalition of movements, political parties and NGOs, as was the case in N. Macedonia. Mistrust of the current opposition party coalition, the centrist/right-wing Union for Serbia, is evident among representatives of social movements who refuse to join it – political (and social) change in Serbia will then, presumably, follow a different path.

Notes

1. From here onwards, N. Macedonia.
2. As will be explained later in the text, several protest initiatives took place before the *#1od5Milliona* protest, but they were mostly of a local character, or focusing on very specific issues.
3. This, of course, goes for the post-2008 political landscape. It is, however, worthwhile reminding oneself about the region's dynamic anti-war, and anti-regime (especially in Serbia and Croatia) protests of the 1990s.
4. Our sample consists of 33 interviews in total. We interviewed 20 representatives of 9 movements from Serbia, and 13 representatives of 4 movements from N. Macedonia.
5. Protest and social movements, in this context, overlap significantly as most of the newly emerged movements primarily act in public through protests, and many mass protests were organized by the (coalition of) social movements, as will become clear further in the text.
6. The protests that ousted Milošević occurred on 5 October 2000, following his reluctance to resign after loosing the presidential elections.
7. RTS. 2017. Šesti dan protesta u Beogradu. [The sixth day of protest in Belgrade]. 8 April. http://www.rts.rs/page/stories/sr/story/9/politika/2694286/protest-poceo-pred-zgradom-vlade.html.
8. RTS. 2018. Deo opozicije podržao studentkinju Tijanu Hegić. [A part of opposition gave support to student Tijana Hegic] 23 February. http://www.rts.rs/page/stories/sr/story/2728/izbori-2018/3048636/djilasova-koalicija-podrzala-studentkilju-hegic.html.
9. Rizaov, G. 2016. Protests in Macedonia Gain Momentum as New Round of Political Negotiations Is Announced. Global Voices, 19 April. https://globalvoices.org/2016/04/19/protests-in-macedonia-gain-momentum-as-new-round-of-political-negotiations-is-announced/.

10. Similarly to Belgrade protests organized by the initiative *Do not let Belgrade d(r)own* [Ne da(vi)mo Beograd], as shall be soon discussed. The objective of the project Skopje 2014 was to rebuild the face of Skopje, capital of N. Macedonia, so that its architecture could testify to its supposed antiqueness.
11. Regarding this criterion, we focused on movements that have shown continuity in organizing protests and similar interventions in the public sphere, and that have managed to gather considerable number of followers.
12. It is worth noting that the following facts explain some specificities of certain movements: Protestiram was a citizens' movement principally responsible for organizing the so-called Colourful Revolution, but many of its activists also participated in other social movements in N. Macedonia; Local Front (from Kraljevo, Serbia) is the only social movement from our sample that takes part in governing structures (some of its members are representatives in the local assembly).
13. Even in cases of social movements that were formally organized before a certain 'triggering event' took place, their public visibility and engagement became prominent only afterwards.
14. Personal interview with activist M.N., August 2018, Serbia.
15. Personal interview with activist D.V., August 2018, Serbia.
16. Personal interview with activist M.P., September 2018, N. Macedonia.
17. It should be noted, however, that a minority of movements here explored have an official programme of the movement.
18. Personal interview with activist J.P., August 2018, Serbia.
19. Personal interview with activist T.P., September 2018, N. Macedonia.
20. Personal interview with activist I.S., September 2018, N. Macedonia.
21. Personal interview with activist T.P., September 2018, N. Macedonia.
22. Personal interview with activist M.P., September 2018, N. Macedonia.
23. Personal interview with activist M.N., August 2018, Serbia.
24. Glasnik. 2017. По членовите на НВО-ата, на ред за вработување се активистите на Шарената револуција. [After being the members of the NGOs, the 'Colourful Revolution' activists are in line for employment] 7 July. http://glasnik.mk/posle-clenovite-na-nevladinite-na-red-za-vrabotuvanje-dojdoa-aktivistite-na-sarena-revolucija/.
25. An exception to this were the narratives of activists from the Student organization in Novi Sad and Collective action Roof over head (Belgrade), which state 'a desire to be proactive in our community' and 'an inherent need for engagement … to help the vulnerable,' implying a more general sense of social engagement.
26. Personal interview with activist T.P., September 2018, N. Macedonia.
27. Personal interview with activist J.P., August 2018, Serbia.
28. Marusic, S. J. 2011. Macedonians Protest Over 'Fatal Police Beating', *Balkan Insight*, 7 June. http://www.balkaninsight.com/en/article/macedonians-protest-after-police-murders-youngster.
29. Personal interview with activist D.K., August 2018, Serbia.
30. Personal interview with activist with M.P., September 2018, N. Macedonia.
31. Personal interview with activist D.V., August 2018, Serbia.
32. The first mass protests in Serbia since Aleksandar Vučić's de facto coming to power in 2012, started in November 2018, several months after the finalization of our fieldwork. The protests, which take place in various towns across Serbia, have activated and animated all the movements from Serbia analysed here.

Disclosure statement

No potential conflict of interest was reported by the authors.

ORCID

Gazela Pudar Draško http://orcid.org/0000-0001-8361-4144
Irena Fiket http://orcid.org/0000-0003-3939-4089
Jelena Vasiljević http://orcid.org/0000-0001-8669-0767

References

Almeida, P., and A. Cordero Ulate, ed. 2015. *Handbook of social movements across Latin America*. New York: Springer.

Babović, M., S. Bajčeta, K. Veličković, D. Petrović, S. Stefanović, and S. Cvejić. 2017. *Da li like-uješ protest?* [Do you like the protest?] . Belgrade: SeConS grupa za razvojnu inicijativu.

Benhabib, S. 1996. The democratic moment and the problem of difference. *Democracy and difference: Contesting the boundaries of the political*, ed. S. Benhabib, 3–18. Princeton, NJ: Princeton University Press.

Beogradski centar za bezbedonosnu politiku (BCSP). 2017. *Stavovi građana o spoljnoj politici Srbije*. [Citizens' attitudes towards foreign politics of Serbia]. http://bezbednost.org/upload/document/stavovi_graana_o_spoljnoj_politici_srbije.pdf.

Bermeo, N. 1997. Myths of moderation: Confrontation and conflict during democratic transition. *Comparative Politics* 29(2): 205–322. doi:10.2307/422123

Bešić, M. 2011. Politički i situacioni prediktori poverenja u institucije [Political and situational predictors of trust in institutions]. *Godišnjak Fakulteta Političkih Nauka* 6: 119–48.

Bieber, F. 2018a. Patterns of competitive authoritarianism in the Western Balkans. *East European Politics* 34(3): 337–54. doi:10.1080/21599165.2018.1490272

Bieber, F. 2018b. The Rise (and Fall) of Balkan Stabilitocracies. *Horizons* 10(Winter). https://www.cirsd.org/en/horizons/horizons-winter-2018-issue-no-10/the-rise-and-fall-of-balkan-stabilitocracies

Bieber, F., and D. Brentin, ed. 2018. *Social movements in the Balkans: Rebellion and protest from Maribor to Taksim*. London: Routledge.

Bieber, F., and I. Ristić. 2012. Constrained democracy: The consolidation of democracy in Yugoslav successor states. *Southeastern Europe* 36: 373–97. doi:10.1163/18763332-03603005

Bosi, L., M. Giugni, and K. Uba. 2016. *The consequences of social movements* . Cambridge, MA: Cambridge University Press.

Cengiz Günay, C., and V. Džihić. 2016. Decoding the authoritarian code: Exercising 'legitimate' power politics through the ruling parties in Turkey, Macedonia and Serbia. *Southeast European and Black Sea Studies* 16(4): 529–49. doi:10.1080/14683857.2016.1242872

Centar za Slobodne Izbore i Demokratiju (CeSID). 2017. *Politički aktivizam građana Srbije* [Political activism of citizens of Serbia]. Belgrade. http://www.cesid.rs/wp-content/uploads/2017/06/POLITI%C4%8CKI-AKTIVIZAM-GRA%C4%90ANA-SRBIJE-2017.pdf

Crowther, W. 2017. Ethnic Condominium and illiberalism in Macedonia. *East European Politics and Societies and Cultures* 31(4): 739–61. doi:10.1177/0888325417716515

Daskalovski, Z., and K. Trajkovski. 2017. *Macedonian Obama or the platform from Tirana: A guide to the integrative power sharing model* . Skopje: The Centre for Research and Policy Making.

Della Porta, D. 2012. Critical trust: social movements and democracy in times of crisis. *Cambio* 2 (4): 33–43.

Della Porta, D. 2014. *Mobilizing for democracy: Comparing 1989 and 2011* . Oxford: Oxford University Press.

Della Porta, D. 2015. *Social movements in times of austerity: bringing capitalism back into protest analysis* . Malden, UK: Polity press.

Della Porta, D., J. Fernández, H. Kouki, and L. Mosca. 2017. *Movement parties in times of austerity* . Malden, UK: Polity press.

Democracy Ranking. 2016. The democracy ranking association. http://democracyranking.org/wordpress/rank/democracy-ranking-2016/.

Dimitrov, N., I. Jardanovska, and D. Taleski. 2016. *Ending the crisis in Macedonia: Who is in the driver's seat*. Balkans in Europe Advisory Group, 4 April. http://www.balkanfund.org/publib/biepag/Ending-the-Crisis-in-Macedonia-Who-is-in-the-driving-seat-web.pdf

Dolenec, D. 2013. *Democratic institutions and authoritarian rule in Southeast Europe* . Colchester: ECPR press.

Đorđević, S. 2006. Renesansa lokalne vlasti – uporedni modeli [Renaissance of the local government – comparative models]. Belgrade:Čigoja štampa.

Đorđević, S. 2011. Decentralizacija i jačanje kapaciteta lokalnih vlasti u Srbiji. [Decentralization and strengthening capacities of local governments in Serbia]. *Anali Hrvatskog Politološkog Društva* 8(1): 179–202.

Dryzek, J.S. 2000. *Deliberative democracy and beyond: Liberals, critics, contestations* . Oxford: Oxford University Press.

Džihić, V., and N. Hayoz. 2016. Questioning democracy and liberalism in the eastern part of Europe. *Religion & Gesellschaft in Ost und West* 44(9–10): 4–8.

Fagan, A., and I. Sircar. 2017. Activist citizenship in Southeast Europe. *Europe-Asia Studies* 69(9): 1337–45. doi:10.1080/09668136.2017.1390196

Fiket, I., Z. Pavlović, and G. Pudar Draško. 2017. Političke orijentacije građana Srbije: Kartografija nemoći [Political orientations of citizens of Serbia: Cartography of impotence]. Belgrade:Friedrich Ebert Stiftung.

Fishkin, J.S. 1991. *Democracy and deliberation: New directions for democratic reform* . New Haven: Yale University Press.

Freedom House. 2019. *Democracy in retreat: Freedom in the world 2019*. https://freedomhouse.org/report/freedom-world/freedom-world-2019/democracy-in-retreat

Fridman, O., and S. Hercigonja. 2016. Protiv Nenormalnog: An analysis of the #protivdiktature. Protests in the context of memory politics of the 1990s in Serbia. *Contemporary Southeastern Europe* 4(1): 12–25.

Habermas, J. 1996. *Between facts and norms: contribution to a discourse theory of law and democracy* . Cambridge, MA: MIT press.

Horvat, S., and I. Štiks, ed. 2015. *Welcome to the desert of post-socialism: Radical politics after Yugoslavia.* London: Verso Press.

Jacobsson, K., ed. 2015. *Urban grassroots movements in Central and Eastern Europe.* Farnham: Ashgate.

Kendall-Taylor, A., and E. Frantz. 2014. Mimicking democracy to prolong autocracies. *The Washington Quarterly* 37(4): 71–84. doi:10.1080/0163660X.2014.1002155

Klekovski, S., E. Nuredinoska, and D. Stojanova. 2010. *Trust in Macedonia* . Skopje: Macedonian Center for International Cooperation.

Kmezić, M., and F. Bieber, ed. 2017. *The crisis of democracy in the Western Balkans. An anatomy of stabilitocracy and the limits of EU democracy promotion.* BiEPAG. https://biepag.eu/publica tions/the-crisis-of-democracy-in-the-western-balkans-an-anatomy-of-stabilitocracy-and-the-limits-of-eu-democracy-promotion/

Knight, J., and J. Johnson. 1994. Aggregation and deliberation: On the possibility of democratic legitimacy. *Political Theory* 22: 277–96. doi:10.1177/0090591794022002004

Lazić, M. 2011. Čekajući kapitalizam [Waiting for capitalism]. Belgrade:Službeni glasnik.

Macedonia National Public Opinion Poll. 2017. Center for insights in survey research, 4-12 March. http://www.iri.org/sites/default/files/2017-5-5_macedonia_slides.pdf

Maeckelbergh, M. 2011. Doing is believing: Prefiguration as strategic practice in the Alterglobalization movement. *Social Movement Studies* 10(1): 1–20. doi:10.1080/ 14742837.2011.545223

Milan, C. 2017. Rising against the 'thieves': Anti-corruption campaigns in the Western Balkans. *Partecipazione E conflitto/Participation and Conflict* 10(3): 826–49.

Mujanović, J. 2018. *Hunger and Fury: The crisis of democracy in the Balkans.* New York: Oxford University Press.

National Democratic Institute (NDI). 2017. Macedonia poll finds citizens concerned about political situation, divided on way out of crisis. April 5. https://www.ndi.org/publications/ macedonia-poll-finds-citizens-concerned-about-political-situation-divided-way-out

Pešić, V., 2017. Dometi i paradoksi Protesta protiv diktature [Achievements and Paradoxes of Protest against Dictatorship]. *Peščanik,* April 21. https://pescanik.net/dometi-i-paradoksi-protesta-protiv-diktature/.

Petrović, J., and D. Petrović. 2017. Konektivna akcija kao novi obrazac protestnog aktivizma. [Connective Action as the New Pattern of Protest Activism]. *Sociologija* 59(4): 405–26. doi:10.2298/SOC1704405P

Pollozhani, L. 2016. The student movement in Macedonia 2014-2016: Formation of a new identity and modes of contention. *Sudosteuropa Mitteilungen* 5/6: 38–45.

RCC. 2017. *Balkan Barometer 2017.* https://www.rcc.int/seeds/files/RCC_BalkanBarometer_ PublicOpinion_2017.pdf

Reef, P. 2017. Macedonia's colourful revolution and the elections of 2016. A chance for democracy, or all for nothing? *Südosteuropa* 65(1): 170–82. doi:10.1515/soeu-2017-0009

Roos, J.E.,, and L. Oikonomakis. 2014. They don't represent us. The global resonance of the real democracy movement from the Indignados to occupy. *Spreading protest. Social movements in times of crisis,* ed. D. Della Porta and A. Matoni, 117–36. Colchester: Rowman & Littlefield.

Rosanvallon, P. 2006. *La contre-démocratie. La politique a l'âge de la defiance* . Paris: Seuil.

Schenkkan, N., Z. Csaky, and N. Stormont. 2018. *Nations in Transit 2018: Confronting illiberalism.* Washington DC: Freedom House. https://freedomhouse.org/report/nations-transit /nations-transit-2018

Sitrin, M. 2016. Horizontalism: From Argentina to wall street. *NACLA Report on the Americas* 44 (6): 8–11. doi:10.1080/10714839.2011.11722131

Snow, D., S. Soule, and H. Kriesi. 2004. Mapping the Terrain. *The blackwell companion to social movements*, ed. D. Snow, S. Soule, and H. Kriesi, 3–16. Malden, UK: Blackwell Publishing.

Stefanovski, I. 2016. From shallow democratization to mobilization: The cases of the 'Bosnian Spring' and the 'Citizens for Macedonia'. *International Journal on Rule of Law, Transnational Justice and Human Rights* 7(7): 43–51.

Tarrow, S. 1995. Mass mobilization and regime change: Pacts, reform and popular power in Italy (1918–1922) and Spain (1975–1978). *The politics of democratic consolidation in Southern Europe: Comparative perspective*, ed. R. Gunther, N. Diamandouros, and H. Puhle, 204–30. Baltimore: The Johns Hopkins University Press.

Trejo, G. 2012. *Popular movements in autocracies religion, repression, and indigenous collective action in Mexico* . New York: Cambridge University Press.

World Press Freedom Index 2014. Reporters without Borders. https://rsf.org/en/world-press-freedom-index-2014

Moving towards EU membership and away from liberal democracy

Věra Stojarová 🆔

ABSTRACT

The article concludes the Special Issue, Illiberal Politics in Southeast Europe, on the retreat of liberal democracy in the region. It focuses on the central themes that link all the papers together: free and fair elections, media freedom, judicial independence, privileged access to public resources and the role of civil society. It seeks to disentangle the causes and consequences of illiberal politics in the region and explores the similarities in the illiberal practices and strategies incumbents use with the aim of staying in power indefinitely. The main argument is that democratic backsliding in Southeast Europe is deeply rooted in the unfinished transitions of the 1990s, which gave rise to new political and economic elites and that blending those two into one resulted in the dominance of the executive over the judiciary and legislature. These new elites became entrenched during the wars and conflicts that affected the region. The enabling factors were of societal origin – clientelist practices, corruption, nepotism and mistrust in politics accompanied by external factors – as well as international pull and push factors (from the EU and Russia) along with a domino effect of democratic backsliding in the region.

Introduction – something is rotten in Southeast Europe

A decline in liberal democracy has been seen throughout Europe and it seems that a new spectre – the spectre of illiberal regimes – is haunting Europe. Until now, the academic literature has focused on the most blatant examples of non-democratic regimes. The countries of Southeast Europe have experienced democratic decline recently and so the direction of academic research has shifted to illiberal practices in the Balkan region. As Bieber and Kmezić point out, there was no single tipping point for the entire region, but the downward spiral began more than a decade ago and was accelerated by the economic crisis in 2008 and the series of crises within the EU (Kmezić and Bieber 2017, 91; Bieber 2018). The aim of this Special Issue is to contribute to the academic debate about the quality of democracy in Southeast Europe. It provides a comparative overview of the rise of illiberal politics in the case study countries with an emphasis on the quality of democracy by looking at the media, judiciary, checks and balances and the whole electoral playing field on which the democratic battle is being fought. The issue concentrates not only on the six Western Balkan countries as potential EU members but also on Croatia, where we have seen similar trends, though in different guises, despite its EU membership. Croatia is an integral part of Southeast Europe and plays an important role in regional security and potentially in democratization overspill, so we could not omit it.

As we have shown in the introductory article, there are many shades of illiberalism and many ways of approaching and defining that term, not to mention illiberal democracy (Zakariah 1997), defective democracy (Merkel 2004), competitive authoritarianism (Levitsky and Way 2010), electoral authoritarianism (Schedler 2013) and simple democratic backsliding (Bermeo 2016; Solska et al. 2018). We understand illiberal politics as a set of policies proposed or enacted by incumbents that create an uneven playing field with the aim of remaining in power indefinitely. These include illiberal socio-economic structures and governing practices as well as specific and targeted illiberal actions against political opponents and key institutions aimed at reducing accountability (Kapidžić forthcoming-a). Democratization might be understood as a process with no linear character but instead potentially reversible tendencies, which might result in de-democratization (Tilly 2007). What we see is not one single pattern of illiberalism throughout the region but rather different forms of illiberal practice. However, in each country one can identify one or more of those and the final character of the regime varies. Our aim was therefore to look at every case with the eyes of local researchers, political scientists specializing in the democratic transition in their respective countries.

The first case study written by Dušan Pavlović examines the slow and general deconstruction of democratic institutions under Aleksandar Vučić in Serbia since 2014. The author focuses mainly on electoral manipulation, media freedom, the autonomy of the judiciary and access to resources and claims that Serbia is on a path towards embracing a more radical version of electoral authoritarianism as illiberal politicians are at present in control of the electoral process and the media and they manipulate public funds for partisan purposes. Pavlović claims that the main responsibility for the decline in Serbian democracy is the incomplete design of democratic institutions and an incomplete transition to liberal democracy, which enabled the rise of illiberal tendencies. The author emphasizes how important the extraction of public funds has been for the hybrid regime in Serbia, noting the role of the political economy behind the gradual demise of democratic institutions in the country: 'Extractive institutions matter because they directly impact other critical segments of electoral authoritarianism (notably, elections and media freedom), but also because they explain the type of leadership they promote in politics' (Pavlović forthcoming, xx). The text gives examples of lack of oversight over public resources in Serbia and describes contracts between the government and private firms (with confidentiality clauses so they stay hidden from the public eye), budgetary non-transparency (most items are expressed in finance legislation as a lump sum whose detailed composition cannot be analysed), rigged public procurement (selecting a private firm that is close to the incumbent), misallocating public funds by state agencies (in the pockets of tycoons and members of the incumbent coalition parties) and last but not least party patronage in public companies and local administration. The claim is that, if public resources are left without institutional oversight, the authoritarian leaders can use them not only for private gain, but more importantly for skewing the level playing field and uninstalling democracy. Therefore, in order to understand how incumbents win elections, we must understand what kind of advantage unrestrained access to public funds provides. The lack of oversight over public resources generates a specific type of leadership – political agents who are prone to violate and abolish democratic procedures in order to embezzle from public finances. This dynamic, according to Pavlović, lies at the heart of the most recent democratic reversals in Serbia.

Borjan Gjuzelov and Milka Ivanovska Hadijevska examine state capture and the institutional and symbolic aspects of the illiberal rule of the VMRO-DPMNE-led coalition, describing the core characteristics of Macedonian illiberal politics in the period 2006–2017. The institutional aspects of Macedonian illiberal politics are evidenced by an uneven access to resources, media and law; the symbolic aspects of illiberal rule are then shown by monopolizing public discourse and mobilization through an ethno-nationalist narrative with an emphasis on antiquitization, anti-communist, anti-minority, and conservative narratives, and concerted discrediting and smear campaigns against political opponents and civil society. The authors argue that the VMRO-DPMNE systematically exploited unfair political competition, enabled by pre-existing weak institutions and populations' clientelist preferences (Gjuzelov and Hadijevska forthcoming, xx). The incumbents constructed a strong nationalist narrative, which appealed to voters along with offering clientelist employment and other benefits to mobilize political support. The multi-ethnic character of the country, the disputed Macedonian national identity, and lack of viable international prospects allowed the governing party to build a strong nationalist narrative that appealed to voters. The text suggests that institutional capture during rule by VMRO-DPMNE is rooted in regime change which created a dominant executive, weak institutional checks and balances, and advanced clientelist practices. Slow economic development, an implementation gap and the ethnification of politics were detected as enabling factors of illiberal politics.

Olivera Komar examines illiberal practices in Montenegro, a country where one man has headed the state for almost three decades. She looks at the control of the media, the use of public resources for electoral gain and control over academic (supposedly independent) institutions. The author argues that 'democratic development in Montenegro went through a formal and institutional transformation, moved towards substantial stagnation, and has returned to the old ways of doing things in new settings. It is a case in which democratic institutions never really took off' (Komar forthcoming, xx). Still, she concludes that laws might be stretched but remain important, elections do take place and there is some space for the opposition in the media. The playing field is nonetheless uneven, and Komar recalls the redistribution and cementing of the position of political and economic elites during the 1990s. The author stresses that voters are the ultimate goal, the outlook of legality is essential, and independent institutions and European standards are often 'used' to assert authority. The author concludes that the preconditions are of a structural nature: personalized politics, an overly strong executive branch, lack of accountability; while contentious political issues enable illiberal politics.

In the fourth study Damir Kapidžić examines illiberal politics in Bosnia and Herzegovina (BiH); more precisely, he studies subnational autocratization. The author looks at three specific cases of illiberal politics: the 'Justice for David' protests and the subsequent related restrictions to the freedom of assembly in Republika Srpska; political control of the media and self-censorship by journalists; and the prevalence of patronage practices by incumbent parties in elections. Kapidžić concludes that, with its substantial subnational variations, Republika Srpska can be described as a competitive authoritarian regime, whereas the Federation of BiH is an electoral democracy. He sees the main drivers in the institutional framework that blend executive dominance with economic power and informal party-political networks, only sometimes accompanied by individual actors' perceptions of threat. At the same time subnational governance includes illiberal politics while consociational institutions and power sharing constrain it from becoming a national problem. In his concluding remark, the author states that 'in order to revitalize democratization in the country, actors need to focus on subnational politics and deep-rooted power structures that blend executive dominance with economic power and informal party networks' (Kapidžić forthcoming-b, xx).

Writing on Kosovo, Adem Beha and Arben Hajrullahu argue that a form of rule has arisen in the country that they describe as soft competitive authoritarianism, in which the elites promote their own interests rather than those of the state and where the state is partially used for party-political purposes to distribute economic resources to companies close to the incumbents. They note the international presence in Kosovo, which 'prohibited efforts by any single political party to put the whole of the country's economy, society, politics and the media under one centralized control'. They identify a lack of accountability as the key component of this illiberal regime, and explore how the political elite began to extend its influence by capturing a number of state institutions, independent agencies and public companies for private gain and prevented parliament from exercising its supervisory role over the government. The authors explore how the rhetorics of democratization, the post-1999 normalization and Europeanization were misused to enable the establishment of soft competitive authoritarianism in the country. They conclude that 'by (mis-)using the macro-politics of "final political status settlement", the "finalization of statehood", and finally the empty and vague rhetoric of "Euro-Atlantic integration" since 1999 the very same political entrepreneurs managed successfully to gain internal power and external legitimacy' (Hajrullahu and Beha forthcoming, xx).

The article by Gentiana Kera and Armanda Hysa looks at the case of Albania and addresses issues related to clientelist practices and the private funding of electoral campaigns with a primary focus on the parliamentary elections of 2017. The authors indicate that it is not only public-sector employees who are prone to abusing state resources, but also business owners and private-sector employees, especially through tax offices and state institutions' biased attitudes to businesses. The analysis shows that there are legally defined limits on donations to political parties by individuals and businesses, which aim to reduce their possible influence on political decisions. However, it also shows that there are serious discrepancies between these legal regulations and practice, and that political parties do not declare their income or expenses in full, which creates options for long-term clientelist relations between businesses and political parties. The authors conclude that the private funding of electoral campaigns impacts free and fair elections and hence democracy itself, and propose the monitoring of expenditure during electoral campaigns as an efficient method of enhancing transparency of political party funding, in order to improve democracy in Albania (Kera and Hysa forthcoming, xx).

Dario Čepo in his article on democratic retreat and failed conditionality in Croatia deviates a little from the regional pattern, as illiberal practices in Croatia are on a much smaller scale than in the other countries of Southeast Europe. 'The spread of illiberal practices seems to be focused on the liberal part of the liberal-democratic nexus, targeting media freedoms, independent institutions and the judiciary. The democratic part, represented by electoral practices, is more or less stable and, to a significant degree, respected by the political elite' (Čepo forthcoming, xx).

What connects the paper to the other articles in this volume is the claim that the current system is a product of the wild economic transition and the redistribution that followed. The political and economic elites who made it to power seem slowly to cement the whole system, preventing new players from entering the game by labelling them as quislings of the Croatian nation; they do so with the help of influential actors such as the Catholic Church and veterans' organizations. 'While there is no outright government censorship, owner-influenced, editor-influenced and self-imposed censorship are rife in the Croatian media ... There are taboo topics that cannot be tackled, including the veterans' groups' collective rights, and the power of the Catholic Church, and when these are put under scrutiny, the backlash is immediate and fierce' (Ibid., xx). The author argues that backsliding was made possible by structural factors, primarily the activities of the Croatia Democratic Union (HDZ) since independence. As Croatia has already joined the EU, the stick-and-carrot policy cannot apply anymore, and even though the EU has some mechanisms to discipline its members, it is unlikely to use them against the Croatian government, which is part of the dominant European party grouping.

Věra Stojarová takes a comparative look at the state of the media in the region, arguing that while the democratic façade remains, the playing field is tilted and the mechanisms used to control the media are very subtle. The author offers three arguments to explain deteriorating media freedom in the western Balkan region: structural factors (state advertising revenue as the main source of income, media owners close to the political incumbents), proximate or external factors (the role of the EU, the deteriorating freedom of the media in the whole region, the stability before democracy) and, last but not least, political-societal dynamics (civil lawsuits against journalists, verbal and physical assaults on journalists) (Stojarová forthcoming, xx). The regimes use the media as mouthpieces for their propaganda and the media can no longer play the role of watchdogs for democracy.

Marko Kmezić focuses on the rule of law in all of the countries of the western Balkans and concludes that behind a democratic façade built on regular elections, the promulgation of legal acts, guarantees of freedom of expression and a declared system of checks and balances is hiding a reality of informal structures, clientelism and control of the media. The author argues that the structural weaknesses of democratic institutions are deliberately exploited by these regimes, which are able to misuse the fragile institutions to their advantage. Kmezić discusses the inherent lack of internal capacities of these states to eliminate the conditions that prevent them from moving beyond the category of *electoral* to *liberal* democracies. 'Rule of law, a functioning prerequisite for the region's convergence to liberal democracy, is absent ... this study maintains that the WB lack the substance not just of liberal, but also of formal democracy' (Kmezić forthcoming, xx). He concludes that the key remedy would be to unlock new party dynamics that would enable these countries to break away from their established patterns of clientelism, informal networks and strong party control over the media and state institutions, and presents this vision using the case of North Macedonia.

Gazela Pudar Draško, Irena Fiket and Jelena Vasiljević focus in their text on the capacity of civil society – or more precisely social movements – to reverse illiberal decline and prevent illiberal retreat. Their paper provides a comparative analysis of these social movements' characteristics and capabilities to fight illiberalism and incite political change in Serbia and North Macedonia. The authors argue that the movements in both countries exhibit similar goals and values and express a commitment to bring citizens back into politics. When looking at the differences, the major finding is that the movements in North Macedonia acted as part of a wider network of political actors collaborating closely with opposition parties, thus enabling the articulation of demands on a larger scale. This is unlike the social movements in Serbia, which so far have not been able to find one common voice and unify in one broader alliance. The authors pinpoint the contexts of the historical legacy and the level of trust in political institutions and organizations. They argue that a lack of professionalization, mistrust in politics and in international players in society, accompanied by weak cooperation between different movements, prevent the transformation of the movements into political actors that could bring about change in Serbia (Pudar Draško et al. forthcoming, xx).

What are the key themes that link these papers? Several, partially overlapping, thematic strands can be discerned: an uneven playing field before, during and after elections; limited media freedom and government control of the media; lack of judicial oversight of executive power; and privileged access to public resources accompanied by limited space for corrective tools from civil society. What also binds them together is their emphasis on the power redistribution that occurred in the 1990s, and the will of the political and economic elites that arose at the time to maintain a grasp on power indefinitely. This resulted in captured states.

Free and fair elections

All the case studies in this Special Issue indicate that the electoral processes during most of the elections in the region have been declared by international observers as transparent, competitive, professional and largely meeting the commitments of democratic elections. However, at the same time, it seems that the elections in the region have shared similar flaws (Box 1).

All of the incumbents in the region, even in Croatia, seem to benefit from a high emigration rate and the fact that voter lists are not kept up to date. In both Serbia and Croatia, there are more voters than inhabitants. In the 2017 elections in Serbia it turned out that there were 800,000 more voters than adults living in the country. The lists do not get updated when voters die, and they include people who do not exist, with fake addresses. Even those who emigrated long ago have been found voting on some electoral rolls; multiple voting has also been recorded. Such malpractice contributes to the instability of the systems, which become more volatile, shaky and unpredictable. One example is a 2018 referendum in North Macedonia whose validity was questioned because it failed to secure the turnout of 50 percent required to validate the nonbinding vote, despite recording the overwhelming support of 36.9 percent of all registered voters. In Albania, it's not only the high emigration rate that contributes to the low turnouts in elections, but also the boycotts quite often announced by opposition parties. In the

June 2019 local elections a 21.6 percent turnout led to an overwhelming victory by the Socialist Party in the majority of municipalities.

The role of an electoral commission is to solve electoral issues and ensure the fairness of the whole process. If necessary, the commission can order a recount or cancel an election. In Serbia, the Electoral Commission is made up of political rather than legal experts and serves the incumbents with its decisions and resolutions, basically tilting the electoral playing field and having a detrimental effect on free and fair electoral competition. The author cites examples in which the Electoral Commission in Serbia served the ruling political elite – when it declined to recognize Vojislav Koštunica's electoral victory in 2000 and when it rejected the application by Luka Maksimović in the 2017 presidential elections. Interestingly, the Serbian Electoral Commission does not distinguish between incumbents; it seems to be ready to make up the numbers and serve Milošević, Vučić or whoever is in power.

Articles covering Serbia, Montenegro, North Macedonia, Albania and BiH also describe vote-buying and pressure on civil servants with aggressive campaigns involving intimidation and job loss threats to the potential electorate, and offers to channel state money to potential voters or of party employment. In these countries, the intimidation of voters in pre-election periods has been monitored, as have blurred state and party activities which do not provide a level playing field for all the parties running in elections. The Montenegrin case study reveals a major incidence of vote buying – during the 2016 local elections, it is estimated that vote buying reached up to 24 percent (Komar forthcoming, xx). The article on North Macedonia also describes how ethnic Macedonians from Albania were given citizenship and identity cards with Skopje addresses so they could vote for VMRO-DPMNE in the 2013 local elections. In BiH, 80,000 workers employed in 550 state-owned enterprises across all sectors of the economy faced losing their jobs if they failed to cast their ballot in favour of the incumbents. All of the articles offer a very similar picture and pinpoint the dependence of the population on the state: almost one-third of all legally employed people in Montenegro work in public administration and thousands more receive some sort of welfare assistance which makes them directly dependent on the state.

All of these actions described raise concern about voters' ability to cast their vote free of fear of retribution. Last but not least, the uneven playing field is tilted further by the political incumbents control of the media in the pre-election period.

Media control

Control over the media is essential for illiberal regimes as it provides inaccurate information in the form of governmental propaganda while reinforcing the merits of the incumbents and at the same time covering up their bad deeds. In regimes where the media appear at first sight to be free, the pressure is indirect and subtler. The media lose their function as the fourth estate and watchdog for democracy and, rather, provide legitimacy to those in power (Box 2).

Voters are bombarded with twisted information, which has a great impact on their decisions during elections. Politicians target journalists and accuse them of being incompetent liars, traitors or public enemies. As the paper on Serbia makes clear, Vučić often points out that some media portray him as a bad guy; he presents this to

ILLIBERAL POLITICS IN SOUTHEAST EUROPE

EU officials to suggest that it is he who is the victim of the media rather than the opposition, so the image of free and fair media is preserved. The BiH analysis shows that the media in RS are under tight political control and those who try to report

Box 1. Illiberal politics and systemic flaws affecting elections.

Illiberal politics and systemic flaws affecting elections
• deliberately inaccurate voter register (multiple voting, voting by dead and emigrated individuals) • politicized (non-independent) electoral commissions • no deterrent to electoral manipulation (vote buying, carousel voting, photographing the ballot and compiling lists of 'guaranteed voters') • voting linked to party employment • voting linked to selective distribution of social benefits • party-induced intimidation of voters and job loss threats • blurring of state- and party-financed activities • partisan control of the media

objectively are labelled as traitors to the Serb people. The Montenegrin paper examines the RTCG which was for some time perceived as a ruling party media outlet; its selection of guests and the tone and direction of its reporting significantly benefited the ruling party. Media loyalty is incentivized through well organized media-political clientelism, as the Macedonian paper shows, conducted primarily via extensive state-financed advertising and the concentration of media ownership in the hands of businessmen close to the government. The Macedonian government was the top advertiser on private national TV stations during the VMRO-DPMNE rule, so buying the loyalty of the media.

In some countries, threats of defamation, insult and incitement to hatred are used to put significant potential pressure on the media. Fear among journalists rises and leads to self-censorship and a curtailing of the plurality of the media. The comparative article on media freedom in the region reveals the interesting fact that Croatia has the harshest laws on insulting national symbols. Mocking the emblem, flag or anthem in that country is punishable by up to three years in prison, whereas in the other countries punishments are either less, or by fine, or there is no provision for them. The paper on Croatia confirms that judicial harassment, through the misuse of libel laws, has become endemic, and there are currently 1,000 ongoing lawsuits against journalists and media organizations. Most of the articles point out the weakness of regulatory bodies, which are politicized and incompetent, and serve the ruling parties. The comparative article presents the complaints of media advocates in North Macedonia about legislation being stuck in the old mechanisms. Broadcasters must comply with detailed provisions that make them vulnerable to political pressure and to being pushed into bankruptcy for small technical mistakes. Such provisions may seem at first sight to foster media freedom, but in practice they suppress it.

Judicial independence

An independent judiciary is an integral part of a functioning system of checks and balances in a liberal democracy and serves as a guarantor of governance based on the rule of law and not on political will. All of the case studies in our Special Issue showed some weaknesses of judicial independence (Box 3). Without exception, all the papers concur that the judiciary has been politicized, serving political rather than public interests. The absence of any autonomy of the judiciary and prosecution is mirrored in both direct pressure on judges and indirect pressure via their election, appointment and promotion in their careers. In Serbia, judges in political and criminally sensitive cases who attempt to avoid political direction are transferred to other cases. Aleksandar Vučić states quite often that he would love to interfere more in the judicial process. The Albanian and Montenegrin cases show that their judiciaries are not very decisive in

Box 2. Illiberal politics and systemic flaws affecting media freedom.

Illiberal politics and systemic flaws affecting media freedom
• political and economic influence and/or ownership of media by ruling parties or proxies of the ruling elite • biased coverage of ruling parties and opposition • acceptance of verbal and physical attacks on journalists by politicians, referring to media as enemies in public discourse • arrests of investigative journalists • media regulatory bodies controlled by ruling parties • use of defamation lawsuits to silence critical media • encouragement of journalistic self-censorship by political elites

obtaining evidence, sending a clear message to party operatives that, regardless of what they do, they can count on the authorities to turn a blind eye as long as they are in the service of the ruling party's cause.

The Macedonian case shows that the judiciary and law-enforcing institutions were under strong VMRO-DPMNE interference that led to double standards that favoured ruling party officials and disfavoured the opposition. This included reshuffling sensitive cases allocated to ideologically befriended judges and arresting opposition leaders on trumped-up charges. Interestingly, even Croatia has not been spared from this. Dario Čepo points out that the judiciary never had an independent, autonomous or institutionally separate role in the Croatian political system and is still one of the least trusted institutions among Croatians. Čepo blames the HDZ for dismantling the judicial system in the early 1990s and completely capturing it in subsequent years by removing judges who *were not capable of understanding their role in fulfiling the national interest* on charges of being either communists or Serbs disloyal to the new state. Interference by politicians in the work of prosecutors and judges goes unpunished, becomes part of daily life and so is tolerated and normalized and weakens liberal democracy.

Privileged access to public resources and the misuse of power

The central themes that link most of the papers and which featured prominently in the texts seem to be the misuse of public resources, clientelism and patronage (Box 4). The Serbian article points out secret contracts between the government and private companies without proper oversight, shady and non-transparent budget spending, the corrupt practices of public companies, party patronage and, most importantly, appointing party activists without experience or knowledge of corporate governance to top positions in public enterprises with only one condition – immense political loyalty to the incumbents. These practices are not limited to public companies but also occur in the private sector – only private firms loyal to

ILLIBERAL POLITICS IN SOUTHEAST EUROPE

Box 3. Illiberal politics and systemic flaws affecting judicial independence.

Illiberal politics and systemic flaws affecting judicial independence
• politically motivated appointment of judges by governing parties
• executive influence and control over judicial institutions
• disregard for judicial rulings
• direct and indirect pressure on judges in individual cases
• pressure on prosecutors not to investigate or to mishandle investigations of incumbents.

the party are selected by state agencies in public tenders. Recent examples include the Christmas tree for Belgrade and the controversial Belgrade Waterfront project. The authors of the piece on North Macedonia reported a similar situation, claiming that the control and misuse of state institutions and resources increased unfair political competition. Moreover, analysis shows that election years have been characterized by an increased number of public-sector jobs and agricultural subsidies, and that private companies have mobilized their employees to vote for the incumbent political party.

The granting of non-merit-based political party employment seems to be consistent throughout the region. In North Macedonia, party clients had not only to demonstrate their political loyalty, but to provide lists of 10 to 30 other people who could be relied on to vote for the party while also being actively involved in party rallies and other activities. Business-political clientelism and uneven access to resources were mirrored in differences in political financing and campaign expenditure. VMRO-DPMNE reported considerably greater income and expenditure than opposition parties which links us back to free and fair elections. It is not only in Albania that companies fund the campaigns of the incumbent party in order to keep doing business and receiving public money through tenders and concessions. As we learn from one of the interviews in the BiH article, there has not been a single BiH party that has not descended into clientelism – the longer they are in government, the more control they have, while most patronage is concentrated at the level of the entities and further shaped by ethnicity. The result is that the dominant party from each ethnicity controls 'its own' companies. The ethnic or national argument is also present in Montenegro – everyone accepts DPS no matter how much misuse of public resources, clientelism and patronage it is responsible for. The alternative is unacceptable as it undermines Montenegrin sovereignty and statehood.

Social movements, civil society and others – a potential threat to the government?

All of the papers in this edition point out the threat social movements pose to governments and the hold on civil society and other independent institutions by the incumbents. The Croatian paper mentions a number of those who are supposedly independent but in reality linked to HDZ: the information commissioner in reality acts against freedom of information; the National Foundation for Civil Society Development gives financial support to organizations whose members are part of the government; the parliamentary Commission for the Resolution of Conflict of Interests and the Croatian Bureau of Statistics have been captured by the party in government; all of these have

Box 4. Misuse of public resources, patronage and clientelism through illiberal politics.

Misuse of public resources, patronage and clientelism through illiberal politics
• partisan appointments to senior positions in public companies • use of non-transparent public contracts • prevalence of non-transparent budgeting, spending and oversight • distribution of economic subsidies according to loyalty and as a reward for voting • party patronage in public employment as well as in private-sector contracts • use of public procurement for patronage and reward

a negative influence on the consolidation of liberal democracy in Croatia. In North Macedonia, independent civil society was a target of a VMRO-DPMNE campaign, which depicted the Open Society Foundation as being close to the opposition and serving the interests of foreign powers. A blatant example of smear attacks in Serbia is that done against Saša Janković, Serbia's former ombudsman. Olivera Komar cites the government's dismissal of the rector of the State University as an example of imposing political control over an independent institution while Damir Kapidžić analyses restrictions on the freedom of assembly in Banja Luka.

What we have seen recently in the region is the large number of calm as well as violent protests against the regimes (including flares, firecrackers, smoke bombs, torching cars, tear gas, confrontation with police and subsequent injuries and detentions or just diverting buses with opposition supporters to undergo a technical check). These include: 2015 and 2016 in North Macedonia; in 2018 in Serbia, a year of all-day Sunday protests known as 'One of Five Million'; in 2019 in Montenegro, a wave of protests against widespread corruption and alleged links between top state officials and organized crime; opposition protests in Albania in 2019 linked to the student protests of 2015–16; in 2019 in Kosovo, protests organized by the opposition party Vetëvendosje against a 'correction of the borders'; and also in Kosovo, for the past three years, a series of citizen-led protests related to justice, widespread corruption and the rule of law. Last but not last, we have to mention the daily protests in Banja Luka coordinated by the Pravda za Davida (Justice for David) movement which echoed another case of Dženan Memić. The BiH protests are significant as they united people across ethnicities and the protests took place simultaneously in Banja Luka and Sarajevo showing inter-ethnic solidarity in two fathers' quests for justice. The regime decided to act and arrested the organizer Davor Dragičević and his wife and a number of other organizers left the country claiming to be under significant political pressure and fear for their lives. Meanwhile, the police forbade anyone to gather in what has been dubbed 'David's Square' in front of the church or in a nearby park.

The regimes in neighbouring countries have reacted in a similar way – in 2015–16 in North Macedonia, many people were injured and detained during demonstrations. In Serbia in 2018, Borko Stefanović, leader of the Serbian Left party, was injured during a physical assault after claiming the Vučić regime was responsible for creating a 'gruesome atmosphere'. This incident was a prelude to the current demonstrations dubbed 'One of Five Million'. One might also recall the unresolved assassination of politician Oliver Ivanović in 2018 in Kosovska Mitrovica by unknown perpetrators, with suspicion falling on the Srpska lista party, the puppet of Vučić in Kosovo.

Republika Srpska is the only example in the region where freedom of assembly is restricted, while Croatia is the only country that has not recently faced any large and

ILLIBERAL POLITICS IN SOUTHEAST EUROPE 225

continuous protests against the governing party. Besides these, the protests share many similarities – violent police intervention, detention and prosecution of opposition leaders and negative and smear campaigns against them (Box 5). The protests across the western Balkan region share the frustration of the citizens – frustration from the unfinished transition, endemic corruption, high unemployment, the judiciary and economy tied to the state and so state capture, losing the already deteriorating media freedom, a skewed playing field during elections, privileged access to public resources for political incumbents, the dependency of civil society and the growth of 'gongos' (governmental organizations) and, last but not least, loss of faith in European integration and no future hope for the region in sight.

Concluding remarks: illiberal democracies or competitive authoritarian regimes

The governing regimes in illiberal democracies are very smart – citizens can still go to elections, organize demonstrations and protests, or criticize the incumbents without risking long-term prison terms. However, these activities might lead to smear campaigns by the government media, financial inspections by state agencies and discrimination in employment. At the same time, it's not only about negative campaigns, but also positive ones. The regime uses its propaganda to give it a new modern façade. The independent institutions exist but are too weak to have any voice or influence; the party equals the state.

Box 5. Illiberal politics against challengers to the incumbent rule.

Illiberal politics against challengers to the incumbent rule
• use of police force during protests • detention, prosecution and imprisonment of opposition leaders • public intimidation, negative campaigns, and smear attacks by individuals in power • threat of dismissal of (public) employees • use of public media to obstruct the spread of civic movements

The only country where there is no alternation of power is Montenegro. There the transformed communist party (the Democratic Party of Socialists, DPS) has enjoyed a privileged and dominant position, ruling independently or in coalition and forming all governments since the introduction of the multi-party system in 1989–90. Still, we cannot classify the system as non-competitive, despite abuse of power by the ruling party. In order to stay in power, the DPS has combined misusing state resources, limiting the opposition's access to the media and imposing topics which produce deep divisions in society, such as national identity, the independence of Montenegro and membership of NATO. The long-term rule of the DPS has also been possible thanks to the very strong charisma of Milo Djukanović (Vujović and Tomović 2019, 130). In the rest of the region, the ruling parties have governed for more than one election period. All of the main parties are dominant parties, which are socially rooted, have strong and active local organizational structures directly linked and accountable to the central leadership (Hasić 2019) and quite often use the opportunity to engage in illiberal politics. Once they change the rules of the game, they remain in power for a longer period of time.

Table 1. Illiberal regimes in Southeast Europe.

Countries (Sub-national level)	Democratic deficits
Serbia	Media independence threatened, judicial bias, fairness at elections disputed, privileged access to public resources, captured state, suppression of the opposition
Montenegro	Media independence threatened, judicial bias, fairness at elections disputed, privileged access to public resources, captured state, suppression of the opposition
North Macedonia 2006/8-2019	Media independence threatened, judicial bias, fairness at elections disputed, privileged access to public resources, captured state, suppression of the opposition
Albania	Privileged access to public resources, judicial bias, governmental ties with organized crime, media independence threatened
Kosovo	Privileged access to public resources, judicial bias, governmental ties with organized crime
BiH (Republika Srpska)	Freedom of assembly, media independence threatened, judicial bias, fairness at elections disputed, privileged access to public resources, captured state, suppression of the opposition
BiH (Federation of BiH)	Privileged access to public resources, judicial bias, media linked with incumbents
Croatia	Media independence threatened, judicial bias

As the Table 1 shows, the regimes are neither fully democratic, nor fully autocratic. They show deficiencies in terms of media freedom, judicial independence, fair access to public resources and an independent civil society. According to the definition of Levitsky and Way, competitive authoritarian regimes are not democracies – competition is unfair and the opposition parties are seriously handicapped in their efforts to challenge the incumbents in elections, the legislature, the courts and other public arenas. Competitive authoritarian regimes fall short on *at least one* – and usually more – of three defining attributes of democracy: (1) free elections; (2) broad protection of civil liberties; and (3) a reasonably level playing field (Levitsky and Way 2010). If we stick with Levitsky and Way's conceptualization, all of the countries would fall under this definition. The worst situation seems to be in the entity of Republika Srpska, Serbia and North Macedonia in 2006/8-2016, where we see the repression of civil opposition movements. These regimes are captured states *par excellence* in which the tentacles of the government octopus envelope the economy and politics as well as society. We saw a change in the governing parties in North Macedonia and Kosovo; however, it is still too early to judge whether the contemporary governing parties manage to break free of the old ways of governing. In Albania, even though the protests were not peaceful and were met with police tear gas and water cannons, the suppression of the opposition did not reach the levels seen in Serbia, North Macedonia, Montenegro and Republika Srpska. Nevertheless, as the situation in the whole region is very dynamic, this might change for better or for worse. Even in the EU member, Croatia, the political elites cement the system by preventing new players entering the game, labelling them as quislings via control over the media and with the help of influential actors such as the Catholic Church and veterans organizations and their hold over the judiciary.

Our argument is that the democratic backsliding in Southeast Europe is deeply rooted in the unfinished transition of the 1990s, which gave rise to new political and economic elites, and the blending of those two into one, and the dominance of the executive over the judiciary and legislature. The enabling factors were of societal origin – clientelist practices, corruption, nepotism, mistrust in politics accompanied with external factors – pull and push international factors (EU, Russia) along with a domino effect of democratic

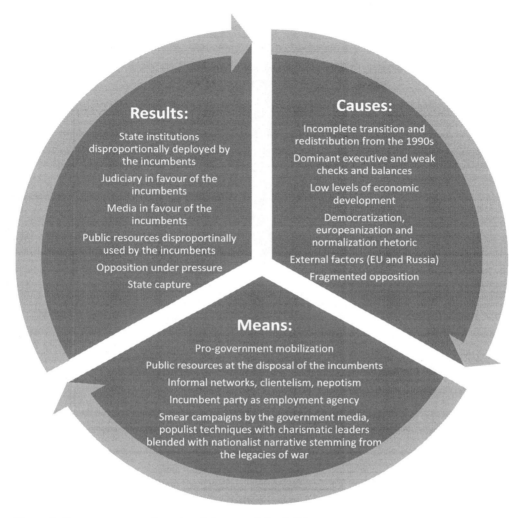

Figure 1. Causes, means and results of democratic backsliding.

backsliding in the region. Last but not least, we cannot forget the roles of conflict and wars which made transition much more difficult than in the rest of Eastern Europe (Figure 1).

Mistrust in politics, a lack of professionalization of the protests and very often fragmented opposition and mistrust in international players often stands in the way of change. North Macedonia enjoyed a change of regime in 2016, but still a lot of the old practices prevail. Kosovo saw a change in the electoral victor in 2019 elections and looked forward to breaking free from the captured state governed by PDK. Only the future will show us whether these two countries do not fall back into the waters of captured states, though run by a different political elite. Still, with every new start with a new idealist elite it makes sense to try to unravel the octopus's tentacles. The rest of the countries remain under the old elites and there is no evidence of any light at the end of the tunnel leading to true and substantial liberal democracy; rather the opposite. They appear to follow the regional trend in democratic backsliding. As repetition is the mother of wisdom let's remind ourselves that democracy is not static but rather a living force, it is the most deeply honourable form of government ever devised by man, so is worth fighting for. The basic conditions remain the same: free and fair elections, media freedom, judicial independence and independent oversight institutions. What makes a difference is how the elites handle them – as at any time they can choose from both good and evil.

Croatia is the only country to have joined the European Union; the other countries are recognized or potential candidates for future membership. Some applied more than decade ago and have started to implement the EU requirements. In 2017, Serbia and Montenegro were described as frontrunners that should join the EU no later than 2025. However, the recent cancellation of the start of EU membership talks with Albania and North Macedonia meant a major setback not only for the two countries, but for the entire region. The European Union is losing its credibility in the region and people ask whether they will ever join the EU, seeing that EU is failing to keep its promises. The European Union has played the role of guarantor of stability in the region and has long preferred stability over democracy. However, if the EU wants to preserve stability, it must not retreat from the region and must seek both stability and democracy by offering credible membership in the EU. Once the states in Southeast Europe lose their faith in future membership, they have many other world or regional powers to turn to and we might see a revival of the Balkan powder keg. Let us not forget that stability as well as democracy in Southeast Europe is important for the future development of the whole of Europe.

Disclosure statement

No potential conflict of interest was reported by the author.

Funding

This work was supported by the research project: 'Current Issues in Political Science III' undertaken at the Department of Political Science, Faculty of Social Studies, Masaryk University.

ORCID

Věra Stojarová ⓘ http://orcid.org/0000-0002-0496-5171

References

Bermeo, N. 2016. On democratic backsliding. *Journal of Democracy* 27: 5–19. doi:10.1353/jod.2016.0012

Bieber, F. 2018. Patterns of competitive authoritarianism in the Western Balkans. *East European Politics* 34: 337–54. doi:10.1080/21599165.2018.1490272

Čepo, D. forthcoming. Structural weaknesses rearing their head: Democratic backsliding in Croatia since 2013 and the role of the dominant political party. *Southeast European and Black Sea Studies* 20, no. 4: xx.

Gjuzelov, I., and M. Ivanovska Hadijevska. forthcoming. Institutional and symbolic aspects of illiberal politics: The case of North Macedonia (2006–2017). *Southeast European and Black Sea Studies* 20, no. 4: xx.

Hajrullahu, A., and A. Beha. forthcoming. Soft competitive authoritarianism and negative stability in Kosovo: Statebuilding from UNMIK to EULEX and beyond. *Southeast European and Black Sea Studies* 20, no. 4: xx.

Hasić, J. 2019. Deviating party leadership strategies in Bosnia and Herzegovina: A Comparison of Milorad Dodik and Dragan Čović. In *Party leaders in Eastern Europe: Personality, behavior and consequences*, ed. S. Gherghina, 17–41. London: Palgrave Macmillan Publishing.

Kapidžić, D. forthcoming-a. The rise of illiberal politics in South Eastern Europe. *Southeast European and Black Sea Studies* 20, no. 4: xx.

Kapidžić, D. forthcoming-b. Subnational illiberal politics and ethnic party dominance in Bosnia and Herzegovina. *Southeast European and Black Sea Studies* 20, no. 4: xx.

Kera, G., and A. Hysa. forthcoming. Influencing votes, winning elections: Clientelist practices and private funding of electoral campaigns in Albania. *Southeast European and Black Sea Studies* 20, no. 4: xx.

Kmezić, M. forthcoming. Rule of law and democracy in the Western Balkans: Addressing the gap between policies and practice. *Southeast European and Black Sea Studies*.

Kmezić, M., and F. Bieber. 2017. *The crisis of democracy in the Western Balkans. An Anatomy of Stabilitocracy and limits of EU democracy promotion*. Graz: BIEPAG.

Komar, O. forthcoming. The elephant in the room: Illiberal politics in Montenegro. *Southeast European and Black Sea Studies* 20, no. 4: xx.

Levitsky, S., and L.A. Way. 2010. *Competitive authoritarianism: Hybrid regimes after the cold war*. Cambridge: Cambridge University Press.

Merkel, W. 2004. Embedded and defective democracies. *Democratization* 11: 33–58. doi:10.1080/13510340412331304598

Pavlović, D. forthcoming. The political economy behind the gradual demise of democratic institutions in Serbia. *Southeast European and Black Sea Studies* 20, no. 4: xx.

Pudar Draško, G., I. Fiket, and J. Vasiljević. forthcoming. Big dreams and small steps: comparative perspectives on social movements' Struggle for democracy in Serbia and North Macedonia. *Southeast European and Black Sea Studies* 20, no. 4: xx.

Schedler, A. 2013. *The politics of uncertainty. Sustaining and subverting electoral authoritarianism*. Oxford: Oxford University Press.

Solska, M., F. Bieber, and D. Taleski, eds. 2018. *Illiberal and authoritarian tendencies in central, Southeastern and Eastern Europe*. Bern: Peter Lang.

Stojarová, V. forthcoming. Media in the Western Balkans: Who controls the past controls the future. *Southeast European and Black Sea Studies* 20, no. 4: xx.

Tilly, C. 2007. *Democracy*. Cambridge: Cambridge University Press.

Vuković, Z., and N. Tomović. 2019. The presidentialisation of political parties in montenegro: A limited semi-presidentialism. In *The presidentialisation of political parties in the Western Balkans*, ed. G. Passarelli, 119–44. Cham: Palgrave.

Zakariah, F. 1997. The rise of illiberal democracy. *Foreign Affairs* 76, no. 6: 22–43. doi:10.2307/20048274

Index

Page numbers followed by 'n' refer to notes, those in **bold** refer to tables and those in *italic* refer to figures.

AAK *see* Alliance for the Future of Kosovo (AAK)
accountability 5
Acemoglu, D. 34n2
Adès-Méval, Pauline 188
advertising 165; political 183
AEM *see* Agency for Electronic Media (AEM)
Agency for Electronic Media (AEM) 144, 148
Agency for the Prevention of Corruption (ASK) 67, 74
Ahram, I.A. 104
Ahtisaari, Martti 101
Ahtisaari Proposal 101
Albania 120, 217, **226**; campaign funding 121, 124–6; Central Election Committee 125, 126; clientelism 121, 126–32; defamation 162, **163**; EU membership 228; INFORM project theoretical model *122*, 122–4, 133n1; in-kind donations 129, 133; LDI, EDI and LCI measures of *8*, *9*, 10, **10**; Macedonians *vs.* Albanians 42–3, 53; media 130; media sector 159, **159**; political pressure on media 167–8; private funding 126–33, 134n7; voter turnout 219–20
Albanian Electoral Code 121, 125
Alliance for the Future of Kosovo (AAK) 106
Alliance of Independent Social Democrats (SNSD) 79, 80, 85, 86–91, 94
Amended Law on Determining the Additional Condition for Performing Public Service (2011) 50
anti-European/anti-American approach 114
Article 88 of Electoral Code 125
Ashton, Catherine 112
ASK *see* Agency for the Prevention of Corruption (ASK)
ASK Council 67
Audio recording scandal 69–70, 73–4
authoritarianism 3; competitive 4, 6
authoritarian tendencies 40
autocratic tendencies 193, 194
autocratization 2, 3, 80; in BiH 81–5, 93–4

Baća, B. 70
Balkan Barometer 168, 172n2

Balkan Contact Group 116n1
Balkan Investigative Reporting Network (BIRN) 186
Beha, A. 107, 217
Belgrade: Christmas tree 223; 2018 local election in 184; protests 198, 199, 209n10
Belgrade-Pristina relations 112–13
Belgrade Waterfront project 30, 34n10, 223
Bermeo, N. 60; democratic backsliding 3; executive aggrandizement 5
Bertelsmann Transformation Index (BTI) 81, *82*
BHRT *see* Radio and Television of Bosnia and Herzegovina (BHRT)
Bieber, F. 11, 19, 40, 60, 105, 214
BiH: LDI, EDI and LCI measures of *8*, *9*, 10, **10**
Blakaj, Elez 114
Bleiburg commemoration 141
Bliznakovski, J. 123
Bochsler, D. 11
Boduszyński, M.P. 42
Boskovski, Ljube 49
Bosnia and Herzegovina (BiH) 79, **226**; autocratization in 81–5, 93–4; brown areas 82; Communications Regulatory Agency 89; defamation 162, **163**; democracy measurements for 81–2, *82*; electoral competition in 83; Electoral Integrity Project 92; electoral registry 183; ethnic party dominance 85–6; illiberal politics in 80–1, 84–6, 94–5, 216–17; *klix.ba* case 166; media control 89–91, 221; media dominance in 183; media sector **159**, 160; patronage in elections 91–3; political pressure on media 166; political system of 80; post-communist power mutation 84; power-sharing 80–2, 94–5; protests 224; Public Service Broadcasting 160; restrictions to freedom of assembly 86–9
boundary control 83
Broadcasting Law (2005) 164
budget non-transparency 29
Bujanec, Velimir 144
Bulgaria 43
Burnell, P. 124

INDEX

campaign funding 121; exploitation of public resources 181–2; legal regulations on 124–6; private 126–33, 134n7; transparency 121, 125, 127, 132
captured institutions 195
Capussela, Andrea 107, 108
Catholic Church 140–2, 218
Cavatorta, F. 189
Cekić, Nenad 26
Cengiz Günay, C. 195
Chesterman, S. 104
civic protests 51
civil liberties 5
civil society organizations (CSOs) 205, 206
clientelism 92, 178, 195, 223, **224**; in Albania 126–32; indirect 182; long term 124; political 123, 133; relational 181–2; short term 124
Colourful Revolution 194, 199, 209n12
Commission for the Verification of Facts [Lustration Commission] 51
competitive authoritarianim 102–3
competitive authoritarianism 4, 6, 40; in Serbia 32, 33
Competitive Authoritarianism (Levitsky and Way) 21
competitive authoritarian regimes 226
competitive authoritarian system 178
competitive elections 6
Comprehensive Proposal for Kosovo Status Settlement *see* Ahtisaari Proposal
confidentiality clauses 28–9
consociational democracy 80–2, 84, 94–5
Constitutional Court, Croatia 147
Constitutional Framework for Provisional Self-Government in Kosovo 103
constitutional liberalism 4, 102
Council of Europe 167
Criminal Code 125
Croatia 215, 217–18, **226**; Catholic Church 140–2, 218; Constitutional Court 147; contentious political issues in 141–2; defamation 162, **163**; democratic backsliding 138, 149, 150; democratic consolidation 138; democratization 138; economic pressure on media 164; electoral law 142, 143; electoral practices 142–3; electoral registry 143; EU and 137, 145–6, 149; EU membership 228; external control 149; fake voters in 184; Homeland War 141; horizontal accountability 145–6; illiberal practices in 148, 150; immigration policy 142; independent judiciary 146–8; institutional oversight 146; internal power sharing 149; LDI, EDI and LCI measures of 8, *8*, 9, **10**, 10–11; media in 143–5; media sector 159, **159**; negotiation with EU 137; party system of 139–40; political actors 139–41; political pressure on media 165–6; political system 137, 139, 149; State Judicial Council 147–8

Croatian Democratic Union (HDZ) 138–42, 148–50, 218; capture of media 144–5; and Catholic Church 140; control over local politics 143; judicial control 147; unrestrained rule 147
Croatian Democratic Union BiH (HDZ BiH) 81, 85
Croatian Journalist Association (HND) 145, 166, 169
Croatian National Television (HRT) 144
cultural trauma 141
Čuruvija, Slavko 168
Cvijanović, Željka 166
Cvjetićanin, T. 91

Dačić, Ivica 112
Dahl, Robert 7
Dalić, Martina 165
Džankić, J. 69
David Dragicević's case 86
Dayton Peace Agreement (1995) 81
D4D *see* Democracy for Development (D4D)
defamation 162, **163**, 172n1
defamation lawsuits 90
Della Porta, D. 197
democracy: BiH's 81–2, *82*, 94; consociational 80–2, 84, 94–5; consociational model of 42; constitutional liberalism and 102; defective 3; electoral 94; electoral component of 4–5; formal 178–80, 189; illiberal 3, 102–4; indices 7; liberal component of 4–6; media and 157, 172; political finance on 124–5; power-sharing 81–5; rule of law and 178–9; Serbia's 19–20, 22–3
democracy-autocracy continuum 2
Democracy Barometer 15n8
Democracy for Development (D4D) 106
democratic backsliding 1, 226–7; Bermeo on 3; causes, means and results of *227*; Croatia's 138, 149, 150; in Serbia 19, 20; in Southeast Europe 7–12
democratic consolidation 138, 181
democratic density 103
Democratic Front 63
democratic institutions 215
Democratic League of Kosovo (LDK) 100–1, 105–6, 111
Democratic Opposition of Serbia (DOS) 22, 23
Democratic Party (DP) 126–30
Democratic Party of Albanians (DPA) 54n3, 54n5
Democratic Party of Kosovo (PDK) 100, 111; emergence of 106; Pronto-Affair 109
Democratic Party of Socialists (DPS) 62, 65, 225; Audio recording scandal 69–70; elements of illiberal policies *68*, 68–9, 73–4; RTCG and 66–8; University of Montenegro 70–3
democratic rupture 7
Democratic Union for Integration (DUI) 40, 52, 53, 54n4
democratization 215; Croatia's 138; in Kosovo 105–9
Dženan Memić's case 86

Derifaj, Danka 165
Désir, Harlem 185
Džihić, V. 195
Đinđić, Zoran 196
disinformation 91
division of power 6
Djakić, Ivan 169
Djakić, Josip 169
Djukanović, Milo 171, 188
Dodik, Milorad 81, 85, 87, 89–91, 94, 166, 171, 182
Dolenec, D. 6, 11, 41, 52, 59
DOS *see* Democratic Opposition of Serbia (DOS)
DPS *see* Democratic Party of Socialists (DPS)
Dragićević, Davor 224
Draško, Gazela Pudar 219
DSV *see* State Judicial Council (DSV)
Đukanović, Milo 76n5

Èalović, Vanja 169
economic liberalization 180
economic pressure on media 164
Èepo, Dario 217–18
Efendic, A. 122, 123
election campaigns: exploitation of public resources in 181–2
elections 189; electoral registers 183–4; exploitation of public resources 181–2; free and fair 180, 219–20; illiberal politics and systemic flaws affecting **221**; media dominance 182–3; patronage in 91–3; paying back 181; phantom voters 184; postal voting 184; quality of 181; vote buying 220; vote coercion 184; voter fraud 184; voter turnout 219–20; in Western Balkans 180–1
electoral authoritarianism (EA) 3, 18; in Serbia 18–21, 23; Schedler on 34n3
electoral campaign funding 134n7; legal regulations on 124–6; private funding 126–33
electoral code 121, 123–4, 167
Electoral Commission, in Serbia 220
electoral component of democracy 4–5, 7–8
electoral political competition 123
electoral politics, in North Macedonia 43–5
electoral registers 183–4
Electronic Media Law (2014) 26
enforcement belt 123
Èović, Dragan 81, 85
ethnification of politics 43, 52
Euro-Atlantic integration 101, 112, 115, 116
European Commission (EC) 74, 114, 138, 145, 156, 178; Macedonian media freedom 47; SCPC criticism 49
European Convention on Human Rights 161
European Court of Human Rights 187
Europeanization 196; in Kosovo 112–15
European Rule of Law Mission in Kosovo (EULEX) 101, 107, 108, 111
European solution 113
European standards 74

European Union (EU) 88, 161, 170, 204–5, 228; *acquiscommunautaire* 123; Croatia and 137, 145–6, 149; enlargement policy 137; 2018 Enlargement Strategy 114; Kosovo and 112–13
executive aggrandizement 5, 60
exploitation of public resources 181–2
extractive institutional design: budget non-transparency 29; contracts with confidentiality clauses 28–9; impact of 32–3; party patronage 31–2; public procurement 29–30; State agencies and other bodies 30–1; Vuèić government and 28

Facebook 160
Federation of Bosnia and Herzegovina (FBiH) 83, 85, 217, **226**
Federation's Federalna Televizija (FTV) 183
Fiket, Irena 219
formal democracy 178–80, 189
frankenstates 7
free and fair elections 180, 219–20; in Serbia 23–5
Freedom House Index (FH) 81, *82*
Freedom House's Report 185
Freedom in the World Index 7
Fukuyama, Francis 177
Fukuyamian eschatology 102
functional rule of law 179–80

Galtung, Johan: positive peace 109
Gašić, Vladan 187
Gërxhani, K. 125
Gibson, E.: boundary control 83
Gjuzelov, Borjan 216
global economic crisis 177
Goode, J.P. 104
Gordy, E. 122, 123
Grabar Kitarović, Kolinda 144
Grabovci, Adem 109
Grèić, Milorad 31
Gruevski, Nikola 46, 48–50, 52, 190, 194, 196, 202, 203, 205, 206

Hadijevska, Milka Ivanovska 216
Hajrullahu, Arben 217
Hamza, Agon 110
Haradinaj, Ramush 114
HDZ *see* Croatian Democratic Union (HDZ)
Helmke, G. 123
historical institutionalism 138
HND *see* Croatian Journalists' Association (HND)
HRT *see* Croatian National Television (HRT)
hybrid media systems 185
hybrid regimes 177
Hysa, Armanda 217

identity issues 196
illiberal democracy 157; concept of 3–4
illiberal politics: concept of 2–7
incremental regime change 3
incumbents 4–5

INDEX

independence of media 168, *168*
indirect clientelism 182
INFORM project theoretical model *122*, 122–4, 133n1
in-kind donations 129, 133
institutional aspects of illiberal politics 40, 45–9, 51–3, 53n1
institutionalism of rational choice 138
Internal Macedonian Revolutionary Organization - Democratic Party for Macedonian National Unity (VMRO-DPMNE) *see* VMRO-DPMNE
International Civilian Office (ICO) 101
International Court of Justice (ICJ) 101
internet access 160
In the Name of the Family 141
Ivanović, Oliver 224
Izetbegović, Bakir 81

Janković, Saša 224
Jankulovska, Gordana 46
Jano, D. 127
journalists: intimidation, physical assault, assassination of 168–70; police's unauthorized surveillance of 186; self-censorship 221
Jovanović, Duško 169
judicial independence 221–2, **223**
Juon, A. 11
Justice for David movement 224
Justice for David protests 86–9, 94, 216
Jutka, Milutin Jelièić 32

Kajsiu, B. 125
Kamolli, M. 129
Kapidžić, D. 102, 138, 216–17, 224
Kera, Gentiana 217
Kezharovki, Tomislav 49
King, I. 104, 107
Klarić, Ivana Milas 146
klix.ba 166
Kmezić, M. 214, 218
Komar, Olivera 216, 224
Kosovo **226**; *see also* soft competitive authoritarianism; Ahtisaari Proposal 101; Assembly 107; D4D 106; electoral registry 184; ethnicity 110; EU integration process 113–15; EULEX 101; Euro-Atlantic integration 101, 112, 115; European solution for 113; EU supervision 107; The First Agreement of Principles Governing the Normalization of Relations 112; freedom of expression 161; independence 101, 104, 109, 115; LDI, EDI and LCI measures of 8, 9, 10, **10**, 11; manipulative political elites in 101; media dominance in 183; media sector **159**, 160; methodological constraints 104–5; misuse of public office 182; Parliament of 107; political elites in 101, 104, 107, 109–13, 115; political pressure on media 168; political status of 100, 103, 113; post-1999 115; SAA 113; and Serbia 109–13, 115; Standards for Kosovo 109; state

building in 102–4, 107; UNMIK and 100, 103–4; visa liberalization 113
Kosovo Anti-Corruption Agency 108
Kosovo Information Service (SHIK) 108
Kosovo Liberation Army (KLA) 100, 105–6, 108
Kosovo Serbs 110, 111
Kostova, Jadranka 47
Koštunica, Vojislav 23, 220
Kovaèić, Siniša 165
Krasniqi, Afrim 126

Lakić, Olivera 169
Law on Political Parties 125
Law on Public Broadcasting Services of Montenegro 167
legal system: abuse of 186–7
Leković, Saša 166
Levitsky, S. 4, 21, 40, 63, 101, 102, 123, 156, 178, 226
liberal democracy 4–6; media in 156–7
liberal politics 2
Limaj, Fatmir 108
Ljajić, Rasim 27
long term clientelism 124
Lunacek, Ulrike 107
Lustration Law 50

Macedonian illiberal politics *see* VMRO-DPMNE
Machiavelli, N. 189
Maksimović, Luka 220
Marković, Dragan 182
Marković, Stojan 187
Mason, W. 104, 107
Matić, J. 186, 188
Matić, V 187
media: bias 183; control 220–1; in Croatia 143–5; democracy and 157, 172; dominance 182–3; in ex-Yugoslavian countries 160; government-friendly 165; hybrid systems 185; in illiberal democracy 157; legitimacy of 171; in liberal democracy 156–7; loyalty 221; privatization 187–8; self-censorship 157, 165, 167, 168
media, in Western Balkans 156, **159**; advertising 165; control 158; defamation 162, **163**, 172n1; economic pressure 164; external factors 170; financial crisis 164; fragmentation 159; freedom 157, 169, **169**; independence 168, *168*; internet access 160; intimidation, physical assault, assassination of journalists 168–70; legislative framework 160–1; overview of 158–60; pluralism 171, **171**; political pressure 165–8; political-societal dynamics 170; regulatory bodies 161–2; self-censorship 167, 168; structural factors 170
media freedom 169, **169**, 184–5, 218; abuse of legal system 186–7; assessment on 185; direct pressure 188; Freedom House report 160, *160*; illiberal politics and systemic flaws affecting **222**; informal pressure 187–8; legacies

of authoritarian past 185–6; in Macedonia 47–
8; in Serbia 25–8; Serbia *vs.* N. Macedonia 196;
in WB countries 157, 160, 170; in Western
Balkans 185–8
media ownership 47, 90; in WB countries 162, 164
Media Sustainability Index 185
Milčin, Vladimir 51
Milinović, Draško 89
Milošević, Slobodan 111, 187, 198, 204, 208n6;
Serbia under 18–19, 22
Milososki, Antonio 47
mistrust 197, 219, 227
Montenegrin Election Law 62
Montenegrin illiberal policy 60–1; control over
independent institutions 70–3; elements of *68*,
68–9, 73–4; misusing public resources 66–8;
overview of 65–6; tilting the electoral playing
field 69–70
Montenegrin National Election Study (MNES) 63
Montenegro 74–5, 225, **226**; Agreement
on the Minimum Principles for
the Establishment of a Democratic
Infrastructure in Montenegro 75n3; civic
opposition 63; defamation 162, **163**; democratic
backsliding 60; democratic consolidation 62;
democratic development in 216; economic
pressure on media 164; EU membership 228;
EU Progress Report 76n10; Freedom in the
World report 63, *65*, 76n5; history 59; illiberal
policies 60–1, 216; journalists, violence
against 169; LDI, EDI and LCI measures of *8*,
9, *10*, **10**; media ownership 164; media sector
159, **159**; patrimonial communism 62; political
pressure on media 167; political system in
59–63, **64**; predominant party system 62;
protests 224; state advertising 165; theory-
building process tracing 61, 74; vote buying 220
multi-party political system 177, 185, 225

National Foundation for Civil Society
Development 146, 223
NATO 204–5
negative stability 107
Network for Affirmation of the NGO Sector
(MANS) 169
Nikolić, Tomislav 23, 181
NISMA 108
normalization: in Kosovo 109–12
North Macedonia 39–40, **226**; *see also* Serbia
vs. North Macedonia, social movements in;
challenges 41, 43; civic protests 45; defamation
162, **163**; democracy watchdogs in 167;
economic pressure on media 164; electoral
registry 184; ethnification of politics 43, 52;
EU and NATO integration 41–3, 52; EU
membership 228; identity issues 196;
institutional and symbolic aspects of illiberal
politics in (*see* VMRO-DPMNE); LDI, EDI
and LCI measures of *8*, *9*, *10*, **10**, 11; legal
framework 52; Macedonian scenario 190;

Macedonians *vs.* Albanians 42–3, 53; media
dominance in 183; media freedom 196;
media sector 159, **159**; mistrust 197; misuse
of electoral registers 184; national identity
and language 43; OSCE/ODIHR election
observation mission reports **44**, 46; party
system in 42; political pressure on media 167;
post-communist transition during 1990s 41–
3; privatization in 42; Przino Agreements
45, 54n6; 2018 referendum in 219;
regime change in 193, 194; SDSM in 42,
45, 50–2; state advertising 165; surveillance
of journalists 186; triple transition 41; vote
buying 220; wiretapping scandal 45

O'Donnell, Guillermo, 179; 'brown areas' 82
OFA *see* Ohrid Framework Agreement (OFA)
Ohman, M. 131
Ohrid Framework Agreement (OFA) 42
oligarchic parties 129
Ombudsman for Children 146
One of Five Million protest 194, 208n2, 224
Open Society Foundation in Macedonia 51
Orbán, Viktor 170

Party for Democratic Prosperity (PDP) 54n5
Party of Democratic Action (SDA) 81, 85, 89
party patronage 31–2
patrimonial communism 62
patronage 223, **224;** in elections, BiH 91–3
Pavlović, Dušan 215, 216
paying back 181
PDK *see* Democratic Party of Kosovo (PDK)
Perković, Marko 169
Petersen, A. 129
Pevehouse, Jon C. 103
Pinterest 160
plurality of media 171, **171**
political accountability 179
political advertising 183
political clientelism 123, 124, 133
political mistrust 197
political parties: competition 59–60; media
dominance 182–3
political pressure on media 165–8
political-societal dynamics 170
Popovac, Josip 144
populism 123
positive peace 109
post-communist power mutation 6, 7, 84
predatory conception of public office 60
predominant party systems 62
prime ministerial republic 107
private funding, for electoral campaigns 126–
33, 134n7
privatization 180; of media 187–8; in North
Macedonia 42; of Serbian media 27
process-oriented approach 4, 40
Pronto-Affair 109, 116
Protest against Dictatorship 198, 199

Protestiram 199, 209n12
Przino Agreements 45, 54n6
public office misuse 182
public procurement 29–30
public resources, misuse of 66–8, 181–2, 222–3, **224**
Public Service Broadcasting (PSB) 160

Radio and Television of Bosnia and Herzegovina (BHRT) 89
Radio-Television Montenegro (RTCG) 66–8, 76n10, 221
Radio Television of Republika Srpska (RTRS) 89–91, 183
Radio-Television of the Federation of Bosnia and Herzegovina (FTV) 89
Radio Television Serbia (RTS) 188
Radio Television Vojvodina (RTV) 26, 188
Radonèić, Fahrudin 90
Rakić, Mirjana 144
Rama, Edi 120
Ramkovski, Velija 48
Regional Cooperation Council Balkan Barometer (2018) 168, 172n2
Regulatory Authority for Electronic Media (REM) 22, 26
relational clientelism 92, 93, 181–2
REMCouncil 34n8
Reporters Without Borders World Press Freedom Index 185
reproductive rights 142
Republic Electoral Commission (REC) 24
Republika Srpska (RS) 79, 83, 166, 216–17, 224, **226**
Richter, S. 178
Robinson, J. 34n2
A Roof Over Our Heads 206
RTCG see Radio-Television Montenegro (RTCG)
RTCG Council 66–7
RTRS see Radio Television of Republika Srpska (RTRS)
Rugova, Ibrahim 101, 111
rule of law 189, 218; democracy and 178–9; functional 179–80

SAA see Stabilization and Association Agreement (SAA)
Šabić, Rodoljub 29
Sanader, Ivo 144
Schedler, A. 34n3; *Electoral Authoritarianism: The Dynamics of Unfree Competition* 21
Schram, A. 125
SDP see Social Democratic Party (SDP)
SDSM see Social Democratic Union of Macedonia (SDSM)
Selaci, Gëzim 107
Selmani, Naser 47
Serbia 101, **226**; *see also* Serbia *vs.* North Macedonia, social movements in; autocratic tendencies in

193, 194; case of *Zrenjaninskenovine* 186–7; collapse of communism 33; consolidation of democracy 22–3; CRTA reports 25; defamation 162, **163**; democratic decline 171, 215; democratic decline in 19, 20; democratic score 20, *23*, 23–4; DOS coalition 22, 23; economic pressure on media 164–5; electoral authoritarianism 18–21, 23, 34n3; electoral registry 183–4; EU membership 228; extractive institutions 21–2, 33, 34n2; The First Agreement of Principles Governing the Normalization of Relations 112; fourth branch of government 33; free and fair elections 23–5; identity issues 196; institutional design 22–3; journalists, violence against 168–9; Kosovo and 109–13, 115; LDI, EDI and LCI measures of *8, 9,* **10**, 10–11; media dominance in 183; media freedom 25–8, 196; media ownership 164; media sector 159, **159**; under Milošević 18–19, 22; mistrust 197; political instabilities in 196; political pressure on media 166–7; post-Milošević cabinets 20, 22; SNS activists 24–5; state advertising 165; voter turnout 219
Serbian Electoral Commission 220
Serbian media: fake news 27–8; financial support for private media 27; Information Act 25; local media 27; print media 27–8; privatization of 27; REM 26; RTS and RTV 26; violence against journalists 28; Vuèić and 25, 27
Serbian Progressive Party (SNS) 24–5, 32; accusations 184
Serbia *vs.* North Macedonia, social movements in 194, 206–8, 208n4, 209n13, 219; attitudes towards EU and NATO 204–5; beliefs and ideas 201; Colourful Revolution 194, 199, 209n12; commonalities and shared characteristics 199–202; contentious political arenas and 198–9; decision-making 201–2; differences 202–6; internal structure and organization 201–2; legacy or burden of previous protests 204; motivation and goals 200–1; Protest against Dictatorship 198, 199; Protestiram 199, 209n12; transcending the constraints of 'single-issue oriented' struggles 203
Sertić, Željko 29
Sharifi, Idavet 167
Shipovic, Miroslav 49
short term clientarism 124
Skopje 2014 50, 199, 209n10
Slavko Èuruvija Foundation 166
Smederevo steel factory 28–9
Smilov, D. 129
Snow, D. 199
SNSD see Alliance of Independent Social Democrats (SNSD)
Social Democratic Party (SDP) 67, 71, 139
Social Democratic Union of Macedonia (SDSM) 42, 45, 50–3, 194, 196

Socialist Movement for Integration 126–8
Socialist Party (SP) 125–7
social movements 194, 223–5; *see also* Serbia *vs.*
  North Macedonia, social movements in
soft competitive authoritarianism 101, 115–
  16, 217; democratization rhetoric 105–9;
  Europeanization rhetoric 112–15; illiberal
  democracy and 102–4; normalization
  rhetoric 109–12
Spaskovska, L. 50
Spaskovski, Blagoje 32
stabilitocracies 11
stabilitocracy 107
Stabilization and Association Agreement
  (SAA) 113
stabilocracy 195, 202
Standards for Kosovo 109
State Audit Institution (SAI) 29
State Commission for Prevention of Corruption
  (SCPC) 46, 49
State Judicial Council (DSV) 147–8
state-owned enterprises (SOEs) 85; as electoral
  prizes 91–3
Stavric, Dejan 49
Stefanović, Borko 224
Stojarová, Vìra 218
strategic electoral manipulation 5
subnational autocratization 81–5
Surroi, Veton 104
symbolic aspects of illiberal
  politics 40, 49–53

Tadić, Boris 20, 23
Tansey, Oisin 106
Televizija Srbije (RTS) 26
Thaçi, Hashim 108, 111, 112
theory-building process tracing 61, 74
Thessaloniki Declaration (2003) 113
Thessaloniki Summit 111
Topić, Tanja 166
toxic leaders 195
trust, in political parties 197
Tuđman, Franjo 137, 139, 147, 149

United Movement of Free Tenants 203
United Nations Interim Mission in Kosovo
  (UNMIK) 100; as benevolent autocracy 104;
  co-optation policy 105; with KFOR 106; UN
  Resolution 1244 on 103–4
University of Montenegro 70–3

UN Resolution 1244 103, 110
US State Department 47

Varieties of Democracy index (V-Dem) 2;
  democracy measurements for BiH 81, *82*;
  Electoral Democracy Index (EDI) 7, 9, 10, **10**;
  Liberal Component Index (LCI) 7–10, *9*, **10**;
  Liberal Democracy Index (LDI) 7–10, *9*, **10**
Vasiljević, Jelena 219
Veseli, Kadri 108, 114
Veselinović, Goran 186
Vijesti 66
Visoka, Gëzim 113
Vladisavljević, N. 15n7
VMRO-DPMNE 216; access to
  law 48–9; access to media 47–8; access to state
  resources 45–6; antiquization 50; clientelist
  employments 46; control over SCPC 49; early
  elections 43, 54n6; electoral politics 43–5;
  incomes and expenditures 46; institutional
  and symbolic aspects of illiberal politics
  40, 45–53, 53n1; lustration processes 50–
  1; reconstruction of national identity 50;
  wiretapped conversations 46, 48
vote buying 220
vote coercion 184
voter fraud 184
voter turnout 219–20
Vučić, Aleksandar 19, 25, 27, 32, 76n5, 166–7,
  171, 183, 186, 188, 198, 202, 215, 220, 224

Ware, A. 124
Way, L.A. 4, 21, 40, 63, 101, 102, 156, 178, 226
Western Balkans (WB) 1, 15n1; EC enlargement
  strategy 156; EU membership 114; media sector
  (*see* media, in Western Balkans)
wiretapping scandal, in Macedonia 45
World Press Freedom Index (2014) 196
World War II 141
Wunsch, N. 178

Yee, Hoyt Brian 121

Žada, Ivan 169
Zaev, Zoran 194, 202
Zakariah, F. 3, 102
Zakošek, N. 6, 180
Zaum, Dominik 109
Zernovski, Andrej 49
Zrenjanin Social Forum 203